LINCOLN CHRISTIAN UNIVERSITY

This is a book that can open eyes and

D0878182

These compelling stories demonstrate that faith in search of understanding, and understanding in search of faith, go on in the most unlikely places. *Finding God at Harvard* testifies to the fact that God can find us anywhere.

Richard John Neuhaus
author, *The Naked Public Square*
Editor-in-Chief, *First Things*

Finding God at Harvard demonstrates that Light can penetrate the darkness of Academia. These poignant stories provide a ray of hope that reflects God's Son as "the Way, the Truth, and the Life."

Kenneth W. Ogden, Ed.D.
Vice-President, Counseling and Education
Focus on the Family

The greatest controversy of our age is the crisis of truth. This book is a wonderfully reasoned defense that ultimately points to the One who is the source of all truth.

Charles W. Colson
Chairman, Prison Fellowship Ministries

When I read Ari Goldman's discouraging story of *not* finding God at Harvard, I wished he could have known the bright and committed Christian students and faculty that I have met at Harvard. They are well-represented in this encouraging and stimulating collection of essays focused on the importance and validity of Christian faith. Here is nourishing and uplifting food for the spirit, as well as the mind. In an intellectual environment of confusion, disillusionment, and cynicism, here are notes of hope, integrity and joy.

Dr. Roberta Hestenes
President, Eastern College

It is only natural that those who seek the truth, be it intellectual or spiritual, will only find what they are searching for in the person of Christ.

Kay Cole James
author, *Never Forget* and *Transforming America*

Finding God at Harvard offers real-world testimony to the so-called Generation-X that, whatever vocation we are beginning to explore and struggling to understand, God can be meaningful no matter where we are or what we're doing—through Jesus Christ.

Drew J. Ladner
Publisher, Regeneration Quarterly

Finding God at Harvard is a wonderful piece of work, bringing together intellectual excellence and spirituality.

John Perkins
author, Let Justice Roll
Publisher, Urban Family

I have long believed that too many believers weren't defeated at our premiere academic institutions; they simply abandoned the territory. Kelly Monroe shows that while many believers left Harvard, God didn't, and he may continue to be found wherever people truly seek him.

Cal Thomas
syndicated columnist and CNBC talk host

This book is desperately needed today for it provides the profound—and only—remedy for a society devastated by secularism.

the late Richard C. Halverson
formerly Chaplain, United States Senate

These stories caused me to think, cry, laugh out loud, and to pray. I was taken in and taken along on their travels, their studies, their service. I felt knitted into the Body in which there is a unique shared living.

Ruth Allderige, writer

With grace, humor and emotion, three dozen authors dispel stereotypes that Christianity and intellectual pursuits are incompatible.

Patrick McGuigan
The Daily Oklahoman

In thought-provoking diversity, their accounts testify to the power of religious discovery and hold life together joyfully in the human confrontation with death and limitation. These essays succeed brilliantly and show convincingly that in an aggressively secular age, spirit is still redemptively at work.

Richard Nunley
The Berkshire Eagle

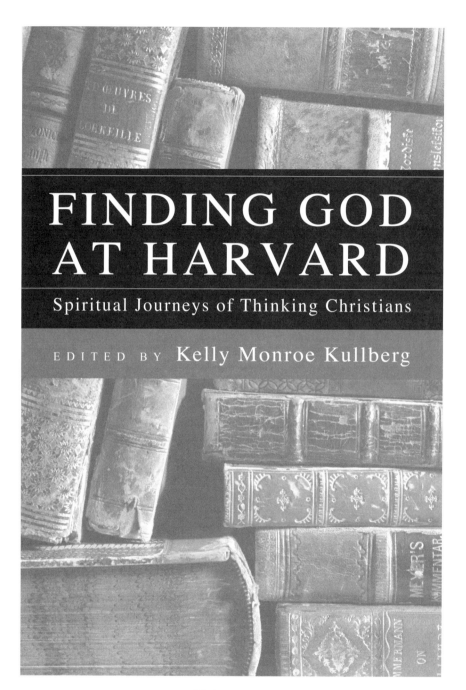

FINDING GOD
AT HARVARD

Spiritual Journeys of Thinking Christians

EDITED BY Kelly Monroe Kullberg

IVP Books

An imprint of InterVarsity Press
Downers Grove, Illinois

InterVarsity Press
P.O. Box 1400, Downers Grove, IL 60515-1426
World Wide Web: www.ivpress.com
E-mail: email@ivpress.com

Copyright © 1996 by Kelly K. Monroe

Revised edition ©2007 by Kelly Monroe Kullberg

All rights reserved. No part of this book may be reproduced in any form without written permission from InterVarsity Press.

InterVarsity Press® is the book-publishing division of InterVarsity Christian Fellowship/USA®, a student movement active on campus at hundreds of universities, colleges and schools of nursing in the United States of America, and a member movement of the International Fellowship of Evangelical Students. For information about local and regional activities, write Public Relations Dept., InterVarsity Christian Fellowship/USA, 6400 Schroeder Rd., P.O. Box 7895, Madison, WI 53707-7895, or visit the IVCF website at <www.intervarsity.org>.

All Scripture quotations, unless otherwise indicated, are taken from the Holy Bible, New International Version®. NIV®. *Copyright ©1973, 1978, 1984 by International Bible Society. Used by permission of Zondervan Publishing House. All rights reserved.*

Permission to reprint "A Hunger for God" by Mother Teresa granted by the author.

Design: Cindy Kiple
Images: Jeff Spielman/Getty Images

ISBN-13: 978-0-8308-3433-8

Printed in the United States of America ∞

Library of Congress Cataloging-in-Publication Data

Finding god at Harvard: spiritual journeys of thinking Christians /
edited by Kelly Monroe Kullberg.
      p. cm.
  Prev. ed published by: Grand Rapids, Mich.: Zondervan Pub. House
c1996. Includes bibliographical references and index. ISBN
978-0-8308-3433-4 (pbk.: alk. paper)
  1. Harvard University—Religion. 2. Christian
biography—Massachusetts—Cambridge. 3. Spiritual
biography—Massachusetts—Cambridge. 4. Harvard
University—Biography. 5.
Intellectuals—Massachusetts—Cambridge—Biography. 6. Church and
education. I. Kullberg, Kelly Monroe, 1960-
LD2134.F56 2007
378.744'4—dc22

                                                                            2006101784

P   20   19   18   17   16   15   14   13   12   11   10   9   8   7   6   5

Y   23   22   21   20   19   18   17   16   15   14   13   12

Contents

————— ৡ২ —————

With the drawing of this Love, and the Voice of this Calling,
we shall not cease from exploration
and the end of all our exploring
will be to arrive where we started
and know the place for the first time.

T. S. ELIOT, CLASS OF 1909

જંડ

    The true Harvard is the invisible Harvard in the souls of her more
truth-seeking and independent and often very solitary [students]. . . .
The university most worthy of rational admiration is that one in which
your lonely thinker can feel himself least lonely, and most richly fed.

WILLIAM JAMES, 1903 COMMENCEMENT ADDRESS

DEDICATION

——— ཨེ§ ———

This book is for those of you who have known this way of love long before we heard. And it is for those who don't know but have a mind for questioning and a heart for hearing.

In memory of writers
Vera Shaw, Brent Foster, Elton Trueblood,
Betsy Dawn Inskeep Smylie, and Mother Teresa

And for our children and younger friends such as
Michelle, April, John, Keya, and Josh; Michelle, Callie, Cory, and
Cece; Emily and Sarah; Elijah Ming; Zach and Ezra; Hannah,
Caleb, Alezah, Micah, Esther, Josiah, Emma, Judah,
and Ruth; Caroline and Hannah; Natalia and Noah;
Benjamin and Jonathan; Joseph and Roger; Julia;
Brendan the Voyager, Mary Kate, and Sophie;
and your parents and your children some day

When the world tells you that you are all alone,
only animal, only image, that evil is good and good is evil,
don't listen—you are made in God's image for joy.

"The thief comes to kill, steal, and destroy.
I have come that [you] would have life,
and have it abundantly." (John 10:10)

"You are precious in my sight.
You are honored, and I love you."
(Isaiah 43:4)

CREDITS

"The Wonder of Being" by Charles H. Malik, 1974, Word, Inc., Dallas, Texas. Used with permission.

"The Grace that Shaped My Life" is adapted from *Philosophers Who Believe,* edited by Kelly James Clark © 1993. Used by permission of InterVarsity Press, P.O. Box 1400, Downers Grove, Ill. 60515.

"God in the Ghetto" by Glenn Loury is used with permission of the *Wall Street Journal,* © 1993, Dow Jones & Company, Inc. All rights reserved.

"Salvation to the Streets" is reprinted with the permission of *Sojourners,* 2401 15th Street NW, Washington, D.C. 20009.

An adaptation of "Thorns in the Garden Planet" by Vera Shaw is used with permission of Thomas Nelson Publishers.

Information on the history of Abimael Guzman and the Shining Path is from Gustavo Gorriti's article "The War of the Philosopher King" in the *New Republic* (June 18, 1990), 15–22.

"Alternative to Futility" by Elton Trueblood is adapted and used with permission of the author and of HarperCollins, New York, N.Y.

Lyrics from "Lovers in a Dangerous Time" by Bruce Cockburn, © Golden Mountain Music Corp., 1984, are taken from the album *Stealing Fire.* Used by permission.

Lyrics from "Joy in the Journey" by Michael Card are used with permission of EMI and Sparrow.

Lyrics from "How Did You Find Me Here?" by David Wilcox are used with permission of P.O.W. and Rondor Music Publishing.

Lyrics from "Galileo" by Emily Saliers, Indigo Girls, are used with permission of EMI and the Hal Leonard Corp.

Lines from "Little Gidding" by T. S. Eliot, from *Four Quartets,* are used with permission of Faber and Faber.

Lines from *100 Love Sonnets* by Pablo Neruda, translated by Stephen Tapscott, copyright © Pablo Neruda 1959 and Fundacion Pablo Neruda, copyright © 1986 by the University of Texas Press. By permission of the publisher.

The photographs in the photo section are by David Herwaldt and the Harvard News Office. The photo of Kelly Monroe on the jacket of the book is by David Herwaldt.

ACKNOWLEDGMENTS

———— ❧ ————

If one must make a book, it is good, for the sake of trees and of readers, to let words say something real. This book says something, and I confess to you that this makes me all the more grateful for friends who dare things together.

I thank editorial volunteers and friends: Kay Hall, class of '87, whose love for God, for Harvard and for life is contagious; Poh Lian Lim Yap, class of '87, who offered encouragement and late-night editorial counsel; Franklyn Ayensu, a former law student from Ghana who gave meticulous attention to many of the essays; and Nishan de Mel, class of '94, a brilliant senior who helped me through one of the extra miles before returning home to Sri Lanka, then on to Oxford as an economist. I'd like to thank Harvard University for administrative support in this project.

I am grateful to each writer for your faith in things unseen. Your patience has helped me through schedule and editorial challenges too numerous to describe here. Something like live versions of this book, Veritas Forums to which readers are invited, often took precedence over the completion of this volume. Thank you, Jerry Mercer, for encouraging Veritas far beyond Harvard in the 90s. Thanks to Veritas leadership, Kurt Keilhacker, Ted and Ashley Callahan, Dan Cho, Craig Hammon, Bethany Sayles, Ana Maria Schlecht, Rich Halvorson, Jason Mann, Katie and Mike Milway, and John Kingston, for continuing and growing Veritas in the 2000s.

In addition to those in the table of contents, writers and readers who contributed to this book project include Ruth Allderige; Jane Bruns; Jody Velz Chang; Daniel Chua; Gary Dietrich; Ruth Gana; Gary Haugen and editors of *Veritas Reconsidered*; John Kingston; Kendall Palladino; Jennifer Parker; Dan Philpot; David Powlison; Fred Reisz; Erick Schenkel; Tim Shah; Robert Siegel; Greg Slayton; Deanna Snyder; Liping Song; Dan Stid; Kathleen Stuebing; Li-Ann Thio; Glenn Tinder; Ed and Kay Monroe VanMeter; Dawn Yip; Meirwyn Walters.

For your encouragement, I thank friends with InterVarsity Press, including my editor, Al Hsu, and publisher, Bob Fryling; InterVarsity Christian Fellowship and IFES worldwide; Cambridgeport Baptist Church; Upper Arlington Lutheran Church; Campus Crusade; the Fellowship House; Young Life; Search; Christian Leadership Ministries; Alpha; Focus on the Family; L'Abri; FOCUS; the Navigators; the C. S. Lewis Foundation; the Maclellan and Templeton foundations.

For friends, like roots, who are strong and deep: Armbrusts, Ausinks, Barnesons, Brenda Birmann, Bruns, Callahans, Carusos, Dan Cho, Edgars, Gauthiers, Halls, Hamlins, Craig Hammon, Hansels, Hansens, Kirstin Johnson, Keyes, Kurt Keilhacker, Kingstons, Kurfees, Lakes, Lataifs, Martha Linder, Glenn Lucke, Tom McCallie, Milways, Moores, Nagys, Roz Picard, Pierces, Ruhms, Shaws, Sisterhens, DJ Snell, Splaingards, Strawbridges, Thurlbys, Ulrings, Webbs, Scott Wilson, Wulfs, and Yaps.

Finally, I wish to thank you, dear reader. Open to our own error, we wish to express large thoughts about life, both deep and wide. We want to build bridges and not walls as we explore together. If you are offended by us, I ask your forgiveness. Though I can say that love is at the core of this, we are not yet the people who, by grace, we will fully become. We are also grateful for your high principles of liberalism and pluralism, and the choice to suspend disbelief long enough to read and to hear.

❧

A note on pronoun use: The reader is asked to consider the biblical insistence that all human beings, male and female, are created in the image of God. Some writers occasionally use the pronouns *he* or *him* intended as inclusive references to human beings. We're grateful for your understanding of this linguistic difficulty in the English language.

PREFACE TO THE 2007 EDITION

———— ❦ ————

Harvard, like many older institutions, tends to add branches while laying an ax to its own root. Yet, as with our own lives, sustainable vitality depends upon a living Vine, a Life-Giver.

The current crisis of education has recently been described by a former Harvard president as "emptiness," and by a dean as "excellence without a soul." Education has been severed from a lifeline, and confusions of identity and belonging, of ethics, and of purpose are evident. We see the outcomes of addictions, sexually transmitted diseases, crime, depression, and even suicide. Ideas have consequences. In our cynical, demoralized and postmodern moment, the pain is acute.

Souls are reduced to bodies. Minds are reduced to brains. Consciences are reduced to political polls. We witness the gradual suicide of secular cultures that no longer drink from the Wellspring of life. Passion wanes for the sacrificial nurturing of future generations of children and students in life-giving faith and vision. We are diagnosed with cultural anemia not unlike the Roman Empire that fell like a house of cards to barbarian tribes. The tree rotted from within. What of twenty-first-century America? Have we lost a proper source of knowledge out of which proper confidence is possible? Have we lost the power to love?

Is there a True North visible in the fog? Has an Author spoken or entered the play to show us his face and to tell us our Story? Without a humble and proper way of knowing truth, *Veritas,* how do any of us know how to think and act? Without revelation and reason, as well as emotion and conscience, "reality" is reduced to a series of private pleasures, pains, and power struggles. One could die of sheer boredom, if not sorrow, living in the flat, grey, secular story.

But most students, and many citizens, want to live in a great story, even if it requires great sacrifice. And we are welcomed to join as protagonists that story which includes an Author who speaks of a good creation, a tragic fall, and the possibility of redemption, because this same Author enters the play as sacrificial hero (in flesh and blood) restoring the world to goodness and beauty.

This same great story animated scholars like Newton, Galileo, Pascal, and Jonathan Edwards; the founders of Oxford, Cambridge, Harvard, Yale, and Princeton, as well as the Red Cross and the Salvation Army; people such as

Mother Teresa, Wilberforce, and Lincoln, and other abolitionists of slavery; artists such as Rembrandt and Bach, and the countless modern equivalents of these lovers and geniuses.

And so, despite the crisis, and despite so much dull but verbose cynicism, we see a new generation of believing scholars becoming the largest and most dynamic student organizations at schools like Harvard, MIT, Ohio State, Texas A&M, and Cal Poly. We hear their songs and laughter; we see their compassion and brilliance. Many of today's students join those before them in lives of service and adventure.

Finding God at Harvard begins where the critiques end. In these pages, students, alumni, professors and guest speakers offer a uniquely coherent, personal, and hopeful response to the emptiness of the modern and post-modern university. On the far side of the world's complexity, the ancient and future vitality of Harvard emerges anew. For at the name, and before the brilliance, of Jesus Christ, knees eventually bend or humbly bow.

This volume is a treasure chest of changed lives. The answers are not words and abstractions, but the actual lives of people who have encountered the secret in whom Harvard is rooted. With enough lives restored, whole cultures can be revived.

Today, a decade after its first release, it is a joy to witness the lives of these writers now so well employed in the adventure of building a kingdom of love on earth. (A postscript at the book's conclusion will provide current biographical updates.) Some battle disease, others discover new frontiers through electron microscopes and radio telescopes. Many nurture children and teach. Some create music, art, and wise public policy. Some live alongside the poorest of the poor on every continent, encouraging and empowering life. According to their callings, each serves. Well rooted, trees bear good fruit.

Many of these writers spoke at the inaugural Veritas Forum at Harvard Law School in 1992. When *Finding God at Harvard* first appeared in 1996, fifteen of the writers gathered as the speakers for the fourth Veritas Forum, in Harvard's majestic Sanders Theater. As the book became a *Boston Globe* bestseller and found its way into various universities and languages, Veritas Forums emerged, now in more than seventy-five universities on three continents, exploring the deepest questions of our times:

- Truth? Whose truth? How would we ever know Truth if we saw it?
- What is it to be human? Am I intended, and desired? What is the life that is *really* life?
- What of twenty-first-century science? What is the language of DNA and the Genome, and the logic of the cosmos and "Big Bang" revealing?
- Where do I belong, and to whom? Do I dare love and parent children? How?

- How can I forgive? And be forgiven, and try again?
- How can I be unbranded, free, and know my heart's desires?
- What does it mean to have a body? How is our desire for intimacy finally satisfied?
- What of our clashes of civilizations, ethnicities and genders?
- Is there hope of justice? Of mercy?
- If God is love, why is there evil and suffering? Does suffering have value?
- How can my heart survive this world and live again?
- What could excite me perpetually?

Before long, *ABC World News Tonight* reported, "Hunger for answers runs deep. When Veritas Forums [emerge within] a university, thousands of students pack auditoriums to participate." In the 2006 book *Finding God Beyond Harvard: The Quest for Veritas* (IVP), I share the story, and stories, of the Veritas movement from Harvard to Berkeley and many schools in between, including my own struggles and crisis of faith beneath the surface.

Though Harvard tends to add branches while laying an ax to its own root, thankfully the tenacious root of Harvard is *Veritas*, Truth—the True Vine who will not die. He has a way of rising from the dead. Thus, nearly four centuries ago, Harvard College was founded for his glory, *In Christi Gloriam*, and its shield bears his offer of true life to us, *Veritas, Christo et Ecclessiae*. In the same spirit, Princeton was founded nearly three centuries ago: "I restore life to the dead," *Vitam Mortuis Reddo*.

The personal nature of this book is unusual in the academy. These writers speak with vulnerable candor. We may sense a Spirit who hovers over ancient ruins, to rebuild. We find the same Spirit brooding, healing and recreating lives. Seeds of God's word, so often sown in tears, germinate life; for the Creator just keeps creating and now offers to animate our lives from within. The One who once breathed into us the breath of life still inspires. He offers wisdom for the true scholar, Word and lilting melody for the deaf, light in our darkness. He is hope when we're downcast and dying, living water for our thirst, and comfort in fear and injustice. He offers himself as the relentless lover who enters only when invited.

Might our ancient door be the golden key to the future? Might our first light remain our True North who shines on the far side of our world's confusion? Perhaps he is the True Vine on whom we might draw, yielding the fruit of love, joy, creativity, discovery, and progress. A Tree of Life in whom all things are new. Love who is alive and will not die, making hopeful a world awaiting its redemption.

Kelly Monroe Kullberg

Introduction:
Found by God at Harvard

L ike Jacob wrestling until daybreak with God himself, the story of Harvard is a struggle with *veritas*—truth. And who cannot say this about his or her own life? We long for character that is—and friends who are—true to life and down to earth. We work to build lives and homes on a solid and lasting foundation. The goal of veritas is not religion. The goal is life.

In *The Search for God at Harvard*, written while *Finding God at Harvard* was also in the making, author Ari Goldman found that Harvard's motto, *Veritas*, "was just another shorthand way of recognizing Jesus Christ, who was seen as the ultimate Truth." But Mr. Goldman was disappointed in his search, which was confined to Harvard Divinity School, upon finding no one to speak of the *gospel* ("good news") and person of Jesus Christ.

In this book we find this gospel and this person by entering the whole university. We meet professors, alumni, and students in the college and ten graduate schools—scientists, philosophers, medical doctors, an Olympic medalist, homemakers, environmentalists, an economist, a sophomore who is battling bone cancer. Their searches and research reveal a high common denominator. Their microscopes, telescopes, and eyes are windows surveying a shared horizon. Through their stories, we see the gospel—the first light of America's first college.

Beyond their work, writers describe their personal stories of wonder, despair, love, and hope. They challenge popular cynicism by sharing with us their questions, turnings, joy, and the one whom they have eventually come to know as Truth.

These stories speak of minds and lives saved from the anesthetic of Godlessness; for eventually nothing is as boring as selfishness nor as exciting as forgiveness, freedom, and obedience to that which is real and gives life.

Writers encourage honest questions because they believe there are real answers. What is it to be human? What are our origins? Of what value is my life and work? What should we do with our bodies? If a loving God exists then why do we suffer? How can nations be reconciled? What about the poor? How can human love last? For them, learning flows from humility and the sense of wonder.

As we learn in the essays and epilogue, there is a grassroots spiritual vitality pushing up once again, not coming from institutional religion but from diverse students, alumni, and a few professors whose treasure hunts are leading to a treasure.

FIRST LIGHT

The college was founded in 1636 that students might be free to know truth and life in relation to Jesus Christ. Thus, the early mottoes were *Veritas* (Truth, 1643), *In Christi Gloriam* (To the Glory of Christ, 1650), and *Christo et Ecclesiae* (For Christ and the Church, 1692).

From the beginning, Harvard had the good liberal sense not to require Christian faith of its students but to nurture their freedom for the search. The display of three open books on the early college seal, two facing up and one facing down, suggested the dynamic relationship between reason and revelation. One of the earliest accounts of Harvard, the College Laws of 1642, reads:

> Let every student . . . consider well the main end of his life and studies is to know God and Jesus Christ which is eternal life, John 17:3, and therefore to lay Christ in the bottom, as the only foundation of all sound knowledge and learning. Seeing the Lord giveth wisdom, everyone shall seriously by prayer, in secret, seek wisdom of Him.[1]

The foundation of their search for truth was the deduction that the first step in learning about the world was to learn about the world's Creator. According to Gary Haugen, editor of the former campus journal *Veritas Reconsidered*:

> One could ask the Puritan to deny the existence of a creator; but from the available evidence in the universe, he concluded that such an assumption required too much blind faith. As their Catholic brother in France, Blaise Pascal, wrote during the same era, "Reason's last step is the recognition that there are an infinite number of things which are beyond it."[2]

Such a recognition produced both humility and curiosity. Professors were to be stewards of a community of seekers who would explore and pass on truth, like a torch, from generation to generation, truth both divine and human—the accumulated arts and sciences of the ages.[3] Thus, the college was *not* founded as a divinity school per se—students were to explore the mind of God for the art of life, and so they applied themselves to Scripture, languages, math,

---

[1]Harvard College Laws, 1642. The earliest known account of Harvard College. Also appears in *New England's First Fruits* (London, 1643), quoted from "Rules and Precepts That Are to Be Observed in the College."

[2]Gary Haugen, "The Puritan Path to Veritas," *Veritas Reconsidered* (1986).

[3]George Williams, *Wilderness and Paradise in Christian Thought*, 150.

logic, history, music, geometry, and astronomy. Yielding joy and not cynicism, a relationship with Christ could be celebrated in every area of life and study. The Christians rejected any dichotomy, later made in the Enlightenment, between reason and revelation—the merger bore life in their garden called the New World.

Though Morison did not personally prefer the Puritan mind, he called their vision and foundation for education the "dynamic motive for the intellectual movement in New England." He maintained that "if not for the passionately sincere religion of these Puritans, there would have been no Harvard."[4]

The Christian remnant has sought to live out the gospel here for nearly four centuries as they have stimulated dialogue in their classrooms and labs; fought, along with Park Street Church, to abolish slavery; sacrificed their lives as "student volunteers" abroad; and, along with diverse classmates, helped the needy in Harvard Square.

BRAVE NEW WORLD

Today's popular *Veritas* shield no longer includes Christ and the church. The book facing down is turned up, possibly to suggest that it is only a matter of time before we know and control all things by our own wisdom. Harvard, like many modern institutions, seeks to excite in its students a passion for truth while tending to ignore the possibility of any transcendent truth worth pursuing.

This creates an environment wherein students feel safer as doubters than as believers, and as perpetual seekers rather than eventual finders (even though finders who are humble remain tenacious seekers).

The secular academy is not entirely responsible for this shift toward relativism, for it reflects, as well as shapes, the world into which its graduates enter. However, this does not limit our responsibility in the university to be a part of the solution after we first consider some of the problems.

A Law School professor recently expressed concern that many professors have become like "priests who have lost their faith, and kept their jobs." Consider the contrast to a 1789 Massachusetts law that instructed Harvard professors to impress on the minds of youth committed to their care:

the principles of piety and justice and a sacred regard for truth, love of their country, humanity, and a universal benevolence, sobriety, industry

---

[4]Samuel Eliot Morison, *The Founding of Harvard College* (Cambridge: Harvard Univ. Press, 1935), chapter 1.

and frugality, chastity, moderation and temperance, and those other virtues which are the ornament of human society. . . . [5]

Without the sacred regard for truth, and love of our neighbor, things fall apart. The "center cannot hold." We have teachers who do not teach, students who do not learn, and ministers who do not minister, using words like "veritas" that now seem empty and adrift.

"What is the biggest problem among today's students?" Billy Graham recalled asking former Harvard president Derek Bok. The president answered, "Emptiness."[6]

This year alone, four Harvard students have taken their own lives, one just after murdering her roommate and "best friend." Two seniors embezzled one hundred thousand dollars raised for charity. Without love, and knowledge of the living God, we forget what it is to be human. Passion dies. Souls lie fallow. Leaves begin to fall, and we sense that it is getting late.

It is no news that classical Christian thought has been politically, socially, and even theologically incorrect at Harvard. Believers are often considered its counterculture. Some students feel marginalized in the classroom, not because they are African-American, Asian-American, and international students but primarily because they are believers.

The *Harvard Gazette* reported in 1993 that the humanist chaplain on the Harvard-Radcliffe United Ministry, a committed atheist whom few students had heard of, has "a huge following: the entire university."[7] The chaplain said, and the paper agreed, that secular humanism is constantly reinforced in the classrooms. Less tolerated is the Christian concept that the gospel and the *imago dei* (beings created in the image of God) lay the surest foundation for humanism, rights, and lasting dignity for all people.

Some students assume that relativism is related to the theory of relativity, a misapprehension lamented by Einstein himself. Relativism is then confused with the fact of pluralism. Many assume moral law to be a social construct rather than a God-given reality of conscience and sense of justice.

A history of science instructor silently presupposes naturalism, chance, and random evolutionary mutations over time. After nine weeks a student asks the instructor to explain her presuppositions, and comment on the possibility of design in the universe. The instructor is first stunned, then disregards the question and the student as impertinent.

In a place with so many words, we learn by asking what the university is *silent* about. There is at least one word that is an embarrassment in the class-

---

[5]President Derek Bok quoted from "Ethics, the University and Society," *Harvard Magazine* (May–June 1988), 40.

[6]As told by Dr. Graham in a 1991 televised program from London.

[7]Debra Bradley Ruder, *Harvard University Gazette*, vol. LXXXVIII, no. 42 (July 9, 1993), 1.

room, as implied by divinity students who refer in their braver moments to "the J word"—Jesus.

Silence, whether expected or self-imposed, barricades from the public square those who might challenge the status quo. Ironically, postmodernism and liberalism, like Christianity, are philosophically committed to celebrating diversity, not abolishing it. We are all guilty, however. Each group has elements that prefer to stifle rather than to arouse ideas.

Instead we should welcome all voices—even ones in the wilderness. In this volume, Rebecca Baer Porteous writes:

> I had become deeply disturbed by many of my classes in which we were no longer able to ask whether or not there is a God. A student who is never challenged to ask such questions may be a student divorced from the possibility that a God exists, and that in knowing a loving God, we might find the purpose of human existence.

In a graduate commencement address, another student said:

> They tell us that it is heresy to suggest the superiority of some value, fantasy to believe in moral argument, slavery to submit to a judgment sounder than your own. The freedom of our day is the freedom to devote ourselves to any values we please, on the mere condition that we do not believe them to be true.[8]

Relativism threatens to extinguish the motive for education. What were once high aspirations are now leveled as neutral, making wisdom, virtue, and freedom feel like empty words with false hopes. Relativism would teach us not to discriminate between preferences of personal and therefore (we are told) equal merit: parental commitment, cyberpunk, drugs, Jesus, Freud, virtual reality, virtual morality. Within our social schizophrenia, there remains no source of legitimate authority and meaning. Absolutely no absolutes. And above all, no possibility of transcendence and joy.

Perhaps this is what novelist Dorothy Sayers meant when she said:

> In the world it is called tolerance but in hell it is called despair. The sin that believes in nothing, cares for nothing, seeks to know nothing, enjoys nothing, finds purpose in nothing, lives for nothing but remains alive because there is nothing which it would die for.

Today's younger generations didn't begin this condition, though we are blindly choosing to continue in it, and the cost is far more than tuition. We see it in each newscast. War, crime, addiction, and "free sex" continue to cost millions of lives, and the secular entertainment media continue to stimulate

---

[8]John C. McCullough. Quoted also by Robert Bellah in his Noble Lectures.

and feed the appetite for abomination.[9] The modern ethic? American roulette—
"Just Say No" and "Just Do It" without the recognition of a moral reality to
decide which to do when. Standing in Harvard Square, a mecca of diversity
and ideology, do we smile at or lament the popular bumper sticker that reads,
"Practice random acts of kindness and senseless acts of beauty"?

The enormous potential of students has been malnourished and under-
challenged. Curiosity about the mind of the Maker, excitement for great love
and virtue, imagination for innovation, and desire for the dignity of work—
these inspired education until the death of God in the minds of many influential intellectuals in our century. A century of technology and so-called progress,
now also called "the bloodiest century in history." Nietzsche's announcement
that "God is dead" appears to have been prophetic.

A NEW CONVERSATION—A NEW CENTURY

Students, however, are too smart to believe everything they read. This
year's Harvard-Radcliffe Christian Fellowship T-shirt says, "Nietzsche is dead."
It is signed, "God."

In *The Culture of Disbelief*, Yale law professor Stephen Carter said what
many believers have felt: "When citizens do act in their public selves as though
their faith matters, they risk not only ridicule but actual punishment."

When *ABC World News* recently visited, they found that students' faith is
marginalized in the classroom. And they found that Christians here are not
protesting but praying—hard. With hundreds of students in Bible studies and
fellowships, the *gospel* is a growing extracurricular reality.[10] The greater challenge is to raise the level of discussion in the classroom itself. Some students
and professors are daring to consider the legitimate presence of the teachings and
love of Jesus Christ in the middle of a college founded for him.

Christians in the sciences consider the Creator's elegance, design, and
power in astrophysics, biochemistry, geology. A cell biologist questions the
potential use of fetal tissue in his lab, and a dialogue begins.

Some business students practice servant leadership and challenge appeals
to social Darwinism. They discuss the need for a moral absolute in ethics. They
challenge child-labor practices and explore the potential of capitalism without greed.

A few students in literature and the arts point out biblical ideas and inspiration, often otherwise forgotten, in the works of Shakespeare, Dante, Bach,

---

[9]A poll taken in the June 1993 issue of *TIME* magazine says that 80% of the television-
viewing population, including children, think there is too much violence shown on television, yet their opinions have little, if any, effect on producers.

[10]See "Christian Groups Bloom," *Harvard Crimson* (December 1994).

Raphael, Rosetti, and Coleridge. They challenge the logic and foundational influence of men like Kant, Skinner, Dewey, Freud, and Derrida.

Christian students at the Law School consider the triumph of grace over law in yielding love and gratitude, which changes the moral choices of human beings. They seek to stand with hurting people who have known neither justice nor mercy.

A freshman asks the art history department to offer a survey course that even includes some of the old masters. With his parents' eighty thousand dollars in tuition, he hopes to learn something about the broad history and inspiration of art and artists, not only the theories of deconstruction and contextualism. "Art history," like literature or philosophy, he says, "enables us to study works of art that . . . penetrate both our minds and our souls. . . . This seems to be an idea that Harvard has all but forgotten."[11]

Those who tire of culture wars and the old categories of "right" and "left" are finding common and higher ground on which to stand. Beyond the ivory tower, a few "pro-life" and "pro-choice" students become friends, by accident, as they roll up their sleeves and work together in a shelter for women and children.

The Harvard-Radcliffe Christian Fellowship (HRCF) documents the need to increase minority faculty hiring, remembered daily in "noon prayer." They join other fellowships on Friday nights to explore "The Fall of the Iron Curtain: The Role of the Church" and "Jesus and the Dynamics of Diversity." They sing and pray with Christian grad students also off to serve the poorest of the poor in inner cities as close as Dorchester and as far away as Kuala Lumpur.

Students begin to learn from the example of those who serve them each day—the women who cook their meals and who clean their hallways. Some students turn to them for prayer and counsel. Meals begin to taste better for students who cultivate the capacity for gratitude.

By grassroots initiative, a thousand students join writers of *Finding God* for the Harvard Veritas Forum in Sanders Theater, where three nineteenth-century shields are illuminated after a century in shadow—*Veritas, Christo et Ecclesiae*. In panel discussions, treasure hunts, films, and concerts, several generations of alumni are united with current students. Together they explore the gospel's relevance to all of life—from astronomy to zoology.

Students are learning that the truth claims of Jesus are not marginal but central to human history—starting in the Middle East and spreading into Asia, Africa, and Europe by the end of the first century A.D. They are seeing that every real scholar, including their professors, should wrestle with the challenge of Jesus Christ; for it is intellectually more honest to question him, and be questioned by him, than to ignore him. The twenty-first century will require such honesty of us.

---

[11]Charles Barzon, "Deconstructing Art History," *Harvard Salient* (March 14, 1994).

ABOUT THESE WRITERS

So Jesus has been ignored; why shouldn't he be? What compels us to reconsider Jesus' claims? In what sense does he awaken and satisfy the mind? Is he Truth, in whom all of life finds unity and coherence (unity in diversity: uni-versity), as understood by the founders of most colleges throughout the world? Is he Truth who makes bridges out of barriers between cultures, ethnicities, and genders?

In what sense, as some claim, did he fuel the Great Awakening, the abolition of slavery on several continents, women's suffrage, civil rights, the liberation of Eastern Europe and South Africa? Did he really inspire excellence in universities, and societies committed to philosophy, painting, music, scientific inquiry, literature, architecture, and family life? Does he still?

The intent of these writers is not to revert Harvard to its Christian past but to raise and explore honest questions of our lives and times—questions about truth and meaning that were once welcomed as central contributions to an education that is both liberal and liberating.

First called to listen, we now speak, not out of intolerance but out of love that is good and real enough to take risks. With the sort of honesty found in these stories, in fellowships, in Veritas Fora now developing around the country, Harvard can generate light as well as heat, for these people choose to "light a single candle more than to curse the darkness." The question "Why is there crime?" becomes "How can I have virtue?" "Why are we angry?" becomes "How can I forgive?" "Why is there despair?" becomes "What is my hope?"

The historicity and consequences of the life of Jesus prevent us from calling this hope "mythological" and "ridiculous." Glance at the New Testament and you will find that he was a revolution of tenderness and dignity for the forgotten and the lost, for those of all faiths and so-called races. He upset cultural norms to exalt women, children, and all those of humble heart. He forgave the repentant. He enthused the weary. He remains the Life-giver, as articulated by writers in this book.

It is rare to find two Harvard people who agree on much of anything, yet here the young and old, the famous and the less known, meet from diverse cultures and professions. They write not as Protestants, Orthodox, Anglicans, or Catholics but as mere Christians. They speak not first as professors and professionals but as humans, imperfect like the rest of us, being saved by grace.

Some suffer alongside neighbors whose dreams are shattered by war, disease, poverty, and drugs. They put down their books and take time to listen to their colleagues in an environment of otherwise relentless competition. Many comfort prisoners, single parents, hospital patients, and the elderly who have also known losses. They are among those who challenge and bring hope to Wall Street, "Third World" and U.S. combat zones, the suburbs, Capitol Hill, and even Hollywood. They hear the cries beneath the words of the poor and the rich, because they are not called to religion but to life.

Our first writer reveals the value of the broken things she has found. In these journeys, each writer *enters into* veritas by caring more about real human kindness than perfect scores on moral reasoning exams. Even in suffering, they find that life is deep, vast, and immensely worth living.

These writers have been touched by moments of grace that inspire life-times of learning. Perhaps this book should be entitled *Found by God at Harvard*, since we have not found and loved Veritas so much as he has found and loved us. But to the extent that life is a treasure hunt, I hope that you will find these stories and writers to be both maps and treasures. We begin by exploring together our questions of this living Truth who loves, and frees us to love.

KELLY K. MONROE

The first Veritas Forum at Harvard, 1992.

Gathering of the writers of *Finding God at Harvard,* at Veritas Forum at Harvard, 1996. L to R: Jeff Barneson, Bill Edgar, Todd Lake, Poh Lian Lim, Habib Malik, Kelly Monroe Kullberg (with microphone), Eve Perera, Rodney Peterson.

Professor
Robert Coles

Veritas shield
from Harvard.

Jim and Vera Shaw

Owen Gingerich

The Harvard Kuumba Singers

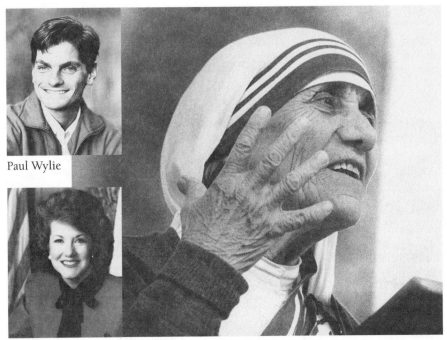

Paul Wylie

Elizabeth Dole   Mother Teresa

The Harvard Graduate Student Christian Fellowship building a medical clinic with Haitian friends.

CHAPTER 1

QUESTIONS AND TURNINGS

৵ৎ

Where is the wise man?
Where is the scholar?
Where is the philosopher of this age?
Has not God made foolish the wisdom of this world?
. . . And the weakness of God is stronger than man's strength.

PAUL THE APOSTLE (1 CORINTHIANS 1:20, 25)

ॐ

We must at all times remember what intellectuals habitually forget:
that people matter more than concepts and must come first. The worst of
all despotisms is the heartless tyranny of ideas.

PAUL JOHNSON, INTELLECTUALS

ॐ

It is not excess of thought but defect of fertile and generous emotion
that marks [many "intellectuals"] out. Their heads are no bigger than
the ordinary; it is the atrophy of the chest beneath that makes them seem
so.

C. S. LEWIS, THE ABOLITION OF MAN

ॐ

I knew I'd disappoint you, if I showed to you this child,
      who is crying out inside me, lost in wild.
Now inches from the water, about to disappear,
      I feel you behind me, but how did you find me here?

LYRICS BY DAVID WILCOX

Questions in
a Quiet Moment

శ్రీ

— R E B E C C A   B A E R   P O R T E O U S —

"What does it mean to lead rich human lives? How can people find a way to lead lives of meaning and purpose?" As a Christian, I knew that there were answers to such questions. But where did they fit into the secular university?

Rebecca Baer Porteous is completing a doctorate in ethics and theology at Duke University, drawing inspiration in part from her father, Richard Baer, who teaches environmental ethics at Cornell. She is currrently teaching in Johannesburg, South Africa, where she and her husband, David, live.

Following graduation from Harvard College in 1987, Becky studied in Zimbabwe and returned to teach sections for Robert Coles' course "The Literature of Social Reflection."

Rebecca joyfully led "dumpster diving" excursions while at Duke and Harvard, because she sees the creative redemption and recycling of that which is wasted or rejected as a symbol of God's work in the world.

"As a child hearing the Bible read aloud by my parents and Anabaptist grandparents," she remembers, "I had learned that wisdom was central to life, something to be sought and valued." Her reflections arise out of this memory.

Questions in a Quiet Moment

— R E B E C C A   B A E R   P O R T E O U S —

Sometimes in a quiet moment I sit and look at the basket on top of my small bookcase. It is filled with pieces of shattered bottles, cracked dishes, broken glass bangles, shards of a clay cooking pot, and a ceramic ring around a defunct spark plug. People often laugh when they come in and see these baskets—several around the room—full of fragments.

As I sit quietly, the broken pieces tell stories of men and women whose lives, like these fragments, were shattered. The first piece of glass in the collection came from an urban housing project in Cambridge, Massachusetts—a broken medicine bottle, recalling to my mind a young black girl with sickle cell anemia who lived in the project. Her life was painful and hurt-filled, with only tenuous hopes for the future. Another fragment used to be a Limoges salad plate, borrowed from friends and carelessly dropped, like a friendship fallen apart by careless handling. The glass bangles came from India—fragile, delicate objects that shattered easily but were cheap to replace, like the lives of some impoverished Indian wives, burned or killed for larger dowries. The spark plug is from Mamelodi, a township outside Pretoria, South Africa. As I hold it, I reflect on the brokenness of those without power in a society in which some are powerful—comfortably successful in the modern world with its technological conveniences—the way I am, at home with my own car, a bank account, and an income. Then I pick up a piece of a Coke bottle and think about lives like mine. Two undergraduates I know of at Duke tried to kill themselves this semester. Despite consuming more than 250 bottles of "the real thing" per person per year, we "successful" ones here in America often end up broken, too, forgotten, used up, exposed, and shattered, like the remains of the Coke bottle lying on the street.

The sad thing is how much of our brokenness we carry inside ourselves. Inexplicably, we can find ourselves hurting the very people we long to love. Unable to keep commitments we once desired, we can become bored with and angry at the people we so desperately wanted to spend time with or be married to. We can run in fear from what we truly would like to say and have been longing to do; we complain, we are bitter and disappointed with our lives, but unsure why. "I do not do what I want, but I do the very thing I hate," the apostle Paul wrote almost two thousand years ago, and which of us wouldn't, if we were honest, agree with him at times? Although we have learned how to get our acts together, to lose ourselves in our work for the sake of success, to consume, to be entertained, in quiet moments we find ourselves like the baskets, full of broken pieces, of splintered memories, of shattered hopes.

Such moments lead me to a cascade of questions. If there were no God, nothing beyond ourselves, how could there be hope? How could we be anything but trapped in a destructive reiteration of the things we hate yet nourish within ourselves? I have often thought that from a strictly atheistic point of view, there can be nothing but material determinism. Tightly linked causal chains. Every action leading to a reaction. Each action a mere response to stimuli. And the stimuli themselves only responses to other stimuli. Without God, without the possibility of something breaking in and freeing us from ourselves and the implications of the destructive choices we have often made, the ways we have felt and acted, how could there be anything but self-created hell? Who of us could really bear to face honestly the consequences of all the ways in which we have lived in a world without forgiveness, without mercy?

As an undergraduate, I wondered: If our lives are determined by impersonal causes, if there is nothing transcendent, why do people sometimes have passion for their work? What motivated people to paint, to teach, to create, to passionately and unceasingly devote their lives to such projects? Why, for instance, did the great novelists take such pains in writing? I was frustrated and disappointed with my English professors for focusing only on the historical background and the stylistic analysis of novels and poems, avoiding discussions about the questions and the thoughts that had impelled authors and artists to write and create. What did they want to say?

In my junior year I switched concentrations to social studies. Karl Marx particularly intrigued me. I wondered what it was that would have inspired a man to devote his entire life to writing, living in poverty and insecurity. At the heart of Marx's more philosophical writings, I found a man asking: "What does it mean to lead rich and purposeful human lives?" As a Christian, I knew that there were answers to such questions. I had learned to ask questions, because I believe that, by God's grace, truth is revealed, not exhausted, by investigation.

But these questions were not addressed in the classrooms. We were asked to understand and re-present Marx's view of history, Rawls' original position, Freud's understanding of humans as sexually motivated creatures, but few professors ever asked us whether or not we considered these views to be true. Classes on human nature, morality, and society systematically eschewed metaphysical questions, even though the theorists under study had themselves often been driven to write precisely because of their desire to answer such questions. What does it really mean to be a human being? This question had been excluded a priori, dismissed as nonempirical and relative, unworthy of academic consideration because the answers were ultimately seen to be purely subjective and emotive.

The "knowledge" one could acquire through the political, social, or natural sciences was often limited to a catalog of observed phenomena, information that would lead to the development of models with predictive capacities. It was enough to describe such a world empirically, suggest how it works and what tinkering with it in a particular way might do, but it was wrong to ask what made a truly good life, not just for Aristotle in the Athenian polis, but for us, now, today.

Over time I became deeply disturbed by many of my classes. A mental world that never asks metaphysical questions, the questions of wisdom, no longer is open enough to ask whether or not there is a God.

Was Sartre right that there is no God and therefore no good and no bad, no moral truth about anything at all? A student who is never challenged to ask such questions, never allowed to think that there might even be true answers to such questions, may be a student radically divorced from the possibility that a God exists, and that in knowing a loving God, we might find the purpose of human existence, and that in experiencing his love expressed in Jesus Christ, we might find a hope for life.

A few years after graduating, I returned to Harvard as a summer school proctor and was struck by the spiritual confusion and hunger I encountered among students. One woman was desperately seeking God from a Christian background but frustrated again and again that she could not *see* God. Several other students had been asking searching questions about what they ought to do with their lives. I challenged them to consider that they would not be able to answer their questions about what they ought to *do* until they had answered the larger questions of who they ought to *be* and *why*. Most people, most career counselors and young people, seem to avoid these ultimate questions facing each of us. Martin Luther King Jr. put it simply: "A man is not a man until he's found something worth dying for."

In the midst of my own brokenness, and the brokenness around me, I have found an answer, a light, and a powerful healing hope that brings forgiveness, a hope that brings wisdom and life. I have found food for an intellectual hunger, an emotional hunger—a hunger and thirst for righteousness that becomes an energy with which to seek, to serve, to celebrate, to worship, and to know.

The Inexplicable Prayers of Ruby Bridges

৯৫

— ROBERT COLES —

I assured my wife I would not pray for those people. First, I would call the police. Ruby couldn't call the police. She would not even call those people rednecks.

Robert Coles is a social anthropologist and research psychiatrist, as well as professor of medical humanities, psychiatry, and literature at Harvard University. He is the author of the five-volume, Pulitzer-Prize-winning series *The Children of Crisis* and books including *The Call of Stories: Teaching and the Moral Imagination, The Spiritual Life of Children*, and *Harvard Diaries*. He is a frequent contributor to the Catholic periodical *The New Oxford Review*.

Professor Coles' life stories, and his gift for telling stories, illustrate the role of narratives in our moral formation. The stories of his friendship, for example, with the physician-poet William Carlos Williams reveal an important influence on Coles' life and career. In his course "The Literature of Social Reflection," he tells the following story to his students.

The Inexplicable Prayers of Ruby Bridges

— ROBERT COLES —

When a federal judge ordered four little black girls to go into two white New Orleans elementary schools, you would have thought that the Devil himself had arrived in that old cosmopolitan port city. Fear and anger erupted into street scenes and demonstrations.

I was drafted into the air force in 1958. A psychiatrist, I was put in charge of a psychiatric hospital in Biloxi, Mississippi. I had my own struggles with certain air force policies and decided to undergo psychoanalysis in New Orleans, where there was a training institute. That is how I came to know that New Orleans was aflame with racial violence and social upheaval.

One day I was early for my appointment, so I decided to go and see what was happening at one of those schools. Outside the Frantz school I saw a mob of people standing and screaming. It was two o'clock in the afternoon, and I realized they were waiting for something. I asked one of the people what was happening.

He answered, "She's coming out in a half an hour."

I said, "Who's she?"

And then I heard all the language about who she was—all the cuss words and the foul language. I decided to stay and watch, even if I didn't get to see my doctor.

Soon, out of the Frantz school came a little girl, Ruby Bridges. And beside her were federal marshals. She came out and the people started in. They called her this and they called her that. They brandished their fists. They told her she was going to die and they were going to kill her. I waited when she left in a car, and I wondered who was going to come out of that school next. But then I found out no one else was in the school. The school had been totally boycotted by the white population. So here was a little black child who was going to an American elementary school all by herself in the fall of 1960. That is part of our American history.

Before going South, I had done some work in Boston at the Children's Hospital, with children who had been stricken with polio during what was the last polio epidemic we will probably ever see in this country. I had studied stress in children and presented my conclusions to the American Psychiatric Association.

In New Orleans, I thought to myself, *Why not do another study right here?* Here too is stress—social stress. I figured I could get in another little study there before I went home. I could present another paper at the American Psychiatric Association.

With the help of Kenneth Clark, a black psychologist in New York, and Thurgood Marshall, then the NAACP legal fund attorney, I eventually established contact with Ruby and her family. My wife and I went to the Bridges' home, knowing the family was under terrific stress.

"How are you doing, Ruby?" I would say to Ruby twice a week, and she would say, "I'm OK."

"Mrs. Bridges, how is Ruby doing?"

"She's doing fine."

I had learned these questions in my study of pediatrics and child psychiatry. One expects children or their parents to answer them with some evidence of turmoil. "Mrs. Bridges, is Ruby sleeping OK?"

"Oh, yes. Ruby's sleeping fine."

"Are you sure she's sleeping fine?"

"Yes."

"Well, how is Ruby's appetite?"

"It's fine."

"Are you sure she's eating well?"

"Fine. "

"How do you think Ruby's doing with her friends when she comes home from school?"

"Ruby's fine when she comes home. She plays and sometimes she reads from the books that she brings home, or tries to read the books. She's just in the first grade learning how to read."

"Does Ruby seem upset at any time?"

"No, Ruby doesn't seem too upset," said Mrs. Bridges.

I said to myself, *Maybe Mr. and Mrs. Bridges do not know how to pick up these symptoms.* I had been used to having parents come to see me from all the well-to-do suburbs of Boston, and you can be assured that parents there knew how to pick up the symptoms. As for Ruby, she was probably more upset than she realized. Eventually she would realize it, or if she didn't, I would realize it. And I would tell her, and if not her, the world. There was a world waiting for our news.

The days turned into weeks and the weeks turned into months. And one day the schoolteacher, who saw Ruby every day, all by herself in the classroom, said to me, "You know, I don't understand this child. She seems so happy. She comes here so cheerfully." The teacher spoke about the way Ruby went through those mobs, escorted each time by the federal marshals.

So I said, "Well, I'm a little puzzled myself, but I think that sometimes people under tremendous stress gird themselves mightily, and it can take time to find out just how upset they are." Then I remembered what I had learned as a resident in child psychiatry: you ask the children to do some drawing. Perhaps their pictures will tell you something.

Ruby did some drawings and they were interesting. She did show that she regarded white people as being bigger and stronger and black people as being vulnerable. And I would point this out to her, and she would say, "Yes, they certainly are stronger, those white people." And I would think to myself, *Well, that is no great discovery for her.*

But I kept on asking her how she was doing and how she was getting on. And what I began to notice is that here was a girl who was six years old, whose parents were extremely poor, were illiterate so that they did not even know how to sign their names. They were going through tremendous strain, day after day, and they did not seem to be complaining, parents or child. What a contrast with the well-to-do middle-class people I had seen in Boston whose children, for one reason or another—all of them white, by the way—were having all sorts of difficulties. *Now, how do you explain that?* I would ask myself. And I did not know how to explain that. I was accumulating all this information, but I was getting rather frustrated.

Ruby Bridges came into New Orleans when she was three years old. Her parents had been tenant farmers near Greenville. We would later learn, in the late 1960s and early 1970s, to call such people culturally disadvantaged and culturally deprived: poor folk, poor black folk.

Mr. Bridges was a janitor. Mrs. Bridges took care of her three small children from morning to night. When she tucked the children in, she went to other homes, got down on her knees, and scrubbed the floors. Then she came home in the middle of the night and was ready for the next morning after just a few hours of sleep. What both parents obviously wanted for their children was a better life than they had had.

One day the schoolteacher said to me, "I saw Ruby talking to those people on the street this morning. She stopped and seemed to be talking to the people in the street." Every morning at eight o'clock there were at least fifty people there waiting for her, and every afternoon another fifty or seventy-five.

We went to Ruby's home that night, and I asked, "Ruby, how was your day today?"

She said, "It was OK."

"I was talking to your teacher today, and she told me that she asked you about something when you came into school early in the morning."

"I don't remember," Ruby said.

"Your teacher told me that she saw you talking to the people in the street."

"Oh, yes. I told her I wasn't talking to them. I was just saying a prayer for them."

"Ruby, you pray for the people there?"

"Oh, yes."

"Really?"

"Yes."

I said, "Why do you do that?"

"Because they need praying for," she answered.

"Do they?"

"Oh, yes."

"Ruby, why do you think they need you to pray for them?"

"Because I should."

"Why?"

"Because I should."

Then Ruby's mother came into the room. She had heard this line of inquiry and she said, "We tell Ruby that it's important that she pray for the people." She said that Ruby had the people on a list and prayed for them at night.

I said, "You do, Ruby? You pray for them at night, too?"

"Oh, yes."

"Why do you do that?"

"Well, because they need praying for." Mrs. Bridges told me Ruby had been told, in Sunday school, to pray for the people. I later found that the minister in their Baptist church also prayed for the people. Publicly. Every Sunday.

I said to Mrs. Bridges, and then to her husband later, "You know, it strikes me that that is a lot to ask of Ruby. I mean, given what she's going through." And they looked at me very confused.

"We're not asking her to pray for them because we want to hurt her or anything," said Mrs. Bridges, "but we think that we all have to pray for people like that, and we think Ruby should too." And then she looked at me and said, "Don't you think they need praying for?"

"Yes, I agree with you there," I said. "But I still think it's a little much to ask Ruby to pray for them."

I talked to my wife. "I don't understand why this girl should be praying for them—she's got enough to bear without that."

My wife said, "That's you speaking, but maybe she feels differently." Then my wife asked, "What would you do if you were going through a mob like that twice a day?"

"I can tell you one thing," I answered. "I wouldn't pray for the people who were doing what they're doing to Ruby, or trying to do to Ruby— telling her they want to kill her, for instance."

My wife constructed the following scenario: "I can just picture you try- ing to get into the Harvard Faculty Club through mobs. What would you do if to get into that club in the morning and leave it in the afternoon you had to go through those mobs, and even the police wouldn't protect you?" (The city police wouldn't, by the way, protect Ruby in New Orleans. Hence the need for federal marshals.)

I assured my wife I would not pray for those people. What we decided I would do was this: First, I would call the police. Ruby couldn't call the police. The police were on the side of the mobs. The second thing I would do is get a lawyer, and fast. Ruby had no lawyer. Ruby had not even been born at the hands of a doctor. The third thing I would do would be to turn immediately on this crowd with language and knowledge. Who are these people, anyway? They are sick. They are marginal socioeconomically, psy- chosocially, socioculturally, and psychohistorically. But Ruby did not have the language of sociology or psychology to turn on this crowd. She would not even call them rednecks.

The fourth thing we agreed that I would do, of course, would be to write an article about what I had gone through. Maybe I would even turn it into a book. But Ruby was just learning to read and write.

Ruby—and, by the way, many other children we got to know in Little Rock and Clinton, Tennessee, and later in Atlanta, who came from humble homes and who were black people in the south in the 1960s—again and again showed this inclination to pray for their persecutors. What was it? Personal dignity? Prayerful dignity? Once, a couple of weeks after the first time I mentioned it, I again asked Ruby about this praying. "Ruby, I'm still puzzled. I'm trying to figure out why you think you should be the one to pray for such people, given what they do to you twice a day, five days a week."

"Well," she said, "especially it should be me."

"Why you especially?"

"Because if you're going through what they're doing to you, you're the one who should be praying for them." And then she quoted to me what she had heard in church. The minister said that Jesus went through a lot of trouble and that Jesus said about the people who were causing the trouble, "Forgive them, because they don't know what they're doing." And now little Ruby was saying this in the 1960s, about the people in the streets of New Orleans. How is someone like me supposed to account for that, psychologically or any other way?

Here I could get very sophisticated and say that perhaps, though Ruby was saying the words, she did not really understand what they meant. When I tried this observation on my wife, she said, "At least she was saying them. I know a lot of people with a lot more money and power—and white skin, to boot—who wouldn't say it."

"Me included," I said. "I wouldn't."

"That's the point," my wife responded.

So now what was I supposed to do? Call Ruby and her family masochists? Say that they were making statements they didn't comprehend? That they had not studied in college, had not read the implication of what Christ meant when he asked this forgiveness for his tormentors, as interpreted by X, Y, and Z philosopher-theologian?

Later, when I would talk about the mobs in the streets in New Orleans, others would tell me how ignorant they were. They were rednecks, the kind of people who would behave that way. That sounded convincing to me. These poor people in the streets, they were ignorant. They lacked education. It sounded plausible.

The only thing is that one day my wife and I started recalling some of our twentieth-century history. Germany in the 1920s and 1930s did not have a large uneducated population. It was one of the most educated nations in the history of the world. There were great universities in a culture rich and finely textured. It was the nation of Goethe and Schiller and Freud and Einstein. There were impressive scientists, artists, musicians. Was there ever a more civilized nation? And then Hitler took over in January 1933. If you read German history carefully, you will know that within months, the Nazis had working for them and with them lawyers, doctors, journalists, college professors, and, I regret to say, ministers, theologians, philosophers, and psychiatrists. Education, tradition, and culture did not stop Germany from embarking on a program of mass genocide.

But there's little Ruby, who had taken no courses in moral analysis or systematic ethics. She hadn't read the books we treasure. Yet somehow she walked through that mob praying for those people. Every day. A year later, when schools had been reluctantly desegregated, she kept on praying. And quoting from the Bible. And quoting those statements, those sayings, those stories, that Jesus uttered in Galilee.

I am not about to argue for some kind of anti-intellectualism. But we do have a lot to learn about what makes for good people in the living of life. I do not mean "good people" in the sense developmental psychologists mean it. For example, "Let's see, Ruby, we have some tests here for you. We'll find out about the stage of your moral development. Answer these various scenarios that we're presenting to you. What would you do under these circumstances? We will then grade you and give you a score." These may be very interesting hypothetical scenarios. But do we know that someone who does well at answering those scenarios, put to one in a laboratory, is then going to go out into the street and be honorable in every-day life? This ought to haunt us.

I remember when I was in college. We would come back to our rooms and a woman would be there, cleaning our rooms and making our beds. We had a name for these women in the Harvard of the 1950s. We called them biddies.

We never knew the name of the woman who did this for us because she was just our biddy. She cleaned up after us. And if we were very thoughtful, some days we might thank her but I don't want to remember how many times we never thanked her. And I don't want to remember how many times we had a smashed beer bottle or two in the fireplace, knowing that she would clean up after us. After all, she was being paid to do that. We gave her a big tip at Christmas time. Never "thank you" or "please." Never any conversation.

At the same time, of course, we were taking courses. Courses, for instance, in psychology, where we would learn about empathy. You would get an A in a course by writing for a whole hour on empathy. But I couldn't tell you the biddy's name. We weren't asked to do that, because that wasn't part of the curriculum, core or otherwise. It still isn't. I watch my children reading books by great philosophers and then I wonder. How can one teach so that what one is teaching engages with a life?

What now does this leave us with? The great paradox that Christ reminds us about is that sometimes those who are lonely and hurt and vulnerable—meek, to use the word—can be touched by grace and show the most extraordinary kind of dignity and, in that sense, inherit not only the next world but even moments of this one. We who have so much knowledge and money and power look on confused, trying to mobilize the intellect, to figure things out. It is not so figurable, is it? These things are mysteries. As Flannery O'Connor said, "Mystery is a great embarrassment to the modern mind."

My Search for the Historical Jesus

— TODD LAKE —

*We all sensed he could be trouble, and we wanted to make sure
he never again became a live issue.*

After graduating *magna cum laude* with a degree in German studies
in 1982, **Todd Lake** deferred entrance to Harvard Law School—
twice—while he mulled over whether law or the ministry would
present the better opportunity for serving the poor. During this time,
he worked as a legislative aide in California on bills protecting
migrant farmworkers' rights and later as a volunteer with the Peace
Corps' environmental sanitation program in Paraguay.

Lake ultimately settled on the ministry and studied at Princeton
Theological Seminary and Southern Seminary in Kentucky. He is
now completing a doctorate in systematic theology in a joint program between Boston College and Andover-Newton School of Theology. In 1989 he married Joy Jordan, a fellow seminarian, a gifted
writer, and a passionate horse-lover. Together they serve as pastors at
Cambridgeport Baptist Church in Cambridge, Massachusetts.

"In the church we are trying to tear down the barriers between
people of different ages, ethnic backgrounds, cultures, and classes
and to encourage friendships across these lines. We want to see a
balance of head, heart, and hands."

A member of the United Ministry at Harvard-Radcliffe, Lake is
frequently invited to speak on Christian apologetics and on the historicity of the New Testament.

My Search for the Historical Jesus

— TODD LAKE —

Religious truth. I had long viewed this as a classic oxymoron. Debates among devotees of the Buddha, the prophet Mohammed, and the Christ seemed as pointless as junior high boys arguing about whose girlfriend was prettiest. Agnosticism seemed the honest person's turf—not a denigration of anyone else's faith but a recognition that proclaiming a personal preference as a universal truth is intellectually dishonest.

I took this tolerant attitude with me to Harvard College, a place where relativism in all things religious is viewed as the birthright of the intellectual. Into my closed universe burst a practitioner of the arcane science of Christian apologetics by the name of Josh McDowell, author of the best-selling book *Evidence That Demands a Verdict*. He asked an intriguing question: "What if Jesus really *had* risen from the dead, vindicating his claim to be God in the flesh?" I thought of the late-night television comedy query "What if Eleanor Roosevelt could fly?" It seemed to me about as likely. And in Mrs. Roosevelt's favor, at least we had historical evidence for her existence.

I was puzzled that McDowell wanted to know *how* I knew anything at all about Eleanor Roosevelt or anyone from the past. It seemed to me that if the issue were her flying or Jesus' rising, the answer was obvious: science taught us that both were impossible. But he pointed out that the scientific method of verifying a claim was predicated on being able to repeat an experiment, and that because neither of the aforementioned subjects could be thus examined, neither could be disproved by science. Science cannot prove or disprove any historical event. McDowell then suggested that the quarrel about Jesus' resurrection was not with science at all. Indeed, those who recognize a miracle as such are already presupposing the truth of science—that is, they assume a uniform functioning of scientific natural laws.

Christians do not claim that Sons of God or resurrections from the dead have ever been part of the repeatable natural order but that at *one* time and place, God became a human being, suffered and died for our misdeeds, and was raised from the dead. This moves Jesus (and Eleanor) from the province of science to that of history and opens the question of the verifiability of historical claims.

I thought about this for a while. This conclusion seemed logical, but I also knew the historical argument would doom the inquiry from the start. The documents that spoke of Jesus had been written by fanatical partisans long after his death, then copied and miscopied for centuries. Christian acceptance of the New Testament was simply another triumph of dogmatic faith over clear, cold reason.

At Harvard, I had not so much come to such conclusions as inherited them. The idea that there was anything left to discuss about Jesus, with the possible exception of his ethics, would have struck most of us as utterly ancient. Moreover, most of us knew enough about Christianity to realize that if Jesus were accepted as the Son of God, religious relativism would take it on the chin. I remember Mother Teresa's speech on the steps of Memorial Church at the Class Day exercise in 1982, where she talked of Jesus incessantly—I mean *incessantly*—and even quoted that verse, John 3:16 (already well known to most of us, thanks to signs in end-zone bleachers). But in a triumph of brilliant editing, *Harvard Magazine*'s account managed to report almost the entire Mother Teresa speech without once hinting that she might even have mentioned Jesus. We all sensed he could be trouble, and we wanted to make sure he never again became a live issue.

This seemed assured, because of the hazy past he inhabited. So I was surprised to learn that even non-Christian New Testament scholars granted that these early Christian documents were, by and large, historically accurate. The article on Jesus in the *Encyclopaedia Judaica* (Jerusalem, 1972) asserts that Matthew, Mark, and Luke were written within the lifetime of eyewitnesses to the events recorded. Even Anthony Flew, committed British atheist, concedes that the earliest New Testament documents bring us to within twenty years of Jesus' death.

Yet all this talk of documentation, it seemed to me, sidestepped the problem of the checkered history of the *transmission* of those documents. Even if a newspaper account is initially accurate, after centuries of hand-copying it will eventually be transmuted into only a garbled version of the original. What hope was there for the New Testament?

As it turns out, the modern science of textual criticism has developed techniques for looking at the thousands of early handwritten copies of the New Testament documents and discerning certain patterns of copying errors made by scribes. The process of arriving at the best readings has progressed to the point that the twenty-sixth edition of the Nestle-Aland Greek New Testament is used by every New Testament scholar, regardless of their faith or their stance toward the New Testament's claims about miracles.

They know what the general public does not: the Greek New Testament documents in our hands—and their modern English translations—

are virtually identical to the ones penned by the earliest followers of Jesus. Indeed, scholars agree that there are more serious textual discrepancies between various versions of *Hamlet* than there are between translations of the New Testament.

This seemed to be an important point. But then again, Widener Library in Harvard Yard has accurately-transmitted copies of *Pravda* from the 1970s in its files. No one thinks that they are therefore faithful mirrors of Soviet events in the 1970s. Couldn't the earliest followers of Jesus simply have concocted his resurrection and the alleged prior supporting miracles and sayings? The answer is yes, but the question is, why would they? What possible long-term motivation could they have had that would not have been nipped in the bud by the first lion brought in to eat up Christians? L. Ron Hubbard, a moderately successful science fiction writer, stated in 1950 that the way to get rich was to invent a religion. He promptly founded the Church of Scientology and made a fortune. On the other hand, the followers of Jesus met with bitter persecution from both the Jews and Romans, as even Jewish and Roman historians, such as Josephus, Tacitus, and Seutonius, attest. It is highly unlikely that people would willingly die for a story they know is fabricated, and yet the earliest followers of Jesus repeatedly paid with their life's blood for claiming that he was God incarnate, the Messiah of the Jews and the only true light for the Gentiles.

But Japanese kamikaze pilots and Iraqi martyr-soldiers also died for their beliefs, not knowing that the assurance of posthumous bliss in exchange for sacrificial suicide may well have been an empty promise. Wasn't belief in the resurrection similar? The difference is this: There was no way for kamikaze pilots to have known whether or not the promise of posthumous honor was true. They could not verify it. But if Jesus had not been resurrected, the disciples would have known. In the relatively small town of Jerusalem, there was no way for them to fool themselves. One is therefore hard pressed to explain the martyrdom of the apostles of Jesus in some way other than that Jesus rose. For if Jesus had not been raised from the dead, his apostles must have fabricated the story themselves. And if so, then their deaths and their refusal to retract their statements of faith contradict every theory of human motivation and behavior. Moreover, the Jewish and Roman authorities, who had placed armed guards at the tomb, had every reason publicly to display the corpse of Jesus if it were in their possession. And let us not forget that the earliest followers of Jesus were devout Jews. They knew they would suffer death here and damnation in the hereafter for lying about God's actions and proclaiming a false, dead Messiah to their contemporaries.

The logic of the Christian position was beginning to overwhelm me, so in true Harvard fashion I did not counter the arguments but simply posed another question: "This information about Jesus is interesting, but to be intellectually honest, wouldn't I have to examine all of the other religions and *their* claims about Jesus?" As it turns out, the pre-Christian religions are understandably silent on the subject, and evidence from the post-Christian ones is inadmissible. The fourth sura of the Koran, for example, suggests that someone else was crucified in Jesus' stead. However, this conjecture was written six centuries after the eyewitness accounts in the four Gospels, much too late to have any historical value. And the traditional "out"—that Jesus may have lived and died but he was just a great moral teacher— ignores the reason for his getting into so much trouble in the first place. It was not "Love your neighbor as yourself" which caused him problems but his extraordinary claim to be the Son of God, the Messiah. This is the crucial claim that has led so many alternative religions, and even some so-called Christian denominations such as Unitarian Congregationalism (which dominated Harvard in much of the eighteenth and nineteenth centuries), to carefully deny either Jesus' deity, sinlessness, atoning crucifixion, or resurrection, even though they accept him as a great prophet and moral teacher.

Ironically, it is the Hebrew Scriptures, written centuries before Jesus was born, which give perhaps the most impressive evidence for Jesus being who his disciples said he was. Virtually all of the central circumstances of Jesus' life found in the Greek New Testament are prefigured in the Hebrew Old Testament: the Messiah was to be a descendant of King David (Jeremiah 23:5; Acts 13:22–23), born in Bethlehem (Micah 5:2; Matthew 2:1–6), attested to by the miracles he did (Isaiah 61:1–2; Luke 4:18–21), rejected in the end as he suffered for the sins of others (Isaiah 53:2–6; Mark 15:1–39), and subjected to the ignominy of being crucified, with his tormentors gambling to decide who would take his clothing (Psalm 22:15–18, John 19:23–24).

Although I was now too intrigued to pretend I would not read the New Testament, I still wanted to exercise my right to be an independent thinker. I decided that the gambling detail, for example, was probably smuggled into the story by the disciples to make the prophecy fit Jesus. It turns out that it was common for Roman centurions to cast lots for the personal effects of the deceased; how would the writers of the Hebrew Bible have known that gambling for a criminal's tunic would become a common Roman practice several hundred years later? All right, then what about this crucifixion thing? Couldn't this too have been contrived to tally with the Hebrew Scriptures? But there also, the same counterargument applied: crucifixion was a Roman invention predicted by Old Testament writers foretelling the death of Jesus centuries before.

I had read the New Testament as literature in high school, but now as I opened the Bible to the Gospel According to John, I knew that I was in the same position as those living in Palestine in the time of Jesus. I could know for myself what he said and did. Whether I became another Judas or another Peter was up to me.[1]

પ્ર

In July of 1979, I knelt down in the kitchen of my family's home in Whittier, California, and asked the resurrected Jesus Christ of history to forgive me for what I had done to others and to God, and to come into my life and make me the person God had created me to be.

In the coming years, my desire to own a Porsche and practice corporate law withered away. Christ gave me the chance to serve the poor through working with a state senator on legislation to help migrant farmworkers and more directly by working as a Peace Corps volunteer. I now pastor a church where we have ministries to the elderly, prisoners, and the hungry and homeless. Jesus Christ continues to transform us, ever so slowly but as quickly as we'll let him, and to use us to transform the world, that we might one day see what we now, thanks to Handel, sing: "the kingdom of this world has become the kingdom of our God and of his Christ, and he shall reign for ever and ever."

---

[1] I found the following books particularly meaningful in examining the case for Jesus' resurrection and the historical reliability of the New Testament:

F. F. Bruce, *The New Testament Documents: Are They Reliable?* (Downers Grove, Ill.: InterVarsity Press, 1981).

C. S. Lewis, *Miracles* (New York: Macmillan, 1947).

Josh McDowell, *Evidence That Demands a Verdict*, vol. 1 (San Bernardino, Calif.: Here's Life, 1979).

He Walked Among Us (San Bernardino, Calif.: Here's Life, 1988).

Bruce Metzger, *The Text of the New Testament* (New York: Oxford Univ. Press, 1968).

Frank Morrison, *Who Moved the Stone?* (Downers Grove, Ill.: InterVarsity Press, 1958).

After the Gang, What?

๛

— EVELYN LEWIS PERERA —

I visited a Divinity School class with a friend. There a "learned professor" declared to us the folly of holding on to a "lingering childhood belief" in immortality.

Evelyn (Eve) Lewis Perera received her A.B. in English from Radcliffe (now Harvard-Radcliffe) in 1961 and her M.A. from Middlebury's Bread Loaf School of English in 1975. She now teaches Christian classics and composition at the Berkshire Institute for Christian Studies in Lenox, Massachusetts.

Her nonfiction has appeared in publications including the *Berkshire Eagle*, the *South Advocate*, *Christianity Today*, *New Oxford Review*, and *Creation Social Science and Humanities Quarterly*. While coeditor of *The Ark*, a small literary journal, Eve has managed her own bookstore-restaurant in Lenox, The Quiet Corner.

Eve is the mother of three grown children. She often swims with her eighty-five-year-old mother and enjoys walking for pleasure. Knitting, crewel embroidery, and the occasional "timid attempt" at watercolor provide artistic outlets. Eve and her husband, Dick, attend Grace Congregational Church. She is involved in a ministry, with several other churches, that reaches out to women prisoners.

After the Gang, What?

— EVELYN LEWIS PERERA —

The late Milton Eisenhower, when he was president of Columbia University, quite perceptively described an intellectual as someone for whom "learning is play." Going by his criterion—although I do not toy with theories about algorithms at the breakfast table—I may at the very least be what the brilliant writer Flannery O'Connor called an "interleckshual." But unlike Flannery O'Connor, I endured many years of grievous difficulty with what I had come, grimly, to think of as biblical Christianity. "There's no learning in that nonsense," I thought, "no play in that boring morality." But all that changed when, like the Prodigal Son (who learned through what began as play that there is more to life's foundation than meets the five senses), I rediscovered God's foundational truths. In the process, I had to let go of pride and rebelliousness, and even relinquish intellectual achievement as the primary basis of my self-respect. I was unmade by God. I came home.

But before all that I attended one of the historic girls' boarding schools, in Maryland's blossom-laden Green Spring Valley. Like many such in the fifties, my school was run by two women whose dealings with others shone with a quiet but living belief. We gave thanks at meals, our desks in the study hall had Bibles for morning prayers, and on Sundays we were each taken to our own church. I loved Sunday evening vespers in the "Old Gym," its aisles lined with black, wrought iron candlestands, and I was content that I was a "Christian." We learned and lived in a cocoon of gentility. But deeper down, for personal reasons, I felt unloved and rejected.

So when I came to Radcliffe in 1957, I was an earnest young woman with an overwhelming desire—one might say mission—to be popular. As a freshman in Moors Hall (now absorbed into North House), I was for the first time in my life part of an "Interleckshual Gang." Being part of a ruling clique had eluded me when it was defined by the number of cashmere sweaters you owned or whether you came back from winter vacation with a tanned face and with white ski-goggle halos around the eyes. But our Moors gang selected for wit and energy, and of those I had plenty. I went to my share of mixers and movies. Shrieking along with the cheerleaders, I attended to the confusing rituals of football, its chilling hours improved by a flask of milk punch brought from the Spee Club or one of the other "final clubs" by my escort. And it was not even beyond me to cut a class or two to have coffee at the old University Cafe on Massachusetts Ave. Once Professor Raphael Demos noticed me heading that way and, looking amused, took my arm to walk me to our philosophy class in Sever Hall. We entered, as did others, under the building's curious and often ironic exterior inscription, "What Is Man That Thou Art Mindful of Him?" from Psalm 8.

A small and dowdy counterpart to my intellectual-social life at Radcliffe was provided by the Episcopal church on Garden Street and by the Radcliffe Christian Fellowship. These meetings were, for the most part, pleasant and friendly—if a bit, well, boring. But when the university's Episcopal chaplain took his life, I no longer felt comfortable at Christ Church.

About that time I visited a Divinity School class with a friend. There a learned professor declared to us the folly of holding on to a "lingering childhood belief" in personal immortality. This brought tears to my eyes, and I felt lonely and uncomforted for months. But finally the pain receded, and Sundays became what they were to remain for the next ten years of my life: an opportunity to sleep very, very late and to read the Sunday *New York Times*.

My Harvard classes did bring me continents of delight. Among my favorites were Alfred Harbage's Shakespeare survey; John Finley's Hum 2, "Epic and the Novel"; and Philip Slater's social relations (pronounced "sock-rell") course on groups, in which the class gradually realized that the class itself was among the groups we were studying. At the end of my freshman year I sat in the Moors second-floor smoker, in between ferocious rubbers of bridge at two and three in the morning, and debated my choice of major, with my filtered Tareytons adding their own gray film to the rising clouds of befuddlement.

At the last moment, for no discernible reason, I chose English over social relations, Harvard's amalgam of psychology and sociology. (I am still not ashamed of my honors thesis about the seventeenth-century Welsh Christian poet Henry Vaughan.) At that time Timothy Leary, now Baba Ram Dass, was in our soc rel department and was beginning to feed LSD to eagerly receptive students. I thank my God, whom I did not know and from whom I was keeping a firm distance, that he protected me from being drawn into such self-experimentation, for I was both proud *and* gullible (a devastating combination), and there is no guarantee that I could have seen any danger in Leary's workshops in self-annihilation—especially with LSD in my system.

Like many young women of my era, I had given no thought whatsoever to job-seeking until, after Christmas vacation of senior year, what I call a "blue panic" began to set in. I prowled Radcliffe's career advisory office and scheduled back-to-back interviews. After a few psychology-oriented interviews, ardently pursued, had led nowhere, I began to think "publishing." I accepted an editorial assistantship at Houghton Mifflin. By the time I started it, I had been proposed to, was engaged, and was about to be married the following fall.

The next year my husband decided, with my enthusiastic assent, to join a group of physicians here in western Massachusetts. Eventually I began teaching freshman composition part-time at a community college. But the Vietnam War shifted into higher gear, and with the drafting of my husband in 1967 we moved to Denver, where he was stationed. We started going to Quaker meetings—my husband's religious background. I became even more involved than he, teaching "First Day School" and leading college students in filmmaking and film seminars. But in the silent meetings, away from the beautiful Episcopal liturgy, it became clearer to me that I did not know God.

My unbelief bothered me, and I became preoccupied with religious questions. On a driving trip to California I stopped at a bookstore and purchased John A. T. Robinson's *Honest to God*. I borrowed other books about religion from the public library. I could not understand why the theologians, who were supposed to know all about God, left me so unsatisfied. For years afterward I found it hard not to be resentful and bitter toward liberal theologians.

Finally I decided that reading the Bible might help. I didn't know how to do that—the words often didn't make sense. I bought a handbook on the Bible by Louis Cassels, the late United Press International religion writer. In the introduction I came to a disturbing paragraph. Cassels said that to understand the Bible properly one must recognize that Jesus Christ did rise from the dead. His tone was kind but firm. I couldn't deal with that, so I closed the handbook and laid the Bible aside.

When we returned east in 1969, a month after the birth of our third child, I resumed teaching, but it was difficult to regain my enthusiasm. The Vietnam War and the assassinations of Martin Luther King Jr. and Robert Kennedy, in addition to the memory of the assassination of the first president I had ever voted for, had left me in sorrow for my country and in despair for its future. When students and local adults with megaphones rallied our campus to protest the war by canceling classes for the November Moratorium, I dismissed my classes. But I wanted to shout to the leaders, "Hey, there's blood on our hands, too!" An oppressive guilt weighed on me. I dragged myself through my responsibilities.

Then one of my students received a brand new Mustang, and for several days the whole class was buoyant with his elation and bravado. I looked on. I had the urge to warn him, "Lay not up your treasure upon earth," but in the end I said nothing. Several weeks later someone smashed into that Mustang and spoiled its brand-new looks. The boy was devastated and we all felt sad for him. Many of the students lived for current pleasures and assumed they could get their own way with almost anything in the long run. So what if man is polluting the planet's waters and exhausting its soil? "We'll just expand the Apollo program and mine other planets! We'll colonize outer space!" I loved them, but their foolishness tortured me. "I think we're living in the last days," I mourned helplessly.

Then my sister Vee called.

Vee had suffered a great deal recently—three apartment robberies and hospitalization for a near-ulcer condition. Things had taken their toll, and she seemed much older than a woman in her twenties. But this time her voice over the phone sounded a good bit younger and livelier. She was accepting our invitation to come for Christmas and wanted to bring her Jewish roommate. "Barbara has never been with a family for a traditional Christmas," she said. "I told her all about you and how your children make papier-mâché ornaments and popcorn and cranberry chains—and how the whole family decorates cookies and hangs them on the tree. She wants to join in!"

I wanted only to die. How could I respond to even one of those kind boasts my sister had made about us, when I was having trouble just getting out of bed? But somehow I concocted a few preparations by extracting help from the rest of the family. Finally the night came when Vee and Barbara would arrive. We waited. Their bus arrived and we rushed to help them carry their suitcases up the driveway in the chilly blackness. When we were all seated in the warm living room, I could do little but stare at Vee: the black circles, the lines, the pallor, were virtually all gone. For the first time in a long while she looked her own age. "What's happened to *you*?" I asked.

"What's happened? Well, I've become a Christian."

I was puzzled. "But I'm a Christian, too, aren't I?" I said defensively. "And weren't you always a Christian?"

"Well . . . no." She struggled to find the words, as if talking to her own sister had suddenly turned what was normally a testimony into a confession. "I mean . . . I mean, I have realized that Jesus really is exactly who he says he is, that he really died for my sins and rose again, and I have decided to entrust my whole life to him." Barbara looked on uncomprehendingly.

After more conversation along these lines, Barbara quietly followed me into the study and closed the door. "I'm worried about Vee," she said. "She's always been ardent, but this . . ." She gestured toward the door of the room where Vee was.

"I know," I replied, "but I'm not sure how we can talk her out of it. She seems so . . . so *determined*." Like FBI agents deprogramming a cult member, we decided to talk to Vee about art and music and poetry and novels and friends—all the things she used to live for. Vee was undaunted when we tried this. She opened our minds to understand the faith of J. S. Bach and Michelangelo, of T. S. Eliot and Blaise Pascal and other great figures in many fields and periods who had been followers of Christ. It seemed she hadn't gone off her rocker after all. Perhaps *we* were the ones out in left field.

I had to make a comeback. After all, she was my *younger* sister. I informed her that according to Buckminster Fuller, Competitive Man would soon evolve into Cooperative Man, and then human behavior would improve, without Jesus and "all that blood" that bothered me.

"Human improvement," Vee said. "How much evidence do you see for that? And how does that theory help you personally? All I know is, I wouldn't want to live a single one of my days without him." Her voice was quiet but firm.

By the time Vee and Barbara left, Barbara and I had stopped fighting not only with her but, in a more important sense, with ourselves. We were not believers, but we were willing to be. Vee gave me a book to read and promised to pray for me. She asked me to read the Bible with an attitude of searching for the things God wanted to say to me. I wanted to protest that reading it with that attitude amounted to a bias. But something in me understood what she meant.

I wrestled through the next few days. Occasionally I would find a verse in the Bible that temporarily quieted the storm inside. Eventually I centered in on one verse, Mark 9:24, presumably recalled from Sunday school, and I began to repeat it over and over while folding diapers: "Lord, I believe; help thou mine unbelief." Not long afterward, I woke up in the middle of the night—and I knew that I believed in the risen Christ.

It would make a conveniently resolved story if everything in my life changed that same night. But even though I had acknowledged Jesus Christ, I was still too proud to repent of all I knew I should repent of. I still had a good dose of what Gerard Manley Hopkins, in his poem *I Wake and Feel*, calls "self yeast of spirit."[1] In fact, I had a nervous breakdown and spent time in a mental hospital. But spirit and mind are closely intertwined. Looking back on my childhood, I realize that painful experiences and unwise actions played a role in the later onset of mental darkness and thereby solidified my will's resistance to retraining.

---

[1] *The Poems of Gerard Manley Hopkins*, ed. W. H. Gardner (Oxford, 1972), 101.

Yet all things work together for good for those who love God. I see now that this episode was integral to the long process of healing and renewal that my loving Creator began in me when I used that verse from Mark's gospel to pray for faith. What had seemed like a period of disorder was part of a necessary restructuring of the self, a process of inner purging such that "my chaff might fly, my grain lie, sheer and clear," as Hopkins writes in "Carrion Comfort."[2] My experience enables me to see the wry wisdom in Dr. Theodore Isaac Rubin's paradoxical description of a nervous collapse as a "cleansing temper tantrum . . . a breakup of a tenuous neurotic structure designed to hold a lot of half-truths about oneself in place."[3] As I opened my life to God and allowed him to dismantle and reorganize, he began to substitute his quality of life—joy, kindness, and patience—for a life of fear, pride, and faithlessness.

Our own efforts to build our personalities are never God's way for us— they hardly work. He must use whatever means necessary to let us know this. Many of us need to lay down our idols and allow ourselves to come to the point where, like Jesus marred beyond recognition by the treatment he endured before his execution, we have nothing lovely about us—for it is then that we might see how unconditionally precious we are to God. God loves and wants the unadorned personality, not the embroidered public self.

If my definition of "success" had been to *feel* good, then my suffering would have felt like failure. But my entire worldview and values were changing. I began to see success and human purpose more connected to *being* good than to feeling good. Thus, painful honesty and suffering became necessary as means to that end. There is still plenty of pain at times, but playful learning and a richer sense of humor, too.

For a time during my restructuring I lost my love of books, as I wondered to what extent intellectual advancement was just a form of self-absorption. Now that I no longer use my love of ideas as a substitute for love of God, as I fear many at Harvard tend to do, I have found a new level of meaning in reading, freelance writing, the teaching of literature, and even owning a bookstore for six years.

I still love to sing "Fair Harvard" and "Mid Crimson in Triumph Flashing"—as the mood takes me. But my life as a Harvard (Radcliffe) alumna really came full circle during my twenty-fifth reunion in 1986. I left a class symposium at the Radcliffe Quad to head down that uneven brick sidewalk on Garden Street. Trying to pretend that the new Broadway–Cambridge Street underpass didn't exist, I got myself through the gates into Harvard

---

[2]Ibid., 99.
[3]*Love Me, Love My Fool* (New York, 1967), 76.

Yard near Phillips Brooks House, where I first had learned to teach by tutoring a little boy. Next to PBH, amidst all the brouhaha, was a refreshment tent labeled "Harvard-Radcliffe Christian Fellowship." There I ran into HRCF faculty advisors Jim and Vera Shaw, some of the student fellowship leaders, and even other alumni—all laughing and exchanging stories about Harvard experiences, favorite professors, living abroad, crazy kids, and God's grace over the years. And I knew then that my college experience need not have lead me to unbelief and the inner leanness that comes with it. "Godless Harvard" was not necessarily unconnected to my life as a believer. Like these other women and men of Radcliffe and Harvard, I too had discovered something of the brilliance of the original vision and foundation of Harvard College—people learning, playing, discovering, and worshiping together under the guidance of the truth, the person Jesus Christ, the one who sets us free, the one who brings us back home.

Disillusioned

— WILLIAM EDGAR —

In the summer after my freshman year I had a job in New York with a textile company, in the stretch-pants department! Meaningless work, and hardly worthy of the authentic existentialist from France.

William (Bill) Edgar was born in North Carolina and raised in France. Returning to the States, he went to St. George's Boarding School in Newport, Rhode Island. After receiving his music degree from Harvard in 1966, he went on to earn a master of divinity from Westminster Theological Seminary in Philadelphia, where he is now a professor of apologetics. In 1969 he married Barbara Smyth. In 1992 he received his doctorate in theology from the University of Geneva.

The Edgars have lived in Greenwich, Connecticut, and Aix-en-Provence, France, where Bill has taught music and philosophy. Their son, Keyes, is now practicing law in France, and their daughter, Debbie, is now studying music at Harvard.

Bill has served as president of the Huguenot Fellowship, the Society of Christians in the Arts, and the *Comité Evangélique de Réflexion sur l'Ethique Médicale.*

He has published many articles and two books, *Taking Note of Music* and *Affrontés à la modernité.* He gives "performance-lectures" on the Christian roots of gospel and jazz at the Harvard Veritas Forum. The Edgars hold a L'Abri-style discussion group in their home on Friday evenings.

Disillusioned

— William Edgar —

I entered Harvard at seventeen, bringing to this cosmopolitan environment that combination of confidence and apprehension so common to entering freshmen. In principle, no challenge was too great for my capable mind and body. I had gained a number of skills which I was sure would enable me to stand up to almost any test at Harvard—or would they?

The first was some ability in the game of soccer. My family moved to Paris, because of my father's business. I basically grew up there, going to French schools and absorbing French culture. At the time, the standards in soccer for Europe were much higher than in America. Moves and skills that Americans struggled with came more easily to me, only because I had competed with talented schoolmates on French playing fields day after day. Sports meant a great deal to me. It was a place to have friends in common cause, to do battle with adversaries, to grow in agility. Soccer stood me in good stead during my high school career.

The second skill was more cerebral. As anyone who has lived in France knows, the school curriculum is quite directive. French literature from the *Chanson de Roland* to André Gide was imposed on us. We learned a good deal by rote, so that my classmates and I all knew hundreds of lines of poetry and could recite the plots of scores of novels. With this in my bones, we moved back to the United States, where I went to a New England boarding school. Because of excellent French teachers there, I continued my investigations of French literature. I fell in love with the later nineteenth-century poets Baudelaire, Rimbaud, Mallarmé. And most importantly, I read the so-called existentialists Sartre, Camus, and Merlau-Ponty. As a young adolescent, my mind was being shaped by these *contestataires*, and I soon began to fancy myself a young existentialist.

I was admittedly a fairly comfortable existentialist. As I look back, I can see the "convenience" of pulling out arguments about authenticity, about the need to avoid "bad faith," and yet claiming to have no standards, no authority to answer to. It was obviously advantageous to embrace the framework of Sartrian freedom: no previous moral system could claim any rights on the honest man. The virtue which I most extolled, believing I had found it in my French writers, was that of honesty, brutal honesty. Going against the stream of American optimism, I was engaging in a sort of secular version of sin. I came to the conclusion that human beings were basically evil, or at least profoundly untrustworthy. I rejoiced in declaring this truth to friends whom I considered naïve.

My third skill, and greatest love, was music. As a child I listened to my father's extensive record collection. He loved both the "great classics" and more popular music, especially jazz. I listened to those records on our old hi-fi until I had memorized each line in the Beethoven symphonies, every riff in Benny Goodman's recordings from the 1930s. We had an old piano in the house, and I spent hours working things out on it that were in my ear. One of our baby-sitters showed me how to play fancy-sounding arpeggios and runs, so that to the very unsophisticated ear I could sound like Rachmaninoff. When I got to boarding school, I had the good fortune to study with a most remarkable music professor. He was a fine organist, and we would get him to play anything from Bach preludes to such modern French composers as Marcel Dupre and Jehan Alain on the chapel organ. I learned music history, harmony, and composition from this man. My greatest discovery was the music of African Americans. Their blues, their jazz, their spirituals, had something not found generally in the white world. It had "soul"!

I arrived at Harvard late in the summer of 1962. Cambridge was a smorgasbord. I loved the city. The abundance of opportunities, from the libraries to the concerts, the science facilities, and, above all, new friends from all over the world, made my new life truly gratifying. To a young man who had been cloistered in a small boarding school for four years, this was the stuff of dreams. My immediate plan was to explore each of these three motivating passions of my life: soccer, French literature, and music. My purpose was not, so I thought, merely to "study" these matters as subjects. They were part of a spiritual journey. Paradoxically, I came as a self-assured young person who was at the same time indeed apprehensive. Almost anyone who goes to Harvard experiences the great freshman humiliation. No matter how "good" you might have been in high school, there you are, surrounded by geniuses, great athletes, privileged people. Faced with a community of such people, how would things go for me?

Things got off to a good start, despite my fears. I went to early soccer. Coach Getchell took me aside and made all kinds of promises to me about starting, about being the penalty kicker. I worked and worked. I ran, I dribbled, I hit the ball. Yet within a few weeks the obvious truth broke through. Many of my teammates had a lot more raw talent than I did. They played better. How could it be? I couldn't run as fast as they. Coach Getchell soon had to tell me that if I worked very hard I could hope to start; otherwise, I would be a valuable substitute. I actually did start in a couple of games, but the pressure to succeed was so great that I often flubbed the things I used to know how to do blindfolded. It was a mediocre season for this kid trained in the Bois de Boulogne.

Well, no great loss. The quest for reality through French writers was more likely to yield its coveted fruit: the full discovery of the authentic life. I took advanced courses in French literature. We read my favorite authors, my friends. However, the lecturers sifted out the psychological and structural significance of each text, dwelling on historical references and manuscript evidence. I began to wonder what this had to do with my rough-and-tumble need for authenticity. Sartre was not taken very seriously. These studies were mostly monotonous. Even the architecture of Boylston Hall seemed to articulate the coldness of the method. I wrote a few papers in which I made an awkward plea for the human dimension and the quest for meaning. In general, the graders liked them, but they commented on my texts as if they were ordinary term papers and not the great contribution that I thought I had made to criticism! Again, many of the other students were better, which was another blow to me.

At least there remained the greatest reality of all, music. I majored in music. With long hair, blue jeans, and my baby-sitter's arpeggios in my repertoire, I walked confidently into Paine Hall to take Music 51, the required theory course. I loved analysis of the great composers' texts. Never had the craft of Mozart been so clearly explained, the intricacies of harmony and voice-leading unraveled so scientifically, so rationally. The teaching I received was of the highest order. Still, something was missing. One of my professors tossed off a throwaway line in a class on theory: "The reason you *play* music is because it is a game." Could this be true? In what way were Beethoven's late quartets or Anton Webern's *Concerto* a game? To me they had been the great clues to the mystery of meaning. Another troubling thought grew out of the music department's lack of attention to jazz and rock in those days. I began to wonder whether they were just some sort of low-order folk music and not the deeply spiritual sounds of the black experience which I had come to treasure.

I did not go through any crisis or a depressive state. Perhaps my security was too great for that. I had the advantage of a good home and was always surrounded by friends who bore one another's burdens. Besides, there were plenty of pleasurable experiences to live for at Harvard. The Signet Society, a literary group that met to discuss aesthetic questions over lunch, meant a great deal to me as an undergraduate. So did the Memorial Church Choir, under the extraordinary leadership of John Ferris. Still, something was missing. What was it? Various trials, such as broken relationships, leaving the soccer team, and getting my first poor grade in

German, were difficult to surmount. But they were only symptoms of something deeper.

Growing up in the 1960s was not easy. It is hard for me to understand the current nostalgia for those years. The very first *Harvard Crimson* we received in Stoughton Hall had the headline "Alport and Leary Dismissed from the University for Administering Drugs to Students." We had entered the Age of Aquarius, which was to deliver mind alterations of the worst kind. We lived with the constant fear of the draft over our heads. Being drafted would mean going to the jungles of Vietnam to fight a war few of us agreed with.

Bourgeois life went on as well. In the summer after my freshman year I had a job in New York with a textile company, in the stretch-pants department! Meaningless work, and hardly worthy of the authentic existentialist from France. Things were growing tense with my parents as well. My world was far apart from theirs. I was not interested in money. Though gloriously won, World War II was over. President Kennedy had been shot. We argued a good deal about basic worldviews. Most painfully of all, I felt an increasing sense of bad faith. Between what I felt I should be able to know and the truth, there was a fair distance. This was the ultimate condemnation of the Sartrian.

Then an unusual thing happened. During my sophomore year I enrolled in a large course to fulfill my "Gen Ed" requirements. Affectionately known as "Hum 2," it was a sweeping survey of the great epics and drama of the West, from the Greeks to the moderns. The lecturer was John Finley, one of the most powerful orators at the university. But the event that would mark my life was not one of his lectures. It was rather the enigmatic teaching of a section instructor. As in many courses, the large group of five hundred students was broken down into units of about twenty. My section instructor was Mr. Harold O. J. Brown. When he walked into the room the first day, wearing a stiff collar and plunking his initialed briefcase on the desk, most of us thought we would be learning Greek poetry at the hands of a relic. In fact, it was to be anything but stodgy.

Mr. Brown made no secret of his Christian convictions. He introduced himself as "an orthodox Christian" and seemed to care a good deal about the distinction between this orthodoxy and other brands. His analysis of our course material was unusual. He described the Greek mind-set as being moral, but with an inaccessible beginning point. God, if there were a god, could not be reached. He was not interested in the world. In contrast, Brown said, the modern mind-set was even more problematic. Because the universe was closed altogether, there was no basis for morals. There was an alternative, however, and it lay in the Christian worldview. Guided by a supreme God who is also accessible to human beings, the world had a meaning. At the same time, human beings were sinful according to this view. I had already come to that view, though for very different reasons. In the material we studied, Christian authors were represented by Shakespeare, Milton, and certain others.

At first, this sounded very strange to me. At the same time, I was attracted by the Christian diagnosis that sees human beings as fallen from their original created goodness. I had always assumed religion in general, and Christianity in particular, were myths, the projection of human need onto a Father in the sky. Challenged by Mr. Brown, I began to take a second look. I discovered that there was an abundance of historical evidence for the accounts of the life of Jesus given in the New Testament. My intellectual objections to the existence of God, to the need for redemption, began to fall away. I spent long hours with Mr. Brown, arguing every point, testing every proposition. My friends began to wonder whether I was all right. I began to take the side of the believer in religious discussions in the dining hall. I can well remember Professor William Alfred sitting with us at meals in Kirkland House, often urging us to consider the possibility of the supernatural, and the authenticity of the life of the church. More and more people crossed my path who were believers, people I somehow had ignored previously.

Many influences converged to redirect my commitments. I had joined the university choir for purely aesthetic reasons. But Sunday after Sunday we performed penetrating anthems and motets. Works like Purcell's *Remember Not Lord Mine Offenses*, Bach's *Christ Lag in Todesbanden*, and many others articulated in powerful ways the truth, the reality of Christ. As I later realized, the Holy Spirit was working in my heart. He did so in a Harvard setting!

The final step came in the summer of my sophomore year, in (of all places) a small village, high up in the Swiss Alps. At the recommendation of Mr. Brown, I visited a Christian community there. "L' Abri," meaning "the shelter," was a place where many students in the 1960s found basic answers to life's puzzles. It consisted of a series of chalets, each of them hosted by a family with a gift for communication. Informal seminars, lectures, and worship services were held throughout the week. The issues discussed ranged from the big philosophical questions to more practical spiritual matters. The director of L' Abri, Francis Schaeffer, was one of the most arresting persons I would ever know. He spoke with great passion and authority. He coined his own phrases to make the Christian message more clear, such as "the God who is there,"[1] the "moral motions" inside each person, and human beings needing "a personal beginning." It took a while

---

[1]See Francis Schaeffer's book *He Is There and He Is Not Silent* for example.

to penetrate his terminology, but in the end, a framework emerged. It was far more than a worldview.

The daily life in this community was quite diverse, but all of it converged on the centrality of the gospel, the "good news" of meaning, victory over evil, artistic expression. Hard physical work was combined with prayer, intense discussions, long walks in the mountains, and Bible study. The Bible was considered God's Word, its message transcultural. Through it, God invites the committed reader to entrust and invest one's whole life in Christ. I did. And I discovered that loving Christ above all paradoxically meant that I had been led to the source by which I now love others, even life itself, more than ever. I did not first become a "good person" but rather an alive person.

When I returned to Harvard as a junior, some things were the same, but others changed considerably. My three pursuits—athletics, French literature, and music—all came alive for me in new ways. I went back to the soccer field. But I did it for fun. With less pressure, I did better. But what really mattered is that I enjoyed it a lot more. Literature also became revitalized for me. In my newfound framework, the structures, the themes, and the symbols had new meaning. While I no doubt fell into some simplistic judgments, I found great liberation in being able to put various pieces into their place in the greater framework. Many of my favorite authors took on greater significance for me. Some I lost interest in and abandoned. Significantly, I became disillusioned with Sartre. His demand for authenticity seemed empty, because he claimed to do without any reference point.[2]

My newfound commitment also had implications for music. I began to test various kinds of music against my newfound Christian aesthetics. This was the beginning of work that would be developed in my later writings on music. I wrestled with questions about meaning in the arts. I read a good deal. The philosopher Suzanne Langer was a helpful guide along the way.[3] Professor Leon Kirchner taught me a great deal about the intricacies of modern music. A great humanist, he seemed to have an answer for the dilemma of modern art: does one have to choose between the pure abstractions of the avant-garde and the comfortable conventions of tradition? He introduced me to Stravinsky and Bartok, whose music was modern

---

[2]I had been influenced by both his periods, before and after 1960, when he moved from his early "existentialism" to a variety of "Marxism." Now I saw problems with both. His earlier commitment to "nothingness" and freedom from "essence" appeared to me untenable, as commitment is already a kind of essential quality. His later left-wing stand on things went so far as to allow for purges and cleansings which frightened me.

[3]*Feeling and Form* (New York: Scribner's, 1953).

in the best sense. Naturally, I also rediscovered the great composers of the past, especially those who worked inside a Christian universe.

I still have not fully understood all that has happened to me. Becoming a Christian means that one's foundation is radically changed. But it takes a lifetime—and, I suppose, an eternity—to become fully conformed to what we are foundationally. Christians live somewhere between the two realities of being newly born and not yet fully mature. I had arrived in the new land, free from the arid places. But much was yet to be explored. I made many mistakes. I tried to convert everybody, from my "pagan" parents to my artist friends at the Signet. Sensitivity and tact were not always prominent!

There were new and different hardships along the way. Some of my friends thought I had become a little strange! Though they did not exactly abandon me, I felt they were studying me. More challenging still, in my newfound faith I felt obliged to seek out other Christians. Some of them were from very different cultures than my own. We met as a Christian fellowship in Phillips Brooks House on Friday evenings. Short-haired blond guys from the Midwest tried to teach me their ideas about "witnessing" and spontaneous prayer. Many of my fellow Christians had what I considered to be appalling taste in music. Yet I discovered that while some of these differences were important, the roots of my great discomfort were more often than not in the vestiges of my Sartrian pride.

I had entered Harvard as a skeptic. Four years later I emerged as a convinced Christian. So much has happened since! I have been to seminary, married with children, worked in France again, and played jazz professionally. Presently I teach apologetics (the defense of the faith) at Westminster Theological Seminary, in Philadelphia. But it all started at Harvard. Whenever I go back and walk around the campus, it all comes rushing back to me. The courses, the choir, the soccer games, and the Christian Fellowship meetings. The irony is that the university's original bylaws affirmed in 1642 that Christ is "the only foundation of all sound knowledge and learning."[4] It was a simple but powerful vision: all of life under the aegis of biblical truth. While that heritage has been abandoned, God can still be found at Harvard. Our son graduated from Harvard a few years ago. Our daughter, Debbie, is there now, and a very active Christian.

A few years ago I attended the twenty-fifth reunion. It was a wonderful occasion. Seeing old friends and meeting new ones, comparing experiences with kindred spirits who had (most of them!) moved on from the 1960s to do many astounding things, was extraordinary. But the high point

---

[4]From "Rules and Precepts That Are to Be Observed in the College," in *New England's First Fruits* (London, 1643).

for me was being invited to preach the sermon at our class's memorial service, the opening event of the reunion. The service was deeply moving. Several of us led in various parts of the service. The names of forty-six classmates who had died were read off, and a bell tolled for each. I spoke on Psalm 90. I appealed to the hundreds of classmates in the church to be realistic about our mortality. I asked them to become disillusioned with inadequate answers. I invited them to believe in the resurrected Christ. During the entire week of reunion activities, I was able to hold conversation after conversation about the deepest things in life. God may still be found at Harvard.

CHAPTER 2

A CRISIS OF MEANING,
AND THE NEED FOR CHANGE

More than any other time in history, mankind faces a crossroads. One path leads to despair and utter hopelessness. The other, to total extinction. Let us pray we have the wisdom to choose correctly. I speak, by the way, not with any sense of futility but with a panicky conviction of the absolute meaninglessness of human existence which could easily be misinterpreted as pessimism.

WOODY ALLEN, "MY SPEECH TO THE GRADUATES"

୨୦୨

Postmodernism opens with the sense of irrevocable loss and incurable fault — a death that "begins" with the death of God and "ends" with the death of ourselves. We are in a time between times and a "place which is no place."

MARK TAYLOR, *ERRING: A POSTMODERN A/THEOLOGY*

୨୦୨

My sin was all the more incurable because I did not think myself a sinner.

AUGUSTINE OF HIPPO

୨୦୨

I freed Germany from the stupid and degrading fallacies of conscience and morality ... we will train young people before whom the world will tremble.

ADOLF HITLER, AT AUSCHWITZ

A Professor Under Reconstruction

— GLENN LOURY —

"Everything be damned" was my view, as long as I got what I wanted, whether it be tenure at the best university, having my name mentioned in the New York Times, or enjoying the favors of some beautiful young woman.

Glenn Loury is professor of economics at Boston University. He previously taught economics and public policy at Harvard's Kennedy School of Government, Northwestern, and the University of Michigan. He holds a B.A. in mathematics from Northwestern University and a Ph.D. in economics from M.I.T. Loury has been a visiting scholar at Oxford University in England, Tel Aviv University in Israel, the University of Stockholm, and the Institute for Advanced Study in Princeton. He has received the Guggenheim Fellowship and has served as an economist on advisory commissions for the National Academy of Sciences.

Glenn Loury has been active in public debate and analysis of the problems of racial inequality and social policy toward the poor in the United States. His essays on these topics have been featured in the *New York Times*, the *Public Interest, Commentary*, and the *New Republic*. The first two pages of this essay are reprinted from his essay "God in the Ghetto," which appeared in the *Wall Street Journal* on February 25, 1993.

He is an active member of his church fellowship and enjoys chess, billiards, and listening to jazz in his spare time.

A Professor Under Reconstruction

— Glenn Loury —

The conditions of black ghettos today reveal as much about the disintegration of urban black society as they do about the indifference, hostility, or racism of white society. Institutional barriers to black participation in American life still exist, but they have come down considerably and everybody knows it. Everybody also knows that other barriers have grown up within the urban black milieu in these last decades that are profoundly debilitating.

The effects are manifest in patterns of behavior involving criminality, unwed childbearing, low academic achievement, drug use, and gratuitous violence. These behaviors, which destroy a person's ability to seize existing opportunity, must be changed if progress is to come.

Here our social scientists, and our politicians, have failed us. For the longest time it was forbidden to speak of the unraveling social fabric of ghetto life. This has changed in the past decade, with the discovery of the black underclass, but the former conspiracy of silence has not been replaced with a meaningful discourse on how this broken world will be mended.

Liberals, like the sociologist William Julius Wilson, have now acknowledged that behavioral problems are fundamental, but insist that these problems derive ultimately from a lack of economic opportunities and will abate once "good jobs at good wages" are at hand. Conservatives, such as the political scientist Charles Murray, see the tragic developments in the inner cities as the unintended legacy of a misconceived welfare state. If the government would stop underwriting irresponsible behavior, they argue, poor people would be forced to discover the virtues of self-restraint.

These polar positions have something in common. They both implicitly assume that economic factors lie behind the behavioral problems, even behaviors involving sexuality, marriage, childbearing, and parenting. Both points of view suggest that behavioral problems in the ghetto can be cured from without, by changing government policy, by getting the incentives right. Both smack of a mechanistic determinism, wherein the mysteries of human motivation are susceptible to calculated intervention. Both have difficulty explaining why some poor minority communities show a much lower incidence of these behavioral problems than others and are apparently less influenced by the same economic forces.

Ultimately such sterile debates over policy fail to engage the fundamental questions of personal morality, of character and values. We do not give public voice to the judgments that it is wrong to abuse drugs, to be sexually promiscuous, to be indolent and without discipline, to be disrespectful of legitimate authority, to be unreliable, untruthful, unfaithful.

The advocacy of a conception of virtuous living has vanished from American public discourse, especially in the discussion of race and social policy. For example, the institution of marriage has virtually disappeared from inner-city black communities. The vast majority of poor black children are raised by a mother alone. But who will say that black men and women should get together and stay together more than they now do, for the sake of their children? Who will say that young people of any race should abstain from sexual intimacy until their relationships have been consecrated by marriage?

These are, in our secular age, no matters for public policy. Government, it would appear, must confine itself to dealing with the consequences of these matters not having been taken up elsewhere.

Luckily, government is not the only source of authority. In every community there are agencies of moral and cultural development that seek to shape the ways in which individuals conceive of their duties to themselves, their obligations to each other, and their responsibilities before God.

The family and the church are primary among these. These institutions have too often broken down in the inner city: they have been overwhelmed by an array of forces from within and without. Yet these are the natural sources of legitimate moral teaching—indeed, the only sources. If those institutions are not restored, the behavioral problems of the ghetto will not be overcome. Such a restoration obviously cannot be the object of programmatic intervention by public agencies. Rather, it must be led from within the communities in question, by the moral and political leaders of those communities.

The mention of God may seem quaint, but it is clear that the behavioral problems of the ghetto (and not only there) involve spiritual issues. A man's spiritual commitments influence his understanding of his parental responsibilities. No economist can devise an incentive scheme for eliciting parental involvement in a child's development that is as effective as the motivations of conscience deriving from the parents' understanding that they are God's stewards in the lives of their children.

One cannot imagine effectively teaching sexual abstinence, or the eschewal of violence, without an appeal to spiritual concepts. The most effective substance-abuse recovery programs are built around spiritual principles. The reports of successful efforts at reconstruction in ghetto communities invariably reveal a religious institution, or a set of devout believers, at the center of the effort.

To evoke the issue of spirituality is not to deny the relevance of public action. There are great needs among the inner-city poor, toward which public efforts should be directed. But we must be willing to cautiously and sensitively expand our discourse about this problem beyond a recitation of the crimes of white racism and public neglect. Some of the work that needs doing involves giving support to the decent and virtuous people in these communities whose lives are a testimony to the power of faith.

But how does this power transform a life, a community, any community? One person at a time. The following is a personal illustration.

⁊S

I want to describe my spiritual journey, not analytically as a theologian might but simply as an observer of what has happened in my own life. I offer this report as evidence of what Christ has done for me, and therefore of what I know he can do for others. I once heard a sermon where the preacher addressed the question of why anyone should believe in the resurrection of Jesus Christ. This is, after all, an extraordinary thing to accept as literal truth. After discussing the biblical text, and after reviewing other historical evidence consistent with the biblical accounts, the preacher added that we have our own personal experience with this risen Jesus Christ. Perhaps the most compelling evidence that one can offer that Jesus Christ is Lord is the evidence that derives from what has happened in one's life. It is such evidence that I offer here.

The fact is that I have been born again. I was dead and now I am alive, not because of my own recuperative powers but due to the power of Christ to mend a broken life, to "restore the years the locusts have eaten." Let me explain.

Although a wonderful and beautiful woman loved me and had agreed to become my wife, I was unable and unwilling to consummate with her the relationship that our marriage made possible. I was unable to be faithful to that relationship. I am not speaking now only of adultery; I was unable to be present emotionally. I was unable to set aside enough of my selfishness to build a life with someone else. Marriage involves give and take, but I gave little. My pride and a self-centered outlook eliminated any chance for a fruitful union.

I was dead in spirit, despite the fact that I had professional success as a tenured professor at Harvard. What more could one ask for? I had reached the pinnacle of my profession. When I went to Washington, people in the Halls of Power knew my name. I had research grants. I had prestige. Nevertheless, I often found myself in the depths of depression, saying, "Life has no meaning." I would say this out loud, with such regularity that my wife came to expect it of me. This is not to say that I was suicidal or psychotic; I was not. For me, there was no real joy. My achievements gave me no sense of fulfillment. Nothing in my life had any sense of depth and meaning. I thought of myself as living on the surface of things. Life seemed to be one chore or contest after another, in which I hoped to score high, to win accolades, and to achieve financial gains. But there was no continuity, no coherence, no thread of meaning which gave these various achievements ultimate significance.

Moreover, I was in slavery to drugs and alcohol. I do not want to be overly dramatic here; this "enslavement" had been going on for many years without apparently impairing my ability to function. There was no sudden degradation of my condition. I did not go off to shoot heroin between seminars, or anything quite so sordid as that. I don't want you to envision some terribly ugly or desperate and sad existence, though it became, in due course, quite sad enough. Rather, there was an ordinariness about this dependency. The fact is, I thought I needed to intoxicate myself in order to enjoy an evening's entertainment, to enliven a visit with my family, to have fun at a party or a sporting event, and so on. This pattern of mild inebriation as a boon to sociability had become part of my life. It progressed eventually to the point of threatening my health and my name. Yet through it all, I never thought there was a problem.

These developments in my life eventually came to a point where, without some intervention, my marriage probably would not have survived. I have to wonder whether or not, without some intervention, my honors and prestige would have been sufficient to forestall the increasing depression. I have to wonder indeed whether or not my involvement with drugs and alcohol would have ruined me physically, professionally, mentally. There seemed not to be any inner brakes.

What happened for me was that some people came forward to offer me words about the gospel (Greek, "good news") of Jesus Christ. People proclaimed to me the availability of salvation and the fact that there was a way out of such slavery. People asked me to consider the words of Jesus. Words like:

> I have come to save that which is lost. (Luke 19:10)
> I have come that you would have life, and have it more abundantly. (John 10:10)

I am the way, the truth, and the life; no one comes to the Father but through me. (John 14:6)

He who has been forgiven little, loves little. (Luke 7:47)

When the Son sets you free, you shall be free indeed. (John 8:36)

One person, whose name I do not know, is especially memorable. I was a patient in a substance abuse program in a psychiatric hospital. Each Friday the program invited a representative of some religious order to speak with the patients about spiritual issues. On this particular day a young woman came from a local church. After the formal session, during which I had voiced much skepticism about "organized religion" because of my disgust at corruption among church leaders, which I knew about growing up in Chicago, she approached me for further discussion. She was gentle but persistent when asking about my plans for the future. She suggested that we read Psalm 23 together, which we did. Though I knew the psalm by heart, I had never considered its promises nor thought of them as having been made specifically to me. This minister suggested to me that though I was quite literally walking "through the valley of the shadow of death," I need "fear no evil," for I did not walk alone. I can only say that I was startled by the implication of these words.

I was due to leave the hospital the next day. She urged that I come to church that weekend, Easter of 1988. Despite the fact that I had not been inside a church more than a half dozen times in the preceding decade, I accepted the invitation. The service was beautiful, especially the music. I recalled the many Sunday services I had attended as a child in Chicago. My family was involved in an African Methodist Episcopal church, a two-hundred-year-old Christian denomination found mainly among black Americans in the United States. And so as a child I loved going to church services, but when I reached my teens, I fell away and stopped going; there was really not much that I had retained from those church experiences.

The sermon was about redemption. I wept quietly for two hours, thinking of all that I had done for which I needed to be forgiven. At the time I did not acknowledge to anyone, not even myself, that I was being touched by the Spirit of God. I did not go to the altar for prayer; I did not join the church or confess Christ as my personal Savior. I fled from that sanctuary as quickly as possible when the service had ended, not even thanking the young woman who had invited me.

But the truth is that something happened, deep inside my heart, on that Easter Sunday morning. Nothing was quite the same again after that. In the months that followed others asked me to come to church and to read the Bible. I followed some of this advice, though not especially enthusiastically. Nothing dramatic happened.

There was, however, a minister and friend I came to know through my work as an economist at Harvard who continued to visit me. He seemed to be genuinely and deeply concerned about me; he would politely but insistently ask me questions about my life. Ray Hammond eventually persuaded me to come to a Bible study. I began to go regularly. After that I began to go to church services regularly as well.

There was no one particular moment when the skies opened up and God came wafting down. Rather, over the months as I began to study the Bible, as I went to church, as I learned to pray, as I began to reflect honestly on my life, and as I began to open myself up to the Spirit of God to minister to me and to move me, I came to realize that there was something dramatic missing in my life. I realized that there was an explanation for the low condition of my life. The many things that seemed out of line were all connected to the spiritual vacancy that I was becoming aware of.

Moreover, I began to feel myself growing and changing. I began to be aware that there was something real to this Christian business. Perhaps my greatest step forward in spiritual growth occurred when I began to think about Christianity not simply as a collection of propositions to be examined, not just as a set of truth claims which I was considering, but rather as the actual means by which a transcendent God has chosen to reach out to and establish a relationship with humanity. In other words, I began to realize that this "Jesus business" is not just an intellectual argument that people are making. It is not just a ritualistic set of conventions that people are engaging in, as I had imagined before. As a smug "intellectual" at a leading university, I was unwilling to even consider, much less accept, statements that Christians were making on faith where I could not see the evidence. I was unwilling to have faith without complete evidence, when I now understand that faith is the evidence of things not yet seen. As my resistance to acknowledge spiritual realities began to erode, I became more willing to entertain the possibility and, indeed, the truth of the spiritual things proclaimed to me. I began to make more room within my heart for the message of the gospel. Things in my life began to change.

Dead relationships came to life. My sense of the absence of purpose gradually lifted. As I began to study the Bible, the depth and richness and profundity of life began to open up to me. I began to see that the possibilities for joy and fulfillment are much greater than I ever imagined. I found myself seeing below the surface and finding a richness of meaning that I dreamed of but never believed to actually exist.

For example, I discovered what for me was a life-changing truth: that freedom (or what I thought was freedom) is not worthy of being one's highest value. My constant quest to be "free" of constraint, to be unfettered, had been the source of much of my unhappiness. Since childhood I had always thought I wanted to "do my own thing." Marriage seemed suffocating, because it meant being obligated to consider the concerns of another. Though already a father from a previous marriage, I did not want to have children, because of the enormous responsibilities. I resented the claims of family and friends if they inconvenienced me.

Yet after becoming a Christian, I learned that the deepest satisfactions and most powerful sense of fulfillment can only be achieved when one is faithfully committed and accountable to others. Holding my infant sons in my arms and experiencing the deep satisfaction of being, daily, the kind of father and husband which I know the Lord has called me to be, I realized that the whimsical passions and fanciful pursuits of my earlier life could never have produced true happiness. In the past I was free only to reap the bitter harvest of loneliness, aimlessness, and hopelessness which my reckless pursuit of personal, sensual gratification had produced. But only now do I know joy beyond my wildest expectation, even though my time is often not my own, and I have since lost the taste for the hedonistic delicacies which I used to savor. Life has such a sweetness. Instead of "Life has no meaning," my wife, Linda, now sometimes overhears me saying, "Thank you, Lord."

With my spiritual growth has come an appreciation of the joy of worship and praise, and an ability to share the gospel and minister to people. This was made possible when I received the baptism of the Holy Spirit—the power that the Lord has made available to all of us who believe. These spiritual gifts at first seemed embarrassing and irrational to me. Emotionalism in worship grated against my intellectual style; it seemed archaic, characteristic of something primitive. Yet in due course there I was, full of joy and prepared to worship not just passively but openly. For I had witnessed what the Lord had done for me; I could not remain silent or studiously passive when my church fellowship would celebrate his glory.

I began to see the impact of this transformation on people around me. At Harvard's Kennedy School of Government, I and other faculty taught a course on ethics. Our students were ambitious, earnest, and ready to claim their corner on public policy truth—or to get their man or woman (or themselves) elected to public office. Our job in this course was to raise philosophical questions, to ask students about justice and right and wrong behavior in difficult situations. I began to consider how my personal spiritual experience and knowledge might inform this task of preparing people to confront the world of politics and public policy constructively.

I began to ask my colleagues questions about the relationships between personal spiritual commitment and the ethics of public service. I even circulated an excerpt of the book *Born Again* by Charles Colson, an infamous figure from the Watergate era. He was convicted of crimes committed while working in the White House and served time in prison. After his fall from power he began a relationship with Christ, and when released from prison he dedicated his life to ministry, especially among inmates.

I found Colson quite interesting on the question of *hubris*, or pride. This was an issue of great significance to me, because pride was a part of the sin in which I was entrapped. I suffered from a vastly inflated sense of my own importance, my own capability, and how I was moving to the top. Nothing seemed beyond my grasp; the rules (whether moral or legal) were for others, not for me. I was an exception. "Everything be damned" was my view, as long as I got what I wanted, whether it be tenure at the best university, having my name mentioned in the *New York Times*, or enjoying the favors of some beautiful young woman.

In his memoir, *Born Again*, Colson described his own entrapment in the sin of pride. When I read it, I thought I saw myself. I also recognized, though not to the same degree, aspects of ambition and self-righteousness so characteristic of many young students at the Kennedy School training for careers in government.

I sought to communicate that, ultimately, personal morality must be the bedrock of professional ethics, and religious conviction can play a central role in empowering a person to adhere to such a moral code. I hoped my colleagues might recognize the limitations of our purely academic approach to the subject, given that, in the end, our aim was to shape the values and character of some future leaders of our country. Academic knowledge in ethics may influence our thinking about what we *should* do, but this is impotent compared to the transformation of our inner lives so that "what we should do" becomes what we *want* to do, and then what we in fact do. It has been rightly said that the longest distance in the world is from the head to the heart.

I am convinced that I was restored in part so that I might encourage others to integrate and enliven their lives in the academy through a relationship with almighty God. Ours can be a spiritually barren landscape. Declarations of faith are rare on campus, and those who make them are often marginalized. Yet as college teachers, we have the awesome responsibility of shaping the minds of young people who are at a critical phase in their development. A way must be found to patiently and respectfully challenge these young people on spiritual as well as conventional academic grounds. The simple, unadorned declaration of one's own experience with the Lord is one means to convey such a challenge.

The quality of my family relationships improved greatly after my conversion. I began to have honest exchanges with a number of relatives. I saw a healing of my breaches with my sister and mother. A new and more fruit-ful bond developed with my two adult children from an earlier marriage with whom I had very attenuated relationships after their mother and I divorced nearly twenty years ago. This healing happened in part because I became willing, as a servant, to look at and to care for those relationships in a new way.

Our marriage, which I thought was dead, came to life. The Lord began to bless my wife and me with a family. We had our first son, Glenn II, five years ago. And now we have a wonderful year-old baby boy, Nehemiah Matthew. Our marriage was miraculously healed—that which was dead is now raised. Because of this encounter with Jesus Christ, the death and vacancy, the emptiness of my life, has been filled. There is life now.

There is nothing unique or special about me to attribute any of this to. I had done nothing to have earned these changes. But the Scripture tells us that this is why Jesus came and lived and died and was raised from the dead—that *all of us* could have this new life.

How do I know that the resurrection and the whole gospel are real? I know not only because of my acquaintance with the primary sources from the first century A.D., or even because of the words of Scripture. I know primarily, and I affirm to you this truth, on the basis of what I have wit-nessed in my own life. This knowledge of God's unconditional love for humankind provides moral grounding for my work in cultural and racial reconciliation, economics, and justice. Jesus Christ provides a basis for hope and for the most profound personal satisfaction. To paraphrase a cur-rently popular rallying cry among many protesters for racial justice: No Jesus, No Peace.

A Crisis of Meaning

— RICHARD KEYES —

What is likely to be able to lead us beyond self-gratification as a life project? Where will these powerful higher meanings come from?

Richard (Dick) Keyes graduated from Harvard College in 1964. Together with his Harvard roommate, Dick won the national championship in the double scull the summer after graduation and lost in the finals that would have qualified him for the Olympics in Tokyo. That summer was a new time of questioning his goals and pursuits. Keyes began a search that took him to L'Abri Fellowship in Switzerland. After much study, travel, and nearly endless discussion, he came to believe in the claims of Jesus.

He then went to Westminster Theological Seminary in Philadelphia, and married Mardi Drew, a graduate of Wellesley. On completing theological studies, Dick became the minister of a church in London, and they both worked with L'Abri Fellowship. In 1979 they returned to Massachusetts to begin a L'Abri study center in Southborough, where the question of meaning in life is constantly a live issue.

Dick and Mardi "have enjoyed the rare privilege (in the modern world) of being able to work together in our home and to share in the raising of our three sons." Mardi lectures widely on issues relating to Christianity and feminism. Dick is the author of *Beyond Identity* and the recent release, *True Heroism*.

A Crisis of Meaning

— RICHARD KEYES —

When I graduated from Harvard in 1964, I sold all my books and concluded that studying was a waste of time. I had enjoyed my time in Cambridge immensely, with many good friends and long discussions in the Eliot House dining room. Although I witnessed the warning tremors of the Kennedy assassination and the start of the Vietnam protests, I had no suspicion of the social upheaval that was to come in the latter half of the decade or of its roots in the history of ideas. The future would continue more or less as the past had done, and would make room for us. My experience of academic life was another story.

I found learning at Harvard to be a fragmented and frustrating experience—trying to grasp and remember isolated bits and pieces of information, most of which evaporated within the first few weeks after each final exam. Undoubtedly I was a late bloomer, and I spent more time in the boathouse and on the river than I should have for the sake of my academic education.

Yet as I look back on it now, this was not the only problem. I was also caught in something of an intellectual double bind. From the beginning of an intimidating freshman year, the wonderful liberal-arts ideal was planted in our minds. We were meant to be at Harvard for a broad education for leadership in our society and beyond. I remember being told, in answer to a query about the mysterious purposes behind the curriculum, "You haven't come to a trade school, after all." The carrot that was dangled in front of our noses was a unified grasp of the field of knowledge, an update on the Renaissance-man vision. But from the other side, there was the daily reality of taking courses from intense specialists within their fields. If they had the broad overviews of knowledge that Harvard's reputation and brochures spoke of, they never told us about it. Perhaps they were closet Renaissance men. More likely, they were not conscious of having any ultimate meaning system at all. In fact, some of my professors seemed to scorn such an idea.

I came to believe the Christian faith through a process of searching and questioning that began in my senior year. It was only later that I began to see what had happened. I realized that my gripe was not with Harvard or with that piece of its curriculum that I struggled through. The problem was even larger than my deadly sophomore history tutorial! A past president of the University of Chicago once remarked that the modern university itself is really a "multiversity united only by a central heating system"—

an irreverent analysis, but one that has the ring of truth. Harvard has only reflected the changes in Western intellectual life over the last several hundred years. These changes not only make it difficult to get a good education anywhere but they have created a crisis in every area of life. Perhaps it is most helpful to see it as a crisis of meaning. This essay offers you a thumbnail sketch.

Men and women who lived with a worldview influenced by animism had no such problem of meaning. Every piece of the world was meaningful. The natural world was filled with vital forces which had to be negotiated with and appeased. One could call it a participatory worldview. Through shamans, priests, and magic, one participated in an imagined, invisible world, with its mysterious interconnectedness to the visible world. Even today the well-meaning Peace Corps volunteer might start to dig a well in a time of drought but be stopped because she or he would be "disturbing the spirits in the ground." We look on this and see fear, ignorance, and superstition, but what we do not see is a lack or crisis of meaning. Every detail of life meant something and was related in some invisible way to every other detail. In their eyes, the entire world was laden with meaning.

Into this world came the classical thought of Greece and Rome, but perhaps even more importantly the biblical tradition of the Old and New Testaments through the extraordinary spread of the Christian faith in the early centuries A.D. Like the premodern worldview that I have described, the Christian faith also saw meaning coming from the invisible world, but in a very different way. The personal Creator was independent of the world he had made. He was neither identical to nor identified with parts of it such as the sun, the earth, or the forces of fertility. He was the one who had made them all. He alone was divine; they were not divine in themselves. Creation was not the source of its own meaning. Its meaning was derived from God alone. Thus, the world was safe to investigate in new ways—it was not magic or sacred in itself. You did not need a shaman at your side when you dug a well.

In fact, investigation, stewardship, and nurture of the world was not just permitted but commanded by God in the first chapters of Genesis. The link between human activities and their meaning was not through a magical participation with an invisible world, mediated by a professional priesthood. It was through this personal God himself, who reigned over heaven and earth. The world and what men and women did in it were significant in terms of their relatedness to him. Most importantly, the human race alone was made in the reflection of God's character, and therefore people were God's unique counterplayers. Their meaning derived from his intimate care and ultimate verdict.

If we skip ahead many centuries, it was still within this intellectual framework that modern science arose. For Newton and many of his generation, the discovery that many natural occurrences in the world were caused not by the direct hand of God but by other natural occurrences posed no threat to faith but rather deepened it. Many of the founders of the Royal Academy of Science were Puritans who saw their scientific curiosity as an expression of their biblical faith, not a threat to it. Science was simply investigating the wonders of what God had created, ordered, and sustained. Harvard College itself was founded as an expression of this worldview. Harvard's motto *Veritas* was implicitly, and later explicitly, related to the early seals *In Christi Gloriam* and *Christo et Ecclesiae*.[1] This did not mean that all truth had to be reduced to some narrow religious formulas or utilized in overtly religious ways. But it did mean that since all truth was truth about God or what God had made, it was ultimately to be used in service to him. A relationship to God through Christ would inform every aspect of life and knowledge and also yield wisdom, humility, and intellectual honesty.

But from the early seventeenth century there arose such an enchantment with the usefulness of scientific discoveries, and with the successes in investigating the empirical world as an object of knowledge, that two directions of thought characterized the European Enlightenment. One was the confidence that everything in the world could be broken down into tiny cause-and-effect relationships, making all reality a huge machine—like a giant clock—of which the whole was no more than the sum of its parts. Great mysteries would all fall before the gradual accumulation of small bits of information accurately collected and quantified. The second direction was the conviction that in order to accomplish this breakdown, the observer had to be as machinelike as possible in his or her observation and description of the world—free from the distortions of imagination and subjectivity. The mind was to become like the (as yet uninvented) photographic plate, recording "facts" dispassionately and excluding the fallible "human element" from the process of knowing. At first these ideas were not intended to be in conflict with the Christian faith (e.g., Bacon and Descartes saw themselves as Christians), but much of history illustrates the law of unintended consequences.

As the Enlightenment took shape, the European mind claimed to have "come of age" and to have banished God as an authoritarian and imaginary presence from the field of knowledge. Enlightened people now had a suffi-

---

[1]For a history of the motto and seal, see introduction. See also Samuel Eliot Morison, "Harvard Seals and Arms," *Harvard Graduates' Magazine* (September 1933).

cient understanding of the natural world and of the doings of humanity to get along without appeal to such authority. The "official" church's narrowness, intransigence, and resort to blind authority accelerated an unnecessary polarization between faith and reason, revelation and human understanding.

As the Enlightenment waned, it had lost some of its earlier confidence in both science and metaphysics. Kant's ideas had fixed certain building blocks in the foundation of modern thought. He separated the worlds of fact and meaning with finality. The facts of the external world were without meaning; meanings were rooted only in human subjectivity. Although among philosophers there was no longer such confidence in the exact correspondence between the external world and human thoughts about it, science and technology flourished as never before under the pragmatic assumption that one was dealing with a real and understandable world. But meaning came to be seen as something arising only from human subjectivity, something that we had to supply and attribute to facts from within ourselves. Since it arose from human subjectivity, it was therefore "personal," a matter of opinion, having no status as objective knowledge.

The far-reaching implications of this fact-meaning split have carried into the fabric of twentieth-century thought and life. They are in contrast to the animists' worldview, in which the whole universe carried meaning within itself, and also the Christian worldview, in which meaning was revealed and sustained in relationship to a caring creator God. The separation between fact and meaning is why people today speak of true and false being categories appropriate for science (the world of "facts") but not for worldviews of ethics (the world of meanings). Meaning today is regarded as private, personal, disconnected from anything beyond the subjectivity of the individual. What is objectively real has no meaning and what has meaning is not objectively real. Meanings, like our tastes for food, are personal and therefore immune from the same falsification or critical analysis used in other areas of knowledge. How can one person's meaning be more true than another's? We can only express our personal preferences.

In modern secular thought, the natural world is no longer seen as meaningful because of its relatedness to God; it just exists as a bare, independent fact. If we want to attribute meaning to it, that is our choice. It is a free country. But we are ever to be aware that the meaning comes from our sentimental and inevitably biased subjective addition and not from the world itself. The German theologian Wolfhart Pannenberg laments that in our secular culture, people see meaning only as "bestowed" on the world by their own sovereign choice, and not "discovered" to be true in the world. Thus, apart from our bestowal, the world is without meaning, or meaningless. Pannenberg said, "Secular culture, the more it develops without restriction, produces the experience of meaninglessness first in public life and finally also in individual life."[2]

When the relationship between fact and meaning is broken, eventually all of life is affected. For example, the meaning of a person's existence in imaging God is severed from the "real" world of fact and relegated to personal opinion, a preferred idea for certain individuals. Simone Weil referred to the impact of this change as having produced a "de-created world," and C. E. M. Joad said that with this new diminished status, a human being was "only the star performer in the zoo." It has become somehow more accurate to speak of a language-using animal or a "naked ape" than to speak of a human person. Science, despite its spectacular successes in the world of facts, is mute when it comes to meanings. Science cannot tell us whether the state should treat a human being as uniquely valuable or as an animal in a cage in a zoo. After all, the world of meaning and value is meant to be a matter of private judgment, severed from any transcendent meaning system or basis for authority. Authority without an ultimate meaning base does not dissolve but tends to concentrate in the state. The twentieth century has taught us painful lessons that value systems without a transcendent base are no match for arbitrary meanings generated by the state for its own purposes.

As the separation of fact from meaning filters down into other areas of our lives, it begins to effect everything. I heard a historian complain that "history is just one damn thing after another." Of course, he is right if history is made up only of facts linked by chronological sequence, disconnected from any framework of meaning.

We see the same thing in the changing attitudes toward sexuality. Although sexuality in a Christian worldview is seen to be a beautiful gift, sexual promiscuity is morally wrong, a misuse of that gift. As a fact within God's world, promiscuity carried this clear meaning—independent of any individual's opinion about or discovery of that meaning. Then as God was taken less seriously and allowed less of a say in the matter, it became morally ambiguous—"frowned upon" but at the same time dignified by being considered a bit naughty. Sexual promiscuity next became psychologically very enlightened, good, and healthy, the way to grow to be a mature and liberated person. The final step in the progression has been the full separation of fact and meaning. Sexual promiscuity is now for many just like having a cup of coffee, putting out a cigarette, or falling off a log—that is to say, without any particular meaning at all. It is "no big deal." Some speak of sex as completely "unburdened with meaning." Rabbits do it.

---

[2]Wolfhart Pannenberg, *Harvard Divinity School Bulletin* (February–March, 1984).

Attributing more meaning to it than to rabbits' reproductive activities is just adding human sentiment to real, hard facts. The Playboy totem of the bunny seems to make this point well.

What is interesting is that the secular culture has not stopped talking about meaning, even moral meaning, in areas ranging from sexuality to careers to politics and scholarship. Think of the proper moral indignation recently voiced against rape, date rape, and sexual abuse. This illustrates the dilemma. Our younger generation has been given a double message. They have been taught that sex is unburdened with meaning. It is only a normal biological function. Just be sure to use a condom. But now those who have been taught this message of "freedom" are outraged when others use it "wrongly" as if human sexuality had no particular meaning. We are told that we are like rabbits, but when we behave like rabbits, we get attacked as morally despicable.

The wonderful ideals of Western civilization and of the modern university—justice, peace, freedom, honesty, integrity, and compassion—all make perfectly good sense in the meaning-laden framework that has been discarded with Christianity. Without that transcendently rooted framework, these very ideals, making up the things that we most value in human experience, are the very things that are out of place. The foundation is pulled from beneath them. A secular culture wants to have its cake and eat it too, to have the meanings derived from Judeo-Christianity but dismiss the source of those meanings. But rather than produce a coherent secular view of life, this has resulted in a cross fire of ideas and predictable confusions. As the sociologist Os Guinness has claimed about modern America, "'Just say no' has become America's most nationally urgent slogan at the very moment when 'Why not?' has become America's most publicly unanswerable question."[3]

If a human being is only a biochemical phenomenon, differing merely in degree of complexity from a tree or a rabbit, why should we think that the high ideals of Western civilization are important? Are they not mirages, secondary effects produced by the peculiar biochemistry of the overheated brain of the human animal? How can we be expected to take *any* ideals seriously, let alone such grandiose and difficult ones as justice, honesty, and compassion? The attempt to create or even retain such ideals on this foundation is an act of intellectual alchemy, plausible only within the lingering afterglow of Judeo-Christian influence.

---

[3]Os Guinness, *The American Hour* (Free Press, 1993), 29.

Some might object that this line of argument becomes alarming only when the fact-meaning separation is pushed to its logical "extreme." They might argue that as human beings, we have an innate pragmatic sense of balance that will always correct our course and keep us from drifting toward the perilous edges of any particular worldview. It is only armchair scholars who worry about the logical conclusions of worldviews and philosophical paradigm shifts. I fear that this line of thought is naïve to the point of being dangerous, especially against the backdrop of the bloodshed and oppression in the major events of our own century. I also find it hard to trust the power of "pragmatic balance," after having seen the disastrous impact of the loss of meaning on so many lives of individuals who have taken the fact-meaning separation seriously. Without these understandings, I believe that our new century holds no substantive hope for human beings.

My fear is not only of the loss of explicit moral meanings in our society, although that is certainly fearful enough. Perhaps more destructive in the long term is that the prevalent secular worldview does little to resist the encroachment of banality on modern life. The nuts and bolts of American life, as I observe them, seem far from the high ideals of Enlightenment promises. Look, for example, at much of the past decade's popular nonfiction, visual art and film, television programming, and new music. Shared themes include the body, easy sex, looking young, surviving loose commitments and broken relationships, a sense of meaninglessness, loss of community, violence, death. You may sense a certain narrowness of vision here.

In an issue of *Harvard Magazine*, the author described with dismay a study at one college where only two attitudes were shared by virtually all undergraduates—"a sense of having to survive and a desire for self-gratification." The author pointed to the danger that "expertise and ambition easily become demonic." But what is likely to be able to lead us beyond self-gratification as a life project? Where will these powerful higher meanings come from? Secularism has been unable to lift us out of consumer materialism. Make no mistake, Western culture could not have been built on the banality of these convictions. Nor will it survive long under their reign.

Our call is not to try to turn back the clock to 1636, any more than the founders of Harvard College tried to turn it back to A.D. 33. But we need a fresh, courageous, and honest reevaluation of the roots of meaning. Could it be that we have cut out the vital center of our culture and relegated it to quaint triviality, indistinguishable from personally meaningful fantasy, and having little to do with the "real" world? If this is so, what better place to begin than to examine where we might have made a wrong turn?

Some will say, "Ah, yes, it would be comfortable and nice to believe in the God of the Bible again, but of course we cannot, because history has moved forward." Coming from the strange combination of fragmentation, doubt, and dogmatism that I had picked up in Cambridge, I did not find it easy to believe. But I gradually began to realize that the post-Enlightenment secular view that divides fact and meaning is itself a faith-held commitment, built on very dubious assumptions. On the other hand, the foundations for Christian truth claims turned out to be much more solid than I had been led to believe at Harvard. Could it be that the Christian faith is unthinkable for many people today more from prejudice, misinformation, and neglect than from honest investigation?

Harvard,
What of the Light?

❧

— HERMANN HAGEDORN —

The Oxford meetings were shot through with laughter. No one preached or pontificated. People merely told stories of personal experiences—tangled lives made straight, marriages remade, families reunited, businesses and churches revitalized.

———————

The biographer of Theodore Roosevelt, Leonard Wood, and other distinguished Americans, **Hermann Hagedorn** was Harvard's poet-in-residence in 1936.

In September, 1936[1], as part of the tercentenary celebrations, the University had assembled some of the world's leading scholars to address the growing crisis in the world. The December 1936 issue of the *Harvard Advocate* carried a response by Hagedorn entitled "The Oxford Group and The World Crisis," from which this story is adapted.

Like many people of faith throughout Harvard's history, Hagedorn's was "a voice crying out in the wilderness" which still speaks to us today of the power of God in the lives of students and society.

———————

[1]During the same year, a small group of students met in Phillips Brooks House, given for evangelical ministry, to form the Harvard Christian Fellowship, which is alive and well today.

Harvard, What of the Light?

— HERMANN HAGEDORN —

Harvard, What of the Light?

Light is not light, that lights the mind alone.
Clear from a far and glowing break of day,
Harvard, you speak: "Light is not light, that lights
Only a part, with cold moon-brightness,
Leaving the rest to darkness and the whole to the storm.
Light, that is light, is light for the whole man."

Oh, light, complete, creative, shining, kindling!
Flame in the mind, flame in the heart, white flame
Upreaching infinitely to white flames,
Austere, obedient in their ordered gyres:
The light you bore, the light that bore you, Harvard!

Three hundred years, Harvard, three hundred years!
Out of your light, like fiery birds upspringing,
Runners, runners with torches!
The wilderness upreared,
Monstrous, with talons raised. The wilderness, blinded,
With head averted, withdrew.
Out of your light, Harvard,
A fire on the hearth, a lamp on the hill, a crackling
Beacon, proclaiming to darkness, the deathless
Creator of light!

Out of your light,
Brave hearts, large minds! Out of your light, heroic,
Indomitable souls! Forerunners, captains, upholders!
Rebels and sages! Prophets! Breakers of idols!
Delvers in darkness! Watchers by lonely headlands!
Summoners of the invisible!
Kindlers of fires!
Out of your light, Harvard!

Out of your light,
Cities and states! Out of your light, resounding
Bells in high towers! White beams, exploring the hidden
Interstices of electrons, the secret vagaries of stars!
Out of your light, light! Out of your faith, faith!
Out of your love, the open hand, the outstretched
Encompassing pity. Out of your listening spirit,
A word, a way! Out of your hushed obedience,
Harvard, a new world!

Light is not light that lights not the whole man.
New worlds grow old. Harvard, what of the unfathomed
Ocean, breaking, deep-toned, in successive tomorrows?
What of the night, Harvard? What of the lamentation
Under your windows, the moaning of multitudes, crying?—
"Light blazes on us, and we shake in darkness,
Light clothes our bodies, and we die of cold."

What of the dearth, Harvard? What of the hunger?
The fear, the fever, the desolation, the icy
Whistling of winds through infinite, arctic spaces,
Dividing man and man? What of the cleaving,
What of the heaving ground, the bodies hurtling
From towers, towers toppling, the terror, the swirling fury,
The trampling feet, the drums rolling? Youth in vacuity,
Gasping for daybreak!

What of the night, Harvard?
A wilderness uprears, with talons raised!
What of the light, Harvard?
The light you bore, you breathed on, you made live?
Once more, Harvard, ships on a stormy sea?
Once more, Harvard, the foot on the perilous shore?
Once more, runners with torches?
Beacons, proclaiming
Once more, once more, the ineluctable Christ?
Harvard,
Once more, the wilderness? And a new world?

VERITAS AND THE WORLD CRISIS

One of the striking features of the symposium of the world's leading scholars, on the nature and the future of man, held in connection with the Harvard tercentenary (1936), was the prevailing pessimism as to our future. Nationalism, armaments, despotism, the decay of liberalism, the conflict of tyrannies, civil upheaval, war. None of the speakers missed the gravity of the problem. And none of the greatest minds in the world, it appeared, offered a solution. There is a deal of talk of trade barriers and international exchange of finance and industry and labor, but the problem obviously goes deeper than economics. There is much noisy debate about dictatorship, democracy, liberty, self-government, leagues of nations, but it is impossible to conceive of a cure of the world's malady in terms of political action. The most learned persons have tacitly admitted that science and education cannot reach the source of the disease.

Through an odd combination of circumstances, in which my personal wishes did not enter (my personal life was as confused as the world about me), I found myself one day in an Oxford college, attending an Oxford Group "house party."[1] I was struck at once by the quality of the people about me, men and women from forty different nations, some of them people of large affairs, all of them extraordinarily released. The meetings were shot through with laughter. No one preached or pontificated. People merely told stories of personal experiences. It seemed to me that I had never met such sincerity. What they said, in varying accents and diverse keys, was that man can be changed. The destructive impulses will give way to the creative and constructive.

Day after day, I saw the evidence passing before me: tangled lives made straight, wrongs righted, marriages remade, families reunited, businesses and business relations placed on a new basis, churches revitalized.

I heard and saw enough to convince me that my despair regarding the future of civilization left two factors unregarded: the power of God to communicate his will to man, and the capacity of man to listen, to obey, and to be changed.

I began to realize that the effort to heal the manifest ailments of mankind by intellectual processes or by international conferences and polit-

---

[1]Hagedorn was part of the First-Century Christian Fellowship, developed at Oxford and Princeton Universities in the early twenties under the Reverend Frank Buchman, a former YMCA secretary who had been active in the Northfield conferences attended by hundreds of Harvard evangelicals before the First World War. By the time the movement reached Harvard in the late twenties, it was known as the Oxford Group, and in 1939 the name was changed to Moral Re-Armament, or MRA.

ical and social mass-movements are superficial and short-lived. The disease is moral and spiritual and can be reached only by moral and spiritual regeneration, beginning with individual citizens. But does it happen? Nothing counts in the answer to that question, except facts.

Here is one: Dozens of "changed" women and men, most of them in their twenties—Americans, British, Dutch, including graduates of Princeton and Yale and Harvard—come to South Africa. These young people are intelligent, high-spirited, levelheaded, and obviously sincere. They speak to students in the preparatory schools and universities. To a generation to which everything in heaven and on earth is shifting or in flux, they dare to speak of absolutes, and they present a quartet of them, the distillation of the Sermon on the Mount—absolute honesty, absolute purity, absolute unselfishness, absolute love. The people they talk to have standards, but they are the relative standards of a timid and compromising social order. The word *absolute* startles them and sets the heart beating faster.

One of the four standards is *absolute love*. A Britisher, hearing it, recalls some of the cutting things he has said of his Dutch neighbor and says to himself, "No, that was not, I suppose, absolute love." The Boer, confronted by the disconcerting absolute, wonders a little uneasily about his determination never to permit a Britisher to cross his threshold. The white man, Dutch or British, thinks of his native farm-laborers. Absolute love? Well, not exactly. The black man thinks of his grudge. Absolute love? Something will have to be done about that.

Something is done. For these visitors do more than present standards; they show where power may be found to live up to them.

"Thirty men and women who could not speak our language," wrote a Norwegian recently, "came to our country and spoke to us about God. And six weeks later all Norway was talking about God." They talked of the four standards; of the barriers between man and man, or man and God, which wreck homes and nations; of daily "quiet times" and the guidance of God through Scripture and prayer. Six months after the arrival of the thirty, the Bishop of Tromsoe tells of amazing changes in the national spirit, declaring that Norway has not known such spiritual regeneration since the Reformation; and four professors of the University of Oslo, in a joint statement addressed to the group, say, "Your visit will be the deciding factor in the history of Norway. You have come at the strategic moment with the right answer." Sparks from the fire leap over to Denmark. Public confessions are made. A new spirit of cooperation between the nations begins to emerge.

Sixteen heads of firms in the textile industry get together to find "God's plan" for their industry. A leading chocolate-importer in Denmark changes his pricing and employee relations. He suspects that his action will ruin his business, but he is willing to face even that. To his astonishment his sales and his profits increase. "You will understand that we are only at the beginning," he writes, "but we are learning gradually, as we go on, that this is the right way. We understand that it will mean a completely changed business life in Denmark, and that economic theory will be rewritten."

Ten thousand gather in Hamlet's castle at Elsinore for a meeting. More than twenty-five thousand come together on the eve of a national election, to bring the four standards of absolute honesty, purity, unselfishness, love, before the minds of candidates and voters, and to show them that the choice which really counts is not political but moral and spiritual.

In Switzerland, after the meetings begin in Geneva, six thousand people pay their income tax on the first day, an unprecedented event.

In Canada, a newspaper publisher pays the government twelve thousand dollars in payment of custom duties evaded. In a Western prison, changed prisoners change their warden and get up a purse to send their chaplain to Oxford meetings, convinced that he needs changing.

In Holland, an engineer, smashed by the depression, invents a new kind of explosive bomb, and two or three countries are clamoring for the patent. But he is changed. The guidance is clear. He tears up the formula.

In Great Britain, a team of a hundred Oxford and Cambridge students spend their Christmas vacation in the East End of London, live with the unemployed, and begin to see them changed by love.

Standards, the guidance of God, the transforming power of Christ, individuals changed, nations changing—a world beginning to restore itself to sanity. These are facts which give meaning to the declaration that the only way to bring order to a nation is to bring order to the hearts and lives of its individual citizens. A leading Danish construction engineer and delegate to the League of Nations refers to those who are changed as "the greatest bridge-builders I know, bringing a new spirit of understanding between social classes and between nations." Not mass movements, not political messiahs, but the change of individual lives is the key to fruitful living, to economic security, and to peace.

What is Harvard's response to this dynamic effort of a resilient and tireless group of men and women, of all denominations and varied racial and social backgrounds, to bring standards back to a social order reeling amidst its relativities? Is it the response of Oxford and Cambridge and Edinburgh, of the universities of Oslo and Copenhagen and Pretoria and Zurich, of the provost of Queen's College, of the primates of India, Norway, and Denmark, the heads of state or foreign ministers of a half dozen continental powers?

Three hundred years ago Harvard laid the foundations of a nation on a basis of faith in God and the absolute standards of the Sermon on the

Mount. Words pass and lose their meaning, but the primal necessities of men remain unaltered. Our bodies require food and drink and periodic rest, and our spirits have needs which are no less peremptory. Civilization is facing extinction because men have assumed that they could direct their personal and communal life on a basis of egoism, tempered by expediency, or an altruism too general to be effective. The result requires no comment.

A more sound base is the one on which Harvard herself once stood—*Christo et Ecclesiae*.

☙

Editor's note: Like many Europeans of genuine faith, these who were "changed" worked to form the Resistance and begin underground efforts to evacuate Jews from Nazi-threatened Europe before and during the Second World War. Some died in concentration camps along with their friends.[2] Many continue to live and share the same message of hope.

---

[2]See, for example, Corrie ten Boom's *The Hiding Place*, the documentary *Weapons of the Spirit*, Dietrich Bonhoeffer's *Letters From Prison* or *The Cost of Discipleship*, and "The Solitary Witness of Franz Jagerstatter," *Sojourners* (August 1993).

A World Split Apart

ॐ

— A L E K S A N D R   S O L Z H E N I T S Y N —

Society appears to have little defense against the abyss of human decadence, such as, the misuse of liberty for moral violence against young people.

A devout Russian Orthodox Christian and a student of mathematics and physics, **Aleksandr Solzhenitsyn** is often considered Russia's greatest twentieth-century novelist. He began writing during a three-year exile period. Before this, he had fought against the Nazis in World War II and was decorated twice; but in 1945 a letter in which he had criticized Stalin was intercepted and, without trial, he was sentenced to eight years of hard labor.

During the period of de-Stalinization, Solzhenitsyn published *One Day in the Life of Ivan Denisovich*, based on his experience in the labor camps. As government control tightened again, his morally courageous writing and speaking did not cease. In 1974 he was exiled once more, this time to the West.

In 1970 Mr. Solzhenitsyn was awarded the Nobel Prize for literature "for the ethical force with which he has pursued the indispensable traditions of Russian literature." He was awarded a doctorate in literature by Harvard in 1978.

On June 8, 1978, Solzhenitsyn delivered this controversial and prophetic commencement address at Harvard, adapted here. The complete text is found in *A World Split Apart* available from the Harvard News Office.

A World Split Apart

— ALEKSANDR SOLZHENITSYN —

Harvard's motto is *Veritas*. Many of you have already found out, and others will find out in the course of their lives, that truth eludes us if we do not concentrate with total attention on its pursuit. And even while it eludes us, the illusion still lingers of knowing it and leads to many misunderstandings. Also, truth seldom is sweet; it is almost invariably bitter. A measure of bitter truth is included in my speech today, but I offer it as a friend, not as an adversary. . . .

A DECLINE IN COURAGE

A decline in courage may be the most striking feature an outside observer notices in the West in our days. The Western world has lost its civil courage, both as a whole as well as in each country, each government, each political party, and, in the United Nations. Such a decline in courage is particularly noticeable among the ruling and intellectual elites, causing an impression of a loss of courage by the entire society. Of course, there are many courageous individuals but they do not have determining influence on public life. . . .

LEGALISTIC LIFE

Western society has given itself the organization best suited to its purposes, based, I would say, on the letter of the law. People in the West have acquired considerable skill in using, interpreting, and manipulating law. Every conflict is solved according to the letter of the law, and this is considered to be the supreme solution. If one is right from a legal point of view, nothing more is required. Nobody may mention that one could still not be entirely right, and urge self-restraint or the renunciation of these legal rights or call for sacrifice and selfless risk; it would sound simply absurd. One almost never sees voluntary self-restraint. Everybody operates at the extreme limit of the legal framework. An oil company is legally blameless when it buys out an invention of a new type of energy in order to prevent its use. A food product manufacturer is legally blameless when he poisons his produce to make it last longer; after all, people are free not to buy it.

I have spent most of my life under a communist regime, and I will tell you that a society without any objective legal scale is a terrible one indeed. But a society with no other scale but the legal one is not quite worthy of humans, either. A society ... which never reaches for anything higher than the letter of the law is taking scarce advantage of the high level of human possibilities. The letter of the law is too cold and formal to have a beneficial influence by itself on society. Whenever the tissue of life is woven of legalistic relations, there is an atmosphere of moral mediocrity, paralyzing our noblest impulses. And it will be simply impossible to stand through the trials of this threatening century with only the support of a legalistic structure.

THE DIRECTION OF FREEDOM

In today's Western society an inequality has been revealed between the freedom to do good and the freedom to do evil. A statesman who wants to achieve something important and highly constructive for his country has to move cautiously, even timidly. There are thousands of hasty and irresponsible critics around him, and the legislature and the press keep rebuffing him. He has to prove that each single step is well-founded and absolutely flawless. Consequently, a person gifted with unusual and original initiatives hardly gets a chance to assert himself. From the very start dozens of traps are set out for him. So mediocrity triumphs with the excuse of restrictions imposed by democracy.

It is always easy to undermine administrative power. And, in fact, it has been seriously weakened in all Western countries. The defense of individual rights has attained such extremes as to make society as a whole defenseless against particular individuals. It is time in the West to defend not so much human rights as human obligations.

Destructive and irresponsible freedom has been granted boundless space. Society appears to have little defense against the abyss of human decadence, such as, for example, the misuse of liberty for moral violence against young people, motion pictures full of pornography, crime, and horror. It is considered to be part of freedom and theoretically counterbalanced by the young people's right not to look or not to accept what is being put before them. Life organized legalistically has thus shown its inability to defend itself against the corrosion of evil.

And what shall we say about the dark realm of criminality as such? Legal frameworks, especially in the United States, are so broad that they encourage not only individual freedom but also certain individual crimes. The culprit can go unpunished or obtain undeserved leniency with the support of thousands of defenders in the society. And when a government starts an earnest fight against terrorism, public opinion immediately accuses it of violating the terrorists' civil rights.

Such a tilt of freedom in the direction of evil has come about gradually. It stems primarily from a humanistic concept, according to which there is no evil inherent to human nature. The world belongs to mankind, and all of life's defects are caused by faulty social systems which merely need to be corrected. Strangely enough, although the best socioeconomic conditions have been achieved in the West, there is considerably more criminality here than even in the impoverished and lawless Soviet Union (which does have a huge number of political prisoners in camps. . .).

THE DIRECTION OF THE PRESS

The media too, of course, enjoy the widest freedom. But what sort of use do they put this freedom to? Here too, the main concern is merely not to infringe the letter of the law. There is little moral responsibility for defamation or disproportion to one's readers or to history. How often do we hear of journalists publicly retracting or rectifying a story when they have misled public opinion or the government? Hardly ever—because it would damage sales. A nation may be the worse for such a mistake, but the journalist always gets away with it. It is most likely that he will start writing the exact opposite to his previous statements with renewed aplomb.

Because instant and credible-sounding information has to be given by the media, it becomes necessary to resort to guesswork, rumors, and suppositions to fill in the voids, and none of them will ever be rectified; they will stay on in the readers' memory. How many hasty, immature, superficial, and misleading judgments are expressed every day, confusing readers without any verification? The media both simulate public opinion and miseducate it. Thus, we may see terrorists heroized, the privacy of well-known people intruded upon, or confidential matters pertaining to national security publicly revealed under the slogan "Everyone is entitled to know everything." But people also have the right not to know, and it is a more valuable one—the right not to have their divine souls stuffed with gossip, nonsense, vain talk. A person who works and leads a meaningful life has no need for this excessive and burdening flow of information.

Hastiness and superficiality are the psychic disease of the twentieth century, and perhaps more than anywhere else this disease is reflected in the media. In-depth analysis of a problem is anathema to the media. It stops at sensational formulas. Such as it is, however, the media in Western countries are in some ways more powerful than even the legislature, executive, and judiciary. But by what law have the press been elected, and to whom are they responsible?

There is yet another surprise for someone from the totalitarian East, where the press is rigorously unified: one gradually discovers a common trend of preferences within the Western press as a whole. There are generally accepted patterns of judgment, and there may be common corporate interests. The net effect is not competition but unification. Enormous freedom exists for the press but not for the readership, because newspapers give sufficient coverage and emphasis mostly to those opinions which do not too openly contradict their own and the general trend. . . .

HUMANISM AND ITS CONSEQUENCES

How did the West decline from what was once a triumphal march to its present sickness? Have there been recent fatal turns or losses of direction? It does not seem so. The West kept advancing socially in accordance with its proclaimed intentions, with the help of brilliant technological progress. And all of a sudden it found itself in its present state of weakness. This means that the mistake must be at the root, at the very basis of human thinking in the past centuries. I refer to the prevailing Western worldview, which was first born during the Renaissance and which first found its political expression in the period of the Enlightenment. That worldview became the basis for government and social science. It can be defined as rationalistic humanism: the proclaimed autonomy of man from any higher force above him, with man as the center of everything that exists.

But evidently, the turn that occurred during the Renaissance was historically inevitable. By sheer exhaustion the Middle Ages had come to a natural end. It had come to be an intolerably despotic repression of human physical nature in favor of the spiritual one. But then in the Enlightenment we turned our backs upon the Spirit and embraced all that is material with unwarranted zeal. This new way of thinking, which has imposed its guidance on us, did not admit intrinsic human evil nor see any higher task than the attainment of happiness on earth. It based modern Western civilization on the dangerous trend of worshiping man and his material needs. Everything beyond physical well-being and accumulation of material goods, all other human requirements and characteristics of a subtler and higher nature, were left outside the area of superior sense. That provided access for evil, of which in our days there is a free and constant flow. Mere freedom does not in the least solve all the problems of human life—and it even adds a number of new ones.

But in early democracies, like America at the time of its inception, all individual human rights were granted because man is God's creature. That is, freedom was given to the individual conditionally, within the assumption of his constant religious responsibility. Such was the heritage of the preceding thousand years. Two hundred years ago, even fifty, it would have seemed quite impossible that an individual in America could be granted boundless freedom simply for the satisfaction of his instincts or whims. Subsequently, however, all such limitations were discarded everywhere in the West. What has occurred is a total liberation from the moral heritage of Christian centuries, with their great reserves of mercy and sacrifice. State systems were becoming increasingly materialistic. The West has succeeded in truly enforcing human rights, but our sense of responsibility to God and society has grown dimmer and dimmer.

In the past few decades the legalistically selfish aspect of the Western approach and thinking has reached what surely must be its final dimension, and the world has found itself in an intense spiritual crisis and in a political impasse. All the glorified technological achievements of progress, including the conquest of outer space, do not redeem the twentieth century's moral poverty, which no one could have imagined even as late as in the nineteenth century. . . .

BEFORE THE TURN

I am not examining here the disaster of a world war and the changes it would produce in society. As long as we wake up every morning under a peaceful sun we have to lead an everyday life. There is a disaster, however, which has already been under way for some time. I am referring to the calamity of a despiritualized and irreligious humanistic consciousness.

We are now finally experiencing the consequences of historical mistakes which had not been noticed at the beginning of the journey. On the way from the Renaissance we have enriched our experience in many ways, but we have lost the concept of a Supreme Complete Entity which used to restrain our passions and our irresponsibility. We have placed too much hope in political and social reforms, only to find that we were being deprived of our most precious possession: our spiritual life. In the East it is destroyed by the machinations of the ruling party; in the West commercial interests suffocate it. This is the real crisis. The split in the world into East and West is less terrible than the similarity of the disease plaguing its main sections.

If humanism were right in declaring that man is born just to be happy, he would not be born to die. But since his body is doomed to die, surely his task on earth must be of a more spiritual nature. It cannot be unrestrained enjoyment of everyday life. It cannot be the search for the best ways to obtain material goods and then cheerfully get the most out of them. It has to be the fulfillment of a permanent, earnest duty so that one's life journey may become an experience of moral growth, so that one may leave life a better human being than one started it. It is imperative to review the general chart of human values. Its present incorrectness is astounding. Assessment of the president's performance cannot be reduced to the question of how much money one makes during his administration or the unlimited availability of gasoline. Only voluntary, inspired self-restraint can raise us above the world's stream of materialism. . . . We cannot avoid reassessing the fundamental definitions of human life and society. Is it true that man is above everything? Is there no superior spirit about him? Is it right that man's life and society's activities should be ruled by material expansion, above all?

If the world has not approached its end, it has reached a major watershed in history, perhaps equal in importance to the turn from the Middle Ages to the Renaissance. It will exact from us a spiritual blaze. We shall have to rise to a new height of vision, to a new level of life where our physical nature will not be cursed as it was in the Middle Ages, but even more importantly, where our spiritual being will not be trampled upon as it is in the modern era.

This ascension will be similar to climbing onto the next anthropologic stage. No one on earth has any other way left but upward.

CHAPTER 3

FINDING HOPE, HEALTH, AND LIFE

ॐ

"Are you thirsty?" said the Lion.

"I'm dying of thirst,' said Jill.

"Then drink,' said the Lion.... "There is no other stream."

C. S. LEWIS, THE SILVER CHAIR

❧

What seemed to be the end proved to be the beginning. . . .

Suddenly a wall becomes a gate.

HENRI NOUWEN, GRACIAS! A LETTER OF CONSOLATION

❧

The Cross is the point where God and sinful man merge with a crash and the way to life is opened—but the crash is on the heart of God..

OSWALD CHAMBERS, MY UTMOST FOR HIS HIGHEST

❧

Now—here is my secret: I tell it to you with an openness of heart that I doubt I shall ever achieve again. . . . My secret is that I need God— that I am sick and can no longer make it alone.

DOUGLAS COUPLAND, LIFE AFTER GOD

❧

Five years ago I came to believe in Christ's teaching, and my life suddenly changed. . . . I heard the words of Christ and understood them, and life and death ceased to seem to me evil, and instead of despair I experienced happiness and the joy of life undisturbed by death.

LEO TOLSTOY, CIRCA 1900

On Gravity and Lift

— PAUL WYLIE —

In the 1992 Olympics, I felt God's pleasure.

While a sophomore at Harvard, **Paul Wylie** earned a position on the 1988 U.S. Olympic figure skating team. As you will discover, Olympic experiences in 1988 and 1992 helped to shape his journey of faith. As a student, he studied, skated, and twice coordinated Harvard's "Evening with Champions" to benefit the Dana Farber Cancer Research Institute. Having concentrated in government, Wylie graduated from Harvard in 1991.

In 1992, after twelve turbulent years of competition, and a nearly disastrous triple axel fall in his final Olympic warmup, Wylie found himself with one last chance to show critics, and the world, what his friends had believed from the beginning — that for Paul Wylie skating can be an extraordinary confluence of body, mind, and spirit — the "celebration of the whole man" envisioned by founders of the modern Olympics a century ago.

In addition to a 1992 Olympic silver medal, Paul received the Olympic Spirit Award for sportsmanship, the Personal Best Award for community service, and the title of USOC Skating Athlete of the Year. More recently, he has won the world professional championship. Paul also skis and bikes. He may return to Harvard as a law student next year.

On Gravity and Lift

— PAUL WYLIE —

The crowd of twenty thousand is electric, and by extension my mind attempts to contemplate the live worldwide television audience. I am a figure skater, a sophomore at Harvard, and for fifteen years I have worked towards this competition. It is 1988, and I finally take the ice in Calgary, one of three American men competing in the Winter Olympics.

The intensity of the focus is overwhelming. This is not a human-scale event, and yet I stand alone at center ice, under the watchful, expectant gaze of the world. As the music starts I move onto a long edge, hearing little but the sound of my blade rumbling across the ice. I notice that my nerves have caused my mouth to dry up such that my teeth stick to my upper lip. I understand that this is not a good sign of how I'm handling the stress. I set up for the first jump in my program, but as soon as I'm in the air, I know something is terribly wrong.

A flash later my hand touches the ice; the blade will not hold. I start slipping and now I realize it: I am falling. All I hear as I collapse to the ice is the empathetic groan of what seems like a million voices. I struggle to get up, hustling to get to the next move, thoughts racing through my mind as I try to cover the disappointment. There is no way of erasing a fall from the judges' minds, nor can I jam the television transmissions to the living rooms of friends and family watching at home. This is live, and I have just blown it.

I have four minutes left and one important choice to make. Either skate through the rest of the program believing that something constructive will come of the mishap, concentrating and performing through to the end, or continue to dwell on the fall and its consequences, inviting more mistakes caused by a negative frame of mind. A Scripture flashes through my mind that helps me with my decision: "The righteous shall fall, but they shall not be utterly cast down." I suddenly grasp God's perspective: he will use our successes and our failures to teach us about ourselves and to show the world his glory. "And we know that in all things God works for the good of those who love him, who have been called according to his purpose" (Romans 8:28). I move on, accepting a new role. I admit imperfection and decide to skate "heartily as unto the Lord"—for God's glory rather than my own "results."

At the end of the program, the audience surprises me with a rousing ovation. They appreciate the comeback after the initial mistake, having sensed the abandon and determination I felt to redeem the rest. The audience forgave the initial glitch, but the judges—well, they never do.

I have learned so much about God and my relationship with him from such experiences. I've seen, in other areas of my life, that God wants to lift me when I fall, and he provides me with a way to leave my mistakes behind, redeeming them and using them for his purposes.

Yet too often I choose to skate long-faced through the rest of a program, abandoning hope once my personal goals appear unreachable. I focus on myself, wallowing in the pity of making a mistake. Or worse yet, I hide my falls, the true condition of my heart, from him. As Adam and Eve ran for cover in the garden, I attempt to cover up the mistake, hoping God wasn't in the audience or that he didn't notice. I smile and pretend that the fall never happened, but I feel the shame and I feel the power of the sins as they break the rapport I have with God.

In a competition, I cannot expect the judges to overlook a fall, but I can look to God, because of his provision in Christ. Once I ask for forgiveness, the scores all become the perfect marks of his Son—but without my confession and the gift of faith, the weight and the gravity of my sin burdens me and I am alone, separated from God. Only when I run back to God and humble myself, realizing that God's Son died to lift me from my sin, can I get up from a fall of any kind.

I suppose life is not always like a flawed program, because as a Christian, you can grow. We are transformed by the renewing of our mind, by study and meditation on the Scriptures. I became a Christian six months prior to attending Harvard, so my involvement in the fellowships on campus as a freshman represented some of my first contact with God's Word and with other evangelical Christians. Several friends and a professor spent time with me, helping me to nurture a deeper understanding of the Bible and of faith as it is lived out.

The first week of school, I joined the Christian Athletes group, which often consisted of two athletes sitting down to a Bible study. I was impressed by the level of the commitment of the leader, Brian Gimotty, to pray with me and to see me grow as a believer. When I left for a week to compete in Moscow, he gave me tapes, a book, and an encouraging note. I can remember closing my eyes to pray in my hotel room in Moscow and sensing a closeness to home and to God, even though I was far away. In subsequent competitions and exhibition tours, Brian and other Christian friends would pray with me over the phone or come to watch and offer support. I knew that they were concerned for my growth as a person more than for my skating ability, and I responded to their genuine help.

During one season, I asked another friend to spend three hours a week going over the heroes and the highlights of the Old Testament with me. Phillip Araoz and I met in my dorm room for a time of prayer and Bible study where we studied Abraham, David, Noah, Gideon, Elijah, Elisha, Joshua, Daniel, and Jonah, just to name a few. Not only did I begin to grasp the bigger picture of Christianity but I began to see God differently. I started to see possibilities for his interaction in every part of my life, in school and especially in skating. Instead of being independent from God, striving to do things for his glory but without his involvement, I tried to imitate the Old Testament heroes by looking to God for solutions. When I started to ask him to bless me with the wherewithal to accomplish the difficult tasks of training and studying at a high level, the contrast was unbelievable.

When I was relying on myself for the solutions, I was trying to spend twenty minutes a day on sports psychology techniques. I would try to visualize perfect jumps in perfect routines. But I would either fall asleep or I would see myself falling, neither of which helped my performance. Dr. Armand Nicholi, a professor of mine who had done some work with the NFL, made a radical suggestion: ask God for help. After all, visualization is not something new but rather it is a secularization of something God would want us to bring to him in prayer, where we begin to see ourselves through the eyes of God. I started spending part of my prayer time on the specifics of my routines, and asking God how to imagine the perfect technique. As I focused on preparation for competitions, my quiet times helped me to process the corrections and instructions my coaches had given me—and I never learned faster.

The Bible served as a concrete motivator and as a source of mental fiber both in my daily routines and in the heat of competition. The words in the Scriptures carry weight, and they are also organic—living and active. When I am tired, saying to myself, "The joy of the Lord is my strength" does a lot more for me than someone screaming, "C'mon Paul, you need to give more." And all battles are won first in the internal dialogue of the mind.

During the four years between 1988 and 1992, I concentrated on finishing Harvard College and trying to maintain a world-class level in skating. I made three world teams but did not finish higher than ninth place in the world championships. Writers started to label me as a "choker," because each year, I did not meet the expectations generated by my performances in the precompetition practices. Calgary was not the last time I fell on the world stage. In fact, the lowest point of my career came at the 1991 worlds, where I made three mistakes, including one bad fall, in the technical program—nearly missing the qualification for the final round. (I was twentieth, and only twenty made the finals.)

I spent many hours on the commute to and from the rink contemplating retirement. At twenty-seven, I would be the oldest competitor in the men's event in the 1992 games—that is, if I could even make the team. There were rumors that I would retire, and many judges and officials whispered that they wished I would. One judge even called my coaches with her suggestion that I hang up my skates and pursue my education in earnest. I was frustrated with the difficulty of pursuing the dual goals of skating and college, and I often longed for a more typical collegiate experience. I was depressed by my shortcomings in skating, and I relied on the encouragement of my parents, my friends, and especially my coaches, Evy and Mary Scotvold, to continue until the 1992 Olympics, when, having graduated from college, I could concentrate on skating. "Don't limit the Lord," was Evy's admonition to me when I began to identify more with the writers' and judges' opinions of me. "All you need is the faith of a mustard seed."

When maturity brings us closer to the ideal of Christlikeness, we fall less. More experienced skaters make fewer mistakes, and they also skate with a greater grace. As a skater refines technique to match the ideal laid out by God in the laws of physics, the jumps and movements become effortless in their appearance, even though it takes years of falling to achieve the skills. My biggest hurdle in skating was performing the triple axel in the technical program. After years of struggle with the jump, I had come to see it as my nemesis. As it was the centerpiece of the technical program, I knew I had to land it to score in the 1992 Olympics, but I battled with inconsistency.

My coach started to subtly change my technique, and I started to visualize it, seeing the jump the way it ought to be. From my quiet times, I began to feel that God wanted me to turn my attitude about triple axels upside down. Instead of seeing the jump as nerve-wrackingly strenuous and difficult, "The Jump I Dreaded" needed to become, well, *fun*. Instead of feeling the pressure to land it in the most stressful of situations, I was supposed to thrill in the privilege of having the youth and the ability to achieve three and a half revolutions. I suddenly realized that God had gifted me to experience some unusual effects of the laws of physics. I would smile and laugh after landing a good one, because it *was* fun. And once I began to understand that feeling, I was able to train with greater freedom and consistency, allowing me to mature through the fear of falling and move on to skating as a true expression. The shift in attitude from dread to fun, even joy, came as I tried to imagine God's perspective on my life. I thought of

Olympic champion Eric Liddell, portrayed in the film *Chariots of Fire*. He is quoted as saying, "When I run, I feel God's pleasure."

In the 1992 Olympics, I felt God's pleasure. Not only did I perform a clean technical program with a triple axel combination but I also landed two triple axels in the long program! The French crowd got behind me, and their cheers spurred me on. I thought back to Calgary, and I knew that God was watching and that he had planned this night for a long time. Like Gideon after his army had been pared down, I understood that God had fought with me, waiting until my career seemed over but then preparing me for the performance of my life. As I ended the final minute of my program, a huge smile on my face, I realized that God had enabled me to rewrite the story of my whole career, with the end result redeeming the years of disappointment. God had allowed me to go into the wilderness, where I tasted some bitter defeats, but then he allowed me to skate my best when it truly counted. How different from the falls of the past, and how like God to cause me to learn from every mistake, for the greater goal of my maturity in him.

When I look back on that moment, it always amazes me to think that the omnipotent God, the creator of galaxies light years away, will give us his strength and grace to help us in all of our struggles—in our relationships, in our careers, and even in things that seem insignificant to others. He sees our hearts, and he wants us to acknowledge our needs and rely on his help. All we need to do is ask—and rise as he lifts us.

Hope in a Secular Age

༒

— ARMAND NICHOLI JR. —

*Hope decreases morbidity. But what is hope? I cannot help but
compare Marx and Freud with another scholar—C. S. Lewis.*

Armand Nicholi Jr., M.D., is an associate clinical professor of psychiatry at the Harvard Medical School and the Massachusetts General Hospital. He is the editor and co-author of *The Harvard Guide
to Psychiatry.* Dr. Nicholi has received international recognition for
research in: the changing structure of the American family and its
consequent impact on children; the drug culture; the epidemic of
suicide among adolescents; and the success of organizations.

He has served as consultant to the U.S. Peace Corps, the U.S. Surgeon General, the White House, the U.S. Department of Health and
Human Services, and the National Football League..

A faculty member of the Harvard Medical School for the past
twenty-eight years, he also teaches a seminar at Harvard College on
the contrasting worldviews of Sigmund Freud and C. S. Lewis.

Hope in a Secular Age

— ARMAND NICHOLI JR. —

We have experienced an explosive increase of all forms of depression in our society, with some eleven million people needing treatment.[1] We now have a national Depression Screening Week. Over a quarter of a million people decide to take their lives each year and some thirty thousand succeed, and we are experiencing an unprecedented epidemic of suicide among children and adolescents. Most of this self-destruction results from depression.

How do we explain this enormous increase in hopelessness and despair? We cannot relate our despair solely to changes in our personal histories. Nor can we relate it solely to the killings in Africa, Ireland, Bosnia, or the random killings in our inner cities. Human history has always known wars and senseless violence. Though science and technology make our lives more comfortable, we still have difficulty making sense of our existence. We arrive on this planet—we have no choice in the matter—and we soon realize that we are not going to be here very long. The hero of our personal story always dies. Yet we have this intense yearning for permanence. About a hundred years ago Sigmund Freud wrote, "Life as we find it is too hard for us; it brings us too many pains, disappointments, and impossible tasks." He then lists some of the sources of our pain: "We are threatened with suffering from three directions: from our own body, which is doomed to decay . . . from the external world which may rage against us with overwhelming and merciless forces of destruction." And here he mentions earthquakes, floods, and other natural disasters which we have witnessed within the past year. Finally he says, "We are threatened with suffering from our relationships to other men. The suffering which comes from this last source is perhaps more painful to us than any other." Freud writes that in order to bear this kind of pain, we use palliative measures—distractions, intoxicants, or denial. Perhaps we distract ourselves by keeping the radio and television on much of the time or by keeping excessively busy or by using various forms of intoxicants and drugs.

Whether in interpersonal or international relations, the basic nature of life seems to be constant over time. How then do we explain the explo-

---

[1]National Institute of Mental Health. Number of U.S. adults with mental disorder, 1990 (March 25, 1992).

sive increase in depression and hopelessness within our society as we enter the twenty-first century A.D.?

Historians and social scientists tell us that we have fewer spiritual resources to draw from than at any time in Western cultural history. Some say that our culture has forsaken its spiritual roots, that we live in an overtly secular society without even the pretense of spiritual values. Many young people today feel that their cultures fail to provide answers to questions of purpose and meaning and destiny. We fail, they feel, to provide some reason for hope. The consequence is that we are now in a cultural crisis and living in what is being called "The Age of Despair." We hear of our "spiritual vacuum" and our "crisis of meaning." How did this secularization of our culture happen?

No two men have made a more indelible impact on the world we live in today than Karl Marx and Sigmund Freud. They have helped change our particular society from one whose values were primarily moral and spiritual to one whose values are primarily material and secular.

Karl Marx, the German philosopher, through his writings—especially his *Das Kapital* and *The Communist Manifesto*—set the stage for the Russian Revolution. This led to the rise of Marxism and to Lenin and Stalin coming to power. Stalin in turn helped make it possible for Hitler to come into power. One can make a reasonably strong argument that without Marx we would not have had World War II, the Cold War, the Korean War, the Vietnam War, the arms race, or the period of world division into communist and noncommunist camps.

Sigmund Freud, the Viennese physician, whose scientific contributions some historians have ranked with those of Planck and Einstein, has given us a new understanding of the development and functioning of the human mind. His ideas have pervaded not only medicine but literature, anthropology, and many other disciplines as well.

In addition to their intellectual legacy, both Marx and Freud left to us an atheistic worldview, or philosophy of life, that has helped erode our society's moral and spiritual values. Both men mounted a direct attack on religious faith, Marx calling religion the "opiate of the people," and Freud calling religion "the universal obsessional neurosis." Freud concluded that God was but a projection of the childish wish for an all-powerful father who would protect one from the unpredictable, harsh elements of nature.

Both Marx and Freud died in London. Marx died at the age of sixty-five, shortly after the death of his wife and several of his children, one by suicide. He died in abject poverty after having been kept alive through the generosity of his only lifelong friend, Frederick Engels. Freud died at the age of eighty-three after a long bout with cancer.

Both men died bitter and disillusioned, with little compassion for the common man. Freud wrote in 1918:

> I have found little that is good about human beings on the whole. In my experience most of them are trash no matter whether they publicly subscribe to this or that ethical doctrine or to none at all.[2]

Both had virtually no friends. Biographers agree that Marx, with the exception of Engels, had no close friends, was coldly arrogant, conceited, and "full of hate." It is well known that Freud broke with each of his followers, none of whom he had been very close to anyway.

As one reads about the end of their lives—of how they finished the course—one notes an overwhelming sense of despair and hopelessness.

As despair and hopelessness characterized the lives of Marx and Freud, so do these same qualities characterize an increasing number of people in our society today.

When a doctor sees a patient who expresses complete hopelessness, he or she thinks immediately of the clinical picture of depression. Depression may be transient, mild and insignificant, or so intense that it paralyzes. Mild or severe, depression affects more people in our particular culture, both young and old, than any other emotional disorder.

I would like to briefly consider several of the essential elements of mild depression affecting everyone at some time; first in terms of how modern psychiatry tends to describe them, and second in terms of what resources, if any, the Scriptures provide to help cope with them.

One feature of depression might also be considered a cause. What often appears to be the cause of despondency in many today is an awareness of a gap between what they think they *ought* to be and what they feel they are. That is, there is a discrepancy between an ideal they hold for themselves, and at times think they measure up to, and an acute awareness of how far short they fall from the ideal.

Other causes of depression are associated with loss: loss of a friendship, a job, a loved one, or a broken engagement or marriage, etc. Loss usually results in grief or mourning, a normal type of depressive reaction, relatively short-lived, self-limited, and not usually requiring medical help. Many, however, suffer depression without an associated loss. And in these people the cause often appears to be the disparity between what they ought to be and what they fear they are.

---

[2]*Psychoanalysis and Faith: The Letters of Sigmund Freud and Oskar Pfister*, ed. Heinrich Meng and Ernest Freud (New York: Basic Books, 1963), 61.

One of my research interests involves people who drop out of college. Many who do so have superb intellectual equipment which, because of emotional conflict, becomes paralyzed. The most frequent diagnosis among these students who leave college is depression. Most often the cause appears to be an awareness of a gap between the ideal self as a gifted, brilliant student—as often they were in high school—and the actual self which, because of real or imagined reasons, they see as a mediocre student in the highly competitive world of a modern college or university. This is but one example. All of us at some time suffer from the awareness of how we fall far short of what we ought to be.

Does a person's faith proffer resources to help with this conflict? I think so. Faith always involves a very personal aspect of one's life. Perhaps, like most people, I find it difficult to speak openly and freely about it. I can only share what I have found meaningful in my own life, in my commitment to Christ, and in my feeble and often faltering attempt to follow him.

The New Testament documents make me acutely aware of an enormous gap between who God demands that I be and who I am. This realization, of course, leads not to despondence but to greater awareness of my need for Christ: for Christ bridges that gap. The Old and New Testament documents tell me that this bridging of the gap was precisely the reason for his presence on earth—to bridge the gap between God and alienated man, between the perfection God demands and who I am. Spiritual rebirth and redemption are based not on good works, such that "no one can boast" (Ephesians 2:9), but on what Christ has accomplished for me. Good works become a *result* of new birth, not the other way around.

The Scriptures, as I understand them, indicate clearly that God is interested not merely in *good* people but first of all in *new* people. For our goodness always falls short. This new birth does not make me less aware of how far short I fall of my ideals and of God's standards; it makes me painfully more aware. But this awareness does not lead to self-hatred and despondency. Instead I have found that through my commitment to God, I, for the first time, have the motivation and the inner strength to take a step toward being who I know I can become in Christ. I often stumble and fall while taking this step or the next step, but when I do fall, I know that he always offers forgiveness followed by the opportunity and the resources to start again. In this way my faith helps me cope with the haunting awareness of the gap between what I ought to be and what I am. God's forgiveness and acceptance makes it easier for me to tolerate and accept myself and helps me more readily accept others.

Another element of depression, closely related to those discussed above, is the feeling of worthlessness, of low self-esteem. As with all feelings experienced by an emotionally ill person, everyone experiences the feeling of worthlessness to a greater or lesser extent. If we peer beneath the surface of the most egotistical person, we find that his or her conceit covers deeper fears of inadequacy and incompetence. College students with the highest academic performances frequently harbor the constant deep-seated fear of being unintelligent. (One sometimes also finds these feelings of inadequacy in older adults who have been immensely successful.) Some people are able to use these fears adaptively, to work excessively hard, and to achieve more than they would without the fears. However, with most of us these feelings incapacitate and discourage, making every effort difficult.

What causes these universal feelings of worthlessness? They have many determinants, not the least of which are the feelings we have toward ourselves in our early years. As children we feel helpless among the adult giants walking about. We feel hopelessly inadequate, less strong, less knowledgeable, and some residual of these feelings remains with us as adults.

Another determinant: in our society, moral and ethical guidelines have become less and less clear, and people's consciences less and less discerning. People nevertheless feel guilty about their behavior. Regardless of unclear external and blunted internal moral guidelines, I see as a psychiatrist the apparent persistence of an inner moral sense, a kind of universal law of right and wrong that makes one feel guilty and worthless whenever this law is transgressed.

I have observed many college students who express *surprise* that their actions produce feelings of guilt. They say they have thought clearly about what they are doing and can give good reasons why they think specific behaviors are not wrong. Yet for reasons they don't understand, they feel guilty and worthless when they break the traditional moral code.

We have already begun to accumulate clinical data that clearly demonstrate that this moral code which has survived the centuries provides guidelines that enhance individual dignity and ensure the greatest pleasure and the greatest good to the greatest number of people. One thing we know: when a person transgresses these guidelines, he or she will, sooner or later, experience feelings of guilt and worthlessness.

Whatever the cause of our feelings of worthlessness, the important question is how we ought to handle them. Some are paralyzed by them—avoiding all activity that involves risk of failure lest they fail and confirm what they feel about themselves. Others work hard to disprove their feelings. And some handle feelings of worthlessness by projecting them. People have a tendency to see others, especially others who differ from them, as worthless or inferior. We do this unthinkingly. We tend to look down on people from other countries, on people with less or with more education than we have, on people with different-color skin or different clothes. This sort of judging goes on and on. Perhaps all of this is but a desperate attempt to cope with our own feelings of inadequacy and worthlessness.

Does faith in God provide resources to help deal with feelings of worthlessness? I think so. Once again the starting point for me is the full realization that in and of myself, as far as my relationship to *God* is concerned, I can do little to improve my worth. But this realization does not lead to despair. For I recognize that my worth is not in what I do or in what success I achieve. The Scriptures state that my worth is in what God has already done for me. "Not by works of righteousness which we have done, but according to His mercy, He saved us. It is the gift of God" (Ephesians 2:8).

An additional characteristic of depression is the feeling of hopelessness: the feeling that there is no way out, that things will only get worse, and that one is completely helpless. Some authorities consider the feeling of hopelessness and helplessness to be the one essential feature that characterizes all types of depression.

The word "hope" is rarely used in our culture. Perhaps hope runs counter to our concept of a scientific world. Many books exist on faith and on love, but few on hope. Dr. Karl Menninger writes:

> The *Encyclopedia Britannica* has columns on love and faith, but not a single word about hope. In scientific circles there is a determined effort to exclude hope from conceptual thinking . . . because of a fear of corrupting objective judgment by wishful thinking. But all science is built on hope, so much so that science is for many moderns a substitute for religion. . . . Man can't help hoping even if he is a scientist. He can only hope more accurately.[3]

Psychiatrists have long suspected that hope fosters health, both physical and emotional. An increasing body of medical evidence documents the deleterious effect that depression and hopelessness have on physical health. As long ago as 1905, Freud wrote:

> Persistent affective states of a depressive nature, such as sorrow, worry, or grief, reduce the state of nourishment of the whole body, cause the hair to turn white, the fat to disappear, and the walls of the blood vessels to undergo morbid changes. . . . There can be no doubt that the duration of life can be appreciably shortened by depressive affects.

---

[3]*The Vital Balance: The Life Process in Mental Health and Illness* (Gloucester, Mass.: Peter Smith, 1986).

A noted physiologist, Dr. Harold G. Wolf, writes: "Hope, like faith and a purpose in life, is medicinal. This is not merely a statement of belief but a conclusion proved by meticulously controlled scientific experiments." For years there have been clues that hopelessness often lays the groundwork for the development of organic disease. These clues have stimulated a number of recent experiments documenting the deleterious effects of depression and hopelessness on health. Let me mention a few from the medical literature.

In an experiment carried out at the University of Rochester School of Medicine, fifty-four patients for open-heart surgery were interviewed preoperatively and several diagnosed as severely depressed. Eighty percent of the patients who died after surgery were in this depressed group. They were the patients without hope.

In another study, of one hundred patients undergoing open-heart surgery, twelve of them were diagnosed as severely depressed before surgery. All twelve of these patients died immediately or in the early postoperative period. In both of these investigations there was no relationship of the outcome with severity of cardiac disease and surgical factors.

In another study, reported in the *British Medical Journal*, investigators found the death rate of bereaved relatives within the first year after bereavement seven times higher than among a control group. They concluded that bereavement, a form of depression, carries an increased mortality risk.

Very recently a study at the Montreal Heart Institute reported in the *Journal of the American Medical Association*[4] that patients hospitalized after a heart attack were five times more likely to die of that heart attack if they were depressed.

More recent studies have demonstrated that grief has a measurable adverse affect on the immune system. In experiment after experiment reported over the past thirty years in the medical literature, the impression, long held by doctors, is that hope plays a significant role in decreasing morbidity.

But what is hope? It certainly is not the same as wishful thinking, for wishful thinking has little ground for expecting a wish to be fulfilled. Neither is hope identical with optimism—for optimism often implies a distance from reality. And according to Webster, hope is not the same as expectation. Webster defines expectation as implying a high degree of certainty—that is, a certainty based on being able to see what obviously is going to happen. By contrast, Saint Paul says, "We are saved by this hope—but hope that is seen is not hope, for who hopes for that which he sees?"

---

[4]*JAMA*, vol. 270, no. 15 (October 20, 1993).

(Romans 8:24). Webster defines hope as *belief* that what is desired is attainable; hope involves trust and reliance.

If hope is defined as belief, trust, and reliance, one cannot help but ask, "Belief in what or whom? Trust in what or whom?" One must have some basis, some reason for one's hope. Hope must be rooted in reality.

Do the Scriptures provide a reason for hope? Do they provide resources to counteract feelings of hopelessness?

The word "hope" appears about one hundred and fifty times in the Old and New Testaments. It has always fascinated me that the Scriptures mention hope with love and faith. Paul, for example, claims: "In this life we have three great lasting qualities—faith, hope, and love" (1 Corinthians 13).

On what is such a hope based? On wishful thinking? On pie-in-the-sky sentimentality? Or Polly Anna-ish optimism that all is going to be sweetness and light? When we turn to the New Testament, we read, " . . . in his great mercy, we have been born . . . into a life full of *hope*, through Christ Jesus *rising again from the dead*" (1 Peter 1:3, emphasis added).

The Scriptures anticipate our deep need to resolve the question of our mortality, by pointing to the resurrection. Psychiatrists have long observed that we do not begin to really live until we have found some answer to the question, "If a man dies, will he live again?" Because we have always lived on a time-space continuum, we have great difficulty accepting the biblical concept that this life is only the first chapter in a book that goes on and on; we have great difficulty understanding the words of Handel's stirring Hallelujah chorus that ring out, "for ever and ever."

From my clinical observations and experiences I cannot help but observe the very limited resources available to one with no faith and no hope. The lives of both Marx and Freud ended in bitterness and disillusionment. Though they experienced extensive hardship and adversity, they apparently lacked the spiritual resources to enable them to finish the course with any sense of hope.

In 1920, when he was sixty-four, Freud lost a young and beautiful daughter. He began to wonder when his time would come, wishing that it would be soon. "I do not know what more there is to say," he writes. "It is such a paralyzing event, which can stir no afterthoughts when one is not a believer. . . ."[5]

I cannot help but compare Freud and Marx with another scholar. Like Marx and Freud, C. S. Lewis was an atheist; however, in his early thirties, after a great deal of struggle with intellectual doubts, Lewis embraced a

---

[5]*Letters of Sigmund Freud*, ed. Ernest Freud (New York: Dover, 1992).

strong faith in Christ. He then used his gifts of keen intelligence and mastery of language to write books which have influenced scores of people, especially people within colleges and universities, in a direction opposite to that of Marx and Freud.

In *A Grief Observed,* C. S. Lewis wrote about his reactions to the loss of his wife—the one person who was to him everything worthwhile on this earth. The book is a magnificent document for a psychiatrist to read, for it expresses with remarkable clarity the process of mourning and grief. Lewis makes you feel it. He describes the anger, resentment, loneliness, and fear, fluttering in the stomach and restlessness—how the world seemed dull and flat, how he could find no joy in his work. Could God in the final analysis, he wondered, be a cruel God? Was God, ultimately, a cosmic sadist?

In the agony of his grief, he tried to pray. Though his need was desperate, he sensed only a door slammed in his face and a sound of bolting and double bolting from the inside.

He felt that God had forsaken him. There was only the locked door, the iron curtain, the vacuum, absolute zero. He soon realized that in his desperation he was not knocking at the door; he was trying to kick it down. Then slowly, gradually, like the dawning of a clear spring day, with the light and warmth of the sun, his faith began to bolster him, to give him renewed strength, comfort, and what he describes as "unspeakable joy." He knocked—and this time the door was opened, and he experienced again the presence of him upon whom his hope was based.

Do the Scriptures promise freedom from adversity and pain? I do not think so. They make it clear that the world has been altered from its original state by our transgression of God's laws, and thus the world is filled with cruelty and suffering and war and sickness and death. But they also point out that the news is ultimately good, that there is cause for rejoicing. For we have been given great spiritual resources to make this first chapter a victorious one. By no means the least of these resources is *hope*.

The Scriptures again speak eloquently: "May the God of hope fill you with all joy and peace as you trust in him, so that by the power of the Holy Spirit your whole life and outlook may be radiant with hope" (Romans 15:13).

He Sent His Word and Healed Them

— MICHAEL YANG —

I experienced the miracle of the new birth, yet I began to wonder how the gospel of healing was relevant in the age of modern medicine—especially here at Harvard Medical School.

As an undergraduate in biomedical engineering at Johns Hopkins University, **Michael Yang** researched the use of polymers to release drugs in the brain for treating tumors. Yang then earned his M.D. in the joint program in health sciences and technology at Harvard Medical School and The Massachusetts Institute of Technology. Concurrently, he worked at Children's Hospital in Boston on a novel technique for transplanting liver cells. Michael Yang was voted "most compassionate" by fellow interns at St. Elizabeth's hospital in Boston. He encourages people to use God-given common sense in caring for their bodies, always giving thanks for the gift of life.

While practicing medicine, Yang is also writing a Christian response to the philosophical objectivism of Ayn Rand, the writer who most profoundly influenced him toward atheism in his early years. Currently, Michael is in his ophthalmology residency at the Doheny Eye Institute of the University of Southern California.

He Sent His Word and Healed Them

— MICHAEL YANG —

I grew up an atheist. While in high school, I had looked at many of the arguments for the existence of God and came to the conclusion that there was no God. Furthermore, my scientific training in high school and college had nurtured in me a mechanistic view of the universe that, as Laplace said, had no need for the hypothesis of God. I did not believe in a God, let alone a Creator who was intimately involved in the affairs of man; and I had already concluded that miracles did not happen. Besides, among the Christians I knew, it seemed that no one truly believed in a God who worked miracles today.

During my first semester at Harvard Medical School, at the suggestion of Christian friends and acquaintances, I began to examine the Bible and to investigate the Christian faith. It was a reasonable request; I had never before read the Bible but only what others had said about it. At the very least, I thought, after reading their book, I would be able to tell Christians more accurately why they were wrong. Unfortunately, or rather fortunately for me, "The word of God is living and active, sharper than any two-edged sword" (Hebrews 4:12 RSV). As I examined the Bible in detail for the very first time, my mind began to change. I saw the distortions and misquotations of those who had argued against the Christian faith, and I saw the philosophical and historical evidences for Christianity. And in the Scriptures I also found a God who worked miracles.

The Bible tells us that Jesus is the Son of God. He claimed to be God incarnate who had power to forgive sins, and he said that he had come to pay the penalty for sin by suffering death in our place. He offered eternal life to everyone who believed in him, because he rose victoriously from the dead. This Jesus not only preached the good news of eternal life but he also did some startling things, like healing the sick. He promised abundant life now and power to those who trusted him. He said that his followers would participate in the transformation of human lives—as they themselves had been transformed—and even in the healing of the sick. These claims posed a challenge to me. As I read Jesus' words, what C. S. Lewis wrote in *Mere Christianity* echoed in some of my thoughts:

A man who was merely a man and said the sort of things Jesus said would not be a great moral teacher. . . . Either this man was, and is, the Son of God: or else a madman or something worse. You can shut Him up for a fool, you can spit at Him and kill Him as a demon; or you can fall at His feet and call Him Lord and God. But let us not come with any patronising nonsense about His being a great human teacher. He has not left that open to us. He did not intend to.

I am one who fell at his feet in worship and experienced the fullness of his grace and truth.

In turning my life over to Christ, I had experienced what Christians call the miracle of the new birth, yet I began to wonder how the gospel of healing was relevant in the age of modern medicine. Indeed, did I dare believe that it was relevant here at Harvard Medical School, a place known as "The Mecca" because of its community of brilliant medical minds and the proximity of several world-famous hospitals. Perhaps there would be no need for the miraculous when the rational scientific method sufficed? However, as I completed my courses in the basic sciences and began the introduction to clinical medicine, I awoke to the limits and deficiencies of medicine. Cause and effect was not always so clear. Treatments were not always entirely benign processes. Even if a patient recovered, his spiritual condition often remained unchanged. His attitude toward life and his relationship with other people were untouched by the physical healing that medicine provided.

But the Jesus I knew from Scriptures promised to heal both soul and body. The prophet Isaiah foresaw a promised Messiah who would not only be pierced for our sins but who would also bear our sicknesses (Isaiah 53:4–6). When Jesus forgave the sins of the paralytic brought to him, and also healed him, he was confirming that promise (Mark 2:1–12). When he taught the importance of faith in obtaining both salvation and physical healing, he was showing us the connection between belief and healing. How often he said to those he healed, "Your faith has healed you" (e.g., Mark 5:34). The Greek word *sozo*, to heal or to save, refers to the restoration of the whole person: spirit, soul, and body. To touch Jesus was indeed to touch the Great Physician.

But was this healing power available today, or was it limited to the first century, as some have claimed? I found that Jesus imposed no such limitations when he commanded his followers to preach the gospel and heal the sick in his name (Mark 16:15–18). The book of Acts testifies to the power of his name, and the Scriptures say, "Jesus Christ is the same yesterday and today and forever" (Hebrews 13:8). Throughout the ages, from the early church fathers to Martin Luther,[1] the message of Christ's healing power for the physically sick has been proclaimed as an integral part of the good news of salvation. It was not an addendum to the gospel invented by televangelists. From the hard streets of New York City and Bangkok to the ghettos of South America and Africa, that message of healing is still transforming lives today.[2,3] Yet in the world of academic medicine, I was afraid of appearing foolish for believing in such a primitive and unscientific approach to healing. But could I do anything less than to try to obey Jesus fully? After much prayer, I resolved to practice the best medicine I could, and I continue to pray that God will grant me the wisdom to do so. However, if given the opportunity, I would have to respond to the call to minister to patients for both spiritual and physical healing. Those opportunities came as I entered my third year of medical school.

The twelfth floor of the White Building at Massachusetts General Hospital is a temporary home to patients with neurological problems. During my monthlong clinical rotation in neurology there, I met an elderly lady in her late seventies. I'll call her Mrs. Welch. She had developed leg weakness several weeks before I met her. She could hardly stand now, and she certainly could not walk. Moreover, her short-term memory deteriorated until she was unable to remember much from day to day. These signs and symptoms pointed to an abnormality in the brain. A computed tomography scan of her head showed bleeding at multiple sites in her brain, and other tests narrowed down the diagnostic possibilities. We thought she probably had congophilic angiopathy—an abnormal depositing of certain proteins in the walls of blood vessels that weakens the vessels and induces hemorrhage. The attending physician in neurology suggested confirming the diagnosis with a brain biopsy and then treating her with steroids.

I first got to know Mrs. Welch when the junior resident, whom I will call J. R., supervising me, asked me to help perform a lumbar puncture on her. Because of Mrs. Welch's age, we had difficulty getting the needle into her spine. Leaning against my shoulder, she cried out, "Lord have mercy!" I reassured her, "The Lord is rich in mercy and abounding in kindness."

When I returned to visit her later, I noticed that she had a Bible on her side table. As part of my neurological examination, I wanted to see if she could follow instructions and if she could read. I asked her to open her Bible to Mark, chapter 11, and read verses 22 through 24:

---

[1]*Martin Luther: Selections From His Writings,* "The Sacrament of Extreme Unction," ed. J. Dillenberger (Garden City, N.Y.: Doubleday, 1961), 354.

[2]David Wilkerson, *The Cross and the Switchblade* (Westwood, N.J.: Barbour, 1963).

[3]Francis MacNutt, *Healing* (Notre Dame, Ind.: Ave Maria Press, 1974), 26–27, 96–97.

"Have faith in God," Jesus answered. "I tell you the truth, if anyone says to this mountain, 'Go, throw yourself into the sea,' and does not doubt in his heart but believes that what he says will happen, it will be done for him. Therefore I tell you, whatever you ask for in prayer, believe that you have received it, and it will be yours."

I asked her to think of her sickness as her mountain and to tell it to move. She said, "All right, Michael." Then I said, "I'll come back tomorrow, and let's see if you can tell me what we read today, all right?" As I turned to leave her room, I saw one of the nurses at the door. I looked into her eyes for a moment. Perhaps I really knew what she was thinking, or maybe it was the Enemy, bombarding my mind with those thoughts: "Who do you think you are, giving this poor old woman false hope?" My heart sank for a moment; indeed, no power of mine could heal this woman. But then I remembered that the words which I had spoken were not my own, and "everyone who trusts in him will never be put to shame" (Romans 10:11).

The next day, I asked Mrs. Welch, "Did we read something from the Bible yesterday? Did we read something about moving mountains?" She said, "Yeah, was it Mark?" Every day, I asked her to read some of the great healing Scriptures, and I encouraged her to tell her mountain to move and to trust God to move it. Three or four days later, as our neurology team made morning rounds, we found her walking about in her room with the assistance of a walker. This was completely unexpected, because she had showed no signs of recovery up to that time, and we had not yet begun to treat her with any medications. J. R. turned to me and said, "I think you cured her with a little bit of love and tenderness." I replied, "I may have shown her love, but it was God who cured her." After a moment's reflection, J. R., who was not a believer, said, "You may be right. She has been thanking God for being healed."

With each day, Mrs. Welch gained new strength, and I asked her to keep on telling the mountain to move and stay moved. Her response to me was a testimony of her faith: "I have to tell the mountain to move, 'cause I sure can't climb it." As Jesus said to the Canaanite woman: "Woman, you have great faith! Your request is granted" (Matthew 15:28).

A week after I first ministered to Mrs. Welch, she was walking up and down the halls of White Twelve with a stick cane in her right hand. Nurses and physicians applauded at the sight of her recovery, for such dramatic recovery was indeed a rare event on the neurology ward. We never did biopsy her brain or give her any steroids. Mrs. Welch's recovery prompted J. R. to say, "Michael, Mrs. Martin is over in the other building. She's been here for over a year. Why don't you go and talk to her sometime? If she gets better, maybe I'll become religious." I regret that I lacked the time to speak with Mrs. Martin, but God was again working a miracle of transformation. He demonstrated his power in healing Mrs. Welch and used the occasion to sow a seed in J. R.'s heart. I pray that he will make it grow.

When I became a Christian, I wondered why miraculous healing seemed so rare and why some are not healed when prayed for. Was it indeed a promise only for the early Christians, or was it because the scientific skepticism of the last two hundred years has slowly infiltrated and eroded our belief in the supernatural ministry of Jesus Christ? Have we perhaps become so busy debating the issue of healing and miracles that we have neglected to act on God's Word with simple childlike faith? When his disciples failed to cure the lunatic son, Jesus rebuked them for the smallness of their faith (Matthew 17:14–20). According to Mark, Jesus *could* do no mighty work at Nazareth because of unbelief (Mark 6). In the same way, is it possible that our disobedience has limited what the Holy Spirit desires to do through us? Indeed, when was the last time you saw someone anoint the sick with oil and pray the prayer of faith for their healing (James 5:14–15)? Who today lays hands on the sick in Jesus' name, with the earnest expectation that they would be healed (Mark 16:15–16)? Are we doers of the Word, or have we unfortunately become merely hearers who deceive ourselves (James 1:22)? Is it surprising then that healing seems so rare?

We ought not be paralyzed by our fears of failure or lose heart because we remember a time when we prayed for the sick and nothing seemed to happen. We may never know fully why healing does not happen in all cases, but why is it that we are willing to give up after a few setbacks and revise the promise of God? God promises rest if we will come to him. However, we recognize that we do not always have rest because we do not come to God and give him our burdens (Matthew 11:28–30). God says love never fails, but our expression of love towards others may fail (1 Corinthians 13). Yet we pray and believe that as we continue in God's grace, he will complete and perfect the work he began in us (Philippians 1:6).

As a physician, I face the challenge of combining sound medical practice with ministering the supernatural healing that I believe is available in Christ Jesus. At times, it seems easier to ask God to heal the sick using only my medical knowledge. To be honest, it would spare me from having to depend as much on him. While I thank God for the gift of medical science, I know its limitations. Through research and study, I hope to contribute to the advancement of medicine, but I don't know many people who have become believers in God as a result of contemplating the marvels of health care. I do know many who have become confident in the abilities of man apart from God. What the world needs is to see once again the supernatural ministry of Jesus Christ. Like the apostle Paul, I want to see God's kingdom come, not in words only but in demonstration of the Spirit and of power (1 Corinthians 2:4).

I saw a demonstration of that Spirit and power in Mrs. Welch's healing. On my last day in the neurology service, Mrs. Welch left the hospital, wearing a glorious smile on her face. We both had reasons to give thanks, for we knew the age of miracles had not passed. Miracles begin with faith. "Without faith it is impossible to please God, for he who comes to God must believe that he is, and that he is a rewarder of those who seek him" (Hebrews 11:6). By faith in Jesus Christ, we receive the eternal life that God offers us. And by faith in him, we will also have victory in this life. Let us have confidence to proclaim and to obey the word of Christ. Then we shall see that, whether in death or in life, "he who promised is faithful" (Hebrews 10:23).

Facing Death, Embracing Life

❧

— BRENT FOSTER —

All the good I will miss in an extended earthly life are but shadows of the real thing.

———————

In the eighth grade in Shenandoah, Iowa, **Brent Foster** went in for a routine medical exam for football. The next summer, says Brent, "doctors told me that they needed to amputate my leg because of cancer. Within twenty-four hours, the surgery was over." Brent went on to play high school baseball, basketball, and tennis. He was elected president of the student body. Tumors in his lungs appeared during Brent's senior year, before he came to Harvard.

This year, Brent was a sophomore, class of 1997, who helped to lead the Harvard-Radcliffe Christian Fellowship. He loved to write, and to read C. S. Lewis and Russian literature. He painted landscapes because, "as we discussed in the Veritas Forum, beauty *means* something. Though it points us beyond itself to the source of beauty, it is not abstract. When you paint a landscape, you become part of it." Brent painted with oils and acrylics because, "whenever I try watercolor, it becomes a big puddle."

The day before Thanksgiving 1994, test results showed that inoperable bone cancer had spread throughout his body. "I guess I'm realizing that dreams don't always come true," Brent reflected. "At times I feel, here at Harvard, that I am a mortal in the land of the immortals. Then I realize that we'll all see some day that life and meaning come from loving God and each other." Brent concentrated in history because, he said, "I like to learn about people in the past—what they lived and died for."

Facing Death, Embracing Life

— BRENT FOSTER —

My old friends and acquaintances back in rural Iowa would describe me as a very bright person with an even brighter future. In fact, the largest paper in the state covered my graduation, calling me "the most accomplished, polished, and courageous student ever to wear the maroon and white" (my school colors). Success followed me everywhere in high school. My peers elected me president of just about every major organization in school, and my academic might won state and nationwide recognition. I more than once found myself in the governor's office accepting official recognition for my achievements, and locally I was famous for playing high school basketball on an artificial leg. All of this culminated in being made a valedictorian my senior year and gaining admission to the most prestigious college in the nation (according to *U.S. News and World Report*, anyway), the first person of my school ever to have done so. Now, here I am an accomplished Harvard student, the world seemingly at my feet. However, there is one little catch to all of this success: I have widespread bone cancer and only several weeks left to live.

These were supposed to have been the best days of my life. Instead I am at the losing end of an eight-year battle with cancer. And although only twenty-one, my body has grown extremely weak and will soon fail me altogether. In fact, every breath has itself become a struggle. After a total of eleven surgeries, a year of chemotherapy, and a month of high-dose radiation, the doctors can do nothing more. From my experiences, I have sometimes wondered if humans were created with more capacity for pain than happiness. Solomon's words from Ecclesiastes often ring in my ears (along with the other ringing noises I constantly hear from chemotherapy damage):

> Remember your Creator in the days of your youth, before the days of trouble come and the years approach when you will say, "I find no pleasure in them"—before the sun and the light and the moon and the stars grow dark, and the clouds return after the rain . . . "Meaningless! Meaningless!" says the Teacher. "Everything is meaningless!"

For me, the days of trouble came early, and I have found little pleasure in them. I know now that the crosses we are sometimes allowed to bear in this world would not be worth the pain if not for Christ. During my darkest hours, such as while lying in an intensive-care bed with seven or eight tubes protruding from my ravaged body, all the neat Sunday school answers I had learned as a kid seemed terribly hollow. There are no pat answers for many terrible and contradictory things in this broken world. Mere words are meaningless, especially in the face of death. At such times as these, the only respite for me is to "remember my Creator." For in Christ there is a meaning deeper than our understanding and ability to formulate into human speech. As Paul so correctly wrote in 1 Corinthians 4:20: "The kingdom of God is not a matter of talk but of power."

God himself suffered much more than even I could imagine when he became a man, and can therefore understand our deepest sorrows. I am always moved when I read the account of Jesus visiting the tomb of Lazarus. After seeing the considerable grief that death had inflicted on his people, Jesus himself wept. Even though he would soon revive Lazarus, Jesus was overcome with sorrow that humanity had been reduced to such a state and consequently forced to endure such pain. I have always placed my hope in the promise that, just as Christ revived Lazarus, he will come and fix our brokenness also.

It is easy to forget this compassion of Christ's, even though he actually chose to save mankind by subjecting himself to suffering. There is a mystery in God's use of suffering to bring renewal and redemption which I don't completely understand. But this redemptive quality of suffering and tribulation is alluded to many times in the Bible and then underscored by numerous examples. For in the words of Paul, "We . . . rejoice in our sufferings, because we know that suffering produces perseverance; perseverance, character; and character, hope. And hope does not disappoint us" (Romans 5:3–5).

He even tells us that weaknesses, insults, hardships, persecutions, and difficulties are necessary "so that Christ's power may rest" on us (2 Corinthians 12:9–10). My life has certainly shown these words to be true, filling many with hope. Through my hardships, much of God's glory has been revealed to me and to others. But if the only good that had come from my hellish years painfully fighting off death was for healthy people around me to passively be inspired, then I would consider God to be the cruelest villain in the universe. Quite the opposite though, God has used suffering primarily to help me, to remake me into someone capable of knowing him better. Although outwardly wasting away, yet inwardly I am being renewed day by day (paraphrased from 2 Corinthians 4:16). The operation has been very painful, but the Great Physician has begun to heal my spirit. It is impossible to describe in a logical manner this transformation, especially to someone who has never been tempered in God's furnace. But all the same,

I have come to know a Creator who loves me so much that he is not even willing to spare me a great amount of pain so that I might have real life with him.

This notion of good coming out of suffering is, I think, still a hard one to understand. When all the distractions and illusions we create for ourselves in life are suddenly washed away, all can appear empty and futile. For me, the dreams, hopes, and plans I once had for this world are gone. All that I built for myself has been knocked down. However, I know now that what remains after such a washing is all I really ever had to begin with: my faith in God, and the hope that things are working according to his will.

Without God, life is meaningless and death even more so. As Psalm 127 says: "Unless the Lord builds the house, its builders labor in vain." I think only after realizing this have I begun to understand what Christ really has to offer. Everything I do in life doesn't have to be in vain, and death doesn't have to be the victor. Christ offers order over chaos, purpose over futility, hope over despair, and life over death.

What I said at the beginning about having a bright future is still true, perhaps even truer now than ever. Although my illness will appear a tragedy to the world around me, those who know God will understand the truth which he brought to us himself by entering human history in the person of Jesus Christ. As recorded in his Word, all good gifts are from above, and all the good I will miss in an extended earthly life are but shadows of the real thing. Real life begins with God. This is not the end for me but just the beginning. I find the concluding words of C. S. Lewis' *Chronicles of Narnia* very fitting: "Now at last they were beginning Chapter One of the Great Story which no one on earth has read: which goes on forever: in which every chapter is better than the one before."

I hope that all who read this will remember their Creator, "before the days of trouble come," so that when forced to really confront the horrible abyss of death, as everyone inevitably will, he will be able to lead you back to safety, sanity, and an eternity of glory.

❧

Editor's note: In the spring of 1995, Brent returned home to Shenandoah, via Gettysburg, to be with his family. That summer, Brent went on to be with his Lord.

Wonder and Wildness:
On Sex and Freedom

૨૬૬

— POH LIAN LIM —

*The challenge is not so much to define the brokenness which has
become so widespread, as it is to recall what wholeness is about.*

*How do we speak across the wall of hostility that has polarized
the debate on these sensitive topics? I believe there is such a thing
as truth—that which corresponds to reality. As a doctor, I deal
with the hardness of reality every day.*

Poh Lian Lim grew up in Kuala Lumpur, Malaysia. She graduated
from Harvard College in 1987, having concentrated in biochemistry,
and received her M.D. from Columbia University, New York. As a
medical student, she served at a rural mission hospital in Zimbabwe
on a Readers' Digest International Fellowhip. She currently works at
South Cove, a community health center serving primarily Asian
immigrants and refugees in the greater Boston area.

Dr. Lim's interests include infectious diseases and public health in
developing countries. In addition to a love of languages and children's books, she speaks on topics as varied as sexuality, AIDS, and
science fiction. She hopes to return to Malaysia after completing her
fellowship training.

Wonder and Wildness: On Sex and Freedom

— POH LIAN LIM —

It is difficult to know what to do with so much happiness.

NAOMI SHIHAB NYE

❧

Love crosses its islands, from grief to grief,
    it sets its roots, watered with tears,
and no one—no one can escape the heart's progress
    as it runs, silent and carnivorous.
You and I searched for a wide valley, for another planet
    where the salt wouldn't touch your hair,
where sorrows couldn't grow because of anything I did,
    where bread could live and not grow old.

PABLO NERUDA, TRANSLATED BY STEPHEN TAPSCOTT

We have all known the happiness and the islands of grief about which the poets write. But when we look around our society today, can anyone deny that there is a mounting uproar of confusion and pain related to these areas of love and sexuality? Divorce, child abuse, AIDS, date rape, sexual harassment, adultery, abortion, premarital sex, homosexual behavior—whether one defines numbingly the problems from the left or the right, the litany has become familiar.

The litany is also painfully personal, as we struggle with broken dreams, both in our own lives and the lives of people we care about. Already I know colleagues and college friends who are divorced, who are all under thirty. Unwanted pregnancies. Friends openly living in "gay" relationships. Someone working through a history of abuse in childhood. The wrenching pain of a breakup. Friends who are living and dying with AIDS.

In fact, the challenge is not so much to define the brokenness which has become so widespread, as it is to recall what wholeness is about.

What does God want of us? He calls us to live fully and gladly for him. The joyous truth of God's goodness is to permeate every part of our lives, including our sexuality. In the bitter debates about sexual morality, we sometimes forget that God invented sex. He could, after all, have created us to reproduce by binary fission. But he made us a two-gendered people, with the capacity to feel exquisite physical pleasure, to long for emotional intimacy, and to give ourselves in stable, enduring relationships. He gave us—and it is a good gift—the responsibility and joy of raising children who issue from that sexual union.

Christians, of all people, should disagree with Woody Allen's quip about sex being ultimately an empty thing (but as far as empty things go it's about the best, the humor sadly continues). Sex, as God purposed it, forms one of the richest parts of human life. Listen to the Song of Solomon as it overflows with evocatively sensual imagery, or the description of marital faithfulness in Proverbs:

> *Beloved*
> Like an apple tree among the trees of the forest
>   is my lover among the young men.
> I delight to sit in his shade,
>   and his fruit is sweet to my taste.
> He has taken me to the banquet hall,
>   and his banner over me is love.
>
> Song of Solomon 2:3–4

> May your fountain be blessed,
>   and may you rejoice in the wife of your youth.
> A loving doe, a graceful deer—
>   may her breasts satisfy you always,
>   may you be ever captivated by her love.
> Why be captivated, my son, by an adulteress?
>   Why embrace the bosom of another man's wife?
> For a man's ways are in full view of the Lord.
>
> Proverbs 5:18–21

God harnesses the power and pleasure of sexual love within the context of marriage, because commitment actually enables love to grow and deepen. He commands purity outside of heterosexual marriage, and faithfulness within it. He considers all sexual wrongdoing to be offenses against himself, above and beyond any harm done to another person or even oneself—which cuts radically across prevailing notions of acceptable consensual adult behavior.

When I came to Harvard in 1983, the sexual revolution had long been over. Students who were sleeping together were noteworthy only as material for mild on-campus gossip. But this aspect of American college life posed a painful shock to me as an eighteen-year-old foreign student from Malaysia. I had become a Christian as a child against strong opposition, in a Buddist family and a Muslim country. Although I lived in the capital city with extensive exposure to American pop culture, my family was typically Asian and strict in our upbringing.

So when a freshman roommate repeatedly had her boyfriend sleep over, I remember being struck by the lack of shame. Something in my spirit cried out against the wrongness. But the weight of cultural opinion here ridiculed Christian convictions. I was unable to articulate any protest other than a rights-based argument that could not accurately represent the reasons for my unhappiness. My roommate resented what she perceived as a religious, judgmental attitude. The tension become so painful that I ended up staying in the library much of that year.

How do we speak across the wall of hostility that has polarized the debate on these sensitive topics? Are Christians the prudes or narrow-minded bigots that secular culture assumes us to be? Can there be sensible, persuasive reasons to live according to biblical teachings regarding sexuality which might make sense even to people who do not share Christian presuppositions?

I will speak as a Christian not simply because this viewpoint has a right to be heard as one among many (although Christians have been reduced to arguing this in many areas). I also believe there is such a thing as *truth*— that which corresponds to reality. As a doctor, I deal with the hardness of reality every day. Doctors are trained to handle hypotheses, but there is also data to contend with and real-life events which happen, which no amount of wishful thinking can change. And if there is such a thing as reality, then what we think about it matters immensely, because there are real consequences to what we believe and act on.

In the course of my medical training, it became increasingly clear that the biblical sexual ethic makes good sense as far as medical outcomes are concerned. The epidemic of teenage sexual activity has brought with it corollary numbers of teenage pregnancies, sexually transmitted diseases, and abortions. There is an association between sexual promiscuity and pelvic inflammatory disease (PID), between PID and infertility as well as with ectopic pregnancies. The causal relationship between cervical cancer and human papilloma virus was discovered through its increased incidence in women with multiple sexual partners. The grim, unglamorous reality of disease—people with herpes, syphilis, hepatitis, AIDS—underscores the lie of the sexual revolution. There may be freedom from conventional morality, but it has not brought freedom from disease or fear or death.

We have an inherent resistance to acknowledging any link between our actions and their consequences. But whether we believe it or not, that link *does* exist. The most difficult place where this applies is in the AIDS epidemic. It also illustrates clearly the complexity of the problem. There has been a demonstrated causal relationship between sexual behaviors and the transmission of the virus. (This is true for both homosexual and heterosexual intercourse.) However, there have also been "innocent" victims— infants of HIV-positive mothers, or recipients of infected blood transfusions, for example. Why innocent people get harmed is part of the larger question of suffering and evil, which I will not attempt to explore here. But the fact that not everyone who smokes gets lung cancer, and some people get lung cancer who never smoked, does not invalidate the causal association between smoking and lung cancer. It is a deadly self-deception if we deny that our sexual behaviors carry consequences that matter.

However, there should be no distinction between our compassion and care for someone with AIDS and someone with lung cancer. We need to be softhearted if we are to be hardheaded. (There can be no greater indictment of Christians than the charge of being softheaded and hardhearted.) In the area of sexuality, if we are to speak the truth at all, let it be with humility, a deep gentleness, and a stubborn persistence.

Abstinence outside of marriage and monogamy within marriage is considered impractical for the purposes of public policy. Nevertheless, even implemented incompletely, it would constitute the single most powerful measure for breaking the transmission of major sexually transmitted diseases. We haven't given it serious consideration because we think it is too hard. That is true—it *is* too hard. Jesus said, "Everyone who sins is a slave to sin." But he also went on: "If the Son sets you free, you will be free indeed."

Consequences are a necessary condition for the existence of any real choices. Nevertheless, God has placed an interval of time between many of our actions and ensuing consequences. He did this in order that we might still choose obedience freely, that we might have a space for grace, for a turning away from the things that lead to death.

I have spoken primarily about the adverse physical consequences because my work in medicine deals with that aspect. There are also social outcomes with which we must wrestle as a body politic. There are emotional costs, as many can attest to from raw personal experience. And in the end, there is a spiritual cost. Human free will necessarily means the ability to turn away from God. That is a real choice, although it is not a good one, and the end of it is death in our spirits.

If we define away our sinfulness, our need for the transforming power of Christ goes unrecognized. It is in trying to live out the requirements of God that we find how far we fall short. The gospel is the amazingly good news that while we were still sinners, Christ died for us. His forgiveness frees us to live by the power of the Holy Spirit, rejoicing in the goodness of God and all his gifts. Including the gift of love and sexuality.

What does God call us to? By Christ's death and resurrection, God has made us accepted in the Beloved, no matter what our pasts have been. We are called to live as people who have been so deeply loved that our bodies themselves are considered temples in which the God of all creation lives.

In the meantime, many of us live with old scars, inclinations that still draw us in wrong directions, or unfulfilled desires. I struggle with being a single woman, with envy and wistfulness and insecurity from time to time. But I am deeply comforted realizing that Jesus also experienced my singleness and loneliness. He went to the cross at thirty-three, knowing for a long time ahead that his destiny was to die. What did he feel as he held children he was blessing? What did he feel as he met women and knew he would never marry? His was a much harder road than I will ever have to walk.

Dietriech Bonhoeffer wrote, "Remember, it is possible to have a fulfilled life even if there are many unfulfilled desires." That is a word of hope for those of us who continue to struggle with singleness or sexual orientation, who may never have some of our deepest yearnings fulfilled. It expresses trust that even for us, especially for us:

> There is a joy in the journey
> There is a light we can love on the way
> There is a wonder and wildness to life
> And freedom for those who obey.
>
> MICHAEL CARD

In the end, it is perhaps not argument but poetry that we need to cry out the agony of this profoundly human struggle, and to sing of our hope—that goodness still remains at the heart of all created things, because there is a gracious Giver.

De Noche
POH LIAN LIM

I am hollow for loving
without return.
I am chambered, echoing
only your name.

falling from wretched fingers,
a handful of shriveled grass
died this long hot shimmering summer,
in the little well-loved garden;
to the eyes worn with wearied hope
the rains never came
(and tears cannot sustain life).

a whole year the wound waited,
willful with venom, throbbing with desire;
alternately a fever and a shaking chill,
bone-deep, world-vast, consuming as a fire.

rising on a morning sweet with spring
the light spills warm onto the windowsill
the violets purr, delighting in the sun.
all the world is radiant blue and gold;

and far beneath, the distant traffic hum
beside the gray-blue Hudson
murmurs ten o'clock silences
and a leisurely cup of coffee.

and wondering if I'm missing much
of that lecture when it's really
so much nicer sitting here,
listening to the gurgle of pipes;

till, piercing deep and twisting
some thought of you comes, swifter than desire
(vivid sunlit flickers of the now-closed past)
pain catches on my breath; I recognize
familiar as only an adversary is,
in one vast inchoate cry
blotting out all affections and appetites merely human,
my old and hopeless yearning.

I wrestle, reaching wildly for a grip
on this pain that lives by the pulsing of my heart;
and in the darkness of my unknowing,
bitter with tears,
flung out like rope into the abyss
paying out endlessly
prayer yet brings easing
for this one night.

I am come into a Presence.
passionate with patience
familiar as sorrow,
stern as a rock that questions dash against
and die like waves away

into a stillness
worn and dear as a mother's hands,
a space of mercy, a space of quiet
a dear and gracious place.

and shall I truly know
some day
that high, glad, lifting joy
that lilting happiness?

I am open to the earth and sky
washed by rain and dried by sun,
the scarecrow stands in empty fields
as happy and as free.
And wheeling seasons circle like the birds
in my embrace
transparent now of any fear

and love has made me hollow
and love has made me whole.

De noche iremos, de noche—*By night we shall go, by night*
que para encontrar la fuente—*seeking to find the source*
solo la sed nos alumbra—*thirst alone our light*
solo la sed nos alumbra—*thirst alone our light*

CHAPTER 4

THE RECOVERY OF LOVE, FAMILY, AND COMMUNITY

❦

The flat soul is what the sexual wisdom of our time conspires to make universal. . . . Are we lovers anymore?

ALLAN BLOOM, *THE CLOSING OF THE AMERICAN MIND*

෨৪

When you're lovers in a dangerous time,
   sometimes you're made to feel as if your love's a crime.
But nothing worth having comes without some kind of fight.
Got to kick at the darkness till it bleeds daylight.

BRUCE COCKBURN, LYRICS TO "LOVERS IN A DANGEROUS TIME"

෨৪

The wind snatched Thanne's wedding veil so that it flew up wild above our heads. I remember how my heart rose on that veil and on Thanne's laughter. All things in that instant were right and good and true—the breathings of my God, who blew the fields, and of my wife, who laughed. My wife.

WALTER WANGERIN, *AS FOR ME AND MY HOUSE*

෨৪

How little people know who think holiness is dull.

C. S. LEWIS, UNPUBLISHED LETTER

෨৪

The sweetest thing in all my life has been the longing …
   to find the place where all the beauty came from.

C. S. LEWIS, *TILL WE HAVE FACES*

Childrearing Interlude

꙳

— KATHRYN DONOVAN WIEGAND —

Like many other women of my generation, I was extremely vulnerable to the you-are-your-career myth. Success was measured in job titles, in salaries, and in the ability to write an impressive entry to Class Notes.

Kathryn Donovan Wiegand graduated from Harvard-Radcliffe Phi Beta Kappa in music in 1977. She is now profitably invested as a homemaker and mother of six in New Rochelle, New York. She and her family enjoy, among other things, the gift of music. Kathy remains active in church music and performance in piano, cello, organ, and guitar.

Wiegand happily refers to herself as "a contemplative mom," even while wiping runny noses and dismantling Play-doh sculptures. The story itself speaks more of her life.

Childrearing Interlude

— KATHRYN DONOVAN WIEGAND —

I winced slightly as I opened the questionnaire—elegantly typeset on twenty-four-pound Strathmore natural-white bond paper. What was inevitable had finally happened: I had been asked to indicate for the Radcliffe Alumnae Directory just how I was putting my Phi Beta Kappa education to use. I looked down the columns of careers that the questionnaire, apparently, had preselected as possibly appropriate occupations for Radcliffe women: ❑ Attorney ❑ Physician ❑ Concert Musician . . . I sensed a minor existential crisis brewing within. Somewhere near the bottom of the sheet I found what (I guess) was *my* occupational cubbyhole: ❑ Childrearing interlude. I went for the box, grateful to not have to mark ❑ Other and then explain at length. Hurrying, I dispatched what had turned out to be a particularly irksome piece of correspondence for a morning just beginning. But later that day the phrase began to trouble me: childrearing interlude. This is not my real life? If this is an interlude, what exactly is the real thing? Something that pays? Something with a title? Something that requires a degree?

Allow me to fantasize where I would be and what I would be doing now without my three-year-old Becky Jane, without eighteen-month-old Danny Boy, and without their daddy, Jeff. As much as the thought distresses my Protestant husband, I think I would have made a good nun, preferably of a somewhat isolated variety—the type out of fashion today—hemmed in by the rhythm of the prayer cycle, buoyed along in spirit by the enigmatic smile of a mother superior, and those swishy robes. I am kneeling on cold medieval stone and pouring my soul into a Gregorian "Magnificat." I am preparing a sparse room for some weary pilgrim. There I am, in the order of Mother Teresa, bathing a dying outcast in a bucket of disinfected Ganges water and in tender remembrance of the suffering Christ.

And about as far removed as one can get from the life of a suburban housewife in comfortable New Rochelle, New York.

Thank God, who saves us from what we think we want. On the other hand, be careful what you want, because you will get it, the saying goes. God *has* given me my fantasy, but not in the exotic form that I thought—actually better. I consider these years of full-time motherhood as a hearty and much needed portion of humble pie. All right, I admit it: having been a music major in college, I do want more from life than wiping runny noses and dismantling Play-doh sculptures. I look forward to having my children in school and spending long, uninterrupted hours playing Bach fugues and composing. Yet I wouldn't trade the lessons I am taking from God, and from my children, for the most fabulous musical career. Although I still direct a choir and enjoy many freelance opportunities, these activities are subsumed under the priority of my family.

But why has God chosen to reveal himself to me in the cycle of diaper changes and not in the rhythm of monastic prayer? The Westminster Confession states that "the chief end of man is to glorify God and to enjoy Him forever." How is that for a priority? The apostle Paul, in his magnificent letter to the Philippians, concurs: "But whatever gain I had, I counted as loss for the sake of Christ. Indeed I count everything as loss because of the surpassing worth of knowing Christ Jesus my Lord."

I certainly am not claiming that full-time motherhood is the vocation of every woman or even every married woman or even every married Christian woman with kids. I do know, however, that none of us—woman or man—can respond fully to the call of God without a death. I recognize this in my own life: I had to die to my idea of a successful musical career or a formal religious vocation. For me, those options would have been gifts which, in pride, I would have brought to God, when what I needed to realize was that I could bring nothing. And from the nothing of death, from the bareness of the cross, has sprung new life in me.

Like many other women of my generation, I was vulnerable to the you-are-your-career myth. Liberation meant losing ourselves in workaholism as grimly as "successful" men of our parents' time did. Success, of course, was measured *de rigueur* in job titles, in salaries, and in the ability to write an impressive entry to Class Notes. Although I did not choose the professionalism celebrated by nearly an entire generation of baby boomers, I carried its ethos with me, and its image within me.

Like a career in music or in the monastery, working on Wall Street, I am sure, can be a lofty and fulfilling life's work. But God called me into this death to self in order to free me to become a nothing—in society's eyes—thereby also freeing me to rejoice with Mary the mother of Jesus that "he who is mighty has done great things for me."

There are, of course, different kinds of death. Some of us will die to the dream of graduate school or artistic accomplishment or marrying rich (of course, no one I know ever thinks about that) or children or health. But every death is an opportunity, an invitation to embrace God if we do not give in to bitterness and self-pity but see our brokenness as a reflection of his on the cross. We cannot approach God in pride and self-sufficiency and still have any hope of knowing him or the meaning of his grace. In dying to ourselves we give up the lordship of our own lives and thereby make space for his.

Philippians 4:7 teaches that quite regardless of your circumstances, there is a "peace that surpasses all understanding" which can "keep your hearts and your minds in Christ Jesus." I still think I would have made a good contemplative in a monastery—and yet here amidst the nursery-like Walt Disney decor of my home, my overwhelming daily experience has been the calm presence of a loving and faithful God. Like Brother Lawrence, who prays amidst the clatter of the abbey kitchen in his book *The Practice of the Presence of God*, I acknowledge God constantly throughout my day.

There are some fairly practical reasons why I find it possible to do this, not the least of which is that parenting continually reminds me of God. Just as David's years taking care of sheep later helped him to understand God's watchful, nurturing side, so has caring for my kids deepened *my* awareness of God's parenting love for me. Indeed, let me, if I may, para-phrase King David's famous psalm the way I imagine Danny Boy or Becky Jane might:

> The Lord is my mummy,
> She's all I want.
> She makes me lie down in my bed.
> Then she takes my hand,
> And then she makes my boo-boos go away.
> She comes with me so I don't fall.

As any mother knows, however, the home front is not all calm presence and contemplation. Indeed, much of my spiritual growth comes from the unending need to exercise patience, gentleness, self-control, and all the other expressions of the fruit of the Spirit mentioned in Galatians 5. Hav-ing a child in the house seems to be the spiritual equivalent of following one of those programmed texts that constantly quiz you to let you know just how well you have assimilated the lesson. The feedback, I assure you, is instant and generous.

But trying as it may be, motherhood is not the intellectual and emo-tional black hole it often is made out to be. (Pause for a moment's tribute to the availability of some sort of regular baby-sitting relief.) Being at home permits me the luxury of controlling my environment far better than my husband can control his, spending his workday yelling hardly audible stock quotes across a noisy, cigar-filled trading room. The kids and I silence the world's barrage by keeping the television unplugged, substituting lots of homegrown entertainment.

In a wonderful essay published in a 1908 issue of the *Ladies Home Journal*, Harvard president Charles W. Eliot offered a culturally prescient appraisal of the modern Radcliffe woman's dilemma in sorting out myth from reality in trying to balance family and intellectual challenge. Said he:

> There is a common impression that to procure for herself a real intellectual life, as distinguished from a life of sentimental or mechanical routine, a woman needs to have some occupation similar to those of men—that is, she needs to keep a shop, carry on a business, have some trade or profession, be skillful in some art which has a commercial use, or be a professional writer, artist, or student. The common life of women in bearing and rearing children and making a home for a family is not thought of as affording the wife and mother the means and opportunities for an intellectual development. Is this a rational view?[1]

After demonstrating some understanding of the challenges of childrearing, Eliot then comments with some astuteness:

> It will be observed that the women who are most apt to lose their chances of obtaining their intellectual life as mothers and heads of families are those who are able to employ servants, nurses, and governesses to do their work for them. They do not so surely secure the natural opportunities for mental growth which the direct and unaided care of children provides.[2]

I can personally affirm the empirical truth of President Eliot's surmisings on natural opportunities. Much of the rhythmic routines of laundry, dishes, and toy-sorting keep my hands busy but leave my mind free to ponder Tolstoy's musings on the inevitability of history. I am enjoying *War and Peace* in ten-page bites, sandwiched between dicing carrots and figuring out how our new whizbang electric juicer works. I memorize music from a hymnal propped open on the kitchen counter while doing dishes.

With their constant store of questions that no one would think to ask, the kids themselves are a source of intellectual stimulation. I like to reconstruct Becky's linguistic concepts from her grammatical errors. It's like doing a crossword puzzle underwater in a foreign language. "Know wha' something?" is one of her newfangled elisions—a combination of "Know what?" and "Know something?" (Becky doesn't have time to waste.) Just today I asked my Harvard classmate Jenifer Nields, fresh out of medical school and

---

[1]William Allan Nielson, *Charles W. Eliot: The Man and His Beliefs* (New York: Harper Bros., 1926), 568.
[2]Ibid., 573–4.

about to begin a residency in psychiatry, if she had any ideas why children love to be chased. Jenifer drew a blank. So I offered my theory to her—that for children, playing chase disarms an actual fear of menacing presences by diffusing it into a ritualized substitute. "You wanna know something?" Jenifer mused. "In medical school we learn but they don't actually *teach* us much."

All told, my fantasy career is not altogether unrelated to the realities of my domestic life. My matins are a six o'clock mug of hazelnut coffee with Jeff as we take in some morning Scriptures. My "Magnificat" may be "Jesus Loves Me" crooned to a tired child. Instead of Mother Teresa's precious outcasts, I serve the ordinary inhabitants of a suburban neighborhood, counting it a privilege to minister to the sufferer of a rocky marriage or of loneliness or of creeping frailty. My current weary pilgrim is an inspirational East African Christian visiting the United States on a mission for his home church and staying in our guest room. Since Mr. Kpawirena speaks little English, I am challenged by the need to communicate with him in freshman-elective French.

As I speculate on my future with God beyond this "childrearing interlude," I am comforted and assured to read that a Dutch woman named Corrie ten Boom was little more than a kindly spinster watchmaker until, at the age of fifty or so, God used her to smuggle Jews out of Nazi-occupied Holland, thereby saving the lives of hundreds. Without the many years of quiet Christian faithfulness that laid a deep foundation for ten Boom's crowning work, would she have dared the hazardous task or subsequently survived her own imprisonment (and even blessed others) in a concentration camp?

Much in me still would prefer to be burning myself out for God in a way that hews closer to the Alumnae Directory's ideal of what a real Radcliffe woman *should* be doing. But I believe that, for now, the Lord desires a less Class Notes-oriented vocation for me. He is molding a handmaid, as he has done for centuries, to sing him praises and to nurture others he has called to himself. I don't begrudge the Lord his creativity—or even his sense of humor—in assigning this would-be contemplative to the front lines of the baby brigade. *Ad Dei Magnam Gloriam.*

The Grace That Shaped My Life

஭

— NICHOLAS WOLTERSTORFF —

I shall struggle to live the reality of Christ's rising and death's dying. In my living, my son's dying will not be the last word.

Nicholas Wolterstorff, a former president of the American Philosophical Association, has a joint appointment as a professor in the philosophy and religion departments, and the Divinity School, at Yale University. He earned his Ph.D. in philosophy at Harvard in 1957, taught for thirty years at Calvin College, and held an appointment at the Free University of Amsterdam. He has given the Wilde Lectures at Oxford and the Gifford Lectures in Scotland.

His many books include *Art in Action: Toward a Christian Aesthetic; Reason Within the Bounds of Religion; Works and Worlds of Art; On Universals;* and *Until Justice and Peace Embrace.* This story is adapted from *Philosophers Who Believe* (InterVarsity Press) and *Lament for a Son* (Eerdmans).

Professor Wolterstorff has also led graduate student discussions on professorship as a calling, the secularization of the academy, and the importance of Christian community for scholarship.

The Grace That
Shaped My Life

— NICHOLAS WOLTERSTORFF —

The grace that shaped my life came not in the form of episodes culminating in a private experience of conversion but, first of all, in the form
of being inducted into a public tradition of the Christian church.

The reformation of the Christian church that occurred in the Swiss
cities during the second quarter of the sixteenth century took two main
forms. One eventuated in the movement known as Anabaptism. The other
became embodied in the churches known throughout continental Europe
as Reformed and in Scotland as Presbyterian. I was reared in the tradition
of the Dutch Reformed Church transplanted to the United States. My parents had emigrated from the Netherlands in their youth. The place was a
tiny farming village on the prairies of southwest Minnesota—Bigelow.

SIMPLICITY, SOBRIETY, AND MEASURE

In his book on English dissenting movements, the poet and critic Donald Davie remarks that it was John Calvin who first clothed Protestant worship with the sensuous grace and aesthetic ambiguity of song. From the
architecture, from church furnishings, from the congregational music, from
the Geneva gown of the pastor himself, everything breathes simplicity, sobriety, and measure.[1]

We "dressed up" on the Lord's Day, dressed up *for* the Lord's Day, and
entered church well in advance of the beginning of the service to collect
ourselves in silence, silence so intense it could be touched. The interior
was devoid of decoration: plaster painted white, ceiling pitched to follow the
roof, peak high but not too high. The only "richness" was in the wooden
furnishings. These were varnished, not painted; as a child I dwelt on the
patterns in their unconcealed woodiness—perhaps because, coming from
several generations of woodworkers, I was from infancy taught reverence for
wood. We faced forward, looking at the Communion table front center, and

---

[1]Donald Davie, *A Gathered Church* (New York: Oxford Univ. Press, 1978), 25.

behind that the raised pulpit. Before I understood a word of what was said, I was inducted by its architecture into the tradition.

Every service included psalms, always sung, often to the Genevan tunes. There was no fear of repetition. The view that only the fresh and innovative is meaningful had not invaded this transplant of the Dutch Reformed tradition in Bigelow, Minnesota. Through repetition, elements of the liturgy and of Scripture sank their roots so deep into consciousness that nothing thereafter, short of senility, could remove them. "Our help is in the name of the Lord, who has made heaven and earth," said the minister, unfailingly, to open the service.

The cycle for one of the two sermons each Sunday was fixed by the Heidelberg Catechism. This catechism, coming from Heidelberg in Reformation times, had been divided up into fifty-two Lord's Days; the minister preached through the catechism in the course of the year, taking a Lord's Day per Sunday. It was doctrine, indeed, but doctrine peculiarly suffused with emotion—perhaps because, as I now know, it had been formulated for a city filled with exiles. The first question and answer set the tone; decades later they continue to echo in the chambers of my heart:

Q: What is your only comfort in life and death?
A: That I am not my own but belong to my faithful savior Jesus Christ.

If the aesthetic of this liturgy was simplicity, sobriety, and measure, what was its religious genius? The only word I have now to capture how it felt then is *sacramental*; it felt profoundly sacramental. One went to church to meet God; and in the meeting, God acted, especially spoke. The language of "presence" will not do. God was more than present; God spoke, and in the sacrament, "nourished and refreshed us," here and now sealing his promise to unite us with Christ.

In word and tone the liturgy I experienced was a liturgy of God's action; it was "Calvinistic." During the liturgy as a whole, but especially in the sermon and most of all during the Lord's Supper, I was confronted by the speech and actions of an awesome, majestic God. Of course, liturgy was our action as well, not just God's. We gave voice, always in song, never in speech, to praise and thanksgiving and penitence. The religious genius of the liturgy was interaction between us and God.

Max Weber argued, in his famous analysis of the origins of capitalism, that the energetic activism of the Calvinists was designed to secure the success that was taken as a sign of membership among the elect. I can understand how it would look that way to someone on the outside; and possibly there were some on the inside, English Puritans, for example, who did think and speak thus. But it has always seemed to me a ludicrous caricature of the tradition as I experienced it. The activism was rather the activism congruent to gratitude. Sin, salvation, gratitude: that was the scheme of the "Heidelberger." Conspicuous material success was more readily taken as a sign of shady dealing than of divine favor.

My induction into the tradition, through words and silences, ritual and architecture, implanted in me an interpretation of reality—a fundamental hermeneutic. Nobody offered "evidences" for the truth of the Christian gospel; nobody offered "proofs" for the inspiration of the Scriptures; nobody suggested that Christianity was the best explanation of one thing and another. Evidentialists were nowhere in sight! The gospel was report, not explanation. And nobody reflected on what we as "modern men" can and should believe in all this. The scheme of sin, salvation, and gratitude was set before us, the details were explained; and we were exhorted to live this truth. The modern world was not ignored but was interpreted in the light of this truth rather than this truth being interpreted in the light of that world.

The picture is incomplete without mention of the liturgy of the family. Every family meal—and every meal was a family meal—was begun and concluded with prayer, mainly prayers of thanksgiving principally, though not only, for sustenance. We did not take means of sustenance for granted; my family was poor. Food, housing, clothes—all were interpreted as gifts from God; again the sacramentalism, and again a sacramentalism of divine action rather than divine presence. Before the prayer following the meal there was a reading, usually from Scripture chosen on a *lectio continua* scheme but sometimes from devotional literature and often from a Bible-story book. Thus, between church and home I was taught to read the Bible as doctrine, as Torah, and as narrative; that there might be tension among these never occurred to me.

THE CENTER

The piety in which I was reared was a piety centered on the Bible, Old Testament and New Testament together. Centered not on experience and not on the liturgy but on the Bible; for those themselves were seen as shaped by the Bible. Christian experience was the experience of appropriating the Bible, the experience of allowing the Bible to shape one's imagination and emotion and perception and interpretation and action. The practice of the tradition taught without telling me that the Bible had to be interpreted; one could not just read it and let the meaning sink in. The center from which all lines of interpretation radiated outward was Jesus—Jesus Christ.

THE FULL PATTERN

I remember my father sitting at the dining-room table during the long winter evenings in our house in the village on the Minnesota prairies, making pen-and-ink drawings. All his life long, I now believe, he wanted to be an artist; but he grew up in the Depression, child of displaced Dutch city dwellers consigned to farming in the New World, and it was never a possibility. There was in him accordingly a pervasive tone of disappointment. He was on intimate terms with wood; but wood was not yet art for him. I have since learned of Christians who see art as a device of "the Enemy," something to be avoided at all costs. I have learned of other Christians who are torn in pieces by art, unable to leave it alone yet told by those around them that art is "from the other side." My father-in-law was one of those troubled lovers of art. But not my father.

I have also learned of Christians for whom the life of the mind is "enemy." That too was not my experience. I take you now on our move from Bigelow to Edgerton, forty-five miles distant, in my early teens. My mother died when I was three. Of her I have only two memories: being held in her lap on a rocking chair when my arms were full of slivers, and seeing her lying still and pale in a coffin in our living room while I ate strawberries. After a few years of loneliness my father remarried and we moved to Edgerton, the village from which my stepmother, Jennie Hanenburg, came. The Hanenburgs were and are a remarkable family: feisty, passionate, bright, loyal. Though our family lived in the village, most of the others were farmers. So after morning church they all came to our house— aunts and uncles, cousins, everybody, boisterous dozens of them. Sweets were eaten in abundance, coffee drunk, and the most dazzling intellectual experience possible for a young teenager took place. Enormous discussions and arguments erupted, no predicting about what: about the sermon, about theology, about politics, about farming practices, about music, about why there weren't as many fish in the lakes, about what building the dam in South Dakota would do to the Indians, about the local schools, about the mayor, about the village police officer, about the Dutch Festival, about Hubert Humphrey. Everyone took part who was capable of taking part— men, women, teenagers, grandparents. I can hear it now: one aunt saying at the top of her voice, "Chuck, how can you say a thing like that?" And Chuck laughing and saying, "Well, Clara, here's how I see it." Then when it was time to go, everyone embracing.

I must mention especially my Aunt Trena, one of the most wonderful women I have known; she also died young. One Saturday afternoon I walked into her house and heard the Metropolitan Opera playing on her radio; to me, as a young teenager, it was caterwauling. So I asked her why she was listening to that. Her answer remains for me a marvel and a parable: "Nick, that's my window onto the world." She had never gone to school beyond the fifth grade; she was then trying to finish high school by correspondence.

Reverence for wood and for art in my father; reverence for the land and the animals in my uncles, sometimes even for machinery; longing reverence for music in my aunt; reverence for the life of the intellect in everybody. In the tenth book of his *Confessions* Augustine imagines the things of the world speaking, saying to him: Do not attend to us, turn away, attend to God. I was taught instead to hear the things of the world saying: Reverence us, for God made us as a gift for you. Accept us in gratitude.

It has taken me a long time to see the full pattern of the tradition. I think it was something like this: first, the tradition operated with a unique dialectic of affirmation, negation, and redemptive activity. On the reality within which we find ourselves and which we ourselves are and have made, I was taught to pronounce a differentiated yes and no: a firm yes to God's creation as such, but a differentiated yes and no to the way in which the potentials of creation have been realized in culture, society, and self. And I was taught, in response to this discriminating judgment, to proceed to act redemptively, out of the conviction that we are called by God to promote what is good and oppose what is bad, and to do so as well as we can; as an old Puritan saying has it, "God loveth adverbs." The affirmation of what is good in creation, society, culture, and self was undergirded by a deep sacramental consciousness: the goodness surrounding us is God's favor to us, God's blessing, God's grace. Culture is the result of the spirit of God brooding over humanity's endeavors.

The tradition also operated with a holistic understanding of sin and its effects, of faith, and of redemption. By no means was everything in society, culture, and personal existence seen as evil; much, as I have just remarked, was apprehended as good. The holistic view of sin and its effects instead took the form of resisting all attempts to draw lines between some area of human existence where sin has an effect and some area where it does not. To the medievals who suggested that sin affects our will but not our reason, the Reformed person says that it affects our reason as well. To the Romantics who assume that it affects our technology but not our art, the Reformed person says it affects art too.

Corresponding to this holistic view of sin and its effect is, then, a holistic view as to the scope of genuine faith. Faith is not an addendum to our existence, a theological virtue, one among others. The faith to which we are called is the fundamental energizer of our lives. Authentic faith transforms us; it leads us to sell all and follow the Lord. The idea is not, once again, that everything in the life of the believer is different. The idea is rather that no dimension of life is closed off to the transforming power of the Spirit—since no dimension of life is closed off to the ravages of sin. But faith, in turn, is only one component in God's program of redemption. The scope of divine redemption is not just the saving of lost souls but the renewal of life—and more even than that: the renewal of all creation. Redemption is for flourishing.

Third, the tradition operated with the conviction that the Scriptures are a guide not just to salvation but to our walk in the world—to the fundamental character of our walk. They provide us with "a world and life view." This theme of the comprehensiveness of the biblical message for our walk in this world matches, of course, the holistic view of sin and of faith.

The grace of God that shapes one's life came to me in the form of induction into this tradition. That induction into tradition should be an instrument of grace is a claim deeply alien to modernity. Tradition is usually seen as a burden, not grace. But so it was in my case. If you ask me who I am, I reply: I am one who was bequeathed the Reformed tradition of Christianity.

I later spent thirty years of my life as a teacher at Calvin College. Or better put, as a member of that community of Christian learning. That community has been for me an instrument of grace, supporting me in my Christian reflections—challenging, correcting, supplementing, encouraging, chastising, disciplining. To know who I am, you must know that I was bequeathed the opportunity of being a member of that community. I miss it deeply. It was an instrument of grace.

CRIES OF THE OPPRESSED

Several experiences have evoked in me a great deal of reflection and reorientation. I was confronted with the faces and voices of people in Palestine and South Africa suffering injustice. And I have felt confronted by the Word of the Lord telling me that I must defend the cause of these suffering people. My tradition yielded me the category: it was a call.

Justice has become for me one of the fundamental categories through which I view the world. I think of justice not so much as a virtue but as a condition of society: a society is just insofar as people enjoy what is due them—enjoy what they have a legitimate claim to. Previously the fundamental moral category for me was responsibility. Now I have come to see that the moral domain is an interplay between rights and responsibilities. To the Other in my presence I have responsibilities; but also the Other in my presence comes bearing rights. The violation of moral responsibility yields guilt; the violation of moral rights yields injury. The proper response to guilt is repentance; the proper response to moral injury is lament and outrage.

Slowly I began to see that the Bible is a book about justice; but what a strange and haunting form of justice! Not our familiar modern Western justice of no one invading one's right to determine one's life as one will. Rather the justice of the widow, the orphan, and the alien. A society is just when all the little ones, all the defenseless ones, all the unprotected ones, have been brought back into community. Biblical justice is the shepherd leaving the corral to look for the hundredth one and then throwing a feast when the one is found.

LAMENT FOR A SON

This was all before. I now live after: after the death of our son, Eric. My life has been divided into before and after.

He loved the mountains, loved them passionately. They lured and beckoned him irresistibly. Born on a snowy night in New Haven, he died twenty-five years later on a snowy slope in the Kaisergebirger, Austria.

Never again will anyone inhabit the world the way he did. Only a hole remains, a void, a gap. My son is gone. The ache of loss sinks down and down, deep beyond all telling. How deep do souls go?

The suffering of the world has worked its way deeper inside me. I never knew that sorrow could be like this. I do not know why God did not prevent Eric's death. To live without the answer is precarious. It's hard to keep one's footing. I can only, with Job, endure in the face of this deepest and most painful of mysteries. I believe in God the Father almighty, maker of heaven and earth and resurrecter of Jesus Christ. I also believe that my son's life was cut off in its prime. I cannot fit these pieces together. I am at a loss. My wound is an unanswered question. Lament and trust are in tension, like wood and string in bow.

To love is to run the risk of suffering. Or rather, in our world, to love is to suffer; there's no escaping it. Augustine knew it well, so Augustine recommended playing it safe, loving only what could neither die nor change on one—God and the soul. My whole tradition had taught me to love the world, to love the world as a gift, to love God through and in the world—wife, children, art, plants, learning. It had set me up for suffering. But it didn't tell me this: it didn't tell me that the invitation to love is the invitation to suffering. It let me find that out for myself, when it happened. Possibly it's best that way.

I haven't anything to say beyond what I've already said in *Lament for a Son*. There's a lot of silence in the book; no word too much, I hope. In the face of death we must not chatter. And when I spoke, I found myself moving often on the edges of language, trying to find images for what only images could say. The book is extremely particular; I do not speak about death, only about Eric's death. That's all I could do. But I have discovered, from what readers have told me, that in its particularity lies universality.

I see now, looking back, that in writing it I was struggling to own my grief. The modern Western practice is to disown one's grief: to get over it, to put it behind one, to get on with life, to put it out of mind, to insure that it not become part of one's identity. My struggle was to own it, to make it part of my identity: if you want to know who I am, you must know that I am one whose son died. But then to own it redemptively. It takes a long time to learn how to own one's suffering redemptively; one never finishes learning.

Though there are strands in the Reformed tradition for which sovereignty is God's principal attribute, I don't think I ever thought of God much in terms of sovereignty. God was majesty for me, indescribable majesty. And graciousness, goodness; God is the one who blesses, blessing calling for gratitude. To be human is to be that point in the cosmos where God's goodness is meant to find its answer in gratitude: John Calvin told me that.

Now everything was different. Who is this God looming over me? Majesty? I see no majesty. Grace? Can this be grace? I see nothing at all; dark clouds hide the face of God. Slowly the clouds lift. What I saw then was tears, a weeping God, suffering over my suffering. I had not realized that if God loves this world, God suffers; I had thoughtlessly supposed that God loved without suffering. I knew that divine love was the key. But I had not realized that the love that is the key is suffering love.

I do not know what to make of this; it is for me a mystery. But I find I can live with that. The gospel had never been presented to me as best explanation, most complete account; the tradition had always encouraged me to live with unanswered questions. Life eternal doesn't depend on getting all the questions answered; God is often as much behind the questions as behind the answers. But never had the unanswered question been so painful. Can I live this question with integrity and without stumbling?

It moved me deeply to discover one day that John Calvin alone among the classical theologians had written of the suffering of God. Whenever he wrote of it, it was, so far as I could discover, in the same context: that of a discussion of injustice. To wreak injustice on one of one's fellow human beings, said Calvin, is to wound and injure God; he said that the cry of those who suffer injustice is the cry of God.

And sometimes when the cry is intense, there emerges a radiance which seldom appears: a glow of courage, of love, of insight, of selflessness, of faith. In that radiance we see best what humanity was meant to be. So I shall struggle to live the reality of Christ's rising and death's dying. In my living, my son's dying will not be the last word.

Perfectionism, Shame, and Liberation

࿊

— R O D N E Y P E T E R S E N —

Harvard had helped me to hide from my emotional self.... My world was soon to collapse fully.

Rodney Petersen is executive director of the Boston Theological Institute (BTI) and is adjunct professor in ethics and business management at Webster University, Geneva, Switzerland. He teaches history in the BTI—which encompasses representatives of all of the major Christian communions, together with three universities. He has helped to facilitate theological education by extension in Eastern Europe and he is active in the Christian environmental movement.

Dr. Petersen is a graduate of Harvard College (1971) and Harvard Divinity School (1974 and 1976) and holds a doctorate from Princeton Theological Seminary (1985). He is an ordained Presbyterian (U.S.A.) minister. His latest book, *Preaching in the Last Days* (Oxford, 1993), illustrates relationships among spirituality, church formation, and political activity.

Perfectionism, Shame, and Liberation

— RODNEY PETERSEN —

I was born in the middle of the twentieth century and raised in the middle of the United States. My nurture was shaped more by Plymouth Rock piety and J. R. Mott's missionary mandate, nuanced by the individualism of Dwight L. Moody, than by the adventures of Tom Sawyer and Huckleberry Finn. Their lives were filled with the adventures that were always around the bend in a river defined for me by moral earnestness and republican populism, filtered through the pragmatism of John Dewey. With my own prayers, and those of my parents—and such exhortations as would have made Horatio Alger proud—I was made to feel that failure was a four-letter word. My contemporaries (perhaps less piously tinged than I) and I went to college buoyed with a sense of optimism. We could enter the political process and help to direct American civic life to new levels of affluence and democratic participation.

The liberation movements of one group or another were the vision of a few, not as yet a reality for many. The political assassinations would become the first shadows on our personal and political horizon, components of the social agenda reaching into and beyond the Clinton presidency.

When our entering class arrived at Harvard, we were asked to read, as a part of an introduction to general education, *The Education of Henry Adams*. I didn't see the point at the time, but in retrospect, there was no book that was more pointed. Adams describes, quite emphatically, the inadequacy of his education in helping to prepare him to confront the modern world. What he omits from the book—his troubled years of marriage and wife's subsequent suicide—is no less pointed than what he includes. There are many possible reasons for such an omission, and it would be gratuitous to speculate here on them all. But what seems clear is that in addition to the insufficiencies that Adams attributes to his education, his schooling also failed him in a way he was not able to perceive. It failed to offer him the resources for confronting, with honesty, his own personal inadequacies. Indeed, it may have offered him the cloak to hide those inadequacies from the world, and even from himself. The university in our day seemed caught in a certain academic "gridlock," and it was unprepared or unable to deal with the emotional fallout many of us were experiencing.

I had been trained by my parents to be *good* and by my early schooling to *get things right*. In important ways my success in both shaped and conditioned my sense of identity and my understanding of self-worth. Harvard was to be the next step in an opportunity to be good and to be right, and to put goodness and rightness, both largely defined in terms offered up by a culture now in crisis, in the service of others—controlling, of course, the distribution of the good and the right as I saw fit. Goodness and rightness were ideals I believed in with my external being, but didn't do the emotional work that would have been required to internalize them. In other words, there was a split between external and internal piety. Paradoxically, by holding them at bay, so to speak, they became controlling and socially defined virtues, because they held up an image to which I had to conform. In retrospect I see this tension as calling up the paradox of freedom and obedience to God. The more we keep God's laws, and our understanding of how we are to fulfill them, at arm's length in an effort to hold on to our freedom (as defined by society's values), the more oppressed we feel and the more imprisoned we become to our own ideas about how good or right we will be. On the other hand, the more authentically we take God's command to obey him and to do what is good and right, the more free we become and better able to deal with the vicissitudes of culture.

I acquired a drive for coherence as I moved from academic department to academic department, finally settling in history. There I hoped to find the perspective as well as the necessary tools to carry me through life. Some of the academic disciplines I encountered along the way seemed never to quite reach at the depths of the human problems of being and understanding as I was encountering them. Others seemed to proceed as if the ethical implications of such did not matter faced with the work of getting on in the world. My search for coherence also led me to L'Abri, an American-Swiss community of Christian theological inquiry with which I had formed a relationship under the auspices of the Harvard-Radcliffe Christian Fellowship. In the summer, together with others, I made my way to Alpine heights to find a way of bringing together Christian faith and academic philosophy, but also an emotional wholeness I did not realize I lacked.

My senior thesis, on the nihilism of Frederich Nietzsche, became an opportunity to bring together the threads of my own inquiry into the relationship of being, understanding, and ethics. It awakened in me an understanding for the tension, later noted by philosopher Allan Bloom, between "socially derived" truths and the "natural" laws of a truth to which all might assent. Or to put this another way, it deepened my appreciation for the

struggle of the gospel and history of Christian intellectual inquiry in relation to topical issues raised by the culture. Unawares, I was venturing down
a path outlined by Augustine and Anselm, that of "faith seeking understanding" (*fides quarens intellectum*). Harvard afforded me the opportunity
to walk down the way of this intellectual quest; it failed through its own
institutional "gridlock" to help me to deal with its own relativity and my
feelings of inferiority and emotional inadequacy. At the time I remember
reading incessantly the books of psychiatrist Paul Tournier, particularly *A
Place for You*, feeling then that although raised with parental care and attention, I had no place.

After graduating from the college, I attended Harvard Divinity School.
On the one hand, I felt a call to the ministry in some sense, and on the
other, I hoped to find through religion some salve for the alienation I still
felt—and perhaps even a source of status to help to cover my feelings of
personal inadequacy. I wanted to subject my growing appreciation for the
coherence of Christian faith to the fullest possible scholastic criticism. The
cultural role that religion plays in relation to basic views of politics and
economics in shaping public life was also an important ingredient in my
thinking. The Divinity School provided the means for further growth in
these areas, if not for reconciliation with myself. I continued to play an
active role in university life but fell prey to shadows and fears of inadequacy which would vent themselves in various forms of romantic, if unreal,
dreams and other forms of denial and mistrust.

In retrospect, it seems to me that success in religion can be a kind of
sublimated success. Higher criticism can be a way of dealing with critical
issues, as well as of avoiding the critical direction of one's life. Deconstruction can be a way of dealing with all that shapes understanding, as
well as a way of avoiding the very fact of expression. Feminism and mas-
culinism can be ways of dealing with all of the resentments that crowd in
upon our deepest self, as well as ways of failing to deal with the fact of that
self in its engendered personal and communally related dimensions.

Despite my intellectual growth at Harvard, the solace that I came to
find in academics and in rowing became a kind of retreat from emotional
development. Although I enjoyed both, they masked a certain inadequacy,
and even shame that I had, rather than offering tools (in the case of academics) and time alone (in the case of rowing) to deal with that perceived
depravation. My ideals, themselves subject to cultural critique, were increasingly elusive. I lived feeling that I had disappointed a nameless "other." I
failed to live up to an abstract standard of acceptability, and the shame I
knew deepened. Such efforts at an idealized perfectionism increased a growing sense of alienation from myself, and perhaps through that self from

others as well. I found it hard to look people in the eye. Their gaze seemed to tell me I was inadequate in the depths of my personhood. I compensated for this by trying to be good, to be better than others in the only way I knew, through an affirmation of the good and the right, but without letting the message of that piety touch my deepest area of being—my self-identity and susceptibility to personal failure. I could talk about God's grace and his acceptance of us but found it difficult to believe it for myself. On one level I believed, but I needed to know how and in what way it could be said that Jesus Christ was, as written in the earliest accounts of Harvard College, the foundation of all sound knowledge and learning. It seemed more abstract than real, despite the ministrations of the Reverend Peter Gomes, preacher to the university, who knew the history of the college and yet held the burden of that mantle with humor.

Piety had become a means for hiding, intellectual growth a way of merely understanding, but faith was yet to be exercised toward the end of emotional and personal integration. I left Harvard, married, and set off for Princeton in order to pursue doctoral studies in the history of Christianity. I worked for the administration in a position that fed my ego. It gave me a sense of self-importance and meaning which I still found more theoretically in my faith. Apart from positions and titles, I felt naked and exposed. I felt vulnerable to my fears of lacking in significance in a secular society that proclaimed it had no need of the church or its gospel—that such, in fact, was now divisive in the development of a common political culture. Such fears entered into my personal relations, and I felt my life to be more theoretical than real. I moved on to my first teaching assignment, feeling like I was teaching church history more than living it. I was able to talk more about the one who is at the center of that story, Jesus Christ, than to let him work in my life. It was difficult for me to trust. Grace was something for others, not something I could appreciate.

My world was soon to collapse fully. All titles and appearances were taken away. I was forced to deal with a shame that plagued my soul, the dissonance between self-appropriated ideals and the realities of my life. I could no longer hide from myself, my need for God, and my need of others. My marriage dissolved in divorce. I was unable to work. I wanted to hit and strike at another, yet I knew in love that such was not the path to take. Most vivid for me, yet elusive, was the way in which Jesus used shame in the story of his encounter with the religious leaders in the incident of the woman caught in adultery (John 8:2–11)—both her shame and theirs—to draw a veil of love around the woman. She was naked before him in every sense and yet fully loved. And I realized that Jesus is not interested in piety so much as in wounded persons. She was literally saved by this love. Her life was changed forever, not by compulsion but by his grace and her gratitude. And I learned that, like the woman's accusers, it was in me to shame others rather than to permit my own fear of worthlessness to become known. Harvard had helped me on my quest toward a certain form of formal understanding, but it had also helped me to hide from my emotional self.

It was out of this experience of loss and exposure that Christ brought me to grace. I was given a fresh vision of the place of the church in society, nurtured in part by Langdon Gilkey's book *Shantung Compound*, the story of his own discovery of the sustaining role a Christian community can have in even the most secular of societies, a wartime prison camp. I experienced that sustenance in a church in France. In this way I also learned the meaning of personal acceptance. Further, the opportunity given to me to teach courses in critical thinking and in ethics in corporate life gave me the opportunity to listen to myself and to deal with my emotions and critical attitude in the context of others. Such an experience taught me the truth that Saint Paul was emphasizing when he wrote in his letter to the church at Rome, "You have no excuse ... whoever you are, when you judge another; for in passing judgment upon him you condemn yourself, because you, the judge, are doing the very same things" (Romans 2:1 RSV). These opportunities gave me a way to think about philosophy and ethics with immediate personal application. Additionally, through work with churches in Eastern Europe I discovered afresh the social significance of a deep and vibrant faith in the lives of those with whom I learned to share. These events began to teach me to trust, not to fear, "though the earth give way and the mountains fall into the heart of the sea" (Psalm 46:2).

More importantly, I realized what Paul meant when he wrote that God's grace is perfected in my weakness. Entrusting myself to the acceptance I discovered in Christ enabled grace to have its way. I found liberation within and from myself. Areas of my life that had been places of insecurity became places for humility, trust, listening, and surprising revelation. If, as authors such as John Bradshaw, Christopher Lasch, and Gershen Kaufman have said, that ours is a shame-based culture ashamed of shame, then perhaps only a shame-based religion can provide the perspective and redemption that we need. In the cross of Christ I found the one who, while constituting in his person the very essence of the good and the right, willingly and fearlessly bound himself to shame. Although crucifixion was a form of execution reserved for those least worthy of respect, the writer of Hebrews notes that Jesus "endured the cross, despising the shame" (Hebrews 12:2 KJV). Jesus' confrontation with and affirmation of shame and refusal to be held by it, a fact to which God's resurrection of Jesus attests, becomes the revelation of God's power to heal shame, and became such for me. My experience of this reality became a wedding of experience and religious truth. As the author of the letter to the Hebrews writes:

> For we have not a high priest who is unable to sympathize with our weaknesses, but one who in every respect has been tempted as we are, yet without sin. Let us then with confidence draw near to the throne of grace, that we may receive mercy and find grace to help in time of need.
>
> HEBREWS 4:15–16 RSV

That grace came to meet my need. It taught me that the place of my weakness, my shame, can also be the place of my strength. It becomes the very place where God works, revealing God's power, drawing me to my neighbor as I become vulnerable and leave the place of denial, self-deception, and mistrust. Conversely, the place of my strength becomes the source of my weakness as I seek to serve and not stand over a sister or brother. Through my weaknesses and strength I find community. Joyce Carol Oates writes of the dangers of social singularity in her short story "Heat" and in other works. The idea of being seen as vulnerable, judged, or even temporarily out of control is something I could not bear. Fear of such drove me to singularity. Harvard teaches us how to be in control, but our generation and social order is not in control. This lack of control is a reality that shapes the violence of the underlying and underclass resentment in our society. It conditions the lives of the students in our schools. They and we struggle with perfection and shame and the quest for liberation. But liberation often brings only singularity.

I can now see that holiness, the integration of being with understanding and ethics, is a social reality. It is worked out through mutual vulnerability as we learn to be served and to serve one another. Gone is the illusion that success means control and autonomy. I am liberated from myself and for others, to discover my own giftedness and to foster that of others without fearing that it will detract from mine. Like other institutions of higher learning today, Harvard is being confronted with a social reality that requires something beyond the development of the giftedness of its students. After some years in eclipse, questions of being, understanding, and ethics are emerging in our public discussion and coming to be seen as inextricably intertwined. Our rediscovered search for values in the university world should awaken in us a desire to probe again into the insights that lie behind that *Veritas* implicit in Harvard's foundation. Perhaps, despite all that we know today, something was then seen that we fail to appreciate today.

A Journey Toward Wholeness

— BETSY DAWN INSKEEP SMYLIE —

Suddenly I found myself flat on my back, being wheeled into an operating room, with a strong possibility that the child in my womb would not survive.

Betsy Dawn Inskeep Smylie, Harvard-Radcliffe class of 1975 and Harvard Divinity School class of 1981, lived in Orchard Park, New York, with her husband and two children. She served as vicar of Ephphatha Church of the Deaf, and diocesan missioner to the deaf. With her husband, John, who is also an Episcopal priest, she wrote *Christian Parenting,* published by Upper Room Books in 1991.

A Journey Toward Wholeness

— BETSY DAWN INSKEEP SMYLIE —

One of the amazing paradoxes of the Christian life is that out of weakness and brokenness comes life. It's right smack in the middle of the whole proclamation—a cross, the symbol of a slow and painful execution. And at every Christian Eucharist, death is celebrated as the means of new life as we feast on the broken body and poured-out blood of our Lord.

For me, one of life's most difficult yet rewarding processes has been to learn to admit and accept my weaknesses and my brokenness, and to relinquish my desire to make myself over. I am learning to turn myself over to God, to await God's healing and leadership in my life.

Rather than give a theological treatise, I would like to tell a few stories about how I have begun to learn this powerful lesson along my spiritual journey.

Like many Harvard-Radcliffe students, I was used to being in control of my life, making the grades, running the show, coming out on top. I had never panicked over an academic event in my life, always being able, no matter how ill-prepared, to pull a rabbit out of the hat. But I remember the evening before my first Harvard final. I recall sitting in a Hilles Library alcove, looking out in the dark on Walker Street, with all my "Soc Sci 15" notes spread out around me. Suddenly, absolute panic set in and I became totally immobilized. I couldn't focus on a page of notes or open another book or imagine how I could possibly survive the night or the next morning. I don't know how long the panic lasted, but it seemed an eternity.

Then suddenly I felt myself and the entire Hilles alcove flooded with incredible peace as I heard the Lord say in my heart, "Don't you know that I love you?" And I knew in that split second that I had a choice: fear or faith, control or yielding. And rather than arguing with God about my obvious and urgent need for a miraculous infusion of (largely unnecessary) information, I said, "Yes, God," and breathed deep and relaxed, knowing it would be OK. Not that I felt God's love would automatically cause me to do well but because I knew that my being was not defined by Harvard's blue books or anyone else's standards, including my own brutal perfectionism. Rather, my being was defined by God's unconditional love for me poured out at the cross. I am grateful that I learned that lesson early in my Harvard career. It was a pivotal one which I had to repeatedly recall.

Another pivotal learning time for me came later in my Harvard experience. I was in divinity school, recently married, and just having completed six weeks of clinical pastoral education in a hospital setting where one of my primary tasks was to care for patients about to undergo surgery.

Suddenly I found myself flat on my back, being wheeled into an operating room, with a strong possibility that the child in my womb would not survive the surgical procedure needed to close my cervix, which was dilating prematurely. I wanted to be awake, so I had local anesthesia and was tipped upside down to take pressure off the cervix. This was a much different position from which to view life in a hospital than my safe role as a chaplain. As I felt myself start to tense up and panic, I began to pray the simplest and most basic Christian prayer, which my husband had taught me. And as I called out to Jesus, he brought me peace and the assurance that this baby, whether in life or death, was in God's care.

My firstborn is now a young teenager, but the lesson I learned so early in her tiny life is one that I, as a parent, must relearn day by day. She is not mine to control. She and her brother, and all of life, are gifts to be received and cared for.

The diagnosis came as a shock to me. I have what is called an "incompetent cervix," which means that it doesn't hold weight when the baby reaches a certain size, and must be tied shut. My husband laughed when he heard the name: "You've never been called incompetent in anything in your life!" He was right. And it was difficult to hear, because it wasn't something I could practice and do better the next time. This almost cost the life of my child and most certainly would preclude my dreams of a large family. I was not omnipotent, gifted, healthy, or in control. And praying the name of Jesus, who had hung upon a cross immobilized and bleeding, brought me great comfort.

Another experience of coming face-to-face with my own inability to control and manage my life and the life of my family came when our second child was diagnosed as being profoundly deaf. Through the shock, the tears, the educational mazes, the anger at doctors, God, and myself, my son has taken me by the hand and lead me into a whole new cultural community and into a new ministry. Now the words of the gospel flow from my hands and find a home in my body as I preach and share the Eucharist in sign language among the deaf community. Through the "weakness" of those with broken ears I see the power of the love of God shining brightly, and I marvel at the abundance of God's grace, which reaches to our deepest losses and fills us with hope.

Jesus has been my lover and Lord, my healer and helper, my joy, my food, my life, for many years now. He continues to show me who I am in the light of his unconditional love and to comfort and heal me in my broken-ness. But he has also taught me how to relinquish my need for control in the good times. He wants to work through my gifts as well as my weaknesses. He allows me to use my knowledge of Scripture, and small grasp of his ways, to touch people's hearts as I proclaim his message of love. He allows me the unspeakable delight of putting the sacraments into the mouths of his people. He allows me to choose faith and not fear, joy and not depression or grumpiness, gentleness and not impatience, in all the mundane occur-rences that make up the everyday life of a former "Cliffie" who happens to be a wife and a mother and a priest, day by day seeking to let God have control in her life.

CHAPTER 5

PLURALISM AND THE GLOBAL GOSPEL

Harvard Square   *Habib Malik*

Christ and Karma: A Hindu's Quest for the Holy   *Krister Sairsingh*

Jesus, More Than a Prophet   *Lamin Sanneh*

Power and Gender at the Divinity School   *John Rankin*

Truth requires a maximum effort to see through the eyes of strangers, foreigners, and enemies.

TAYLOR BRANCH, *PARTING THE WATERS: AMERICA IN THE KING YEARS*

ॐ

Are we by nature fated to suppress the deepest we know lest we offend?

CHARLES MALIK, *A CHRISTIAN CRITIQUE OF THE UNIVERSITY*

ॐ

To justify Christianity because it provides a foundation of morality, instead of showing the necessity of Christian morality from the truth of Christianity, is a very dangerous inversion...

T. S. ELIOT, *THE IDEA OF A CHRISTIAN SOCIETY*

Harvard Square

— HABIB MALIK —

Good news and intolerance are mutually inconsistent.

Habib Malik received a Ph.D. in modern European intellectual history from Harvard in 1985. Since 1989 he has been adjunct professor in the School of Philosophy at the Catholic University of America in Washington, and has taught history at the Lebanese American University in Beirut, Lebanon.

Malik was born in Washington, D.C. in 1954, at which time his father, Charles Malik, served as ambassador of Lebanon to the United States. Habib received a B.A. in history in 1977 from the American University of Beirut. He took his senior year at Princeton and went on to do graduate work at Harvard, where he wrote his dissertation on the history of the early reception of Kierkegaard's thought, soon to be published in book form.

Dr. Malik worked with CBN News for a time, reporting from Beirut. He was the Middle East associate at the Institute of Religion and Democracy in Washington, where he investigated issues of religious liberty. He has lectured widely and has published many articles on Arab Christians, Islam, Middle Eastern politics, and Lebanon.

Harvard Square

— HABIB MALIK —

A s a Christian and a student who spent eight years in Cambridge, Massachusetts doing graduate work in history at Harvard, I had the opportunity to experience pluralism firsthand. If there is one place where contrasting ideas, antagonistic worldviews, and dissimilar lifestyles come face-to-face and coexist, sometimes uneasily and not always interactively, it is on the east bank of the Charles River, or one should rather say the "left" bank.[1] It is not without reason that the city has affectionately been dubbed the People's Republic of Cambridge. I arrived in Cambridge as a believing Christian and eventually—no small feat—left with my faith intact, indeed even strengthened.

Cambridge is the quintessential public square, and Harvard Square has earned a reputation as a Mecca for the nonconformist, the newfangled, and the new wave of every shade. Cantabridgians come in all shapes, colors, mentalities, and proclivities. They live in an atmosphere that allows them the freedom either to associate or to remain apart, or both. It is this that nurtures—or, depending on one's view, feverishly fuels—the panoply of outlooks they represent. This pluralism flourishes under the shade of a single overarching assumption: that the autonomous other's freedom of self-actualization is something to be valued.

Because of the symbiotic—if not necessarily sedate—relationship between the university and its home city, some of this Cantabridgian kaleidoscope osmotically permeates the walls and lecture halls and inner recesses of the college, only to be reflected back in rarefied form onto the surrounding community. In fact, it may be accurate to say that Cambridge would not have become the gathering place for such animated diversity were it not for the presence of Harvard in its midst.

How hospitable to the committed Christian is such a modern, secular, pluralist environment, sustained as it is under an elaborate civil and legal system of rights, permits, and interdictions?

There are ways of surviving, even flourishing. During my time at Harvard, I affiliated with that old stone bulwark Saint Paul's Catholic Church

---

[1]The Harvard Business School, on the *west* bank of the river, is no retreat from antagonistic worldviews, either.

on Arrow Street and its Catholic Student Center, and I became close with active Christian students on campus. I helped found the Harvard-Radcliffe Conservative Club, some of whose members were believing Christians, and launched the club's paper, the *Harvard Salient*.[2] It was not always easy, but for me, pluralism in a secular context does not in any way imply relativism. I have never regarded the famous Harvard mottoes of *Veritas*, or Truth, and *Christo et Ecclesiae*—For Christ and the Church—as mere relics of the university's Puritan past, superseded naturally and inevitably by the superior secular imperatives of an obviously more enlightened and tolerant present. On the contrary, belief in truth, and specifically in "the Way, the Truth, and the Life," means that all ultimate claims and positions are necessarily arranged hierarchically according to their proximity to, or remoteness from, this truth. The horizontal leveling of everything, so much a hallmark of modern secular thinking in the West, is therefore unacceptable. I believe that there are fixed and timeless standards against which all things are measured and judged.

On the other hand, hierarchy based on the truth of Jesus Christ is not a license for intolerance. Good news and intolerance are mutually inconsistent—and a Christian is governed at all times by the kerygmatic duty to proclaim, in word and deed, the Good News of Christ. He does this, as it were, in the public square, by creatively encouraging in his interlocutors a healthy and sincere posture of searching through dialogue. Thus, a Christian who is committed to the true expression of the gospel respects the total freedom of others, even others different from himself. Yet out of love, as authentic opportunities arise, out of the constant yearning to find fulfillment in others through the Ultimate Other, he shares Christ's joy with them. The affirmation and celebration of such joy and, on the other hand, the fundamental openness to others are not mutually exclusive or incompatible projects.

I am not, of course, preaching tolerance for its own sake, nor am I romanticizing the bohemian cafe subculture for which Harvard Square is famous, where street musicians in bandannas and leather, tattoos and tiedye, serenade with guitar and dulcimer the unwritten themes of Cambridge life—liberal affability, egalitarian respect, and discreet experimentation. What I *am* saying is that respect for freedom is a deeply religious (or prereligious) concept. For freedom is the vital ingredient, the necessary ontic glue, the central underlying assumption of the entire Judeo-Christian conception of humanity and existence. In the language of theodicy, God took "the risk of freedom," preferring to create beings with the free ability to

---

[2]The *Salient* is still the college's most widely read conservative newspaper.

reject him over the "safer" but less perfect, and less loving, alternative of creating automatons. Freedom is therefore a gift and an open avenue that leads toward, but equally often away from, the divine.

Freedom is the ineluctable substratum of the human condition. Freedom allows for perfectibility, permits the realization of purpose, gives real meaning to sanctification, and safeguards our interaction with others and with the Other. It is the principal distinguishing hallmark of humans, as far as I know the only free creatures aside from the angels. When Dostoyevsky defined a person as "a creature who walks on two legs and is ungrateful," it was a wry way of noting that even the perversity of our ingratitude somehow raises us above the rest of the animal kingdom, for in it we express our God-given freedom to be ungrateful even for the gift of freedom itself. In one sense, freedom is more primary than reason as a defining characteristic of humanness, for as humans we are free to be irrational, as Dostoyevsky's *Underground Man* brilliantly illustrates.

But freedom is not groundless; its reach may be utopian, but it is rooted in the earthly soil of social relationships, and to flourish it requires all the care of a delicate plant. Any form of sustainable freedom has a context, and it is within that context that one is totally free. Everyone's personal profile, those inescapable elements that define the contours of personhood—gender, background, color, personality, genetics, historical circumstances—is a given situational premise that sets a limiting context. The human person is all these elements, but he is also much more precisely because, within his given limitations, he manifests total freedom of development—the freedom to be, to become, to achieve self-actualization.

But ultimately, what makes possible as well as delineates such freedom of self-actualization is that God has given us the capacity to respond to transcendental beckonings with boundless creative communion and to derive strength and direction, power and purpose, inspiration and instruction, from such exchanges. We are grounded but we are not determined. We are grounded by and in the necessity of referencing ourselves to otherness, to Spirit, if we are earnest about nurturing our freedom to its fullest. Ultimately, the entire religious animus is relational in that it is oriented toward the Supreme Other, toward God. Far from circumscribing freedom, however, the necessary spiritual ingredients of personhood in fact *guarantee* freedom by serving to delimit the scope and encroachment of determinism.

Although it is communion with God which makes our freedom possible and inspires it, it is the given presence of others which here on earth gives content to the exercise of our freedom, and not only to the exercise of our freedom but to our personality. It is in and with and through others that we find the greatest fulfillment. And since sameness and cloning are not the order of existence, the presence of others means diversity. Pluralism.

Philosophically, authentic pluralism may be defined simply as the mutual coexistence and interaction of integral non-objectified others. (Now, if you said this in Harvard Square, they would immediately understand you; but even if not, you can guarantee they would grant you the benefit of the doubt—and give you space to flesh out your thought.) An illustrious body of writings reflect on the role, nature, and requirements of pluralism. In modern political philosophy, beginning with Hobbes and certainly since Locke, the major contractual theories of civil society and government all have assumed diversity and aimed to accommodate a plurality of outlooks.

But for pluralism to function and flourish in an overall unifying political framework, certain universals must be accepted across the board by all—a minimum set of hierarchically arranged, shared values that comprise, as it were, the ground rules of the pluralism game. Beyond this, today's secular West would add that each person or group is entitled to full autonomy of opinion and the practice of whatever lifestyle they choose. This has, for better or worse, come to be part of what freedom means in modern Western society.

Is this elaborate civil system hurtful or helpful to Christians? I believe it is more the latter (although there are undeniable elements of the former), for freedom lies at the root of what it means to be human, what it means to be like God, and what it means even to be able to express faith in God and to share faith with others. Committed Christians ought not to shy away from the bustling arenas of secular pluralism in the West, for these domains are inherently dynamic and governed by freedom under the law. The entire impetus of the New Testament is to explain the work God has done to set us free—from the coercion of sin, the ravages of guilt, the fear of death, and the bondage of laws that were arrayed against us. Having been set free by Christ, who respected our freedom to reject him until such time as we were ready to contemplate the fundamental things that pertain to salvation, can we adopt any other approach than to extend the same genuine respect to others who struggle with questions and attitudes and uncertainties? Instead of opting for isolation and the easy alternative of erecting our own clean-cut "City on the Hill," we must accept the challenge, helping to effect a lasting transformation and renewal of the world around us, wherever we find ourselves. Remember, Saint Paul preached a crucified Christ in the Agora, or central square, in ancient Athens.

A defense of pluralism and tolerance is not meant as a cover for moral and intellectual relativism, nor is it intended here to provide an excuse for skirting the troublesome and thorny issues of the day. Neither is such a defense a justification for privatizing all religious conviction in the name of getting along superficially well with everyone. It is rather a challenge—a civic and biblical ideal goading Christians on toward a closer, more genuine, and more vigorous engagement with the diversity that daily surrounds them.

Throughout the world, far beyond the discussion grounds of Harvard Square, there exists a plurality of hostile worldviews in places where the possibility of dialogue has been eviscerated and has been replaced often by a violent strain of intolerance: Bosnia, Lebanon, southern Sudan, Nagorno-Karabakh, Los Angeles, and Bensonhurst, New York, are relatively recent flashpoints. But here too, the believer in the incarnation, crucifixion, and resurrection of Jesus Christ, the believer in the God who freely created free beings, has a role to play. As in any other place, his task here is not an easy one: he has to remain faithful to his deepest beliefs against all odds, yet genuinely available to those around him; firmly rooted in Christ, yet open to a diversity of passions, stances, and opinions. He has, in other words, to continue to love. And faith and love are tested and made perfect by freedom. In the end it is unshakable faith and unconditional love which, for the Christian, become his greatest witness.

Christ and Karma:
A Hindu's Quest for the Holy

— K RISTER S AIRSINGH —

I despised the "uncultured" lower-caste Hindus, and I distrusted Muslims. I was a cauldron of bigotry and prejudice. I knew I had done things for which I would have to pay in some other life. I could only conceive of a downward spiral. I felt there was no way out.

Born in Trinidad to a priestly Hindu family, **Krister Sairsingh** graduated from Yale University in 1971 and received his Ph.D. from Harvard University in religion, specializing in historical and philosophical theology. Krister served as a chaplain to graduate and international students on the staff of Harvard's Memorial Church. His wife, Nancy, is completing her Harvard doctorate in Russian art history. Together they are raising two sons, Jeremy and Daniel. The Sairsinghs live in Moscow, where Nancy studies and Krister teaches theology and philosophy.

Christ and Karma:

A Hindu's Quest for the Holy

— KRISTER SAIRSINGH —

From time to time I am asked questions such as: Why did you become a Christian? Why did you leave the great and ancient religion of Hinduism, with its deep mystical and philosophical outlook, for Christianity, a relative newcomer in the history of religions? What did Christianity offer that Hinduism did not?

This essay is not a defense of Christianity to its intellectual and cultured despisers but a simple narrative account of my spiritual journey to Christ. Conversion to Christian faith changed my values, transformed my mind, and affected every area of my life. But it was just the beginning of a thrilling adventure of faith, of a journey into the infinite and inexhaustible reality of God.

Although I was raised with the belief that all religions are valid paths to the spiritual life, my friends and family members took it for granted that only Hinduism, through the disciplines of yoga and bhakti, offered a path to spiritual perfection and divine self-realization. While we respected other religions as fragmentary manifestations of the divine reality, we believed that only the great gurus and swamis of the Hindu tradition attained that perfect God-consciousness which is the true end of religion. To be holy, so I thought, was to realize one's own divinity, to actualize one's divine selfhood through the disciplines of meditation and yoga, nonattachment, and a radical self-renunciation. The notion that God, out of pure love, seeks out the human and enters into relationship with the human person was an altogether foreign notion to me. Holiness had little to do with human relationships, with a dedication to sacrificial service and reconciling love in human community. Ultimately, these pursuits were just distractions from the true ends of religion. I understood a genuine liberation of the soul to be a liberation from all forms of personal existence. Salvation meant deliverance from embodied existence, from the relentless cycle of karma.

As a young Hindu boy, I was fascinated with people who claimed to be holy. I often visited one such holy man. He was my uncle. It was common knowledge that shortly after the conception of their only child, he took a vow of silence and celibacy and entered a trancelike state through meditation and the practice of yoga.

His silence amazed me. I remember how his son (my cousin Rabi) and I would gaze into his face hoping for some response—a word or even a smile. But not once did he turn to smile or speak. He died without his son ever having heard his voice.

We grew up in the home of our maternal grandfather who was a wealthy and influential leader in the Hindu community which makes up a third of the island's population. With the daily round of religious ceremonies, there was never a dull moment in this large extended family. When swamis from India stayed at our home, I would take long walks with some of them to the sea just to be in their presence. For me they embodied the ideal of the holy. I looked forward to the day when I would have one of these swamis as my guru.

An important event for our family, and indeed the whole Hindu community, was the visit of Swami Advaitananda from India to the island. He spent a week in our home. It was during this visit that he became my guru and gave me a mantra—a short Sanskrit prayer to be repeated many times in my meditation. Although he soon returned to India, I treasured the memory of him and daily adored a picture of him.

My mother and her younger sister began to travel with a group of young women through towns and villages to promote the teachings of the swami. Both of these sisters had arranged marriages. Although most arranged marriages seem to work out well, neither my mother's nor her younger sister's turned out as they had hoped. Eventually both returned to their father's home and, with the assistance of learned gurus and pundits, dedicated their lives to the study of the many volumes of Hindu scriptures and commentaries which we owned. They were kept in the puja room, a room set aside for the practice of yoga and devotion to Hindu deities, whose images rested upon a specially built altar. On the wall of the room, there hung pictures of some of my heroes—Swami Yogananda, Swami Sivananda of the Divine Life Society, and, of course, my guru.

Since I was the oldest child, my mother diligently taught me from the *Bhagavat Gita*. But it was the stories from the *Ramayana*, and the lives of the great rishis and sages, which really captivated me. I also looked forward to reading Swami Sivananda's journal, *Divine Life Society*, which occasionally arrived in the mail. At an early age I was captivated by *Autobiography of a Yogi* by Swami Yogananda, from which my mother often read to me. I dreamed of becoming a holy man like him. Every day, after ritual purification, I would enter the puja room to do japa yoga, offer incense to the deities, and chant Sanskrit mantras to Shiva, Krishna, and Saraswati, the goddess of wisdom.

As I grew up I took enormous pride in our ancient Hindu scriptures and traditions. During my years in high school I cultivated the friendship of Hindu boys who shared my pride in the heritage of Hinduism. Over lunch we would discuss Indian philosophy and read the poetry of the Indian Nobel laureate Rabindranath Tagore. Occasionally we read poems which were written by the leader of our coterie, whose literary passion and fierce loyalty to Hinduism deeply inspired us.

During my final year in high school, he became my best friend. We were both concerned about the threat of Islam and the growing influence of Christianity upon some sectors of the Hindu community. We took such zealous pride in our religious traditions that we made a pact to devote our lives to a defense of the Hindu way of life. He went on to obtain a Ph.D. in Indian history at a leading British university and is now an accomplished academic in the field.

My oldest uncle, a devout Hindu, had obtained his degree in English literature from the University of London and had returned home with an impressive library which began to open up new literary horizons for me. I began to drink deeply from the romantics, especially the poetry of Keats and Wordsworth. The essays of Hazlitt, Charles Lamb, and George Orwell, and the literary criticism of Matthew Arnold, deepened my appreciation for the Western intellectual tradition. My uncle showed me how one could be a scholar well-versed in Western literature and also devoted to the spiritual ideals of Hinduism. He moved within both worlds with remarkable ease.

A younger uncle went on to pursue graduate studies in philosophy and art history at the University of Chicago. As I look back, his counsel and influence upon me would prove to be decisive in the direction which my life eventually took.

We all grew up in the same family bungalow—grandmother, uncles, aunts, and cousins. After the death of Grandfather, my maternal uncles assumed leadership roles in the family. Several members of the family, including my mother, had become disciples of Pundit Janki Prasad Sharma, the presiding spiritual head of the Hindu community. He came to our home frequently to officiate at special religious events. As he entered our home we would await his blessings while we bowed at his feet. There was a measure of pride in belonging to this family for whom the quest for the holy was a daily affair.

Towards the end of my final year of high school, I had a bizarre experience which caused me to question the efficacy of my faith. I was sitting on my bed studying chemistry late at night in preparation for final examinations. I felt a slap on my face as I was thrown upon the bed. I felt as if something was physically strangling me. I could not easily breathe or move.

Since I could not speak, I began to repeat in my mind the mantra which was given by my guru. When that did not work, I tried the Gayatri mantra, the most sacred mantra of Hinduism. But that brought no relief. I thought that perhaps I had offended Shiva and had fallen under the wrath of this deity of creation and destruction, as he is sometimes referred to. Perhaps when I danced before his image and offered incense, something which I regularly did, I may have performed my ritual obligations carelessly. Finally, after much struggle, I broke free. I began to wonder if there were other powers in the universe which could deliver me from the fears that had begun to torment me—fear of death, fear of the unknown.

The next morning, I related my experience to Singh, an Indian classmate, a former Hindu who had become a Christian. I wondered whether he had an explanation of what had happened to me. I went to Singh for advice because there was something different about him, a light that pervaded his presence. He struck me as someone who might be connected with the spiritual world. He seemed convinced that there was a direct link between what had happened to me and my way of worshiping. The worship of idols, he argued, made me vulnerable to demonic attack.

Naturally I was deeply offended by his simple-minded explanation. Although I made it clear that I did not accept his attack on my religion, I wanted to know if there was anything I could do to prevent the reoccurrence of that terrifying experience. Singh suggested that I consider Jesus. That sounded harmless enough. Accommodating Jesus within the pantheon of divinities which I worshiped should not be too difficult, I thought. Like most of my Hindu friends, I believed that whatever power Jesus displayed, he acquired it from the great gurus of India. But Singh was claiming much more for Jesus than I could accept. Jesus, he said, had power over all other powers in the universe, including the Hindu deities and all the swamis and gurus who had ever lived. Although I found this to be a most arrogant and offensive claim, I thought that if it were true, it would mean giving Jesus a place of primacy within my Hindu worship. The idea was mind-boggling. And yet there was something attractive about it. Could this Jesus possibly rescue me from the terror and dread which had enveloped my soul?

At the urging of Singh I began to read the gospel accounts of Jesus to learn more about him. He struck me as utterly unique, different from anyone I had known or read about. There remained, however, a curious mixture of attraction and ambivalence towards Jesus and his claims. When I read his saying, "All power is given unto me in heaven and in earth" (Matthew 28:18 KJV), not only did I feel drawn to the bearer of such power, I was also perplexed, because of its disturbing implications for the entire edifice of Hindu gods and goddesses. Did Jesus really have more power than Shiva or Krishna? I wanted to know.

What astounded me most was Jesus' claim to have power to forgive sins. I understood the fundamental principles of my religion well enough to know that within the Hindu scheme of things, there is no such thing as forgiveness for one's wrong actions. The law of karma—that whatever wrong we do we will have to pay for in some other life—rules out the very idea of forgiveness. According to the law of karma, reincarnation is therefore necessary in order to pay for the sins of a previous life. One's present life is determined by one's previous existence, while one's future existence is shaped by one's present life. Each soul is held to be responsible for its own destiny. The law of karma offered a simple and attractive explanation of the mystery of suffering in the world. People suffer because of their own evil action. But reincarnation as a necessary working out of the law of karma was never good news to me—even though I knew it undergirded the whole fabric of my religious and moral world.

Like many other Hindu families, we nurtured a hope that ritual baths in rivers or the ocean on certain holy days might lighten the load of karma and procure some sort of remission of sin. But I was never convinced by that. I knew full well that the grim and relentless law of karma said otherwise. There was no way out of the endless cycles of birth, suffering, and death except through the perfection of holiness and God-consciousness. This could be attained, so I believed, through a renunciation of the world, the extinction of all human desires, and the dissolving of the mind and its state of ordinary consciousness through a lifetime of yoga. Such rigorous asceticism called for a radical rejection of any belief in the goodness of the created order. It would require that I deny this life rather than celebrate it. I thought of my uncle who had renounced the world, his wife, child, and all human relationships in his quest for holiness and spiritual release (moksha).

As I read the Gospels I became much more aware of my human failings, that I was a creature governed by unruly desires rather than the virtues of compassion and generosity. It dawned on me that I was often unkind to the numerous beggars who knocked at our gates. Whatever charity I showed was born not out of compassion and kindness but out of a desire to build up good karma, to secure a better birth in the cosmic wheel of existence. I began to see how hard I had tried to distance myself from the "uncultured" lower-caste Hindus and how much I distrusted and despised Muslims. There was a feeling of desperation, because I knew that I would have to suffer the consequences in some other life for all my evil actions. In some ways, the teachings of Jesus even compounded my feeling of distress, because he taught that we would be judged for our thoughts, attitudes, and words, not just our deeds. I knew the depths of my prejudice and bigotry. Spiritual liberation—release from the cycle of birth and death—seemed humanly impossible. I could only conceive of a downward spiral. I felt there was no way out.

Who was this Jesus who could break the bondage of karma, who said he had the power to forgive sins? I had to know. I delved deeper into the Gospels. Over the next six weeks, I went into the sugarcane fields to pray, hoping that something of God's truth would be revealed to me. More than anything else, I wanted the truth.

In Plato's *Phaedo*, Socrates is reported to have said, "If you will take my advice, you will think very little of Socrates and much more of the truth." But with Jesus it was altogether different. I soon came to recognize that according to the teachings of the Gospels, the question of ultimate truth is inseparable from the person of Jesus. Jesus said that to be free, one must know the truth. But the truth was not some metaphysical construct, not some esoteric concept. The truth was enfleshed in the person of Jesus. I had to reckon with the gospel teaching that Jesus is the way, the truth, and the life. The logic was clear. In order to know the truth, I had to know Jesus.

As the weeks went by the person of Jesus began to exercise a powerful hold upon my imagination. I could not easily evade his call to follow him. It became clear to me that he was no mere seeker after God; he bore witness to God. In him the truth of God's reality could not be denied. As I read his words in the Gospels, I thought that he was speaking directly to me. It was as if he were telling me that he could actually come to me and forgive my sins, undo the past, loosen me from the terrors of death, break the bondage of karma, and make me truly free.

For a while I tried to incorporate Jesus into the pantheon of deities arrayed on the altar of the puja room. Each morning, after I offered incense and chanted mantras before the altar, I would then turn to recite the mantras to the picture of Jesus beside that of Gandhi and other gurus whose pictures lined the wall of the puja room. I had begun to include Jesus in my prayers. But I had the uneasy feeling that Jesus did not belong to their company, that he was without equal, and that he would not wish to be honored in a way that made him one among many, just another avatar among others. It soon dawned on me that he did not belong to the company of the gurus or even the deities on the altar. He was unique, utterly different. I did not know how to worship and honor him. And yet in the depths of my heart, I desired to adore him.

One night, after meditating on the account of the death and resurrection of Jesus in John's gospel, I asked Jesus to forgive my sins, to set me free from the bondage of karma, and to become the Lord of my life. I had come to believe that he was the only one who could do that. In the puja room I recited the Gayatri mantra to Jesus, but that night I confessed my sins, surrendered my life to him, and worshiped him as Savior and Lord. I knew that something eventful, something life changing, had happened.

When I awoke the next morning, I walked towards the puja room. As I looked at the images on the altar, I knew there and then that I could never return to them. They instantly lost all attractiveness for me. I closed the door of the room with the deep conviction that I belonged to Christ and that from then on my devotion and affections were to be set upon him. It was not to religion but to Christ I was drawn.

I had never been inside a church building. I knew that the one to whom all power in the universe has been given had drawn me to himself, forgiven me, taken away my fears, and given me a peace and joy I had never known. But even so, I was reluctant to identify myself publicly as a Christian. What would I say to my Hindu friends and relatives? Shortly before surrendering to Christ, my closest friend made it clear that if ever I became a Christian, we could no longer be friends.

I began to confide in the Indian classmate who first urged me to read the Gospels. When he learned of my decision to follow Christ, he introduced me to the minister of a house church in our town. The minister, a former Muslim, invited me to attend the service. On my first visit, I felt a little out of place, because nearly all of the people there were either former Hindus of a lower caste or former Muslims. There were some people of African descent. My upbringing, such as it was, had predisposed me to avoid close contact with such people. But they had a love for one another that cut across racial and religious lines. I was surprised to discover that my dislike and distrust of these people had vanished. And soon I began to embrace them as my own brothers and sisters. It was there, in that house church, with the encouragement and biblical preaching of Reverend Hamid, that I was taught, baptized, and nurtured in the Christian faith. I became a keen participant in the life of the church.

Just around the time of my conversion, my mother was offered a privileged position. The leaders of the Hindu community had chosen her to take up a resident position at what was then the largest Hindu temple in Trinidad. There she would have to give lectures on special occasions and see to it that the temple's daily ceremonies were properly conducted.

Dedicated to the cause of the Hindu Women's Federation and rigorously ascetic in her quest for self-realization (the knowledge that the real self within is divine), she became an influential voice for the renewal of Hindu piety. Pundits and gurus often came to her for the clarification of obscure sacred texts. She was looking forward to life at the temple and had made the necessary arrangements for the care of the younger children.

I pleaded with her to wait a few weeks before taking up residence in the temple. Her suitcases had been packed; she was ready to go. Perhaps it was because I was her eldest son—but why she agreed to wait at all still remains a mystery to me. Every day for the next three weeks, however, I read from the Gospels to her as we discussed the teachings of Jesus, his power, and the significance of his death and resurrection.

My mother later admitted that she was baffled by the sudden transformation of my life. She noticed that I was no longer fearful; ferocious thunderstorms no longer terrified me. Quietly she would watch me as I followed the lightning patterns in the sky from my bedroom window and sang hymns to the Creator. She told me she could not understand how such joy could have filled my life in just a few weeks, while she who had spent her whole life in meditation and yoga still felt oppressed by the burden of karma.

My mother normally would begin her daily meditation and yoga at four every morning. But now, she later told me, she would prostrate herself on the floor of the puja room, crying out for the truth. Within three weeks she too had become convinced by the teachings of Jesus. She asked Jesus to forgive her sins and become the Lord of her life. She thought that it would be enough to follow Jesus as a secret disciple, and for a while she tried to do so. She knew, however, that what had happened to her, the experience of conversion and the attendant joy of belonging to Christ, meant that she could not assume the position in the temple.

It was a scandalous affair in the Hindu community. Friends and relatives were shocked and outraged. Pundits and priests came to the house to find out if the rumor was true. The leader of the opposition party in the national government, a devout Hindu, attended a religious festival across the street from our home, and from there, on the loud public-address system, he launched a verbal attack upon our family—for by then, within six weeks of my conversion, my grandmother, mother, brothers and sisters, and my cousin Rabi, an aspiring guru, had all openly professed faith in Jesus Christ as Lord of their lives and Savior of the world.

My cousin Rabi and I removed the altar and all the images from the puja room and converted it into a sanctuary for Christian reflection and prayer. The Bible, *The Imitation of Christ* by Thomas á Kempis, and *The Yellow Robe,* a biography of Sadhu Sundar Singh, an Indian Christian, were the only Christian writings we had in the puja room.

What had been a deeply devout Hindu household was now a place frequented by African Trinidadians, former Muslims, and lower-caste Hindu converts. What was even more astonishing—they were eating at the same table with us. The singing of hymns and late-night prayer meetings with these people had become common practice in our home.

My mother's youngest sister came from India to take the position at the temple. Naturally she was saddened by the changes which had taken place in the home. It was from that very home she had left over a decade earlier, after her husband's death, for Banaras Hindu University. She had entrusted her only child, Rabi, to the care of my mother.

My oldest uncle was even more displeased. He was the head of our home and executor of my grandfather's estate. He left home and moved with his wife near the university where he taught English literature. I recall his last words to us: "Let Jesus Christ take care of you. I am leaving."

One of the dreams of my life was to follow in the footsteps of my uncles and study abroad at a great university. Most of my high school friends had left for universities in the United Kingdom and Canada. It appeared as though I would have to spend the rest of my life teaching at the elementary school in a small village not far from home. But then something unexpected happened.

My mother's youngest brother interrupted his graduate studies in art history and philosophy at the University of Chicago and returned home to relieve me of the responsibility for our family. He began to open up new worlds for me. My uncle encouraged me to read Dostoyevsky, Kierkegaard, Tillich, the *Saturday Review,* and the *New York Review of Books,* which arrived in the mail every couple of weeks.

He urged me to apply to liberal arts colleges in America to study philosophy and theology. He promised that if I did not receive a scholarship, he would sell part of his inheritance to come up with the money. I had no difficulty choosing where to study, since the only university which admitted me with a full scholarship was Yale. The cultural officer of the USIS office of the American embassy knew me, since I often went there to read the journal *Christianity Today* as well as books by Carl F. H. Henry. With great excitement, she immediately took me to meet the ambassador, and the embassy bought me a plane ticket.

Nothing could have prepared me for culture shock at Yale. During my first year, an emeritus professor, Kenneth Scott Latourette, recognized this and for much of the year sat with me for Sunday breakfast.

In a lecture hall full of upper classmen and graduate students, I was the only freshman enrolled in Hans Frei's course "Contemporary Christian Thought." One morning during a lecture on Kierkegaard's *Philosophical Fragments*, he was able to tell from the look on my face that I understood little of it. Before I left, he asked me to come to his office every two weeks with all my questions about the wilderness of modern theology. He became my mentor and eventually the adviser of my senior thesis on Bultmann's historiography. During the writing of this essay, he allowed me access to his unpublished writings, including the manuscript of *The Eclipse of Biblical Narrative*, now an enduring classic in the field of hermeneutics.

Another Yale professor whose writings, personal example, and friendship had an enduring impact upon me was the Hegel scholar Merold Westphal. Professor Westphal was the faculty adviser of the Yale Christian Union, which provided Christian fellowship during my college years. He was an example to us of the Christian as a rigorous academic with a deep commitment to biblical Christianity. With his encouragement, I stayed on to teach for a year in the religious studies department at Yale as a Carnegie Teaching Fellow. After that I enrolled in the Ph.D. program in the study of religion at Harvard University. Under the direction of Richard Niebuhr, the son of H. Richard Niebuhr, I completed a dissertation on the subject of the idea of the divine glory in Edwards' Trinitarian theology.

Whether I am speaking at churches, the Socratic Club, Christian fellowships, or the Veritas Forum, two themes have become central. They are the holiness of God and the uniqueness of Christianity among the religions of the world. Here in Moscow, Russia, where I now teach theology and world religions, I find myself returning to Jonathan Edwards' Trinitarian vision again and again as I try to expound the Christian doctrine of God in my lectures.

According to Edwards, America's greatest religious philosopher, the quest for true spirituality, for the holy, has less to do with a renunciation of God's good creation and more to do with being in rightly ordered relationships. And if we humans are to attain any measure of holiness, it must be through our relationship to the triune God as well as living in rightly ordered relationships with our fellow humans.

The divine love is expressed not only internally within the Trinity; there is also an outward expression of the divine love. In this outward expression of love, God creates, preserves, and redeems. The God of Christian faith is not trapped in heaven. The God of Christian faith is free to come down, show his face, save fallen human beings from sin and death, and bring lost humanity into glorious communion with God. The love of God means that God in Christ has offered himself for us and in so doing has reconciled to himself those who in faith repent and turn to him. This is the good news of the gospel which drew me to Christ, which changed my life, and which, I believe, offers the only real hope for the whole world.

Jesus, More Than a Prophet

— LAMIN SANNEH —

Seen in the light of the cross, all of human nature, indeed all of history, appears to gather at one sharp, poignant place.

Lamin Sanneh was raised a devout Muslim in the Gambia, West Africa. Fluent in four African languages, Sanneh pursued a master's degree in Arabic and Islamic studies at the University of Birmingham, England, and later in Beirut, Lebanon. He spent eight years teaching at the Harvard Center for the Study of World Religions. In 1989 he was tenured at Yale University as the D. Willis James Professor of Missions and World Christianity, and as professor of history.

Based on research he has undertaken in West Africa, Europe, and the United States, Sanneh argues that, far from stunting indigenous cultures, Christian missions more typically reinvigorated cultures by encouraging local people to translate the concepts of the gospel into their own cultural-linguistic terms. It thus took root in ethnic cultures all over the world, extending the dispersion of Pentecost that began at Jerusalem two thousand years ago. A challenge for Christians is to help lead Western theology out of its "enclave" by exposing it to rich insights and idioms of other cultures.

Lamin Sanneh is the author of *West African Christianity: The Religious Impact*; *Translating the Message: The Missionary Impact on Culture*; and *Encountering the West:*. He and his wife, Sandra, a native of South Africa, are the grateful parents of two children. Their son, Kelefa, is an undergraduate at Harvard, and their daughter, Sia, is at St. Paul's School in Concord, New Hampshire.

Jesus, More Than A Prophet

— LAMIN SANNEH —

In my boyhood days in the Gambia, when the annual Muslim fast of Ramadan was approaching, there was a tremendous atmosphere of excitement among us, a feeling of community solidarity, of belonging together. I looked forward to it with great enthusiasm, and I welcomed this time appointed for Muslims everywhere to adore and submit to God, the focus of our religious devotion. Sometimes, though, I wanted to escape from its rigorous observance; there was a feeling that God is stern and inflexible in his demands. But along with this, there was a great sense of accomplishing the discipline of fasting that God had laid down (Qur'án ii:180). Of course, the feast day that followed the end of the fast month was a glorious day. I enjoyed the food and going to the prayer ground with all my friends in my clean robes; there was an uplifting feeling of being accepted before God by fulfilling our obligations to him.

I went to an all-Muslim government boarding school where on special days we would pray the whole night and, as the dawn was breaking, our hymns of praise would ascend to God—it seemed that with the daybreak God's mercy was breaking upon us. This is the sort of religious discipline I had as a Muslim, much of which has stayed with me, and I am very grateful for it. It has become an invaluable part of my adult life.

You may therefore wonder why, despite all this, I became a Christian. The very tradition and culture that gave meaning and depth to my life stirred profound questions in my mind: questions about God and humanity, about life and death and ultimate reality. These sent me back to the Qur'án, and there one thing in particular drew my attention: the Qur'án testifies to Jesus Christ as a prophet and an apostle of God, but not as the crucified one, for in the Qur'án "somebody else" was put in Jesus' place (Qur'án iv:155). I was interested in the teaching of life after death, and it struck me that if God was indeed personally involved in rescuing Jesus from the cross by taking someone else—whoever it was—and somehow exchanging him for Jesus, as the Qur'án says, then God surely bore responsibility for the death of this nameless victim.

I had no direct experience of a Christian community, though in my town, which was the headquarters of the colonial district administration, there were a few members of the Creole Christian community, but they were not religiously active and were dying off in any case from old age. So all I knew about Christians came from the unflattering picture the Qur'án paints of their religion, including the fact that Christians believed the scandalous idea that it was Jesus himself, the Son of God, not someone else, who died on the cross. Consequently, I became very interested in the life of Christ. This both terrified and excited me: it terrified me because I was in danger of exceeding the bounds of honor which Muslim orthodox teaching had allowed, and it excited me because I was following my religious inclinations. However, I was reluctant to freely pursue this path of unorthodox inquiry, and so I made a secret wish for God to save me from proceeding with it, and from the inevitable embarrassment that would result. I had started work in a government hospital, and at the end of the month I saved a few pennies from my wages and offered them to Muslim street people to pray that God would save and protect me from this attraction to the Christian gospel.

As hard as I tried, I could not run from the questions: Who died on the cross? If we don't know his name, how can we know the God who put him there? But suppose Jesus did die on the cross, and suppose God intended it to be so; how would that change our knowledge of God? I reflected on the suffering and the heartbreak which are part of life, hopes that are often dashed to pieces, for even in my relative youth I had known of tragedy in my family and in that of others, such being the precarious nature of life in an Africa just emerging from its middle ages. It seemed to me that deep down at the center and core of life, the cross and its anonymous burden was declaring something about the inner integrity and mystery of life which rang true to all authentic experience.

If we can put a face and a name to the anonymous victim of the Qur'ánic crucifixion, we could do worse than let that victim be Jesus. Of all the characters mentioned in the Holy Book, Jesus was the one for whom the cross was most intended, and therefore of all individuals, the one who came closest to it, whatever the effectiveness of the divine rescue. In such a case, it would follow that God actually did demonstrate his solidarity with humanity by visibly entering our world and defeating death itself, allowing us to understand life in a wholly new way, with redemptive love able to overcome human wickedness and reveal the true face of God. Seen in the light of the cross of Jesus Christ, all of human nature, indeed all of history, appears to gather at one sharp, poignant place. It all began to make sense to me. The need for the cross seemed so compelling and true to the way life is.

My acceptance of Jesus thus arose from the authority I accepted in the Qur'án. Much later I received a copy of the Bible as a gift, although I actually believed that the Bible, or its essence, had been lost, as the Qur'án teaches. After reading the Bible, or the portions of it I read first, namely the *Acts of the Apostles* and the *Epistle of Paul to the Romans*, I came upon the fantastic teaching of God's justification of me by faith. I was stunned by God's magnanimity, more so because I had no personal cultural pedigree in Christianity, nor could I boast of my personal ability to discover a formula for capturing God for myself.

It is hard to explain to modern people, to post-Vatican II Christians in particular, who have never known a religion of strict rules and regulations, what it felt like to be crushed beneath the burden of having to obey God's inscrutable ordinances and how, by contrast, the intervention and interposition of Jesus on the cross felt like a godsend. In a way that is hard to put into words I felt truly unshackled, released from a crippling incapacity to seek to please God. I did not know anything of formal Christian theology, but I came to see that only God can give us the grace to accept his unconditional love for us, since culture, experience, and habit will instill in us a cultivated indifference to revealed truth—precisely where Islam rubs in the salt with regard to human incompetence before God and, by implication, before those who claim to speak for God. (That is one of the reasons why the secular West feels so helpless before religious fundamentalism.)

One of the greatest stumbling blocks to a realization that God loves us as we are is our effort to be good, to impress God with our acts of service and kindness. Or sometimes we go to the other extreme. We become despondent or cynical about our sins; we confess them endlessly to God and try to play on divine pity—and thank goodness, there is plenty of it! Yet the wonderful thing is that, according to the New Testament, God loves me just as I am—this has made a tremendous difference in my life.

As might be expected, it was difficult to find a Christian community, and Muslim friends who felt scandalized by my conversion abused me harshly. In these situations God showed me that the cross of Calvary is a constant, unchangeable fact which can transform our lives at every moment, whatever the situation. A Christian writer said that we surrender not when *circumstances* are miserable but when *we* are miserable. All failure, all weakness, is a failure and weakness of internal trust. We can survive that strange midnight in which is born the strangest and most awful kind of hope. Whatever our feelings may be, God's love abides—tried and proved on the cross, set and sealed in the empty tomb. There is no escaping from, or faltering in, God's trustworthiness. This is partly the secret of the psalmist's words "Where shall I flee from thy presence?" God's presence is in the love that abides, surrounding and embracing us. The apostle John said, "See what love the Father has given us" (1 John 3:1 RSV), and the apostle Paul repeated the sentiment when he said, "God shows his love for us in that while we were yet sinners Christ died for us" (Romans 5:8 RSV). God's love is the unshakable foundation of personhood.

By assuming human form, with everything implied in that, God achieved for us a stupendous breakthrough in Jesus Christ. Rather than rendering Jesus immune to the tragedy and consequences of human disobedience, God was put at risk and, through Christ, entered human history and thus by divine self-choosing became the supreme subject and victim of history. Christ's suffering is a full-blooded encapsulation of the original divine intention of unconditional love. And by this love we are restored to fellowship with God. God, through Christ, would feel our pain and sorrow. Put to grief in the unspeakable agony of human sinfulness, Jesus became the human measure of God's capacity to take on our condition, the Suffering Servant who unenviably receives the tribute of God and the obeisance of humanity. The Suffering Servant is God's self-portrait and the unflattering witness to the wretchedness into which history has fallen, as the catastrophes of the twentieth century bear witness.

Our perception of this truth is indispensable to our obtaining a right and fulfilling relationship with God. Redemptive suffering is at the very core of moral truth and of personal integrity, and the prophets were all touched by its fearsome power. But only one embodied it as a historical experience, although all, including the prophet of Islam in his historical trials and tribulations, walk in its shadow. Those who consult their hearts will hear for themselves the persistent ordinance proclaiming God's ineffable grace.

The apostle Paul speaks of us as pots of earthenware containing a treasure: the gift of "God with us." If we are grasped by the truth which alone can set us free, then it is incumbent on us to make that the proof of our faithfulness in history and community, in sharing and service.

After further study of Islam and Arabic in England and in Lebanon, I went back to Africa, seeking to help churches get closer to Muslim communities. When we really come to know God's love as expressed in Christ, we want to testify to it and to place ourselves at the service of God and our fellows. The only way we can make God known is by sharing with others the way God gives himself to us—sacrificially, lovingly, affirmingly, solicitously.

I began my Christian life with the firm conviction that God was leading me to ordination. However, it became clear that I would have to seek another path of fulfilling my vocation. After my formal academic training I started teaching, first in vocational centers concerned with Christian-Muslim relations, and then in academic appointments at universities in Africa and Britain. Eventually I was invited to the Center for the Study of World Religions at Harvard, where I taught courses in the Divinity School. I was able to return to my interest in theology and included it in my historical work on religion. While at Harvard the idea occurred to me to write what eventually became *Translating the Message* (1989), now in its fifth edition.

There were a number of outstanding issues in *Translating the Message* that I felt needed attention. The result is my recently published book *Encountering the West: Christianity and the Global Cultural Process*. My experience of teaching at Harvard was at the root of the formulations I have advanced in *Encountering the West*. The major challenge for Christianity in our society, I felt, was not science, narrowly defined, but the attitude that culture, our kind of culture, is capable of compensating for the loss of religious faith and indeed of replacing religion altogether. I saw many of us willing to settle for culture as the ultimate source of personal identity, and for the secular national state, defined in ethnic or racial terms, as the highest form of individual obligation. This cultural attitude disarms the gospel by reducing religion to cultural forms or by elevating cultural forms into normative standards. Religious reductionism thus opens the way for cultural absolutization and the corruption that afflicts both religion and culture. I felt I ought to say something about how the cultural implications of Christian translatability may offer relevant insights on the distinction we ought to draw between the absolute and the relative, the universal and the particular, truth and values, the one and the many.

One of the most vexing questions for my generation of Harvard faculty and students was whether Christian distinctiveness does conflict with the demands for pluralism and diversity and therefore whether Christian missions were an exercise in intolerance and bigotry. The uncomfortable conclusion from this line of reasoning is often that all those who converted to Christianity in Africa and Asia were disloyal to their own cultures and were evidence, too, of Western religious imperialism. Many of us at Harvard carried with us this silent, implicit embargo on those forms of Christianity that resulted from the Christian missionary movement, even though the norms of liberalism we practiced required our acceptance of Africans and Asians, among others, whether Christian or not.

Many of us did not see the irony of judging the fate of hundreds of millions of African and Asian Christians by our own a priori convictions rather than by the rules of inclusiveness and giving space to others to speak for themselves. Thus did these colonized populations become twice stigmatized, once under colonial subjugation and once again in the anti-missionary prejudice of enlightened liberalism. Even if I only wanted to rescue liberalism from this contradiction, let alone help them to question the wholesale dismissal of the history of the missionary movement, I would have to lower their barriers of hostility towards so complex and vast a movement. Harvard changed the course of my professional life for good by confronting me so starkly with this issue and with the double duty it laid upon me. And since I also see the hand of God in all this, I have to say that Harvard was God's instrument for what has become an absorbing and fulfilling field of academic endeavor for me and my colleagues in this country and around the world.

In *Encountering the West* I attempted to describe how I view my vocation in terms of my multicultural roots. The book is something of a personal intellectual testament by one who was educated on four continents and who carries within him some of the formative strands of several distinct cultural traditions (the African, the Islamic, the Christian, and the modern West). Often these four strands are unalterably intertwined, and when one strand is drawn out to provide a perspective, the others resonate in sympathy and can result in synthesis. Such multiculturalism is becoming increasingly common in our thrust towards global mutuality.

One of the consequences of this education, for me, is that I find the notion of cultural purity, and the attendant exclusiveness, unsatisfactory and untrue to life—whether in the exclusion of the religious from the secular or in the complete identification of the two.

As I reflect, I praise God for the way he raised me up and for everything he has given me. I praise him, too, for all the tremendous gifts and treasures bestowed on me in the discipline of my Muslim upbringing. He wants me to use these gifts to his glory, to declare that the inner secret of all my upbringing is Christ Jesus, enthroned on the right hand of God, and to declare this in love, in humility, in patience, in service, and in thanksgiving—in everything giving thanks to the Lord.

Power and Gender at the Divinity School

— JOHN RANKIN —

I saw how many women have only experienced the Bible as the bludgeon of male chauvinists.

John Rankin earned a Th.M. at Harvard Divinity School in 1991. John and his wife and four children live in the northwest hills outside Hartford, Connecticut. He has also received an M.Div. at Gordon-Conwell Theological Seminary. John is president of the Theological Education Institute, a private school designed to bring the fruit of a seminary education to the community, with particular emphasis on equipping the church for social outreach and dialogue.

John also sponsors the Mars Hill Forum series on university campuses, where he invites leading skeptics to pose him their toughest questions.

Power and Gender
at the Divinity School

— JOHN RANKIN —

When I began my theological degree at Harvard Divinity School in 1987, I did so precisely to make an evangelical faith accountable to a theological challenge.

Though raised in a macro-evolutionary, agnostic, Unitarian context, I came to faith in Jesus Christ in 1967 at age fourteen. It was in the Episcopal liturgy at prep school in western Connecticut where I had my first exposure to Christian orthodoxy.

My pilgrimage began with an intense prayer life. I first heard the gospel preached by black evangelist Tom Skinner in 1970, when for the first time I learned that there were others who believed as I did. Through involvement in Fellowship of Christians in Universities and Schools (FOCUS) and InterVarsity Christian Fellowship (IVCF), I became grounded in my faith before pursuing my M.Div. at Gordon-Conwell Theological Seminary on the North Shore of Boston.

In college at Denison University, I majored in history and also took many classes in religion. I studied under one professor who personally studied under Rudolf Bultmann, and another professor who studied under Paul Tillich. This exposure to liberal theology, and the lack of any rigid "dogmatisms" in my youth, was helpful in my later studies.

First, since my coming to faith was both intellectual and supernatural in nature, I was eager to pose and think through hard questions. I knew God to be true, and believed that truth never fears being challenged, and that truth alone can afford understatement.

Second, my faith did not begin with a doctrine concerning the inerrancy of Scripture. Rather it began with a personal relationship with Jesus Christ, and as I became introduced to Scripture, its authority became clear to me. Thus, as I studied Scripture and was exposed to its most severe critics, I saw its divine inspiration in the classical evangelical sense. This is important, for I am convinced that in our apologetics the starting point is not the argument of Scripture's inspiration but the demonstration of it through love, a sound mind, and spiritual power. The Bible is so powerfully true in all it claims, and so beautiful in its revelation of the God who loves us, that the greatest challenge for Christians is not to dogmatize about it in the face of skeptics but to live it.

Third, coming into the evangelical milieu from the outside, I was always encouraging fellow believers to be more confident in their faith. By that I mean that many Christians choose the safest route in this life, allowing certain enculturations of their faith in order to gain various measures of worldly acceptance. This is true in arenas of scholarship as well as family life and the workplace. If we truly believe Christ is risen, then we will brook no compromise with this worldly system. Our proclamation of faith will be bold, loving, and unambiguous, and we will become effective salt and light for the kingdom of God.

When I went to Harvard Divinity School, at the recommendation of Krister Sairsingh, I was eager to make my faith accountable and to learn more in the process. Krister and I also believed that those who think the least of the gospel can often only open up to its love if first they are able to pose their toughest intellectual questions.

Currently I am working on a book, *The Ethics of Choice*. These biblical ethics are rooted in Genesis 2:16–17, where the first words in human history, of God to Adam, are positive words of freedom. "In feasting you shall feast" (literal Hebrew: *akol tokel*) is the only positive definition of freedom among origin texts that I have found. Other world religions start with negative freedom, freedom from being violated, as opposed to freedom for creativity and joyous choices. This is one of many confirmations of the divine inspiration of Genesis 1–3 and all Scripture. It begins before the human experience of sin and brokenness.

One central aspect of the ethics of choice is the reality that God does not force his love upon us—it is always a gift. I believe that the most potent objection to the gospel in our culture is "Don't impose your religion on me." This fear of coercion drives many people away from even hearing the gospel, and since the image of God is made for choosing God's love and not being forced into it, such an objection should concern us deeply.

It was these biblical ethics I wanted to test at Harvard Divinity School. I believed that if the gospel is true, and if I had a reasonable grasp of its essence, then I would only prosper in my faith by studying in such a context. And this is what happened. Harvard Divinity School has no creed, it is a prime place for the training of Unitarian-Universalist ministers, and it welcomes many homosexual students. If there was one unifying theme at Harvard "Div," it was opposition to the "trinity" of evil in our society—racism, sexism, and classism. No bigotry was allowed against anyone, except for the periodic bash against "fundamentalism." There were quite a number of evangelicals studying there, too. But, in truth, most kept a low profile and avoided theological conflict vis-à-vis the distinctives of an evangelical confession. Perhaps I had too much temerity or naïveté (or faith?), and I waded right into an unabashed apologetic for evangelical Christianity.

The first semester, I signed up for a class, "Religion and American Public Life," taught by Dean Ronald Theimann, an excellent professor. He set the stage for the students to give oral presentations of papers they had written.

My first presentation was a paper on Richard John Neuhaus' landmark book *The Naked Public Square*. In that context I suggested that evangelical Christians were uniquely free not to force their faith on others. Our basis for such freedom rests on the conviction that we do not defend God's truth but it is his truth that defends our faith. Accordingly, we are secure in faith, and we do not need to convince others just to reinforce our beliefs. We seek to persuade others simply because of the nature of God's love for them.

I then said that the only people who seek to force their beliefs on others, by whatever means, are those who are insecure in what they believe. They are, in some measure, captives to a herd mentality. I expanded this idea by noting that only a biblically based faith has the ethics for such loving confidence, and that those who pull away from the plenary inspiration of Scripture pull away into insecurity and, ultimately, coercive ethics in issues of public policy.

After I was done, one student passionately protested. He said that if I truly believed there was a heaven and a hell as described in Scripture, then I should take people like him and bang their heads against a brick wall until they believed (metaphorically speaking, of course).

My reply was that if I could do that or would do that, the only result would be a cracked skull (again, metaphorically speaking). Belief must be chosen, and indeed, when one looks at the ethics of heaven and hell in Scripture, one discovers the terrific love of God whereby the only people who go to hell are those who refused to go to heaven—those for whom self-righteous bitterness was chosen over humble reconciliation.[1] The rest of the class agreed with me ethically, and Dr. Theimann gave a hearty amen, not to my evangelical faith but, again, to its ethics.

My most instructive experience at Harvard Div was a class in "Property and Christian Ethics." Actually there was not much "Christian" in the ethics, as a disclaimer given at the beginning of the class made clear. It was indeed a class in feminist ethics, taught by a visiting scholar, Janet Farrell Smith, and that is why I took the class. We were thirteen women and two men.

---

[1] C. S. Lewis examines the moral nature of hell in similar fashion in his delightful book *The Great Divorce*.

One reason I studied feminist ethics, both before and during my time at Harvard, is that I believe that the evangelical pro-life worldview has not addressed the reasons why women might be attracted to ideological feminism. We have excelled through crisis pregnancy centers in reaching out to many women. But how can others hear unless we understand and love them and give opportunity for the love of Christ to transcend their pain? It is too easy in the theological and political polarizations of the day to simply hurl rhetorical missiles at those on the "other side" of an issue. This is not the nature of truly biblical faith.

In the class itself, I was once respectfully challenged by a couple of women students as to why I was an evangelical, given that I seemed to be "a nice guy and intellectually competent." Thus, how could I believe the Bible was inspired by a loving God, since it was so clearly written by male chauvinists? I responded that they misunderstood the nature of Scripture, and they responded by challenging me to read two books which they were sure would convince me otherwise. The books were *Bread Not Stone* by Elisabeth Schüssler Fiorenza and *Texts of Terror* by Phyllis Trible.

So I read them, was challenged by their passion and erudition, and decided to do my term paper in response. It also became part of my double thesis for the Th.M. degree, entitled *Feminism, the Bible, and Definitions of Power*.

Schüssler Fiorenza approaches Scripture with a "hermeneutics of suspicion," saying that whatever portion of Scripture does not affirm women according to a certain definition must be jettisoned. She looks for a "canon within the canon" that is free of patriarchy and male dominance. Trible reviews four Old Testament texts where signal evil is done against certain women, and concludes this is because the God of the Old Testament is the creation of a patriarchy which seeks the dehumanization of women. I have to admit, these critiques were most challenging, but only insofar as true biblical hermeneutics were overlooked.

Namely, whether one is evangelical or liberal, it is clear that Genesis 1–3 is the interpretive foundation of all Scripture. In these chapters, the cardinal doctrines of creation, sin, and redemption are introduced and defined. Whether or not one takes these chapters as historically accurate and divinely revealed, as I do, or as mythological, as do Schüssler Fiorenza and Trible, Scripture nonetheless on its own terms distinguishes between the order of creation on the one hand and its reversal in the introduction of human sin on the other.

Thus, male chauvinism and a whole host of other sins are described in the Old Testament, but as the result of sin. The Old Testament saints are not plastic figures, demigods of unreality, but real people with faith in the midst of their sins. Scripture is uniquely candid and evenhanded with all people.

Accordingly, when we take Scripture on its own terms, with a "hermeneutics of trust," we see how male chauvinism is the result of sin. We also see how all power that God the Creator uses, masculine pronoun and all, is only the power to bless and benefit us as his image-bearers, never to trample and destroy. Only Genesis, among all world religions, affirms the humanity of women as made in God's image, joint heirs of eternal life with men. Other world religions in their origin texts do no better than to treat women as dust, demons, animals, and/or less than men in intrinsic worth. This is one reason why theological feminists such as Schüssler Fiorenza and Trible love Genesis 1:26–28. Their hermeneutic failure, I maintained in that paper, was not taking into account Genesis 3:16, which shows the "war between the sexes" beginning as the immediate fruit of sin.

I made an oral presentation of this thesis in class, and when I was finished, there was a moment of silence. Then one woman leaned forward and said, "That sounds so good—are you sure it is biblical?"

As I unpacked this question and began listening to my classmates, I began to see how so many women have only experienced the Bible as the bludgeon of male chauvinists. They saw the Bible as the fictional account of a patriarchal God, created by men for the exploitation of women. I received no criticisms, by the students or professor, that I was inaccurate in my view of what Scripture truly says on its own terms.

My time at Harvard Divinity School was delightful. I found that the gospel, when presented on its own beautiful terms and in eager accountability to the skeptics and violated alike, only prospered my faith.

Through this process, and in view of my present ministry on college campuses and in political activism, I have concluded that the most potent and attractive apologetic for the gospel revolves around the articulation of Genesis 1–3 in contrast to competing worldviews and in the context of current cultural debates. In comparison with the origin texts of all other religions, as received and understood on their own terms, only Genesis has a positive definition of human nature, human freedom, women, verifiable history, the scientific method, and a definition of law that opposes tyranny.

From such a basis, we can represent Jesus as the one who came not to condemn (Satan does that) but to save. In Christ is the "yes" and "amen," and if we want to help dispel the darkness in this culture, it will not be by character assassinations, polarized partisanships, or idolatries of certain political positions. It will be by the love of Christ positively preached, with our partisanships always openly stated and always accountable to being humbly cross-examined, by friend and foe alike, in the sight of God, in whom all truth resides.

CHAPTER 6

MONEY, RACE, AND
THE GOSPEL OF MERCY

From Prophets to Profits at Harvard Business School
Robert K. Massie Jr.

In Sorrow, Joy   *Ruth Goodwin*

Conversion: One Journey Outside the Gate   *Jeffrey Barneson*

Salvation to the Streets   *Anthony Parker*

I want to cry out loudly to my colleagues and students:

"Do not serve Harvard, but God and his beloved Jesus Christ, and speak words of hope to those who suffer from loneliness, depression, and spiritual poverty." But I myself have come to the painful discovery that when I am chained by ambition it is hard for me to see those who are chained by poverty.

HENRI NOUWEN, *SEEDS OF HOPE*

ॐ

Blessed are the poor in spirit, for theirs is the kingdom of heaven.
Blessed are those who mourn, for they will be comforted.
Blessed are the meek, for they will inherit the earth.
Blessed are those who hunger and thirst for righteousness,
    for they will be filled.
Blessed are the merciful, for they will be shown mercy.
Blessed are the pure in heart, for they will see God.
Blessed are the peacemakers, for they will be called sons of God.

JESUS, THE GOSPEL OF MATTHEW

From Prophets to Profits at Harvard Business School

৯৩৫

— R O B E R T K . M A S S I E J R . —

Human beings can never be happy as long as they build their
lives around false gods—that is, things that seem to grant life or
power but in fact cannot.

In the fall of 1984 **Robert K. Massie Jr.**, a young Episcopal priest
from New York City, enrolled as a doctoral student at the Harvard
Business School. He went on to serve as a Harvard University Fellow
in Ethics and the Professions in 1987, to complete his doctorate in
business policy in 1989, and to initiate and direct "The Project on
Business, Values, and the Economy," which is a program of The Center for Values in Public Life at Harvard Divinity School.

Professor Massie has also taught at Yale Divinity School, where
he completed his master of divinity in 1982. He earned his A.B. in
European history, at Princeton University in 1978. He frequently
writes and lectures internationally on ethics in public policy, the history of the South African divestment movement, and medical and
business ethics.

His parents, Robert K. and Suzanne, coauthored *Journey*, a novel
about their experiences as a family coping with the challenge of
Bob's hemophilia. Their interest in the disease also inspired them to
write *Nicholas and Alexandra*, first published in 1967.

From Prophets to Profits

— ROBERT K. MASSIE JR. —

On the fourth day of classes our marketing professor, Mark Albion, inquired of the members of Section F whether or not we would like to introduce ourselves to one another. After all, he said, we were going to be spending an entire school year together in the same room, and we might like to know who our section-mates were.

As we went around the room I counted two lawyers, eight consultants, nine accountants, seventeen engineers, and twenty-three bankers. Twenty-five of my classmates had gone to Ivy League schools, and thirty-five had majored in economics or business administration. Of those who had worked for large corporations before business school, four had worked for oil companies, three had worked for Procter & Gamble, three had worked for IBM, and two were currently on leave from General Motors.

One fellow had been a captain in the Cold Stream Guards and had led a platoon in Northern Ireland; another, a Marine Corps lieutenant who had served in Beirut at the time of the airport bombing. Also among our ranks were an architect, a Canadian ski instructor, an Australian veterinarian, a former assistant to the prime minister of Japan, and me—an Episcopal priest who had left a position at Grace Church on Tenth Street in Manhattan to pursue graduate studies in the relationship between economics and Christianity. Figuring I could always return to the parish, I leapt into an experimental year at the West Point of corporate capitalism, the Harvard Business School.

Before I was permitted to begin doctoral work, the school understandably felt that I ought to learn some of the basics about business, and so they placed me in the first year of the M.B.A. program. Thus it was that in September of 1984 I found myself sitting with eighty-eight other nervous "first years" in the windowless amphitheater known as Aldrich 8.

During my first few days at Harvard, I could not stop thinking about a woman I had known my last summer weeks in New York. She used to sit curled up in a ball in an alcove just to the left of the front steps of Grace Church. The smell of urine and the clouds of flies were overpowering. Even when the temperature reached ninety degrees, she huddled in her filthy winter overcoat, and she never touched the small cups of water and juice I would bring to her. At night or in a rainstorm she would disappear, but she would always return in the morning.

I tried to speak to her, but she never responded to anyone—that is, until a New York City medical team arrived, and then she cursed them violently and insisted she was fine and just wanted to be left alone. And so she sat on the steps, and every day I would talk to her and bring her water that she did not drink, until finally the summer ended and I moved away.

The truth is that I barely remember what happened those first weeks. Suddenly I was yanked from the cool Gothic halls of Grace Church, where my days had been spent preaching, teaching, counseling, and working with the destitute street people of New York, and I was dropped into the world of a business school, with its perplexing courses on marketing, accounting, managerial economics, and organizational behavior. Instead of relying on the language of theology, a language filled with words such as salvation, redemption, forgiveness, and grace, I was abruptly required to speak with an entirely new vocabulary, which consisted of phrases such as depreciation tax shield, cumulative probability distribution curve, product cannibalization, net present value, and subordinated convertible debenture. Instead of pondering the apostle Paul's logic in his letter to the Romans, I found myself designing a consumer and trade promotion campaign for Vaseline Petroleum Jelly.

It was also my fortune (or misfortune, depending on whom you talk to) to belong to the first M.B.A. class to be required to purchase individual personal computers. In the summer we had all been mailed archly worded letters announcing that we would be expected to buy an IBM portable computer, through the university, for a mere $3,200. At about the same time, an article appeared in the *Wall Street Journal,* questioning the machine's value, popularity, and future prospects. A spokeswoman for IBM responded with what she considered decisive evidence of the portable's merits: the Harvard Business School was ordering eight hundred for its incoming students. Even I, a computer illiterate, realized that this was not an auspicious sign.

Since I had touched a computer only two or three times in my life, I brought mine home in early September and approached it with some of the awe one might expect from a Cro-Magnon man before a TV set. Fortunately I was able to assemble it, figure out that a floppy disk was something one put in a disk drive, and find the "on" switch. I was immensely reassured when the floppy disk "Exploring Your IBM Personal Computer" began its little tutorial with a squeaky rendition of the opening bars of Mozart's Fortieth Symphony.

In the opening weeks of class I also discovered that the Business School relies exclusively on the case method to teach business skills. This means that you are confronted with a detailed account (including reams of numbers and charts) of some business problem an executive is facing. You must begin by figuring out what's going on (often the most difficult task), then somehow derive a solution, and finally prepare some remarks so that you will have something to say if you are the hapless student chosen at random to make the opening presentation the next morning. The analytical process is repeated with little variation approximately four hundred times during the school year, giving rise to a famous school adage: "First they scare you to death, then they work you to death, then they bore you to death."

The Business School gives tremendous weight (often fifty percent of one's grade) to classroom participation, and I realized early on that I would have to overcome my paralyzed silence. This was difficult, because my classmates who had the benefit of several years in business were hurling words and concepts around the room with alarming and ferocious alacrity.

Even more difficult than mastering the language was the problem of what identity I should adopt in the classroom. I had made it very clear on my application that I was not leaving the ministry and that I intended to teach or return to the parish, but the moment I began classes at Harvard, I became an anomaly wherever I went. At Business School I was peculiar because I was a minister; with church friends and other ministers, however, I was equally peculiar because I was in business school. This tension between the life of faith and the life of business was exactly what I had come to the Business School to reflect on, but it was distressing to find the tension so soon and within my own person. I found it very tricky to know how to act in class.

Once in a while I spoke up about what I thought were broader political or ethical issues raised by the cases. Was it really necessary to close this plant and throw hundreds of people out of work? Did any sane human being really want overpriced deodorant socks to be conveniently available in supermarkets? What effect might these massive shampoo-marketing efforts we were planning have on the families we had targeted? Isn't it possible that this highly profitable hospital chain might be earning money by excluding the poor? The class seemed to tolerate my outbursts but rarely supported them.

Once I tried to break out of the mold of class ethicist, just to see what it was like. We were discussing the problems of a men's cologne that was declining in popularity. I raised my hand and said, "It's all image and air anyway, so let's capture that air with a campaign built on the most expensive sort of snob appeal." The professor looked startled. "This, from a man of your background?" he said. The class laughed.

I still don't know whether he meant it as a compliment or a reproof. In any case, I never again recommended something I didn't believe in. I stuck to the role I had been granted as a liberal bellwether, a miner's canary who, as long as he didn't pipe up or keel over, certified that ethical boundaries were being respected.

With all the long hours of class, there was lots of time to look around the room and daydream. One thing that always struck me was the abnormal percentage of physically attractive people at the Business School. The men are generally tall, square of jaw, and highly athletic; the women are distinctively attractive and frequently preppy. Rare indeed were unshapely figures, stringy hair, nondescript faces, pasty complexions—to say nothing of disability or disease or the other signs of human mortality. The people at the Business School actually looked like the people in ads for Caribbean vacations or for expensive liquor; they looked like *winners.*

Sometimes in my daydreams I would remember what it was like to stand in my vestments in the sanctuary of Grace Church, with the great *Te Deum* window behind me, the long nave aisle leading to the rose window of the narthex before me. On the table in front of me lay the polished silver paten and chalice given by generations now long gone, the fair white linen, the open prayer book, and the simple sacramental elements of bread and wine. I remember the powerful sound of five hundred voices singing:

> Holy, holy, holy Lord,
> God of power and might,
> Heaven and earth are full of your glory.
> Hosanna in the highest.
> Blessed is he who comes in the name of the Lord.
> Hosanna in the highest.

I would watch the people approach the altar rail, all sorts of people—the young and the old, the mighty and the frail, the honored and the despised, the joyful and the tortured—all would kneel, all would stretch out their hands to receive something that a material world cannot give: hope, forgiveness, and deliverance. All would come, and I had the privilege to glimpse their eyes and see their longing assuaged, not through anything I had done but through some mysterious yet evident love that was reaching out to them.

As the year progressed I got to know the students better, and the more friends I made, the more I suffered from a dilemma. On an individual basis, I found many of my section-mates to be truly charming and thoughtful people. Despite the competitive pressures, mathematically minded students willingly helped those who were struggling with numbers. When a student's mother and a professor's father died during the school year, the outpouring of emotions and donations was immediate and genuine. Some people even found time to participate in volunteer activities, such as becoming a Big Brother or organizing a blood drive.

I benefited all through the year from many people's friendship and assistance. Joel Poznansky, for example, picked me up and drove me to school on several days when I had hurt my knee. The night before the accounting final, Jeremy Freedman spent an hour with me on the phone and cleared up some of my questions, thereby allowing me to squeak through. And I was delighted when a dozen classmates from almost as many denominations formed a little Bible study and fellowship group. We met every Tuesday for lunch and talked about our backgrounds, our beliefs, and our doubts. Before each exam we would briefly meet to pray, to ask God for perspective on the whole ordeal.

Some of my classmates offered me the opportunity to minister to them in moments of personal distress. One woman described her painful separation from her husband and daughter; another man told me in moving detail about the death of his father. On different occasions three people burst into tears as we talked, pouring out fears about their futures, and frustrations with the relentless pressure of the first year. And at least a third of the class approached me at one time or another to tell me privately that they agreed with some objection I had raised in class and to confess that they found it difficult to know how to support such objections.

During one three-day case series, we studied a cold remedy that introduced no new medical features into the marketplace and whose advertising budget would represent sixty percent of its retail price. I decided to keep quiet and see what people would say. After the second day, nine people came up to me separately to inquire why I had not yet objected to this "piece of crap." I encouraged them to speak up, but they blushed. Even one professor remarked, again privately, that the product was terrible. But in three days of class, no one openly objected.

And thus the dilemma: privately and personally the students were warm human beings, but publicly many adopted aggressive, cynical, and callous styles. In the fall we saw a movie on the coal miners' strike in Harlan County, Kentucky, and the sight of the overweight miners' wives brought wave after wave of cackling derision. When, in a discussion of textile workers in England, it was revealed that a woman who had sewed for twelve years for one hundred dollars a week might lose her job, the class was almost unanimous in its feeling that she deserved to be laid off, since she was being paid too much.

Moreover, all day long the students talked about money. Discussions about money in "Managerial Economics" or "Control" (the Business School's term for accounting) or "Finance" always had a clinical quality, as though money were a force with its own properties and principles, like electricity. At meals, though, the conversation would turn to money as something to be pursued for the freedom and pleasure it gave. People would talk about how much a person used to make or how much someone had inherited or how much they would earn. At one lunch students were surprised and titillated to hear that a second-year student graduating in the class of 1985 had "broken the barrier of 100 K" by landing a job with an investment bank for what turned out to be a starting salary of $140,000. One day I asked a fellow student what he most wanted to do in life. "What I most want to do is make a great deal of money," he said amiably.

To keep my sense of perspective, I tried, with uneven success, to maintain a regular discipline of daily prayer and Bible readings. The morning before my finance exam the lectionary pointed me to a passage in the gospel of Mark:

> As [Jesus] was starting out on a journey, a stranger ran up, and, kneeling before him, asked, "Good Master, what must I do to win eternal life?" Jesus said to him . . . "You know the commandments: 'Do not murder; do not commit adultery; do not steal; do not give false evidence; do not defraud; honour your father and mother.'" "But, Master," he replied, "I have kept all these since I was a boy." Jesus looked straight at him; his heart warmed to him, and he said, "One thing you lack: go, sell everything you have, and give to the poor, and you will have riches in heaven; and come, follow me." At these words his face fell and he went away with a heavy heart; for he was a man of great wealth.

It might seem unfair to generalize about the attitudes of sixteen hundred M.B.A. students. Though the students as a whole were conservative, there was a smattering of liberals dispersed through the sections. Though the general attitude toward ethics was that it wasted time, there were some students who thought and said otherwise. By the end of the year, however, I came to feel that these students were the exception that proved the rule and that there was a strongly shared perspective, a faith, as it were, common to almost everyone there.

The first article of faith in the HBS doctrine was an unquestioning conviction concerning the economic and moral superiority of large-scale corporate capitalism. The basic justice and integrity of current economic arrangements were never publicly challenged. There were many corollary tenets to this central creed, notably that:

- Competition is always the most efficient means of distributing resources.
- Government is always inefficient and something to be reduced, controlled, and mocked.

- Monopolies are bad if you are on the buying end but good if you can achieve them in your own industries (this is called building market share).
- American workers are fat, slow, and inefficient, and labor unions are a destructive force.
- Poverty and unemployment are the result of inefficiency and primarily the fault of the poor and the unemployed.
- Almost any marketing or promotional campaign can be justified on the grounds that if a consumer actually buys the product, it must be to fulfill some "need."
- Individual greed always aggregates to a larger good, therefore the rabid pursuit of materialism is only a good thing.
- The earth's resources exist to be used by those who are aggressive and smart enough to get to them first.

Since the case method requires the professor to ask questions and play students' responses off each other, I often wondered how my professors really felt about these matters. Were they also so cynical? Did they endorse the primitive social Darwinism that prevailed among the M.B.A. students?

By Christmastime I got up the nerve to visit different professors to inquire about the curriculum and about their feelings on ethics in business. Many of them, in contrast to the students, were eager to talk about the profound moral and philosophical problems in modern business. I even detected a certain frustration with the students' narrow focus.

The more I talked to the professors and listened to their comments in class, the more it seemed that they had a definite mission they were seeking to achieve through the design of the curriculum. Not only did they intend to turn out well-rounded general managers, but many of them also hoped by doing so to arrest or reverse America's decline as a manufacturing nation and world competitor. The constant theme in the case material was that Japanese firms have outperformed American firms because they have designed marketing programs that are more responsive to consumers, organizations that are more sensitive to employees, and factories that take seriously the contributions to quality and production offered by workers. The message to us was direct and simple: American managers must become more attentive listeners, more humble, more interested in the long term than the short, and more devoted to the company's success than to their own careers.

Although this was what the curriculum stressed, the *culture* at the Business School, harking back to an earlier, more arrogant time, emphasized the reverse. Students were graded on a forced bell curve, which rewarded people with prior training and work experience and automatically failed the bottom ten to fifteen percent in each class. The stereotype most admired by students was that of the "tough, hands-on manager," someone who justifies his or her high pay by being the crisis solver, the problem fixer, and the head basher.

At no period is the emphasis on individual success and achievement more evident than in the frenzied winter mating season, when recruiters arrive on campus. Throughout the fall students rewrite and edit their résumés, join organizations such as the Finance Club, the Marketing Club, the Investment Banking Club, and the Venture Capital Club (in part to get their names included in special club books), and pore over annual reports and lists of alumni in the Career Research Center. Then the recruiters arrive and the students begin a swirling dance of first-, second-, and third-round interviews and callbacks that lasts for three weeks. Attention is paid to the most minute details of performance and appearance. "I was going out the door to an interview," recounted one friend, "and my roommate stopped me and asked me with alarm, 'What are you doing!?' I didn't know what he was talking about. 'You can't go to an interview with a bank wearing BROWN SHOES!' He made me change them."

Occasionally I came to the Business School in a suit, because I had appointments in town immediately after class, and each time, my section-mates playfully inquired if I had "given in" and decided to interview with Goldman Sachs or McKinsey. "Come on, Bob," one good friend of mine said. "Those consulting jobs look pretty good, don't they? Wouldn't it be fun to tell other companies what to do? Wouldn't you like to make $1,300 a week for a summer job?"

Though I usually responded that I would be working as a research assistant during the summer, I inwardly agreed: it *would* be fun. And my wife, Dana, and I could use the money. Our rent took half her pay as a professor, our television displayed fuzz, and our car looked like it had barely survived an air raid.

But whenever I would start to fantasize or worry about "all the money I really deserved to be making," I would look through the Bible, and the fever would leave me. One passage that struck me combined words of warning with words of support:

> We brought nothing into the world, so that we can take nothing out of it; but if we have food and clothing, we may rest content. But those who want to be rich fall into temptation and are trapped by many senseless and harmful desires that plunge people into ruin and destruction. For the love of money is a root of all kinds of evil, and in their eagerness to be rich some have wandered away from the faith and pierced themselves

with many pains. But you, man of God, must shun all this, and pursue
justice, godliness, fidelity, love, fortitude, and gentleness.

FROM PAUL'S FIRST LETTER TO TIMOTHY

The spectacle of hundreds of students desperately searching for work
was not without irony when one remembered the ease with which these
same students proposed shutting plants and firing workers who had been
employed for twenty-five years. The students, however, do not consider
themselves to be in the same league (dare I say species?) as workers; they
have become *managers*. Having put up as much as $40,000 for tuition,
endured two years of cases and cold calls, and earned a degree from Harvard, they feel they *deserve* a job. They believe that they are now entitled to
a high salary and to the unquestioned right to make decisions about other
people's lives.

That pervasive sense of entitlement bothered me more than anything
else. It made me realize that as much as I loved being a member of Section
F, as proudly as I wore my "F Troop" baseball cap, the sectional system is
designed to create and reinforce a sense of managerial elitism. High pressure
and close contact for nine months create bonds, and the bonds create a
sense of a peer group, and the peer group forms a culture that sets it off
from the rest of the world. Like those who have been through boot camp or
some peculiar initiation rite, the students who survive the first year at the
Harvard Business School become the members of a club, and by definition,
a member of a club is a better person than a nonmember.

I came to the Business School because I had stood outside of the corporate club for years and criticized it. I had criticized it in part because I did
not understand what businesses actually did and because I had been on the
receiving end of business activity all my life—of its products, its advertising, its pollution, its political clout. After my year at Harvard, I understand
more and so I am less critical about some things. I now understand, for
example, how extraordinarily difficult it is to run a business, how many
complex and divergent parts—finance, marketing, sales, production, distribution—all have to be coordinated. And I have come to believe that there
is nothing wrong and, in fact, much that is good about a few people coming together, pooling their resources, and trying to provide a service or a
product for which they earn a return on their investment. In other words,
I have become a fan of small business.

However, the question I brought to the Business School—what is the
relationship between such economic activities and the Christian faith?—is
going to require a good deal more work. For one thing, the question has
been debated by theologians since the beginning of the church; it is a derivative of the thorny problem of how closely or distantly the church should

participate in the institutions of the world. Over the centuries some have argued, at one extreme, for complete withdrawal from society, whereas others have simply baptized whatever the culture approves as good with a sprinkling of holy water.

For the serious person of faith who commutes between a church on Sunday and a corporate job on weekdays, who is drawn by the hope and joy and freedom of the gospel yet must live amidst the rules of the marketplace, such extreme answers offer little solace. Church leaders fortunate enough to have money to set aside cannot escape the difficult question of how to invest those funds in a manner consistent with their beliefs. And on a global level, no person who professes that all human beings are beloved children of the same God can be complacent in a world where hundreds of millions live in subhuman poverty.

As the year progressed I came to realize that the most profound question posed by a place like the Harvard Business School is a question common to every human endeavor: what greater goal or God are we individually and collectively called to serve in life? The biblical logic that governs my faith says simply that human beings can never be happy as long as they build their lives around false gods—that is, things that seem to grant life or power but in fact cannot.

And so as a minister in a business school, I found myself wondering all year what the school is really teaching. Some might argue that it communicates a useful and value-free body of knowledge the same way a school for auto mechanics communicates certain functional skills. But an alternative view occurred to me when once during the course of the year I returned to a gathering of the members of Grace Church, and someone welcomed me back as "one of our three seminarians who have gone off to study." Another speaker commented, "I know we live in Orwellian times and war is peace, but I never thought I would hear the Harvard Business School described as a seminary. But I don't know. Maybe it's true."

Author's note: Things have changed at the Harvard Business School since this article was written. First-year students are now introduced to the ethical dilemmas of management in a module at the beginning of their required curriculum.

In Sorrow, Joy

৵৽

— RUTH GOODWIN —

*I decided I could not live the rest of my life being motivated by
anger. There had to be another way.*

Ruth Goodwin came to Harvard Business School on Fulbright and
Frank Knox Scholarships, from a career in international development
assistance with the Australian Foreign Affairs department. She served
in Ethiopia in the mid-1980s during the ongoing famine.

After graduating from business school in 1992, Ruth and other
Christian graduate students learned from and served the poor along
with inner-city churches in the Bronx and Coney Island. Remaining
in New York, she now works with Women's World Banking, which
aids women in development around the world.

This story was first drafted during the Gulf War in the United Arab
Emirates, where Ruth traveled to be with her parents, who are professors and fourth-generation medical missionaries among those with
leprosy and other diseases. Ruth completed the article when she
returned to Harvard after the Gulf War ended.

In Sorrow, Joy

— RUTH GOODWIN —

We were standing on a plain high in the rift valley mountains of Ethiopia; a cold wind was blowing and the sky was overcast. The surrounding mountains were grey-brown and barren; the military lookout posts were the only signs of life on the mountains. Even the village was almost deserted except for the military. But there, on the plain, sitting silently in orderly groups, were thirty-five thousand people. People devastated by their circumstances, haggard and gaunt, dressed only in grey-brown cotton, with no shoes. People waiting in hope of food. It was a morning in early 1988; the world had long forgotten there was drought or war here.

Our attention was drawn to an emaciated man, young girl, and woman clutching a bundle of grey-brown rags, hunched under a grey-brown blanket and moving slowly toward us. "Why don't they sit and wait patiently like everyone else?" I wondered. The woman gently parted the rags to show a tiny red wrinkled face who opened her mouth and started to wail. They wanted to know where to get milk for the newborn; it was more important than grain.

Their story was not uncommon. They came from a mountain village with no access by road. There had been no rain again last year, and all their food had run out. They had wanted to wait until the child was born before starting out on the trek to the food distribution center. But when they had nothing left to eat and the baby still had not arrived, they had to leave. The journey through the mountainous war zone had taken them seven days. The baby was born on the mountainside just three hours earlier. The mother had no milk to feed the baby. She only had energy left to ask for her child to be fed.

Working amongst such suffering changed me. I found I could not live with my conscience if I knew hundreds more might die if I did not act. I knew God loved them just as much as God loved me, and if there was something within my power to show that love, to alleviate some suffering, I would try to do it. I felt the burden of personal responsibility. Even after I left Ethiopia, the burden remained.

I became angry. I became angry because only a few care enough about the suffering of others for it to make a difference in their lives. Some appreciate the agony and injustice many have to endure in this world; few act to change it. I imagined those few as guards who keep vigil through the dark night of human existence while others sleep, ignorant in a dream-world. I was angry with anyone who chose ignorance over wisdom, acceptance of the status quo over change, or who chose a self-centered life over a selfless one. I silently railed at the self-indulgent who occasionally thought about my friends who lived in poverty, but never cared.

I wanted power, real power to marshall international forces for the alleviation of the suffering I had seen. I decided to come to Harvard to get an M.B.A. Harvard and this degree, I reasoned, might help me get into a position where I could influence governments and peoples to take serious action.

Then, in Harvard's relentless environment, I realized that despite my faith and vocation, I had no real peace and little joy. I decided I could not live the rest of my life being motivated by anger. There had to be another way to live, but I needed more time to think it over. So I went traveling. I felt the terror of war while in the Gulf. I drank with the dying. I was poor. I saw spectacular sunsets. I danced at marriage celebrations. I was loved.

I experienced again what Scripture means when it describes the whole of creation as screaming in the pains of childbirth, and what it means for each person, be they head of state, father, or child, to live with the consequences of having the freedom to abuse or to love. I understood that alienation from God is the worst form of pain, which only Christ's love can heal. And I came to know that suffering and pain will only truly end with the ultimate triumph of God's love when Christ returns. This is the nature of the world as I can see it.

I also experienced for the first time something of the depth of God's love for each individual and his joy in the beauty he has created. I understood some of God's pain as he sees how we have chosen to hurt each other and abuse creation. I know that God does not abandon those who suffer; his love can be experienced in spirit as well as in body. God asks those who will listen to receive his love and to share it with the suffering. Yet so many choose not to listen, receive, or share that love. Neither will they be part of the triumph of love over suffering, life over death.

I am no longer angry, but I still grieve over suffering and injustice. I now know, however, that it is only love which will ultimately overcome it. I know what love is: that Jesus Christ gave his life for me. I want to share that love and my new life with my brothers and sisters.

I can now enjoy beauty, love, and laughter, instead of seeing only suffering and pain, for when I come to Christ, I am given new passion for life and its richness. In Christ there is hope for a world of beauty. A glimpse of wild gazelles on a mountain, spontaneous laughter, and the experience of love are no longer tinged with sadness. And I know what it means to experience peace which passes all understanding, to be able to live in a world in which there is both joy and sorrow.

Conversion: One Journey Outside the Gate

৵৻

— JEFFREY BARNESON —

Disturbing as it was to see Christian friends carried off and placed in riot wagons, the event planted a seed in me which began my third "conversion."

Jeffrey Barneson is a chaplain with the United Ministry at Harvard-Radcliffe and InterVarsity Christian Fellowship. In addition to working with the Graduate School Christian Fellowship, a ministry he has advised for twelve years, he is currently a student at the John F. Kennedy School of Government at Harvard. With a background in engineering (B.S., Stanford) and an interest in computer-aided design, he has served as a teaching assistant at the Graduate School of Design at Harvard. An avid cyclist, he serves as faculty advisor for the Harvard Cycling Team.

Since 1984 Jeff has led groups of graduate students to work and learn in impoverished villages and cities in Latin and North America during their summers.

Conversion: One Journey Outside the Gate

— JEFFREY BARNESON —

Loose the chains of injustice . . .
share your food with the hungry
and . . . provide the poor wanderer with shelter. . . .
Then your light will break forth like the dawn,
and your healing will quickly appear. . . .
Then you will call, and the Lord will answer. . . .
The Lord will guide you always;
he will satisfy your needs in a sun-scorched land
and will strengthen your frame.
You will be like a well-watered garden,
like a spring whose waters never fail.
Your people will rebuild the ancient ruins
and will raise up the age-old foundations. . . .
You will find your joy in the Lord,
and I will cause you to ride on the heights of the land.

ISAIAH 58:6–14

෨ς

A friend once told me that coming to faith in Jesus involves three successive conversions: conversion to Christ, to the church, and to the world. While my own experience is somewhat less linear, I do recognize those categories and some of the issues raised by each. This is not to say, however, that one merely completes them like solving integrals in a calculus problem set, finishing one and then going on to the next. Conversions are not so orderly. In fact, my experience has been that each of the categories merge together and influence the others. Recognition of what the church and world are, for example, influences how I view God, myself, and what I am called to be and do.

The first of these, conversion to Christ, is an individual, existential choice to believe in the person of Jesus. It is based on the personal conviction of sin and recognition of Christ as the means of salvation. Understanding our failure, in the face of God's grace in the life, death, burial, and resurrection of Jesus, we place our faith in him. More than that, we give over our lives, acknowledging God's reign in all that we are and do. I made this decision as a youngster in a Baptist church, walked an aisle, and was baptized as outward testimony to the profound event that had taken place in my soul. While we might debate the merits and validity of childhood conversions, something stuck and God grabbed the place at the center of my life.

Conversion to the church was a natural next step for me; after all, that's what Christians did. "The Bible knows nothing of a solitary believer," I was told. I believed it. In the same way that weddings link together families that previously may have had nothing in common, Christians are, for better or worse, joined with other believers. Warts and all, they are the people who have identified with Jesus, and they are, in very practical ways, my people. However, it wasn't until much later, after I'd spent time with Christians in Central America and worshiped with believers in the inner cities of the United States, that I realized the radical nature of the community of faith with which one is identified as a Christian.

Conversion to the world is rooted in the recognition that Jesus had a fundamental identity with the poor of his day; Christians, by extension, are called to a similar alignment. If the church is the people who have identified with Jesus and following Jesus means casting our lot with them, then we must recognize a parallel relationship to the poor, the people with whom Jesus himself identified. This is not to say that the rich have no place in God's economy or that Jesus simply disregarded them. In fact, Jesus had much to say to those who controlled resources and the means of production in his time. Rather, it suggests that Jesus' life and ministry involved a bottom-up operation rather than a top-down strategy. Renunciation of power and privilege in favor of "downward mobility" characterized the life and ministry of Jesus and defines the posture for those who would follow him.

My own journey down this road has been both experiential and theological. It has been a dialectic involving engagement and reflection, beginning when I was a college student when a series of events crystallized the issue in my life. On one occasion I was attending a Stanford film series on the rise and decline of Western civilization. The analysis of one film suggested that the driving values in American society are "personal peace and affluence." Considering only for a moment my own goals, I had to acknowledge the unmistakable truth in the critique.

Later that evening as I was walking home, I noticed a disturbance at the university administration building. Police were arresting students who had been sitting in to protest Stanford's investments in South African corporations. As I watched the police carry student after student from the building,

I realized that many were Christians I knew from meetings on campus. This was profoundly unsettling for me, since my categories for Christian activity had always been safely within "conventional church activities" and never outside the law. Disturbing as it was to see my friends carried off and placed in riot wagons, the event planted a seed in me which began my third "conversion."

The theology which most directly influenced me was taken directly from the Bible. Both Old and New Testaments are filled with images depicting God's fundamental concern for the poor, the forgotten, the stranger. There are literally hundreds of references which call for the people of God to take action on behalf of the oppressed (Micah 6:8 and Isaiah 58 are two well-known texts), leaving little excuse for the small sample of issues which have so captivated the attention of certain segments of the church in our own time. However, the most compelling example of this call for me was the example given by Jesus himself. Consider the picture of Christ presented in the letter to the Hebrews, chapter 13, verses 11–14:

> The high priest carries the blood of animals into the Most Holy Place as a sin offering, but the bodies are burned outside the camp. And so Jesus also suffered outside the city gate to make the people holy through his own blood. Let us, then, go to him outside the camp, bearing the disgrace he bore. For here we do not have an enduring city, but we are looking for the city that is to come.

Despite its clarion call, Christians have tended to overlook the uncomfortable invitation of this brief passage, "Jesus . . . suffered outside the city gate to make the people holy through his own blood. Let us, then, go to him outside the camp, bearing the disgrace he bore." The reference to the area outside the gate and camp is likely an invitation to the dump. *Gehenna* was the name given to the place which received all the trash from the city of Jerusalem. Previously, during the reigns of Kings Ahaz and Manasseh, it had been a site of pagan worship, even human sacrifice. By the time of this letter's writing it was the perpetually burning city dump, which served as a figure for the place of final punishment. As with similar places today outside virtually any Third World city, it contained both the physical garbage as well as the human refuse of society. Those who scrounged for the half-rotten food and the aluminum cans of their day were alongside Jesus in his suffering and will be our companions as well when we go to him "outside the gate."

In recent years, I have been privileged to join Harvard graduate students in visiting and working alongside Christians in a variety of settings "outside the gate." We have built homes with widows and children in the highlands of Guatemala and with campesino farmers in Honduras. We have worked on schools for handicapped children in the shanty towns of Lima and assisted with construction of a church-medical building in the Dominican Republic. Another year, students from the Business and Design Schools assisted a pastor in Haiti in developing a business and constructing a bakery which employs over a dozen people in a mountain community near Port-au-Prince.

Each of these settings has brought their own challenges physically, intellectually, and spiritually. For example, some of the contemporary sociological literature twelve of us came across while preparing for a short micro-enterprise consulting project in El Salvador one spring suggested that a misguided hope for heaven could only pacify the poor, leaving them no incentives to struggle for change in their condition. In our experience, exactly the opposite was true. It was precisely *because* the poor looked for and anticipated a "city that is to come" that they were able to bear the shameful conditions and work for change where they live. Christians in the shanty towns of San Salvador have no trouble recognizing that here "there is no enduring city." Nothing material can command their devotion and no person or government can demand their allegiance, because they are devoted to and looking for that "city which is to come."

Last summer ten of us joined and worked with small Baptist congregations in two troubled neighborhoods in New York City. On Coney Island we worked with homeless persons living under the boardwalk and others who live in housing project towers.

We were left with several questions: What would happen, for example, if a dozen Christian M.B.A. and M.P.A. students chose to live on Coney Island, work with local churches, and start several small businesses? Is it possible, over a period of five or six years, that such a group might help to revive the local economy and create meaningful employment for hundreds of persons? We later worked with churches and FCS Urban Ministries in Atlanta, where this vision is working. Could such a practical ministry of business development be the missing ingredient necessary for the church to recover its credibility in the eyes of people who see it as an irrelevant or destructive institution? Would preaching of the good news of Christ be heard as never before if Christians showed the city God's love in more practical ways?

Salvation to the Streets

৵৽

— A N T H O N Y   P A R K E R —

Death comes at an early age for too many young black people today. And Four Corners is no different.

Anthony Parker graduated in 1993 with his M.Ed. from the Harvard Graduate School of Education. Parker became involved with Azusa, the Christian community described in this story, while at Harvard. Anthony, his wife, and their two sons live in Dorchester, part of Boston's inner city.

His love for teenagers has led him to be a teacher of history and social studies at Newton South High School. Parker is a voracious reader and a freelance journalist. He has written for *Africa News* and for *Sojourners* in Washington, D.C., where he was associate editor. Before coming to Harvard, he attended Earlham College.

Salvation to the Streets

— ANTHONY PARKER —

I t was so sad yet so unsurprising.

Several of us from the Azusa Christian Community in Boston had gathered on the corner of School and Washington Streets to pray for Robert Smith, better known as "Man," who was shot a few nights before on that same corner. While we were gathering to pray, a fight broke out up the street. Two women were determined to break a bottle over the head of a man and maybe the woman he was with, too. Several of our group ran over to intervene. The police were called. They arrived after the fighters had already left.

No one in the group knew why those women and the man were fighting, cursing, screaming, and willing to tear off their clothes in the freezing weather and snow. That kind of rage and anger—the kind that disappears as quickly as it erupts—is dangerous. It requires a healing that secular institutions and good works alone cannot offer.

So our little group prayed. We prayed for "Man," for the spiritual salvation of the people fighting, and for the collective soul of our black community.

The Azusa Christian Community is an intentional community of black men, women, and children who are committed to the complete renewal—spiritually, culturally, intellectually, and politically—of the black poor people in inner-city Boston. The members of Azusa—most of whom were educated at Harvard, M.I.T., and other elite academic institutions—choose to live among the black poor in the Four Corners and Codman Square neighborhoods in North Dorchester. While holding full-time jobs to support ourselves and our families, or while struggling through graduate school, we also act as surrogate parents for an ever-expanding army of angry, emotionally unstable young black people.

In 1984, when most of the members of the then African People's Pentecostal Church were still undergraduates, the three main pillars of their worldview were food distribution, political campaigns, and intellectual discourse. Although Christians, their spiritual maturation had not yet caught up with their political and intellectual acumen.

Our community has developed from a Harvard Christian student organization known as the William J. Seymour Society to a maturing church of about twenty adults and a score of children and teenagers. We are an eclectic bunch: single mothers, a police officer, students, a lawyer, business people, and teachers. Most live within a six-block area in Four Corners and Codman Square, with some living in Roxbury and Cambridge.

Given the deteriorating circumstances of the black poor and the alienation between urban black youth and older, mainstream black leadership—especially within the black church—it is a particularly thorny proposition to inspire young black people to seek justice in Jesus and in the Bible. But such is the task and calling of Azusa.

Named after Los Angeles' Azusa Street, where the first black Pentecostal church was located in the early 1900s and where the first Pentecostal explosion in the United States was sparked during a revival preached by William J. Seymour in 1905, Azusa takes its call seriously. It is a daily challenge that may find some of its members in court, in public schools, and in the streets, bearing witness to the fact that "our struggle is not against flesh and blood, but against the rulers, against the authorities, against the powers of this dark world and against the spiritual forces of evil in the heavenly realms" (Ephesians 6:12).

Our calling is to bridge three worlds: the biblical, the political-economic, and the cultural. The formal name given to Azusa's street ministry is the Dorchester Uhuru Project. Based on aspects found in the Christian-led Southern Freedom Movement and the Students Nonviolent Coordinating Committee's Mississippi Freedom Summer project, the Uhuru Project is a multifaceted campaign designed to organize citizens around those issues most critical to their everyday lives—health care, public safety and crime, education, employment, and adequate housing.

We seek to empower black youth by first attempting to teach discipline and Christian values. The hallmark of Azusa's ministry in Four Corners is the belief that salvation is the greatest equalizer. Conversion and spiritual growth move people far beyond mere political analyses and community service. Our organizing and evangelism is the object of an intensified corporate prayer life. Understanding the role of the Holy Spirit is one of the most vital dimensions of our ability to successfully minister at the corporate and individual levels.

Azusa founder and pastor the Reverend Eugene Rivers has said that:

> the level of violence in these inner cities requires a level of spiritual power so intense that we encourage folk who don't understand the importance of the Holy Spirit for ministry not even to bother. All that could possibly happen is that you will get worn out or run out.

Eugene should know. Two years ago more than a dozen bullets crashed through the windows of Eugene and Jacqueline Rivers' home, one of them missing their son Malcolm's head by an inch as he slept in his bed.

Our worship, like our street ministry, is enthusiastic and bold. We function as "a voice of one calling . . . prepare the way of the Lord" in Boston. Our vision over the next five years is to reach one thousand young blacks, particularly urban black males, ages eighteen to thirty-five. It is black men who are murdered and incarcerated in highest numbers and have the lowest life expectancy of any group in the U.S. "It was the poor black mothers, sisters, and daughters of black men that encouraged us to organize among the black males," Eugene said.

Perhaps, but pain does not discriminate, especially in the inner city. "There's a lot of woundedness around the issue of gender on all sides in the black community," Jacqueline Rivers reflected, an elder in the Azusa community. She is director of the Boston office of the Algebra Project, a national organization that focuses on making algebra easier for inner-city middle school students to understand.

Twenty-one-year-old Sophilia Robinson has a three-year-old son, Marquis. She told me, "The girls need just as much help. Teenage girls need to know not to have children now; they need to know to go to school. There should be workshops for single mothers and programs to get girls off welfare, to make them want to finish school and do something for themselves."

Another Azusa friend, Michelle Shaw, a Harvard-trained lawyer, left a high-paying job downtown to work in a small law firm located across the street from Dorchester Municipal Court in Four Corners. She has spent considerable time, energy, and expense at "being there" for several fifteen-year-old girls from nearby Jamaica Plain. Michelle attended the girls' graduations from middle school this summer—in some instances, standing in for a parent or other relative who could not come. With the breakdown of the traditional family, increasing violence in the schools, drugs, rising numbers of teenage AIDS cases among blacks, and a sexually permissive culture, it is imperative that Christians step in to help parent this generation of black children.

Another aspect of Azusa's work is the Community Youth Technical Exchange Program (CYTE). CYTE is run by Alan Shaw, a Ph.D. candidate in computer science and media technology at M.I.T. and head of his own company. CYTE teaches neighborhood youth how to fix basic electrical appliances and offer their services to the residents of Four Corners for a small fee. CYTE also teaches them graphic design and how to use computers. The youths make business cards for themselves, set their goals, and work on following through on their commitments to the neighborhood.

Individual initiative and achievement, neighborhood economic clout, a skill, and confidence in one's ability are just a few of the values learned through CYTE—values needed for the survival of any at-risk community in the country.

"Too many of our young people are in prison. As Christians, we can't give up on them," said Eva Thorne, a graduate student in political science at M.I.T. Eva is involved with Azusa's Youth Advocacy Project, which tracks at-risk youth in close consultation with probation officers, lawyers, and judges. She continued: "For the gospel to be truly life-transforming and powerful, it should be able to reach the most despised among us."

The growing number of young black men who have dropped out and remain unemployed provides ample evidence of the education system's failure. And many of the teenage women one sees walking along the streets have small children in tow—their fathers in jail, in the hospital, on the run, or dead.

Can you imagine death without the assurance that being a Christian brings? Death comes at an early age for too many young black people today. Four Corners is no different.

I pondered this as I sat outside the chapel of a funeral home in Mattapan on a cold, rainy evening. I was at a wake, with several other community members, for a man I had never met. Only thirty-six, he had died of AIDS.

Living in the inner city is often painful. Living in the inner city is often expensive—like when my family's car and Michelle and Alan's car were hit by bullets during a drive-by shooting. But we at Azusa are integration's success stories. Most of us have undergraduate degrees, have or are completing master's or doctoral degrees. Our income or income potential is excellent. We are, if you will, the "house Negroes," sharing space on the same plantation with the "field Negroes."

The culture of Harvard can foster an exclusivity that is not easily broken. Being black is not necessarily an advantage in trying to evangelize among the poor and disadvantaged—when you are neither, and when you may sound different, look different, and have no concrete or intuitive feel for the rhythms of hard-core street life. As Azusa begins to expand and perhaps take on a working-class flavor, a clash of two cultures is imminent.

How we prepare for this future is critical as new leadership is groomed to handle urban ministry. A true test of discipleship, as lived in the context of our community, is a challenge to young, gifted, and educated black men and women to recognize our own spiritual poverty apart from Jesus Christ and to humbly share the richness and power of God's love with our disadvantaged young friends.

"I think one of the most significant components of the education I received here in the fellowship has been around the issue of class,"

Jacqueline Rivers said. "I think we can become one with the poor. But I think we have a long way to go. We have to rely heavily on the spirit of God and God's ability to love through us, guide us, and to correct us in everything we do. God's ability to transform is the key. We've had a lot of time to work that out, just among ourselves."

There is a consensus in the community that the estrangement between black elites and the black poor can best be resolved through relationships. Eva Clarke, a former elder in the church, says, "Most women want something better for their children, so that's a bond. My hope is just to communicate concern, support, and love for the women in the neighborhood."

We rest and find our strength in the love of God. He is patient and watchful. It is his love that cries out in Deuteronomy, "I set before you death and life. Now choose life."

Our attempt to live out the biblical mandate to serve the poor is coupled with the other biblical command to conversion—an acknowledgment that any change in a person's circumstances must begin with God. The act of conversion is empowering in ways that simply feeding the hungry, clothing the naked, and housing the homeless are not. Freedom must start at the individual level, with a personal experience of transformation, and then move upward to the family, through the church, and finally spill over into the wider community. I have come to understand that the seed and purpose of community is Christ-centeredness.

CHAPTER 7

GOVERNMENT AND THE GOSPEL OF JUSTICE

The great illusion of leadership is to think that others can be led out of the desert by someone who has never been there.

HENRI NOUWEN, *THE ROAD TO DAYBREAK*

෩

When citizens do act in their public selves as though their faith matters, they risk not only ridicule, but actual punishment.

STEPHEN CARTER, *THE CULTURE OF DISBELIEF*

෩

Shoot us simply throught the heart —
peasant worker human beings —
we do not die we never have.
Who else will plough the fields in spring
when earth hard with winter softens sweet for men.
We build with thatch and brick,
adult gratitude for children and their voices.

MENO LOVENSTEIN, *AGAINST A GARDEN WALL*

Crisis and Faith

༝ৡ

— ELIZABETH DOLE —

I had God neatly compartmentalized, crammed into a crowded file drawer of my life, somewhere between "gardening" and "government."

Elizabeth Dole received a Juris Doctorate from Harvard Law School in 1965 after completing a master of arts degree in teaching at Harvard's Graduate School of Education (Radcliffe Program) in 1960. A former trustee of Duke University, she has more recently served on Harvard's Board of Overseers.

On February 1, 1991, Mrs. Dole began her tenure as president of the American Red Cross. She has also served six United States presidents in a career that has seen her named by the Gallup Poll as one of the world's ten most admired women.

In 1990 she resigned as the twentieth U.S. secretary of labor. From February 1983 until October 1987, Mrs. Dole served as secretary of transportation. Under her leadership, the United States enjoyed the safest years in its history, in all three major transportation areas— rail, air, and highway.

A native of Salisbury, North Carolina, Mrs. Dole was chosen by a significant margin in a poll conducted by *McCall's* magazine as the woman most likely to be the first female president of the United States.

Crisis and Faith

— ELIZABETH DOLE —

I consider it one of the greatest possible privileges to share with fellow travelers a little of my own spiritual journey. Like most of us, I'm just one person struggling to relate faith to life, but I am grateful for the opportunity to speak from the heart about the difference Jesus Christ has made in my life. But first I must mention a political crisis—one from which I have learned some important lessons. Now, this is a political crisis involving high stakes, intrigue, behind-the-scenes negotiations, influence in high places, and even an element of romance.

Where have I learned of this crisis? On the front page of the *Washington Post*? No. The newspapers haven't carried this story. The political crisis I am referring to occurred around 2,450 years ago. And we learn about it in the Bible—in the book of Esther.

Esther is the saga of a woman forced to make a decision concerning the total commitment of her life—a decision she was reluctant to make. She had to be vigorously challenged, and it is this part of her story to which I can so easily relate in my own spiritual journey. For while the particulars of her challenges may differ from those you and I face, the forces at work are as real as the moral is relevant. The basic lessons Esther had to learn are lessons I needed to learn. Thus, the story of Esther, over the years, has taken on great significance for me. Indeed, it reflects an individual's discovery of the true meaning of life.

The story takes place in the ancient kingdom of Persia, where there lived a particularly faithful man of God named Mordecai. Now, Mordecai, a Jew, had a young cousin named Esther, whom he had adopted after the death of her parents and raised as his own daughter. In fact, Mordecai had raised a young woman literally fit for a king, for Esther grew into a woman of extraordinary grace and beauty.

One day, Xerxes, the king of Persia, ordered a search for the most beautiful single women in his kingdom so that he could choose a new queen—a sort of "Miss Persia Pageant." Esther, above all others, found favor in the eyes of the king, and this young orphan girl, her Jewish background still unknown, was crowned queen of Persia. The king was so delighted with his new queen that he threw a magnificent banquet and even went so far as to lower all the taxes.

Meanwhile Mordecai, out amongst the people, learned to his horror that a top government official had developed a very careful plan to put to death all of God's people, the Jews, throughout the entire kingdom. Of course Mordecai immediately thought of Esther, and he sent an urgent message saying: "Esther, you must do something. You may be the only person who can persuade the king to call off this terrible plan."

But Esther wanted no part of this. Her response to Mordecai was: "All the king's officials and the people of the royal provinces know that . . . any man or woman who approaches the king in the inner court without being summoned . . . [will] be put to death. The only exception to this is for the king to extend the gold scepter to him and spare his life. But thirty days have passed since I was called to go to the king."

In other words, Esther was saying, "Mordecai, you don't understand protocol. I have to follow standard operating procedures. Chances are that if I do go to the king, I just might lose my head!" Mordecai had no sympathy with Esther's refusal to help. Tens of thousands of her own people stood to lose *their* heads. So Mordecai felt compelled to send a second message to Esther—and it is this second message that resonates deeply with the spiritual challenges of my own life.

I once heard a very insightful pastor, Gordon MacDonald, highlight three distinct themes in Mordecai's second appeal to Esther—three challenges which strike at the heart of Esther's reluctance.

The first theme is *Predicament*: "Esther, think not that you'll escape this predicament any more than other Jews. You'll lose everything you have if this plan is carried out—all the comforts, all the fringe benefits . . ." It seems that Mordecai is saying, "If the thing that stops you from being a servant to thousands of people is your comfort and your security, forget it. You are no more secure in there than we are out here." Esther shares the predicament.

The second theme is *Privilege*: "If you keep silent, Esther, at a time like this, deliverance and relief will arise from some other place. God has given you, Esther, the privilege to perform. If you don't use that privilege, he may permit you to be pushed aside and give your role to someone else."

The third theme is *Providence*: Mordecai says, "Esther, who knows but that God has placed you in a royal position for such a time as this?"

Finally Mordecai's appeal struck home. Esther's response was: "Go, gather together all the Jews . . . and fast for me. Do not eat or drink for three days, night or day. I and my maids will fast as you do. When this is done, I will go to the king, even though it is against the law. And if I perish, I perish."

Now that is total commitment. Indeed, the story of Esther is for me a very challenging and humbling one. For there came a time in my life when I had to confront what commitment to God is all about.

My witness contains no "road to Damascus" experience. My spiritual journey began many years ago in a Carolina home where Sunday was the Lord's Day, reserved for acts of mercy and necessity, and the gospel was as much a part of our lives as fried chicken, and azaleas in the spring.

My grandmother, Mom Cathey, who lived within two weeks of her one hundredth birthday, was my role model. I remember many Sunday afternoons with other neighborhood children in her home—the lemonade and cookies (I think that was what enticed us), the Bible games, listening to Mom Cathey as she read from her Bible (now one of my most cherished possessions).

She practiced what she preached, and lived her life for others. In a tragic accident, Mom Cathey lost a son at the hands of a drunk driver. The insurance policy on his life built a hospital wing in a far-off church mission in Pakistan. Although Mom was not at all a wealthy woman, almost anything she could spare went to ministers at home and missions abroad. And when it became necessary, in her nineties, to go into a nursing home, she welcomed the opportunity. I can still hear her saying, "Elizabeth, there might be some people who don't know the Lord, and I can read the Bible to them."

I love to find her notes in the margins of her Bible, notes written in the middle of the night when she couldn't sleep. For example, I find by Psalm 139 this notation: "May 11, 1952, 1:00 A.M. My prayer: Search me, O God, and know my heart; try me and know my thoughts. And see if there be any wicked way in me, and lead me in the way everlasting."

I wanted to be like Mom Cathey. In many ways she was my Mordecai. I cannot remember an unkind word escaping her lips in all the years that I knew her, or an ungracious deed marring her path. My grandmother was an almost perfect role model. From an early age, I had an active church life. But as we move along, how often in our busy lives something becomes a barrier to total commitment of one's life to the Lord! In some cases, it may be money, power, or prestige.

In my case, my career became of paramount importance. I worked very hard to excel, to achieve. My goal was to do my best, which is all fine and well, but I am inclined to be a perfectionist. I discovered that it is very hard to try to control everything, surmount every difficulty, foresee every problem, and realize every opportunity. It can be pretty tough on your family, your friends, your fellow workers, and on yourself. In my case, it began crowding out what Mom Cathey had taught me were life's more important priorities. I was really competing against myself, not others.

I was blessed with a loving family, a Christian upbringing, the opportunity to study at Harvard, a beautiful marriage, and a challenging career.

Only gradually, over many years, did I realize what was missing—my life was threatened with spiritual starvation.

I prayed about it, and I believe, no faster than I was ready, God led me to people and circumstances that made a real difference in my life. I found a tremendously caring pastor who helped me see what joy there can be when God is the center of life, and all else flows from that center.

A spiritual growth group gave me renewed strength as I began to meet each Monday night with others who shared my need to stretch and grow spiritually. I was strengthened through Bible study with other Senate wives. I learned that Sundays can be set aside for spiritual and personal rejuvenation without disastrous effect on one's work week, and suddenly the Esther story took on fresh meaning.

I finally realized I needed to hear and to heed those challenges Mordecai so clearly stated. Mordecai's first challenge—*Predicament:* "Don't think your life will be spared from the slaughter, Esther. If you try to save your life, you'll lose it all!" It's a call to total commitment, to literally lay her life on the line.

But I can sympathize with Esther's dilemma. She had all the comforts, a cushy life, and when you get all those things around you, it can build up a resistance to anything which might threaten the comfort and security they seem to provide. I know all too well how she felt. Maybe you do, too. I enjoy the comfortable life. I had built up my own little self-sufficient world. I had God neatly compartmentalized, crammed into a crowded file drawer of my life, somewhere between "gardening" and "government." That is, until it dawned on me that I share the predicament, that the call to commitment Mordecai gave to Esther is like the call which Jesus Christ presents to me.

"If anyone would come after me," Jesus tells us in Matthew 16, "he must deny himself and take up his cross and follow me. For whoever wants to save his life will lose it, but whoever loses his life for me will find it. What good will it be for a man if he gains the whole world, yet forfeits his soul?"

Those are hard words to swallow when you are busy doing your own thing, but it is the most compelling logic I have ever heard. For if Christ is who he says he is—our Savior, the central figure in all of history who gives meaning to a world of conflicting priorities—then I had to realize Christ could not be compartmentalized.

It would be different if I believed that Jesus was just a man, as some do. Then I could easily have compartmentalized him. Or if I had believed he was just a good teacher of morals, then perhaps I could have put his book away on my shelf. Or if I had thought that he was just a prophet. Even then I might have been tempted to file him away.

But I knew that Jesus Christ was my Lord and my Savior, the risen Lord who lives today, sovereign over all things. And I knew it was time to cease living life backwards, time to strive to put Christ first, preeminent, with no competition, at the very center of my life. It was time to submit my resignation as master of my own little universe. And God accepted my resignation.

Mordecai's second challenge was *Privilege*: "If you don't take this privilege seriously, Esther, God will give it to another." This too was a challenge I needed to hear. God began to teach me that it is not what *I* do that matters but what a sovereign God chooses to do through me. God doesn't want worldly successes. He wants my heart. In submission to him, life is not just a few years to spend on self-indulgence and career advancement. It is a privilege, a responsibility, a stewardship, to live according to a much higher calling—God's calling. This alone gives true meaning to life. Mordecai's warning to Esther is sobering. God forbid that someday I look back and realize I was too distracted by things of this world, too busy, too driven, and therefore my work was given to another.

The third challenge concerned *Providence*: "Esther, who knows but that God in his providence has brought you to a royal position for such a time as this?" What Mordecai's words say to me is that each one of us has a unique assignment in this world, given to us by a sovereign God, to love and to serve those within our own sphere of influence. We have been blessed to be a blessing; we have received that we might give.

The challenges Esther needed to hear were challenges I needed to hear, and continually need to hear: the call to total commitment.

But there is one last lesson I had to learn from Esther—the way in which her heart responded. Esther called on her fellow believers to pray and to fast. And then she cast herself—indeed, her very life—upon God in dependence on him. "If I perish, I perish."

And how did God work in this situation? What was the outcome of Esther's commitment and dependence on God? Scripture tells us that the king extended the golden scepter, sparing Esther's life, that his heart went out to her cause, and that God's people were gloriously rescued! Esther could have played it on her own wits and charm and just left God out of the picture, but she knew her cause would only succeed if God were with her, and so she rallied others to join her in a spirit of humble dependence through prayer.

I have often found myself faced with tasks demanding wisdom and courage far beyond my own—in decisions both big and small. I am constantly in need of God's grace to perform life's routine duties with the love of others, the peace, the joy, inherent in God's call. I have had to learn that dependence is a good thing. And that when I have used up my own resources, when I cannot control things and make them come out my way, when I am willing to trust God with the outcome, when I am weak, then I am strong. Then I am in the best position to be able to feel the power of Christ rest upon me, encourage me, replenish my energy, and deepen my faith—power from God, not from me.

Yes, the story of Esther is actually a story of dependence. It is a story not about the triumph of a man or a woman but the triumph of God. He is the real hero of this story. And in the same way, I have come to realize there can be only one hero in my story, too: God in Jesus Christ.

Total commitment to Christ is a high and difficult calling and one that I will struggle with the rest of my days. But I know that for me it is the only life worth living, the only life worthy of our Lord. The world is ripe and ready, I believe, for men and women who will accept this calling, men and women who recognize they are not immune from the predicaments of the day, who are willing to accept the privilege of obedience, and who are ready to see that the providence of God may have brought them to such a time as this.

How Did We Not Know?

૭૬૬

— PETER CLARK —

Harvard's case studies also contributed to my sense of alienation from poverty. Then I found myself flying on an aging DC-8 into Ayacucho, Peru's heart of darkness. My real life case study was beginning.

The son of missionary parents, **Peter Clark** grew up in Honduras. He graduated from Wheaton College in 1984 and, two years later, from Harvard's Kennedy School of Government with a master's degree in public policy. He spent the next five years as the country director for World Relief in El Salvador, following the 1986 earthquake. In 1992 the United Nations awarded the Habitat Scroll of Honor to the World Relief El Salvador Housing Reconstruction Program.

In 1991 Clark led a group from the Harvard Graduate School Christian Fellowship to help transform a former city garbage dump in San Salvador inhabited by eight thousand people escaping war, drugs, and the memories of terrorism.

Peter recently completed his Ph.D. dissertation in education at Cornell University on the political economy of international development. He is frequently invited to offer management courses in Eastern Europe. Each summer Peter and friends tour a developing country, by bicycle.

The names of Peruvians in this story have been changed for their protection.

How Did We Not Know?

— PETER CLARK —

You cannot understand until you see.
OLD INCAN PROVERB

❧

The blood of the martyrs is the seed of the church.
TERTULLIAN, IN *APOLOGETICUS*

❧

At least two of the great human tragedies of the twentieth century took place under the penumbra of a complicitous silence. Allied soldiers who liberated Nazi concentration camps during the waning days of World War II could not erase the memory of mass graves and ovens, of meat hooks, and of thousands of gaunt Jewish faces crying tears of joy upon realizing they had been freed. And those who went to Cambodia after the fall of the Khmer Rouge and saw the stacks of human skulls from the killing fields also tried, sometimes in vain, to make sense of a world turned upside down. Witnesses in each case often say that one of the most troubling questions for them was: "How did we not know?"

My years at Harvard's John F. Kennedy School of Government have begun to fade, with time, into one long vigil of overlapping case studies. I can no longer remember what I suggested President Kennedy should do to solve the Cuban Missile Crisis, where I told the government of Bangladesh to drill new wells, or why I said I admired Chicago's Mayor Daley.

But I do remember how eager I was to graduate and begin applying some of the analytical skills I had acquired. As a child of missionaries, raised in Latin America, I grew up with the poverty of the Third World, and I wanted to "do something about it." As a Christian, I wanted to use my concentration in international development to help create practical solutions to human suffering. So I spent my first five years after the Kennedy School coordinating a large earthquake reconstruction program in San Salvador, El Salvador. The job brought with it many of the challenges we had studied at Harvard: How do you mobilize community support for a housing program? What contacts do you make in the Salvadoran government to get the project going?

In many respects, I had an ideal job for someone who wanted to accomplish something tangible for the poor—including extensive funding. Yet I sensed something was missing. I was comfortably ensconced behind a psychological curtain that kept me strangely removed from understanding and empathizing with the poor. Harvard's case studies had sharpened my mind, but in a subtle way they had also contributed to my sense of alienation from poverty. I felt as if I were somehow hovering over the world, casting a sweeping critical eye on "development problems," analyzing their "structural causes," and resolving "situations" with a few quick strokes.

But then God brought my career to a turning point, a moment when the barrier of detachment was broken, pierced, one might say, by the sudden, rushing realization that much of the world actually lives out the case studies I had merely studied at the Kennedy School. These were real people in real contexts with real-life problems. Not only that, but many of their problems were enormous—much larger and more frightening than in the cases we had studied. Thus I found myself, on the morning of March 3, 1991, flying on an aging Faucett Airlines DC-8 into Ayacucho, Peru's heart of darkness.

My real-life case study was beginning.

Peru, March 1991—The eastern slopes of the Peruvian Andes, that swath of land that runs from Peru's northwestern border with Ecuador to its southeastern border with Chile and Bolivia, now constitutes the chief battleground on which the "People's War" is being waged between the Peruvian army and the guerrilla group that has come to be known (and feared) as the Shining Path. The fighting has been fiercest on the mountain slopes nearest Ayacucho. And for ten traumatic years, the Indian Quechua-speaking evangelical church has been caught in the cross fire.

"Just this past year thirty-two of our churches in the presbytery of Union Pichari have been burned to the ground," a church leader from IPNP (National Presbyterian Church of Peru) tells me in Lima. "This is happening because we are currently the largest evangelical denomination in the region, and also because many of our churches happen to be located on the Shining Path's supply routes."

At the general hospital in Ayacucho, the face of forty-five-year-old León Huaman Huacho, a Quechua Indian Pentecostal, every now and then convulses with silent sobs that seem to well up from deep within as he describes a nighttime killing by the Shining Path in his Andean town of Ccano. Just a few weeks earlier, members of his family were gunned down in church while they knelt in an all-night *vigilia* (or prayer meeting). He tells me:

"Thirty-three were killed, seven wounded. Since 1984 our small town of three hundred people has been forced by the army to organize into civil defense. Two months ago the local army post there was closed, and the army people left. Then the Shining Path threatened that we were going to pay, because we were servants of the military. At about 11:00 P.M., while our church was in an all-night prayer meeting, about forty men drove up in several trucks. They locked the church doors and then they began shooting. They had FAL rapid-assault rifles. Then they poured gasoline on all the benches and set the church on fire, people, everything. As the guerrillas ran out, my wife was there. She says they yelled, 'This is how dogs die.'"

It is ironic that the Quechua evangelical church, while being persecuted by the Shining Path, is also distrusted by the Peruvian army. Some Quechua Indians, frustrated with destitution and powerlessness, have joined the Shining Path, making the Quechua church the frequent target of army massacres. I have seen this catch-22 before in the mountains of Guatemala, where Mam, Quiche, Kakchiquel, Ixil, and other Indian groups are trapped in a no-win situation. It seems also that the government confuses the church's biblical stance against greed, selfishness, and corruption with the Shining Path's extreme anticapitalist ideology. Yet where church members have joined the rural civil defense, they have become natural military objectives for the Shining Path. Many church members have died in community-wide massacres that occurred when Peruvian army redeployments, having pressed civilians into defense patrols, then departed, leaving these Indian villages almost defenseless against the Shining Path's inevitable "just retribution against collaborators."

৯৽

Why is all this happening? Why are Peruvian evangelical Christians the target of violent persecution? To understand that, one must first understand how the Shining Path, or *Sendero Luminoso*, came to be.

Lima, Peru—My introduction to the Shining Path is a poster plastered to an exterior wall of San Marcos University in Lima. It depicts Abimael "Gonzalo" Guzmán, founder and leader of the movement, looming over a road filled with workers and peasants marching towards him. The road is bathed in a kind of apocalyptic light—a shining path. The caption reads: "President Gonzalo Guides Us by the Light of Truth." There is no mistaking the messianic theme here. For Abimael Guzmán, however, it was orthodox communism rather than Christianity that promised redemption from oppression.

After a stint as a philosophy professor, Guzmán was sent to study at China's elite Red Guard School. In 1968 he resumed his former philosophy post in Peru, firmly committed to dogmas of the Chinese Cultural Revolution—dogmas that would serve as the "guiding lights" of the Shining Path. "Prolonged People's War" was to be the chief insurrectionary model.

An eventual split with China reinforced the Peruvian group's isolation. The split also drove it to seek financial independence by gaining control of the drug trade in Peru's eastern jungles. Fortified with careful political indoctrination of its members, the Shining Path took to the path of violence, claiming fifteen thousand lives since 1980, five thousand in the state of Ayacucho alone.

Abimael Guzmán's vision is to turn the world ultimately toward communism. He criticizes Soviet communism for turning its back on Stalin, for not going far enough. He views his movement as the de facto government of Peru, and the true spiritual center of world revolution. His tools of choice are systematic sabotage, ferocious terrorism, and stringent adherence to ideology ruthlessly purged of all sentimentality.

The seven survivors of the recent Ccano massacre are arrayed in beds in the dimly lit surgery ward. In the far corner lies a five-year-old boy riddled with five bullet wounds. Sixty-three children lost one or both parents.

Huanta, Peru—I catch a ride in a Toyota on its way to Huanta, a picturesque town thirty-five miles north of Ayacucho. Huanta is headquarters to Radio Amauta. Apart from periodic Shining Path tapes with "revolutionary" messages (which the station staff must air if they have any interest in continuing to live), Radio Amauta's one-kilowatt transmitter beams evangelical programming in Quechua to parts of central and southern Peru. The twisting highway takes us past long lines of civil defense *ronderos* making the trek to Ayacucho. Not all seem able-bodied; some are old men, some too young. A few carry World War I vintage rifles; others have just pieces of wood painted to look like rifles; others carry poles with a knife blade tied to their end.

One of the passengers in the car—Lorena Mercedes Cruz—is a young, bright economics graduate of the University of San Cristobal and an active member of the Presbyterian church. Still single, Lorena has taken in ten children orphaned by army and Shining Path massacres and decided to raise them by herself. Together they survive with the help of church subsidies and thank-yous from aging peasants. "The first few months I had them," Lorena tells me, "whenever we went into town, they would whimper and cling to my skirt every time they saw a soldier. I cannot imagine what they have seen in their brief lives."

In Huanta, we sit down with several Presbyterian church leaders, including Hector Castro, IPNP's current president. Stories of past attacks tumble out: The Espiritu Alto church, on the outskirts of Huanta, was dynamited by the army in 1987, because authorities feared the church building might be used by the Shining Path on nights when there were no services. In 1988 the Shining Path attacked civilians on the highway between Ayacucho and Huancavelica, killing twenty, eight from the local Presbyterian church. During an indiscriminate army offensive in 1984, six leaders of the Presbyterian church in Kallqui were pulled out of a prayer meeting and shot. In September 1990 the Shining Path blew up the large Presbyterian church in Huancavelica. In June 1989, during an evening evangelistic service in the Presbyterian church in Carhuauran, the Shining Path killed nine. And on and on.

I am aware of the spiritual-ideological roots of the Shining Path movement but astonished by the level of the atrocities. I find myself asking again, "But why are *churches* being targeted by the Shining Path?"

"Some denominations have been preaching that the Shining Path is a demonic movement and have actively opposed it," replies Hector, the IPNP president. He continues, choosing his words carefully:

> "We have tried to maintain an officially neutral position, preaching against violence on *either* side. However, I suspect the Shining Path does not trust us completely because of our church's origins with American missionaries. They claim we are a foreign ideology wrapped in the trappings of religion, offering the Quechuas spiritual panaceas to keep them in poverty."

Indeed, in the early 1980s, inflamed with anti-Western, antireligious sentiment, the Shining Path drove IPNP's American founding missionaries from their homes in the central Peruvian Andes, leaving denominational control to indigenous leadership. But only two percent of IPNP members have received any professional training. More than eighty percent are still illiterate; seventy percent are poor peasant farmers. Their faith, in many cases, is extremely deep, but they need to be at least functionally literate to coordinate the complex activities of a large denomination with 182 different congregations.

Despite this poverty, the Shining Path defines the evangelical church as a part of the status quo infrastructure, an entity promoting a form of social cohesion, identity, and pattern of belief that runs counter to the one they intend to propagate. As such, it must be weakened relentlessly and systematically until it collapses. People's War orthodoxy clashes with Christianity as each of them stakes claim on the soul of the Indian—one for indoctrination, the other for life. Churches are thus targeted in order to "decapitate Christianity"—for when the church leaders are silenced, then the "body will melt."

Those are not mere words. "A revolution is not a dinner party nor the writing of an essay," states a piece of Shining Path dogma borrowed from Mao Tse-Tung. "A revolution is an insurrection, an act of violence by which one class overthrows another." But these are poor, defenseless Quechua Indians, shot in the back while they prayed. They do not fit the profile of a "class that needs to be overthrown" by violent revolution. That, however, is not a logic accessible to those steeped in "Gonzalo thought," a potpourri of Maoist, Marxist, and Leninist thinking spiced up with Guzmán's own theorems.

The return drive from Huanta to Ayacucho affords time for reflection. I can barely take in the majesty of the mountains and soaring Andean condors. I am more moved by the dignity of the church and their humaneness under unbearable suffering. And I am struck by their exemplary faithfulness in the face of what surely must look to many as meaningless tragedy, even desertion by God. But *they* do not seem to think that God has deserted them, for the power of God is manifested daily to them in a thousand little deliverances and in a tranquillity that transcends understanding. They are thankful to be alive. They trust God to deliver them from evil, but if that is not his will, they seem prepared to die as a way of participating in the sufferings of Christ. Their faith has reordered their relationship to the world and to the future in a way that I rarely have encountered in people who do not have faith in some larger reality or some final justice, but even more than that, who do not have some inward sense of joy and integrity that sustains them.

Like the martyrs of the Old Testament, or Christians in the first-century church, these Peruvians live out the existential tension between God's infinite ability to protect his children against harm and, on the other hand, the mystery of suffering for the sake of the kingdom. It is the tension embodied in the life of Jesus himself, whose moment of greatest shame and weakness—on the cross—was also the moment of his greatest spiritual victory, the triumph over satanic evil. It is the tension inherent to the concept of a God whose perfect strength is shown most clearly in the weakness of human vessels. One senses that the Shining Path has underestimated the resilience of the Peruvian church, its ability to renew itself in faith, and the depth of its roots in the Christian message of ultimate redemption for those who endure to the end. In attempting to "decapitate the church," the Shining Path overlooked one little thing—the fact that the head of the church is Jesus Christ himself.

Back at the general hospital in Ayacucho, Hector Castro, the Quechua pastor, says to one of the wounded women from Ccano, "I hope this does not make you lose your faith."

"I am ready to join my Lord at any time," she replies.

ᘒᔆ

Since the mid-1980's, the Peruvian government has strictly censored news reporting on Shining Path "activity." Few international reporters make it into the Ayacucho region, because of its remoteness and its security problems. As a result, widespread international public opinion on the killings being committed year after year has been nearly nonexistent. News of the massacre at Ccano, for example, has probably never made it to the outside world—or, for that matter, into a Kennedy School case study.

And yet there are simple things people can do to help the Quechua-speaking church in Peru. They need assistance that is channeled not to bureaucratic non-Quechua agencies based in Lima but directly to Quechua church leaders with deep local roots, in a way that enables them to design their own church-based solutions. Politically, they need the moral force that is generated by international public awareness and by polite but firm contact with the Peruvian government concerning the mayhem against the church.

The persecution of Quechua Christians in Ayacucho and its surrounding regions has not reached the proportions of what was experienced by Jews in Europe in the 1940s, by Cambodians under Pol Pot, or by Russians (including Christians) under Stalin. But what is clear is that the seeds of a new incomprehensible evil are being sown in the Peruvian highlands. "There is in Peru," Hector told me, "an old Inca saying that goes, 'You cannot understand until you see.'"

As "lights in the world," we who have been given those opportunities that come with affluence, literacy, and access to the media have a deep obligation to uncover evil, especially where the evil is launched against a helpless and silenced people. Time may come when we ask, perhaps a little too late, "How did we not know?"

ᘒᔆ

Ithaca, New York, 1996—Five years have passed since my time in Peru, but the memories have not faded. The faith of the Quechua Indians has helped to reunite my own heart and mind. I have also come to see how unhinged people can become if left to their own Godless philosophies and ideologies. For this reason, I hope that I will never do development work that does not take into account the complexity of human motives and the breadth of human needs.

Cambridge, Countries, and Christ

— ROBERT BESCHEL JR. —

Lincoln did not sink into moral cynicism, neglecting the pursuit of justice because people disagreed over exactly what justice was.

In 1981, **Robert (Bob) Beschel** left his internship in college ministry at University Presbyterian Church in Seattle to move to Cambridge. Beschel received a master's degree in public administration from the Kennedy School in 1983, and an A.M. and Ph.D. from Harvard's government department in 1991. He has been affiliated with Harvard's Center for Science and International Affairs as a fellow since 1984, and he served as coordinator of the Kennedy School's program on avoiding nuclear war from 1985–1986.

After serving as a consultant to the Carnegie and Ford foundations, and the U.S. Defense Department, Dr. Beschel was then named executive director of Project Library—the Kennedy School's program to facilitate the process of democratization and economic revitalization in East/Central Europe. He is currently a consultant with the World Bank, specializing in Eastern European transitions to market economies and democracies.

Cambridge, Countries, and Christ

— ROBERT BESCHEL JR. —

I came to Harvard in the fall of 1981, hoping to understand how moral norms and values could best be integrated into U.S. foreign policy. In my formative years, I had watched the *realpolitik* of Richard Nixon and Henry Kissinger give way to the resurgent moralism of the Carter presidency. Like many Americans, I had initially welcomed this development, being uncomfortable with detente's moral ambivalence and the willingness of its proponents to sacrifice normative values on the altar of international stability. As a Christian, I was convinced that there had to be a better way to integrate faith and practice, to reconcile the often contradictory demands of American ideals and American interests.

The late seventies were heady times for the student of ethics in international affairs. As the Carter presidency went on, it became obvious that its emphasis upon morality and human rights was adrift in a sea of irreconcilable contradictions. Ultimately, Carter's policies were replaced by Jean Kirkpatrick's provocative yet overdrawn distinction between "authoritarian" and "totalitarian" regimes. Foreign policy idealism was still in vogue, but it was a very different type of idealism, one that achieved moral clarity only by simplifying many difficult ethical dilemmas. I entered the university convinced with all of the hubris of youth that a better way had to exist to resolve complicated issues of pragmatism and principle, and that—with God's help—I could play a role in finding it.

A decade and three advanced degrees later, after untold hours of listening to Harvard's brightest minds addressing this issue, countless discussions probing the role of morality in foreign affairs with Christian and non-Christian colleagues, and writing a dissertation that explored the interaction between moral values and pragmatic concerns in the making of U.S.–Soviet policy, any comprehensive understanding of the proper integration of ideals and interests in American foreign policy still eludes me. I believe that God desires for us to act morally and has provided useful precepts to instruct us how to do so. Yet, both literally and figuratively, the Devil is often in the details.

To be fair, the question of appropriate ethical behavior in the international arena is a difficult one, complicated by conflicting standards, incomplete information, differing perceptions, and the need to cope with the realities of power.

In spite of the steady expansion of the law of nations over the past few centuries, the international milieu remains highly fragmented in terms of values. Considerations of justice seldom have uniform meaning, and differing ethical standards inevitably lead to different judgments as to the moral validity of a particular course of action.

This point is illustrated nicely by the American invasions of Grenada or Panama, both of which occurred while I was a graduate student. A state moralist, who places ultimate value on the sanctity of borders and on the principle of noninterference, would oppose these actions for violating the sovereignty of another country. A Marxist would condemn the invasions as imperialist. A realist could either support or condemn U.S. policy, based upon its ultimate cost as well as its contribution to regional stability. Others would support the outcome that best promoted the spread of political freedom and democratic governance, or which most improved the daily lives of the local population. Clever international lawyers would find ample legal precedents to argue either side. Christian thought provides surprisingly little guidance as to which standard should apply, although the traditions of pacifism and the Just War have existed since antiquity. In my view, the former achieves moral clarity at the cost of effectiveness; the latter was formulated in a more distant era and fails to adequately address a range of modern problems, such as intervention to prevent domestic chaos, violence, or genocide.

Thoughtful observers rightly shy away from placing disproportionate emphasis upon any one tradition or criterion, attempting instead to obtain a morally just solution by viewing the problem through multiple ethical lenses. Although sensible, such an approach is not without its own complications. Even with perfect objectivity, the morality of an issue such as military intervention is almost impossible to evaluate, in part because to do so requires weighing the moral equivalent of apples and oranges (how can we properly compare the value of social improvements in the lives of Grenadians or Panamanians against the virtues of political freedom or international stability?), and in part because decisions surrounding the use of force often rely upon criteria such as proportionality and last resort that are extremely difficult to assess, even in retrospect.

Ethical questions are made even more intractable by broad differences in perception and worldview. One man's terrorist is another man's freedom fighter; one state's norms of civilized conduct are another state's institutional tools of dominance and oppression. Cognitive psychologists have demonstrated that the notion of human beings as rational and dispassionate observers is largely a myth. Despite our best efforts towards objectivity, whenever we attempt to assess the justice of a particular international problem, we bring with us a host of explicit and implicit assumptions (indeed, an entire worldview) that inevitably affects how we assign motives, interpret facts, and weigh trade-offs.

In addition to problems of value, perception, and lack of information, considerations of power ultimately cast a shadow over any discussion of the role of morality in international affairs. Justice divorced from the power to enforce it is often meaningless. Yet, as Christian thinkers from Augustine through Reinhold Niebuhr have eloquently pointed out, the requirements for wielding power often compel believers to take actions they would otherwise shun. Christians have traditionally responded in three ways to this dilemma. Some, such as Quakers, Mennonites, and Anabaptists, have chosen to withdraw and to separate themselves from institutions and activities they view as inherently evil. Others, such as the famous American realist Hans Morgenthau, have been skeptical that faith and political practice could ever be reconciled.

Rejecting either extreme, I have found myself in the company of the many believers who have attempted to find that muddled middle ground between ineffective moralism and unrepentant realism. (Or, in the more eloquent words of Reinhold Niebuhr, "to move in the vast and morally ambiguous realm of the political community with as much integrity as possible, and with a humble awareness of the taint in all competitive positions in the political spectrum."[1]) Although uncomfortable with this conclusion, I now believe that comprehensive, definitive ethical solutions are likely to be unobtainable for all of the reasons outlined above. Most decision makers will therefore be confronted with the need to act morally in the face of unique, discrete situations in which few "textbook solutions" exist.

This observation need not drive us to despair. On a personal, case-by-case basis, it may indeed be possible for a statesman to act upon his or her Christian beliefs and, in doing so, make the world a better place. During my years at Harvard, my colleagues and I have come upon several guidelines that can help the student of ethics in international affairs navigate through moral dilemmas, however imperfectly. For me, the first and most important is the realization that any ethical schema devised and implemented by human beings will be imperfect. The mind of God and the reality of creation

---

[1]Cited from *Reinhold Niebuhr: A Prophetic Voice in Our Time,* ed. Harold R. Landon (Greenwich: Seabury Press, 1962), 122.

are simply too complex and varied to be captured by the simple standards we seek to establish. There will always be more to heaven and earth than is dreamt of in our philosophy; as the prophet Isaiah warns, his thoughts are not our thoughts and his ways are not our ways.

In making this observation, I am not arguing that we should neglect biblical injunctions in formulating foreign policy, nor that we should take lightly the precepts of international law. But we must appreciate our limited ability to grasp the entire truth in any situation, and recognize that the mechanistic application of any rule, be it divine or secular, is a very dangerous enterprise. The very standards by which we seek righteousness can often become a trap as we follow in the footsteps of the Pharisees and attempt to substitute legalistic adherence to rules and regulations for the much more challenging enterprise of seeking to follow in the footsteps of the living God.

In this context, ethicists since Augustine have noted that moral behavior is at least as dependent upon internal disposition as external regulation. At the moment of decision a step of faith is required, in which the policy maker stands alone and selects from among the many competing and conflicting considerations the factor or principle that will ultimately be decisive. In making this choice, the statesman will be left to work out his or her own salvation with fear and trembling, and the proper place to begin is on our knees, searching our hearts and humbly requesting God's guidance.

Christians also have an obligation to understand the facts, both theological and pragmatic. God is not a god of disinformation, but a God of truth, *veritas*. This requires a great deal of hard work in studying the issues. It also means engaging in dialogue with brothers and sisters who hold differing views. God works through community and diversity, and Christ continually demonstrated to his disciples they had much to learn from those whom they frequently sought to dismiss.

Questions of vocation and calling are also important. If it is to function effectively, the church must be big enough for prophets, priests, and kings. We need those, often on the outside, who call us to greater holiness. We need those on the inside who can comfort and encourage the flock, bind up the wounded, and care for the brokenhearted. And we need those who are willing and able to work within the system and change it for the better. There should be a place within God's kingdom for radical reconstructionists and thoughtful incrementalists, and both vocations need to be respected.

Finally, I believe that appropriate ethical behavior often requires a unique blend of humility, courage, and compassion. In this respect, I have often been drawn to the example set by Abraham Lincoln. The American

Civil War was in many ways a profoundly religious struggle, the irony of which did not escape the president. "Both [sides] read the same Bible and pray to the same God, and each invokes His aid against the other," Lincoln stated during his second inaugural address. "The prayers of both could not be answered. That of neither has been answered fully. The Almighty has His own purposes." Yet Lincoln did not sink into moral cynicism, neglecting the pursuit of justice because people disagreed over exactly what justice was or because God's transcendent plan was moving in a way unfathomable to mortals. Rather, he sought to proceed on the basis of what he believed to be correct and to act on the courage of his convictions. Even more importantly, he recognized the fact that his judgment was limited, which required him to temper the pursuit of justice with the pursuit of mercy. His concluding paragraph is one of the most famous in American public discourse:

> With malice toward none; with charity for all; with firmness in the right, as God gives it to us to see the right, let us strive on to finish the work we are in; to bind up the nation's wounds; to care for him who shall have borne the battle, and for his widow, and his orphan—to do all which may achieve and cherish a just and lasting peace, among ourselves, and with all nations.

Interestingly, in a letter to a friend two weeks later, Lincoln noted that—although this speech may eventually be ranked as one of his best—he did not believe that it would be immediately popular. "Men are not flattered by being shown that there has been a difference of purpose between the Almighty and them," he wrote. "To deny it, however, in this case, is to deny that there is a God governing the world."[2]

---

[2] Abraham Lincoln's letter to Thurlow Weed (March 25, 1865). Both quotes are cited from *Abraham Lincoln: His Speeches and Writings*, ed. Roy P. Basler (Cleveland: World, 1946), 792–93, 794 respectively.

CHAPTER 8

SCIENCE, TECHNOLOGY, AND THE EARTH

৵৻

Why is there something instead of nothing? Why do all electrons have the same charge and mass? Why do we see design everywhere? Why are so many processes so deeply connected?

ALLAN SANDAGE, *VERITAS RECONSIDERED*

❧

I do not know what I may appear to the world; but to myself I seem to have been only a boy playing on the sea-shore, and diverting myself in now and then finding a smoother pebble or a prettier shell than ordinary, whilst the great ocean of truth lay all undiscovered before me.

SIR ISAAC NEWTON, *MEMOIRS OF NEWTON*

❧

There is nothing I long to know with greater urgency than this: Can I find God, whom I can almost grasp with my own hands in looking at the universe, also in myself?

JOHANNES KEPLER

❧

Galileo's head was on the block. His crime was looking up the truth.

INDIGO GIRLS

❧

From Cambridge to California, a growing number of scientists are becoming more open to theological considerations . . . a drift prompted, they say, by recent advances in biology, particle physics, and especially cosmology.

ANTHONY FLINT, THE *BOSTON GLOBE*, JULY 12, 1993

Christianity and the Scientific Enterprise

— CHARLES THAXTON —

The Dutch professor maintained that Christianity had played a vital role in fostering the development of modern science. As a Christian I wanted to believe him; as a scientist, I was yet skeptical.

Charles Thaxton received his Ph.D. in chemistry at the Iowa State University, Ames, Iowa. He was a postdoctoral fellow at Harvard University for two years, where he studied history of science, and he held a postdoctoral appointment in the biological laboratories at Brandeis University for three years. Dr. Thaxton has coauthored *The Mystery of Life's Origin*, and *Light Through a Prism: A World View Approach to History of Science*, and served as academic editor for the high school biology supplement, *Of Pandas and People*. As president of Konos Connection, a nonprofit educational organization helping people relate modern knowledge and Christian values, he has lectured within the U.S. and Europe. In January 1992 he moved with his family to Prague, Czechoslovakia, a base for further teaching in Eastern Europe. He held appointments at the Slovak Technical University in Bratislava, Czechoslovakia and the Biomathematical Institute in Craiova, Romania. Dr. Thaxton is a Fellow of both the American Institute of Chemists, and the American Scientific Affiliation. He is married and has two teenage sons whom he is homeschooling with his wife Carole.

Christianity and
the Scientific Enterprise

— CHARLES THAXTON —

As a student in the 1960's I remember the derision heaped upon Christianity whenever professors or students mentioned it in the classroom. Serious thinkers, it seemed, had replaced mythical Christian doctrine with a far superior, more scientific view of reality. Christianity and Science were seen, necessarily, as in conflict.

Like most other Christian students of the time, I remained silent, intimidated by the superior knowledge of my mentors. Only several years later did I learn to discern the difference between science, and metaphysical naturalism masquerading as science.

While at Harvard in 1971, I had the good fortune of hearing a visiting lecture series conducted by Professor Rejer Hooykaas, a highly regarded historian of science.[1]

Hooykaas presented, what was to me, a new and provocative argument. The Dutch professor maintained that Christianity had played a vital role in fostering the development of modern science.

I remember my reaction well. As a Christian I wanted to believe him; as a scientist, I was yet skeptical. Hadn't many learned scholars already dismissed Christianity as an incredible intellectual position? Surely Hooykaas was mistaken. Perhaps, I misheard him. Though intrigued, I simply could not accept an argument that ran counter to the dominant perspective of my education to that point. I had a Christian heart, but, as yet, a pagan mind.

Nevertheless, Hooykaas' argument fascinated me. I began a reading program to examine his claims. I found other historians and philosophers of science who had recognized that a distinctly Christian worldview had inspired early scientific investigation. P. E. Hodgson in reviewing Stanley Jaki's *Science and Creation* said:

> Although we seldom recognize it, scientific research requires certain basic beliefs about the order and rationality of matter, and its accessibility to the human mind . . . they came to us in their full force through the Judeo-

---

[1]Rejer Hooykaas, *Religion and the Rise of Modern Science* (Grand Rapids: Eerdmans, 1972).

Christian belief in an omnipotent God, creator and sustainer of all things. In such a worldview it becomes sensible to try and understand the world, and this is the fundamental reason science developed as it did in the Middle Ages in Christian Europe, culminating in the brilliant achievements of the seventeenth century.[2]

Alfred North Whitehead added:

In the first place, there can be no living science unless there is a widespread instinctive conviction in the existence of an *Order of Things*. And, in particular, of an *Order of Nature*. My explanation is that the faith in the possibility of science, generated antecedently to the development of modern scientific theory, is an unconscious derivative from medieval theology.[3]

Perhaps, Christianity had played a greater role in the development of modern science than I had imagined. I wanted to know more. If the Christian concept of creation in the late Middle Ages had motivated scientific inquiry, what could have discouraged it before then? In Europe, at least, the answer was clear.

The dominant view of reality in medieval Europe was essentially Greek, having been coopted by the Church and adapted for Christian service. It offered no motivation to investigate nature by observation and experiment. To the Greeks, reality consisted of forms and essences, not material things. In a world where ideals subordinate material reality, observing "what is" becomes less important than reasoning "what ought to be."

The Greeks viewed nature as a living organism imbued with attributes of divinity. Nature was eternal and self-existent, not created. Nature was considered impregnated with final causes, with divine purposes and as such was self revealing. They had only to be apprehended by the mind, and hence, the significance placed on intuiting axioms and principles from which all particular truths could be derived by deductive reasoning. It followed form this view that Greek knowledge of nature and reality rested on the authority of the "system builders": Euclid in geometry, and Plato and Aristotle in philosophy, etc. As a corollary to the Greek view of truth, sensory experience did not lead to new knowledge. It could only provide illustrations for what was already known through reason. Sensory experience was no more relevant to the Greek science of nature than it was to Euclid-

---

[2] P. E. Hodgson. "Review of Science and Creation" (by S. L. Jaki) in *Nature*, vol. 251, October 24, 1974, 747.

[3] A.N. Whitehead. *Science and the Modern World* (New York: Free Press, 1967) 3–4, 12–13.

ean geometry. Therefore Greek science of nature was never experimental. The Greeks' conception of nature and reality led them to distrust the senses.

The medieval world picture inherited from the Greeks was that of a vast hierarchy of beings extending from the deity in the Empyrean heaven at the outer edge of the universe, through a graded series of angels inhabiting the ten concentric crystalline spheres surrounding the central earth, to the levels of men, animals, and plants on the earth itself which formed the system's cosmic center.

A sharp qualitative distinction separated the terrestrial and celestial domains of the universe. Not only were the two domains composed of different types of materials, they had different motions. The terrestrial environs consisted of earth, air, fire, and water, each with rectilinear motion which had a beginning and an end. The heavenly bodies (above the moon) were composed of a more perfect fifth essence, with eternal circular motion.

The linchpin for this medieval cosmology was Aristotle's view of motion through constantly applied force. But as Butterfield remarked,

"It was supremely difficult to escape from the Aristolian doctrine (of motion) by merely observing things more closely. . . . Escaping it required a different kind of thinking-cap, a transposition in the mind of the scientist himself."[4]

Late medieval Christianity supplied just such a transposition of thought through a greater familiarity with Scripture, and an emphasis on the doctrine of creation. Through the advent of the printing press the ideas of Scripture were much more widely disseminated. People could discover for themselves that both Old and New Testaments regarded the material world as substantial, real, and good. A premium was placed on the value and essential trustworthiness of sensory experience, especially in some of the more prominent authority based passages. For example, after Moses reiterated the Ten Commandments, he reminds the people that he is not the authority. The Commandments on stone only solidified the message all the people heard. Says Moses, "Ye heard the voice."[5] The Hebrews had an empirical test for identifying a false prophet.[6] Saint John introduces his first Epistle with an empirical emphasis: "We have heard," "we have seen," "our hands have handled."[7] Jesus said to the doubting ones after his resurrection, "Handle me and see."[8]

Though for many centuries the Church had openly acknowledged God and his creation, the medieval Church's view of nature remained essentially

---

[4]Ibid., 16–17.
[5]Deuteronomy 5:23.
[6]Deuteronomy 18.
[7]First Epistle of John 1:1.
[8]Luke 24:39.

Greek. But with greater appreciation of the value of sensory experience within a created universe, more and more people began to think through the implications of belief in creation for their view of nature. According to M. B. Foster: "The modern investigators of nature were the first to take seriously *in their science* the Christian doctrine that nature is created"[9] (emphasis his).

A created world is contingent upon the will of the creator, and need not necessarily conform to our a priori reasoning. These early scientists emphasized observation using the five senses and experimentation, in order to gain new knowledge.

Francis Bacon (1561–1626) maintained that finding new facts required new methods. He set out to reformulate scientific method to give the empirical, inductive process a more central place. Part of the genius of modern empirical science was precisely its use of recurring natural events to provide observable checks on hypotheses. No more would scientists content themselves with speculative reason unchecked by sensory experience.

Bacon also repudiated the Greek search for final causes in nature, which he maintained were inscrutable to man. According to Bacon, the Greeks were simply wrong in their approach to nature because they failed to regard it as created.[10] Creation may have been a mere doctrine in earlier centuries, but to many in the late Middle Ages it supplied the impetus to rethink the ancients' view of the natural world.

Realizing the implications of a created nature opened the door to emphasizing the importance of sensory experience. Empirical science follows directly from belief in a created and therefore contingent nature. Not until the end of the seventeenth century would Newton reach a new understanding of physical reality. In the meantime, a certain sense of delight and fascination came in exposing cracks in the Aristotelian edifice.

The voyages of discovery into the fifteenth century not only opened up the New World with new trade routes, but they also gave empirical proof that ancient knowledge was both incomplete and in many instances wrong. The explorers contradicted the ancients by experience. They, for example, did not fall off the edge of the earth when sailing uncharted waters.

Once a "transposition" in thinking occurred, allowing for meaningful experiential checks on ideas, the new empiricists found the universe replete with evidence repudiating the ancient cosmology.

In 1572, a new star appeared in the skies over Europe. The star remained visible for a year and a half, even in the daytime. The star hovered

---

[9]M. B. Foster, 1934. Mind. Vol. 43, No. 172, p. 446.

[10]T. F. Torrance. *Theological Science*. (London: Oxford University Press, 1969) Ref. 2, p. 70.

clearly above the moon. Yet, according to established Aristotelian views, the heavens were supposed to be changeless. Some of the learned professors refused to acknowledge the new star, calling it an optical illusion. But for everyone else it was clear evidence that the Aristotelian system was in deep trouble. What's more, the evidence was empirical.

Another blow to the Church's Aristotelian picture came with the comet of 1577. The comet not only signaled more change in the heavens, but since it must have passed through the supposedly impenetrable crystalline spheres, its appearance contradicted Aristotle's view of the heavens.

Copernicus had taken the bold first step, refashioning the world picture. He put the sun at the center in his system, thus making the earth just one of the planets. Copernicus did keep to circular motion for the planets, however. Later, Kepler would discover on empirical grounds the orbits were elliptical.

By the end of the seventeenth century Newton had synthesized the work of Copernicus, Tycho Brahe, Kepler, and Galileo by achieving a unity of heaven and earth, all equally subject to mathematical analysis. Newton banished the Aristotelian terrestrial/celestial dichotomy that had dominated intellectual thought for nearly two thousand years.

The modern scientific enterprise was now ready to explore by the senses, combined with mathematics, the structure and ongoing operation of the universe. Christian thought had done much to inspire this new form of inquiry. As for my own study I concur with C. F. von Weizsäcker's conclusion that modern science is a "legacy, I might even have said, a child of Christianity."[11]

---

[11]C. F. von Weizsäcker. *The Relevance of Science.* (New York: Harper and Row, 1964), 163.

More Than Machines

❦

— OWEN GINGERICH —

It is my prayer for you that you can use what science has to offer, but also your God-given creativity and consciences, to direct our world away from its present suicidal course.

Owen Gingerich, since 1968 professor of astronomy and history of science at Harvard University, is also senior astronomer at the Smithsonian Astrophysical Observatory in Cambridge. Trained as an astrophysicist at Harvard, his research interests have turned increasingly to the history of science, and he has become a leading authority on Copernicus and Kepler. He is a member of the Academie International de l'Histoire des Sciences, the American Academy of Arts and Sciences, and the American Philosophical Society.

In recognition of his scholarship, asteroid 2658 has been named "Gingerich," and Poland has awarded him its Order of Merit, Commander Class, specifically for his Copernican studies. In 1984 he won the Harvard-Radcliffe Phi Beta Kappa Prize for Excellence in Teaching. Among his recent books are two anthologies of his earlier articles, *The Great Copernicus Chase and Other Adventures in Astronomical History* and *The Eye of Heaven: Ptolemy, Copernicus, Kepler*. He and his wife, Miriam, are active members of the Mennonite Congregation of Boston.

More Than Machines

— OWEN GINGERICH —

I have always been interested in the nature of science: how or whether it describes a physical reality, its claims to truth, and the relation of these claims to other beliefs, including religious faith. One can find some of these answers by doing science, as I did for many years. One can also learn about the nature of science by examining historically the way scientific knowledge accumulates and changes. So today I'm heavily involved in a historical exploration of the growth and development of science.

For longer than I can remember, I have been fascinated by the stars. My parents said it all began on a stiflingly hot night in Iowa, when my mother moved cots outside for sleeping—and as a five-year-old I discovered the stars. Later, in a liberal arts church college in Indiana, I built my own telescope, but I studied chemistry, because that seemed so much more useful for mankind than something as arcane as astronomy. (In those days we didn't yet say "humankind.") Through a quite unpredictable series of circumstances I had an opportunity to spend a summer at the Harvard Observatory as an assistant to the famous astronomer Harlow Shapley, and this inflamed my enthusiasm for the celestial science.

But still I held back, uneasy about the justification of astronomy as a career choice. At that point my college math professor gave me some advice. "If you really want to be an astronomer," he said, "you ought to go for it. After all, we shouldn't let the atheists take over any field." So I applied to the Harvard graduate program in astronomy and was accepted.

At Harvard I found a whole gamut of religious viewpoints, from militant atheism to kindred Christian spirits, and in between a majority uninterested in religion though sometimes willing to concede, in a lofty Platonic fashion, the internal consistency of my own beliefs. I struggled with mathematics and physics and astrophysics, but I also snuck off and audited courses in geology and paleontology, topics that were too dangerously close to evolution to be taught at my undergraduate college. And I met Unitarians and Catholics and Christian Scientists—all foreign to my Anabaptist background—and I even met contemporaries who devoutly believed that we could be completely understood as machines. Out of that eclectic crucible I gradually refined my own understanding—still incomplete—of what science and faith are about.

A few years ago I had occasion to reflect on these topics when I was invited to give a commencement address at another small liberal arts college, and it is those remarks that I would like to share with you. I began with a humanist-scientist I much admired, the late Jacob Bronowski. Our paths had crossed a few times, and I always found these encounters enormously stimulating.

In one of his many splendid essays, Bronowski said that the world is divided between those who think of men as machines, and those who refuse to accept the idea of men as machines. "I have a great many friends who are passionately in love with digital computers," he wrote. "They are really heartbroken at the thought that men are not digital computers." It was plain that Bronowski did not number himself with them.

That was somewhat unexpected, for Bronowski was a scientist, and the way science works is to treat everything from atoms to stars and to men and women as machines. Science tries to extract from nature those laws that govern natural phenomena, whether it is the fall of an apple, the path of a comet, photosynthesis in a blade of grass, or the way the HIV virus dismantles the human immune system. Science seeks explanations of naturally recurring events, and it treats phenomena, no matter how complicated, as the combination of many simpler machines, all running like clockwork or computers, all strictly determined by rules of nature. Ideas and beliefs that are not relevant to the theory in any functional way are all left out, a fact that can be unnerving for interested onlookers.

There is a story about the time the famous French astronomer Laplace called on Napoleon. Laplace had developed the so-called nebular hypothesis, about how the solar system originally formed from a cloud of dust and gas. Napoleon asked Laplace what place God had in his theory, to which the astronomer replied, "Ah, I have no need for that hypothesis."

This has often been interpreted as an arrogant, atheistic statement, but actually Laplace was just doing his job as a scientist. It is the goal of science to explain the world around us in naturalistic, machinelike fashion, and that was precisely how Laplace attempted to describe the formation of the sun and planets. No matter what we believe about ultimate reality, as scientists we attempt to be rational mechanists. As an astronomer, I consider the formation of the solar system in mechanical terms. Were I a paleontologist, I would treat the fossil record in evolutionary terms. Were I a neurologist, I would treat the working of the brain as if it were just a determined electrochemical system, a machine. Properly conceived, these are simply models, pragmatic approaches that scientists adopt to make their data conceptually manageable. When pressed, most scientists would say their models are not literally true, although much of the time they act and often speak as if these descriptions are true.

Many people in America today feel threatened by a mechanistic scientific system that does not explicitly recognize the hand of God in its explanations. Science is, by its very nature, godless. But that does not mean that science is anti-God or atheistic. It merely means that science attempts to answer the "how" of the universe—how galaxies formed, how hemoglobin came about, how life arose—and it has virtually nothing to say about the "who," the designer or creator. "The heavens declare the glory of God," says the psalmist, and I believe that is true in many wonderful ways. Indeed, a powerful message of the Bible is to say that the universe has come into being through God's designing hand. But that is not the same thing as the scientific description of how things could come to be in mechanical terms.

The scientific approach is, for better or worse, a mechanistic procedure, but one that has worked with remarkable efficacy in painting a picture of how things work and enabling scientists to use those explanations to predict and discover many new and unexpected features of the universe.

I can sympathize with people who find this incomplete and unsatisfying and who wish that a broader philosophical structure could be placed into biology textbooks, but I think they are wrong when they suppose that the opening chapters of Genesis could substitute in any way as a scientific account of the formation and development of life.

Equally, however, I think many of my scientist friends are wrong when they accept the scientific picture as all that there is. In the opening scene of his Cosmos TV program, astronomer Carl Sagan intoned, "The cosmos is all there is or ever was or ever will be." That can be taken as a powerful statement of faith, not in God but of faith in atheism. "Really?" his associate producer responded when I told him this. "We just put it in because it sounded poetic."

Poetry or not, Carl Sagan has tried hard to persuade me that deep down we are nothing but machines, that the love he has for his wife can ultimately all be understood merely as electrical and chemical impulses.

My faith is different. Like Jacob Bronowski, I am loath to believe that we are merely machines. I look to transcendent qualities of the universe that lie beyond the realm of science but which are nevertheless just as real in the way I perceive the universe. That's a rather lofty and abstract way of saying that I think there's more than just meaningless mechanism in the universe. I shall come back to that more explicitly, but first, at the risk of ruining your day, I want to wade through some deeper philosophical waters.

When we try to build a strictly machinelike view of the universe, our system of scientific explanation seems to run up against certain limitations.

In the 1920s, as physicists explored ever more deeply into the world of the small, they found a barrier to our ever establishing a complete, deterministic description of the universe. The German scientist Werner Heisenberg formulated what is called the "uncertainty principle." One way to understand this concept is to imagine how we could locate the position and motion of a tiny atomic particle. In order to see it, we would have to shine light on it, but the beam of light would in itself disturb the position of the atom. The more precisely we could pin down the position, the more we would disturb its velocity. The end result is that at some fundamental level, the fine structure of the universe is basically indeterminate. We simply can't find simultaneously both the position and motion of a particle with complete precision.

Some may argue that the uncertainty principle does not make the universe less machinelike. We merely end up with a more sophisticated view of what a machine is. My view is that free will and the uncertainty principle are complementary and mutually enriching. Like the chemical occurrences in the brain that for Sagan constitute the basis for love, "underlying mechanics" is no more fundamental or real than our psychological and theological understandings of free will. Apparently, Heisenberg himself leaned toward the complementary view—the idea that at some deep level, the uncertainty principle allows for free will by pointing to the radical unknowability of human agency.

Nearly twenty years ago Heisenberg gave a public lecture at Harvard, and in the discussion period one of my graduate students asked if he had ever thought about the relation of his uncertainty principle to free will. At this, the other physics students in the audience—uncomfortable in a positivistic environment toward moralizing about hard science—hissed so loudly that Heisenberg did not bother to answer. However, later one of Heisenberg's younger colleagues, Carl Friedrich von Weizsäcker, came to visit, and we had an opportunity to speak with him privately, so my student again asked if Heisenberg had ever given any thought to the problem of free will when he was formulating the uncertainty principle. Von Weizsäcker's immediate answer was: "Oh yes, all the time."

Now, the scientists have by no means solved the thorny philosophical problem of freedom versus determinism, but we have found within our own framework that events can never be predicted with absolute certainty. Thus, we can never say that an event is impossible, only that it is exceedingly unlikely. Science cannot, for example, ever rule out the miraculous, even on its own scientific terms.

As a scientist, I work within a mechanical framework, even though there are cracks in the foundation, because the scientific system of prediction and explanation is so powerful and successful. There is much about myself that can be profitably understood as a mechanical product at the end of a four-billion-year chain of evolution.

But as a human being, I am also entitled to believe that these are not the ultimate answers. Not only am I entitled to believe that human beings are more than machines, I proclaim it!

For me, the most crucial part of Genesis 1 is not the sweeping, universal portrait of creation by a divine being who stands beyond as well as within the universe. Rather, it lies in the declaration in verse 27 that God created humankind in his own image. So quintessential is that idea that it is immediately repeated lest we miss it: "God created man in his own image, in his own image created he him, male and female created he them." The biblical account does not tell us much about the relationship of God to the universe of science but a great deal about the relationship of God to the divine aspects of humankind. Succinctly put, the stance of the biblical account is that God is not only creator and designer but that there is within each of us something of the divine: consciousness, creativity, and conscience.

Consciousness, particularly self-consciousness, is such an astonishing gift, an endowment that seems to set us off from all the rest of creation. To have a concept of time, of our place in it and our earthly mortality, is a distinctly human capacity. As Theodosius Dobzhansky, perhaps the greatest geneticist of our century, remarked, no other species was impelled by natural selection to evolve in similar ways.

Creativity is that divine spark that allows us to rise above the machine. Whether it is great music or literature or philosophy or science itself, there is something wonderful and inexplicable about creativity. We can, to be sure, build conditions where creativity flourishes, but I doubt that creativity itself can ever be satisfactorily explained in mechanical terms.

Conscience, the ability to decide between right and wrong, is for me the God-given attribute that separates us from the creatures who, millions of years ago, made the footprints we now find as fossils on the Laetoli plain of Africa. The biblical story of the fall of man is the story of learning the difference between right and wrong, and the awesomeness of taking responsibility for our choices.

After I discussed the verse about humankind being made in God's image in one of my many campus presentations, two members of Mr. Moon's Unification Church approached me, saying that they had generally liked my lecture, but that I had got it wrong about Genesis 1:27. The most important part of Genesis 1, they said, was verse 28: "And God said to them 'Be fruitful and multiply, and fill the earth and subdue it.'" I had to disagree. When

I mentioned creativity, I did not mean procreativity! When your grandparents were born, around 1900, the world population was one and a half billion. In the last seventeen years, the world has added to its population as many people as were alive in 1900. The relentless pressures on our biosphere caused by overcrowding include problems of waste disposal, depletion of fossil fuels, destruction of the ozone layer, acid rain, depletion or pollution of water supplies, sterilization of soil through intensive use of pesticides and chemical fertilizers, to name some of the most important. These are the challenges to young people today, and it will take all your God-given consciousness, creativity, and conscience to cope with them.

It is creativity that has allowed scientists to bring to earth the secrets of the stars: as Arthur Eddington wrote so presciently in 1920, "If indeed, the sub-atomic energy in the stars is being freely used to maintain their great furnaces, it seems to bring a little nearer to fulfillment our dream of controlling this latent power for the well-being of the human race." Perhaps nuclear power or hydrogen fusion will provide creative answers to some of these pressing world problems. But back in 1920 Eddington added four more chilling words to his statement: "It seems to bring a little nearer to fulfillment our dream of controlling this latent power for the well-being of the human race—or for its suicide."

You are indeed machines, victims of genetic circumstance and environmental imprinting, unable to change many of the awesome problems facing the world. But you are more than machines! You are endowed with the God-given gifts of consciousness, creativity, and conscience. You are not merely churning along in predetermined paths, unable to change anything. It is my prayer for you that you can use what science has to offer, but also your God-given creativity and consciences, to direct our world away from its present suicidal course.

Let me close with the familiar words from Reinhold Niebuhr: "God give us grace to accept with serenity the things that cannot be changed, courage to change those things that should be changed, and the wisdom to distinguish the one from the other."

Why Be a Scientist?

— GREGORY HAMMETT —

One motivation for going into fusion energy research, was that I felt this would be a way to work out Jesus' great commandment to love our neighbors as ourselves.

Gregory Hammett, class of 1980, remembers that he "couldn't decide whether to major in physics or economics or politics or philosophy" until the end of his junior year at Harvard. He is now a physicist on the research staff of Princeton University's Plasma Physics Laboratory, which does research on fusion energy.

Hammett traveled frequently in his youth, as his father was in the air force. Greg was born in Japan and went to high school in Georgia. He received his A.B. in physics from Harvard in 1980 and his Ph.D. in astrophysical sciences from Princeton in 1986. He has done research on fusion devices at Princeton and in England. His current research concerns the effects of turbulence on the efficiency of fusion devices, and involves developing theoretical models of plasma turbulence for simulation on the new generation of massively parallel supercomputers. Thankfully, he says, some balance in his life is provided by his wife, Kate, "an artist who does abstracts and stand-up comedy."

Why Be a Scientist?

— Gregory Hammett —

I vividly remember one particular sunny afternoon in 1977 sitting on my neighbor's floor in my freshman dorm, Wigglesworth, contemplating what field I should major in, what career path I should take, what I wanted to do with my life, and what the purpose of life was, anyway.

I eventually became a physicist doing research on fusion energy. Although I have been happy with my career decision, I still ponder some of the big questions. Part of my reason for going into science was to pursue the inborn curiosity we all have. We feel a sense of awe when we learn how energy can be converted from one form to another or when we see the beautiful patterns of ordered chaos in abstract mathematical equations or their physical realization in waves on the beach, clouds at sunset, or even cream swirling in coffee. But beyond enjoying this exploration of the world, one set of big questions I have as a scientist is the same as I would have in any career—Is my field, science, helpful to other people? And if so, how? And why help other people at all? I would like to tackle some of these issues here. Why be a scientist?

There is wide disagreement on how to answer questions about the benefits of science and technology, and how they fit into the larger scheme of God's plan for humankind. Many people view science as embodying the greatest achievements of mankind, with which we will someday build utopia. Certain popular science magazines are proponents of this view. At the other extreme are those who blame science for unleashing a Pandora's box of horrifying capabilities and destroying what *had* been utopia. (I am reminded of how an empty Coca Cola bottle brought modernity and hence greed and violence to an idyllic bushman tribe in the hilarious comedy *The Gods Must Be Crazy*.) Both extremes are distortions of the truth. We should, I believe, neither deify nor demonize science. If we are honest, we will not lose perspective of the successes of science, nor will we forget its limitations or, more importantly, the limitations of human nature.

In many ways, the average person today is healthier, safer, and materially more comfortable than even a king was two hundred years ago. His court jesters can be summoned with a push on the remote control of the television. Mass-production techniques have reduced the cost of many products to a tenth or less of their original cost, including the personal computer with which I am writing. Fear of famine is a thing of the past in much of the modern world, thanks to farm technologies involving machinery, irrigation, fertilizers, pesticides, improved plant varieties, and transportation and storage advances. An abundant food supply, along with basic sanitation and modern medicine, has led to dramatic drops in mortality rates. Thanks largely to drops in infant mortality rates, a person born today in North America has an average life span of over seventy years, compared to thirty-five to forty years at the end of the eighteenth century or only twenty to twenty-five years in the first century. Although infant mortality is still a serious problem in many parts of the modern world, including even certain urban areas of the United States, in the 1600s two thirds of all infants died in their first year after birth.

Despite all of these technological benefits, twentieth-century people are no happier than first-century folk, and for a variety of reasons: the escalation of expectations, the impermanence of technological fixes, the surprising side effects of certain technological "advances," and finally the nontechnological nature of humankind's fundamental problems. All of these represent "hidden costs" that sharply qualify the promise that science and technology hold for human happiness. I'll discuss each of them briefly.

First, escalating expectations: Expectations can be part of a healthy attitude. It is good for a child to be proud to be able to play a simple tune after a few piano lessons and yet still desire to learn more complicated ones. But I am not sure it is healthy to be so driven that one is dissatisfied even after mastering Liszt and performing to an ovation in Carnegie Hall. Each technological advance provides a temporary thrill, but it soon becomes routine, an old toy. Barely a dozen years ago, PCs were welcomed as a major advance over the old typewriter. But the powerhouse computers of recent years are now viewed as quaint antiques. Curiously, a more powerful computer seems not to have reduced the total time I spend typing: I now type more documents and spend more time revising them. "Timesaving" devices rarely save time.

Rising expectations can be part of a destructive, obsessive perfectionism that is never satisfied. It is possible to satisfy our needs, impossible to satisfy our greeds. As Alan Verhey points out, "If we can travel faster by car than horse, we now want faster cars. If we can have a child when we could not have one before, we now want a particular kind of child, say, a bright, blond boy."[1] Verhey fears that this escalation of expectations in the field of genetic engineering will continue "until we have reduced our options to a perfect child or a dead child." By not providing what it seems to promise—genuine fulfillment—science keeps us yearning for still more thrills, gad-

---

[1]Alan Verhey, *Christianity Today* (February 7, 1986), 27.

gets, conveniences, and even power. There is no clearly recognizable point at which it becomes enough. This lack of contentment, this sin of insatiable desire in the human race, can be traced all the way back to Adam and Eve. (Their progeny have not evolved very far, if at all.) Though God provided lavishly for them in the Garden of Eden, they wanted more. They wanted to become *like* God.

The next limitation of science and technology is that technological fixes are impermanent. Cars rust. Moving parts wear out. Hard disks conk out. Penicillin-resistant strains of bacteria develop. The best health system can't prevent the aging of the body, and eventual death. Sometimes it seems as if everything around us is cursed; as soon as we finish pulling up the weeds in one part of our life, they start coming up in another (Genesis 3:17–19), constant reminders that we live in a fallen world.

Third, new technologies often have surprising side effects. Consider some examples: Chemically, freon is usually very inert, so the discovery of its impact on the ozone layer was quite surprising. There are now so many people burning so much fuel that air pollution is a problem and we are beginning to worry about possible global climate changes. As the Amish point out, technologies can have social side effects as well. Television has drastically undercut family interaction. Modern transportation has aided the dispersion of the once close-knit extended family. Higher-skill technologies have cut the opportunities for stable jobs for some in our society. But what these unintended consequences often point to is the abuse or selfish use of technology. Like money, technology sometimes merely aggravates preexisting human problems. The true culprit is the fallen human heart, which has the capability of turning virtually everything it invents into a two-edged sword—a blessing or a curse.

For example, computer recognition of the human voice, if and when it is perfected, will probably replace the word processor keyboard with a microphone, doing wonders for sore backs and tired fingers. But it would also enable intelligence agencies or corporate "big brothers" to greatly expand their eavesdropping capabilities. The capacity for evil is in the heart, not in advanced technology.

This brings us to the fourth limitation of technology, which is that many of our main problems are not even technological at all. The United States has the best medical technology in the world, but millions cannot afford it. The technology exists to feed and immunize every child on the planet, yet tens of thousands die each day of hunger and illness. These are complex social problems that cannot be fixed by technology alone. Technology can make the pie bigger, but it cannot guarantee everyone a large enough slice.

The source of much human happiness and despair lies in the social or personal realm—far outside the reach of technological solutions. Many of the same things make twentieth-century people happy as they did in the first century: a loving family, a living wage, a shared meal, good friends, the birth of a child. Despair too has causes which have changed little over the centuries. The complexities of issues such as poverty go far beyond the problem of material resources to issues of skills, family support, discrimination, political gridlock, alcohol and drug abuse, and hopelessness. And yet social institutions are sometimes the problem rather than the solution. Inefficiency and corruption may subvert the best programs. Governments may liberate or oppress. The media and even the universities may enlighten or indoctrinate. Families may build up healthy personalities or deform them through abuse and neglect. Humans are a great paradox, having the potential for wonderful good, but with a terrible propensity for evil (we were made in the image of God, but we have fallen).

Against such a backdrop, it is easy to understand why it has been said that one of the most observably verifiable doctrines of Christianity is the fallen nature of humankind. We have only to look at our own sin to know that the classical problems of mankind—pride, lust, envy, greed—are still with, and within, us. Scientific progress treats some of the symptoms but not the underlying disease. We still search for the meaning of life and struggle with the meaning of death.

"God has not abandoned us," declared Billy Graham in his 1991 Central Park crusade, "*we* have abandoned God." We have tried every kind of substitute for God: science and technology, money, psychologies, philosophies, individual freedom, drugs, sex. Blaise Pascal (the great seventeenth-century French scientist and philosopher after whom the computer language is named) reflected on mankind's fruitless search for happiness without faith and concluded that within every human heart is an infinite "God-shaped void" that only God can fill. In his *Pensées*, Pascal observes:

> All men seek happiness. This is without exception. . . . Some seek good in authority, others in scientific research, others in pleasure. . . . And yet, after such a great number of years, no one without faith has reached the point to which all continually look. All complain, princes and subjects, noblemen and commoners, old and young, strong and weak. . . . A trial so long, so continuous, and so uniform, should certainly convince us of our inability to reach the good by our own efforts. But example teaches us little. . . .

Drawing on his groundbreaking scientific studies of the vacuum to inform his understanding of the human condition, the French philosopher concludes:

What is it, then, that this desire and this inability proclaim to us, but that there was once in man a true happiness of which there now remains to him only the mark and empty trace, which he in vain tries to fill from all his surroundings, seeking from things absent the help he does not obtain in things present? But these are all inadequate, because the infinite abyss can only be filled by an infinite and immutable object, that is to say, only by God Himself.[2]

We cannot fill our own emptiness; we need help from outside ourselves. God has provided that help through Jesus, the promised Messiah. Jesus offers escape from the finality of death, the ultimate problem which science can never conquer. (For the reader interested in exploring the evidence for Christianity, I recommend three thoughtful little books.[3]) Our fundamental problems are spiritual, the corruption of the human heart. Jesus offers to redeem us and to transform our hearts and lives. This transformation is not instantaneous, and I must confess that there have been many times when I have failed as a Christian and deeply hurt others around me. But God's forgiveness, and the great sacrifice that made it possible, grant us the grace to keep on trying, to continue on his upward path rather than degenerating further in a downward spiral.

My central point is this: at the heart of many of our problems that we try to fix through technological or social means is the root spiritual problem of our fallen nature, and hence our need for redemption. But a spiritual solution does not mean that we are to abandon all physical and social concerns in favor of a "spiritual" approach. Jesus himself was concerned with the whole person; he healed people both physically and spiritually. He said to the paralytic both, "My son, your sins are forgiven," and also, "Rise, take up your pallet and go home." Indeed, knowing that there is an eternity gives new meaning and relevance to this life: death is no longer the end; what we do now can have eternal implications.

Moreover, a spiritual perspective gives the moral framework needed to wisely use the tools of technology, and the motivation to counteract the side effects when necessary. Cultivating a spiritual perspective reins in our greed and puts a healthy damper on the escalation of expectations, helping us to be satisfied with what we have and enabling us to turn our attention

---

[2]Blaise Pascal, *Pensées*, ed. R. M. Hutchins, Great Books of the Western World (Chicago: Univ. of Chicago Press, 1952), vol. 33, p. 244. From section number 425 of the Brunschvieg edition of the *Pensées*, or number 148 of the Lafuma edition. This excerpt has been slightly reordered.

[3]C. S. Lewis, *Mere Christianity* (New York: Macmillan, 1952). Paul Little, *Know Why You Believe* (Downers Grove, Ill.: InterVarsity Press, 1968). Moishe Rosen, *Y'shua* (Chicago: Moody Press, 1982).

to those in greater need. Jesus calls us both to abandon the beguilements of this world and at the same time to be involved in it. The physical takes on new meaning once we recognize the spiritual, with which God has involved his physical creation in many ways. God has given spiritual meaning to physical acts such as caring for those in need. "For I was hungry and you gave me something to eat, I was thirsty and you gave me something to drink, I was a stranger and you invited me in, I needed clothes and you clothed me, I was sick and you looked after me, I was in prison and you came to visit me" (Matthew 25:35–36).

The good which can be done in the physical and social realms is just as real as the evil which can be done. God's creation is not an illusion: a physician heals the real hurts of a real person. A farmer feeds real people who experience actual hunger. In our modern economy, we do not frequently come face-to-face with the needs we are meeting, but the mechanic who fixed the farmer's tractor, the garbage collector who disposed of or recycled the mechanic's trash, and the scientist who invented new recycling methods all play vital roles.

My motivation for going into fusion energy research, apart from enjoying science and math, was that I felt this research would be a way to work out Jesus' great commandment to love our neighbors as ourselves. I went to college in the late 1970s, in the middle of the energy crisis. I was quite conscious of the economic disruptions it triggered both worldwide and on the personal level, and of the threats of war over oil supplies. Energy needs are still a long-term problem. Fusion energy has the possibility of being both abundant and environmentally acceptable. It would not produce greenhouse gases which add to the risk of global warming, and its radioactivity would be thousands to millions of times less hazardous than that of fission reactors. Much work remains to make fusion an efficient and practical reality, but we are now fairly confident that we can make fusion work technically.[4] Yet like all other technologies, however worthy, it cannot solve all the problems of the whole person.

As someone who works in the physical sciences and follows developments in various scientific, technological, and public policy areas, I see the valuable contributions that people in various fields—from engineering to economics, from medicine to business, from politics to plasma physics—can make, and have made, to improve the quality of human life. (Often we don't appreciate the advances that have been made until the car breaks down or the electricity goes out.) However, the solutions to many of our

---

[4]J. G. Cordey, R. J. Goldston, R. R. Parker, "Progress toward a Tokamak Fusion Reactor," *Physics Today* (January 1992), 22.

problems do not lie in more knowledge. If that were the case, then we in the twentieth century would be much more content than all who have come before us. The challenge is often whether we can use our knowledge responsibly and whether we can direct it in a caring way toward others. That implicates the human heart, not so much the mind, and points to our need for God's transforming work in our hearts.

If we are to help the whole person, we must have a proper balance in our approach to physical, social, and spiritual problems. Jesus set an example of caring for both the spiritual and physical needs of people, and he also gave us a reason to follow his example: "This is love: not that we loved God, but that he loved us and sent his Son as an atoning sacrifice for our sins. Dear friends, since God so loved us, we also ought to love one another" (1 John 4:10–11). The world needs good doctors and lawyers (seventy-five percent of my freshman class wanted to be one or the other). The world needs good fathers and mothers, teachers and preachers, farmers and cooks, businessmen and politicians, and even scientists. But whatever we do, we should do it out of love for each other, out of a love which springs from the great love of God.

Thorns in the Garden Planet

୬ଽ

— VERA SHAW —

The gospel offers hope for the pollution of the planet by first recycling the human spirit. But where do we begin?

After graduating from McMaster University, Canada, as a science concentrator, **Vera Shaw** became an industrial chemist. She married her college classmate Jim Shaw, and they moved to Boston in 1945 where he joined the Harvard faculty. For fifty years they have served as faculty advisors to the Harvard-Radcliffe Christian Fellowship. The Shaws are loved by scores of alumni for their prayer, friendship, and quiet encouragement over the years.

For fifteen years Shaw has been chairman of the Conservation Committee of Sutton Island, Maine, where they spend their summers. Her recent book *Thorns in the Garden Planet: Meditations on the Creator's Care* (Nelson, 1993), from which this essay is adapted, is the result of her "garden notebook," in which she continually wondered "what patterns and purposes relate the inner environment of the person to the endangered environment of the planet?"

Mrs. Shaw reminds us that Harvard College was founded to be a *garden* in the wilderness of the New World—a college which cared for truth, and beauty, to be enjoyed from generation to generation.

Thorns in the Garden Planet

— VERA SHAW —

Forty thousand people gave evidence of how desperately the world must seek an answer to the problem of environmental pollution. From all walks of life and cultural backgrounds, they traveled to participate in the international meetings on the environment at the 1992 Earth Summit and Global Forum in Rio de Janeiro. The urgent nature of the talks was underscored when several environmental groups reckoned that the following things happened during the twelve days of the Earth Summit: 600 to 900 species of plants and animals became extinct; 482,000 acres of arable land became desert; over one million acres of tropical forest were destroyed.

I thought of Rachel Carson's classic book *Silent Spring* and her dedication of the volume to Albert Schweitzer: "Man has lost the capacity to foresee and to forestall. He will end by destroying the earth."

In Rio a small group held a daily discussion on "Biblical Themes on the Environment." We discussed practical examples of how our belief in God, as creator, affects our priorities and daily habits in the way we use natural resources. We spoke of a theology of contentment and gratitude. We spoke of real wealth in terms of scattering and planting resources (like seeds) rather than gathering them. We discussed how our relationship with God enriches the ways we enjoy creation. Most of all, we wondered how Jesus Christ would have us understand and respond to the integrity and degradation of the environment.

My thoughts returned to a quiet ocean island where we spend summers in Maine. There, many years before, I first considered the meaning of another environment—the interior environment of the human spirit. There I discovered the words of author George Eliot: "There is a great deal of unmapped country within us." On that island, I also discovered the paraphrase of Psalm 139 of Oswald Chambers as he spoke of the hidden depths of his spirit, unknown and unexplored:

> Thou art the God of the early mornings, the God of the late at nights, the God of the mountain peaks, and the God of the sea; but, my God, my soul has further horizons—O Thou Who art the God of all these, be my God. I cannot reach to the heights or to the depths; there are motives I cannot trace, dreams I cannot get at—my God, search me out.[1]

---

[1]Oswald Chambers, *My Utmost for His Highest* (New York; Dodd, Mead, 1937).

This hidden environment of the human spirit is seldom mentioned in our concern for our more obvious environmental problems. Many biblical passages maintain that what is hidden in our hearts controls our actions and our relationships. The pollution of self-centeredness and self-interest needs to be recognized if we are to get to the roots of the environmental pollution of the planet. Job 32:8 affirms the reality of the hidden self: "There is a spirit in man. . .[that] gives him understanding." Much of Christ's teaching concerns the pollution of this inner environment and the glad news of the redemption, renewal, and recycling that he offers.

Is there a theology of the environment inherent in the Christian faith? Is Jesus' message of the kingdom of God "within us" relevant to the global discussion of the moral and ethical problems of pollution?

The messianic traditions of both Jews and Christians look forward to resolving the disharmony between God, humanity, and nature. The apostle Paul described the relationship between man and nature in his letter to the Romans, emphasizing that renewal of the earth is inextricably linked to man's renewal:

> The creation waits in eager expectation for the sons of God to be revealed. For the creation was subjected to frustration, not by its own choice, but by the will of the one who subjected it, in hope that the creation itself will be liberated from its bondage to decay and brought into the glorious freedom of the children of God.
>
> ROMANS 8:19–21

Paul goes on in the passage to say that as part of the creation, we ourselves groan inwardly as we wait eagerly for our own redemption. How accurate a description of our human condition even now, almost two thousand years later.

The heritage of Scripture includes a love for the whole creation. The psalms overflow with a sense of the beauty and grandeur of the creation and the Creator. Paul maintains in Romans 1 that since the creation of the world God's invisible qualities—his eternal power and divine nature—have been clearly seen, being revealed from what has been made. God's delight in his creation in Genesis is carried forward in the garden theme throughout the Old and New Testaments and culminates in the book of Revelation, when access to the Tree of Life is restored. The Creator's care for the creation is seen in the three gardens in the Bible: the Garden of Eden, a garden of beginnings; the Garden of Gethsemane, a garden of suffering and cleansing; and the garden of the Resurrection and new creation. Each garden tells its own story. In each garden, the Creator, who gives us life and responsibility, engages us in a dramatic dialogue which reveals our relationship to himself, the earth, and our neighbor.

Eden: The Garden of Beginnings

The story of Eden gives insight into the cause of our environmental problems. God gave man, male and female, the wonderful responsibility to till and keep the garden (the Hebrew for "keep" can also be translated "preserve.") It is a beautiful image—the sovereign Lord created his masterpiece and then created man and woman "in his image" to preserve and care for the garden and to walk in deep friendship with himself. God established the Sabbath as a day to rest, a day to remember, and to recognize the Creator's care with joy. The Sabbath celebrates creation in the renewing power of rest. And the Sabbath was for the land as well, affirming the Creator's concern for the preservation of the earth.[2]

Yet while surrounded by the abundance of the perfect environment of Eden, enjoying all its wonderful resources, man decided that no restrictions should limit his control. Man believed all creation was for his satisfaction and he alone should decide how to use it. His fascination with evil polished the forbidden fruit. God honored man's free will. In Eden, man's choice to turn from God's love in order to become his own god, in turn, polluted the garden's perfection and destroyed its harmony.

Gethsemane: The Garden of Suffering, Obedience, and Cleansing

In Gethsemane, God through his Son, Jesus Christ, prepared to pay the enormous cost of cleansing and renewing all creation. The first Adam represents all mankind in turning away from God and placing his own will at the center of his life. The Second Adam, Jesus, represents the new man as he comes to the garden in communion with God, seeking to put God's will at the center of his life. He shares with his friends the fruits of the earth, bread and wine, which are his "body and blood." He prayed not only to know God's will but to do God's will, which was to become the suffering servant. From that garden he is taken to Jerusalem, where he is crowned with thorns[3] and nailed to a forbidden tree to die for our sin, that we would be forgiven and free to live again in friendship with God.

---

[2]Just as the seventh day of each week was a day of rest, so every seventh year was a year of rest for the land (Leviticus 25:1–7). Each Sabbath year, no crops were planted, for the land was to remain fallow in rest. The year of Jubilee was the ultimate celebration—after seven Sabbaths (the fiftieth year) the land, other resources, and even debt were equitably redistributed. The land was never sold, nor new land purchased, for all the land belonged to God. Each generation inherited the stewardship of earth and human community.

[3]Thorns—a symbol of autonomy, rebellion, and conflict—were a warning to Adam as he left Eden. And thorns were made into a crown that Jesus, the Second Adam, carried to the cross.

The Garden of the Resurrection

And finally, near the cross and the empty tomb, the garden of the resurrection makes known the possibility of redemption and renewal for man and earth. With this strength we work to bring the kingdom of God to earth. While in one sense "the kingdom of God is within you," we also look forward to a "new heaven and a new earth," where once again we will live in deep fellowship with God, where "he will wipe away every tear from [our] eyes. There will be no more death or mourning or crying or pain, for the old order of things [will have] passed away" (Revelation 21:4).

The apostle John tells us that what started in a garden will end in a "heavenly city" filled with people from all nations, praising God:

> [I saw] the river of the water of life, as clear as crystal, flowing from the throne of God and of the Lamb down the middle of the great street of the city. On each side of the river stood the tree of life, bearing twelve crops of fruit, yielding its fruit every month. And the leaves of the tree are for the healing of the nations.
>
> REVELATION 22:1–2

These meditations help me begin to recognize God's redeeming care for the whole world, his provision to deal with the thorns both within us and in our world, and his promise to make all things new.

Environmental responsibility is part of the core of Christian life and faith. From Eden onward, the story of the Bible is the story of a God who seeks to fully redeem and re-create that which, and those whom, he made and loves. Indeed, the Christian message offers hope for the alarming pollution of the planet by first redeeming and recycling the human heart and spirit.

But how is this practical in our daily lives? With the mind and spirit of Christ, we become gardeners, or stewards, of the earth in its fullness. Transformed lives are marked by maturity, wisdom, and self-control. We reject the driving, groping pace of consumerism and careerism. We name and constructively solve real problems. We develop the capacity to love, and to share with those in poverty so that they are not forced to use the earth's resources in unsustainable ways. We seek to understand and live out an ecology of life that preserves both interior and exterior environments. We develop the vision to see dumping grounds as gardens, and then roll up our sleeves.

We can no longer afford to focus on the present at the expense of the future. When we look into the New Testament, we see that Jesus not only lived a profound ecological ethic but he created a redemptive community to live out creative solutions to any challenge the world could offer.

In 1962, just as *Silent Spring* was published and the environmental movement was in its infancy, Harvard professor of church history George Williams wrote and lectured on the biblical mandate for conservation and stewardship of natural resources.[4] He asked, who "can better mount the watchtower and sound the alert for the care of the earth?" Christians, with their sense of nature as a creation (which implies the Creator), strategically located with their ministries, properties, educational programs, and publications, can be especially effective if they remind the world of the call to stewardship of the creation. We must be reminded of the importance of daily choices and habits. Do we buy products that protect the environment? Do we diligently recycle? Do we encourage projects that deal effectively with toxic waste, water and air pollution, and conservation of resources?

Williams asks, "Are we in the end conquerors of the cosmos or carers for our fellow creatures, stewards of creation or exploiters, ruthless like some of the beasts or redemptive of them all and therewith mankind, manipulative or reverent toward life in all its mysterious plenitude?"[5] These are deep questions raised in the biblical tradition and deserving of examination in the present environmental and moral crisis. In the words of environmentalist Calvin DeWitt, "a true grasp of faith leads us to a vision of harmony between human beings and nature, and the new life that has come to us through our relationship to Jesus Christ implies power to achieve that vision."[6]

After developing a multitude of recommendations, the final words of the 1992 Earth Summit were fitting: "Let's begin!" But where do we begin? Donald Conroy, president of the North American Coalition on Religion and Ecology, challenged the great assembly of the Global Forum with these words:

> Begin where you live. Tend your corner of the garden planet. Learn the environmental history of the area where you live, and what influences are protecting or destroying its natural beauty. Then learn to be among those who work together, as neighbors around the world, to preserve the beauty of life in the threatened garden planet.

---

[4]George H. Williams, "Christian Attitudes Toward Nature," *Christian Scholar's Review* II (1962). See also *Wilderness and Paradise in Christian Thought,* lectures by author.

[5]Ibid.

[6]Calvin Dewitt, *Growing Our Future,* ed. Katie Smith and Tetsunau Yamamori (Hartford: Kumarian Press, 1992), 9–13.

CHAPTER 9

RENEWING EDUCATION: A LIGHT IN THE YARD

Education begins to do its full work only when the materials of learning, ably and imaginatively presented, penetrate into the very marrow of the learner and set up there a process of desiring that will not be stilled.

HARVARD PRESIDENT NATHAN PUSEY, EMERITUS, 1955

᭝

You could not wish to have been born in a better time than when all is lost.

SIMONE WEIL, *FIRST AND LAST NOTES*

᭝

What else can save us but your hand remaking what you have made.

AUGUSTINE OF HIPPO

᭝

If I can fathom all mysteries and all knowledge,
    and if I have a faith that can move mountains,
    but have not love, I am nothing...
Love is patient, love is kind.
It does not envy, it does not boast, it is not proud...
Love does not delight in evil but rejoices with the truth.

THE APOSTLE PAUL, *1 CORINTHIANS CHAPTER 13*

Judeo-Christian Versus Pagan Scholarship

৯ৎৡ

— H A R O L D   J .   B E R M A N —

To be a scholar is to search for truth. And to search for truth is to be open to the possibility that some discovered truth will lay claim to one's allegiance. In my own case, the truth that "set me free" first appeared to me at the outbreak of World War II, when I was twenty-one years old.

Harold J. Berman is the Ames Professor of Law Emeritus at Harvard Law School. In 1985 he became the Woodruff Professor of Law at Emory University and a Fellow in Russian Legal Studies at the Carter Center.

A prodigious scholar in the field of Soviet law, Professor Berman's work also includes international trade, legal history, jurisprudence, and law and religion. He has authored twenty-five books and some three hundred articles.

Harold Berman graduated from Dartmouth in 1938 and the London School of Economics in 1939. "At that time I was a lukewarm believer in Judaism," he said. "I was, and still am, very conscious and proud of my Jewish heritage." After serving in the U.S. Army from 1942 to 1945, he went to Yale Law School.

As a young law professor from Stanford, Berman arrived at Harvard Law School in 1948 on a visiting professorship — and stayed for the next thirty-seven years.

Judeo-Christian Versus Pagan Scholarship

— HAROLD J. BERMAN —

The founders of Harvard University were convinced that the pursuit of scholarly knowledge would lead to discovery of truth, not merely in the secular sense but also in the Christian sense—that is, truth which discloses the glory of God. They believed that God is revealed both in nature and in us and that therefore the study of natural and human phenomena will disclose God's purposes.

In the past century, we have moved very far from that vision of the purpose of scholarship. Today the lectures offered by the faculty, the class discussion, and the books assigned in the various sciences and humanities give little if any recognition that God even exists—much less glorify him. Our intellectual life, our thinking, has been largely divorced from our religious faith.

Faculty, students, and administrators now think of themselves as members not of a religious community but of an "academic" community—named after the Greek hero Academus. It was in a grove dedicated to Academus—I think we may call him the unknown god of our universities—that Plato in about 390 B.C. founded his famous school, an "academy" dedicated to the pursuit of wisdom. The modern academic community has come to stand in sharp contrast with the Christian community, which is dedicated to the worship of the *known* God—the God who, we are told by Paul in his first letter to the Corinthians, had confounded the wisdom of the secular and made it foolish.

"The Lord knoweth the thoughts of the wise, that they are vain" (Psalm 94:11). The Lord knoweth the thoughts of the eminent historian Professor So and So, that they are vain. God hath made foolish the writings of the distinguished economist Professor This and That. Where is the scribe, Professor ABC of the Divinity School? Where is the disputer of the world, Professor XYZ of the Law School? "Hath not God made foolish their wisdom?" (1 Corinthians 1:20). If the wisdom that we are pursuing is vanity, surely we should cease to pursue it. But is there not another wisdom, a wisdom of God, for us to pursue?

What is the difference between the wisdom of God and the wisdom of the world?

The wisdom of the world assumes that God's existence is irrelevant to knowledge and that truth is discoverable by the human mind unaided by the Holy Spirit. Christian wisdom, on the other hand, seeks God's guidance, the guidance of the Holy Spirit, in order to discover the relationship between what we know and what God intends for us. God is the Lord of our minds as much as he is the Lord of our "hearts." Nothing is discovered without his help. I believe that if we open our minds to the inspiration of the Holy Spirit and pray for his guidance in intellectual matters, we shall discover new truth which will astound those who believe that God's existence is irrelevant to scholarship.

The pagan scholar says, "Facts are facts." He treats nature and society as objects, as things to be dissected and analyzed by his brain. The Judaic or Christian scholar sees not merely nature and not merely society but nature and society as creations of God separated from, and yet still bearing witness to, their Creator. Heaven and earth are still his handiwork and still declare his glory. They reflect his purposes for humankind. The Judaic or Christian scholar attempts not only to see this reflection but to participate in it, to commit himself to exemplifying it.

But isn't a fact a fact? Are not the facts we seek to discover, as natural and social scientists—facts about the moon or about history or about life— the same facts to a Jew or a Christian as to a pagan? In one sense, of course, they are. That the sun rose this morning is a fact recognized by atheist, polytheist, Hindu, Muslim, Jew, or Christian. But in another sense, that is not so. For a fact is never seen in isolation from other facts. The phenomena of space and time may be seen from many different perspectives. As a matter of fact, the sun, of course, did not rise; the earth turned.

A Judaic or Christian perspective reveals certain facts that otherwise cannot be known. It reveals that human history is part of God's plan for the universe and that every fact of the universe is an event in the life of God. The Judaic or Christian scholar strives to find God's purposes, God himself, in the subject of his scholarship. He or she must therefore be a prophet, and more than that, an apostle.

It is customary to treat the historical controversy between science and religion as a dead issue—and it is, in the old sense of science as the hard physical sciences. We are no longer troubled by the claim that the natural sciences disprove religious truth. But there is a far more serious conflict between religion and the modern, broader conception of "science" which *should* trouble us: that is the conflict between the secularism of so-called modern "scientific" thought, especially in the social sciences, and the Christian insight that humans are more than a natural phenomenon, more even than observers of natural phenomena, that humans are rather creatures of God who partake also of God's creative powers.

The modes of analysis which dominate our intellectual life today are essentially pagan modes of analysis. They are inherently skeptical modes of analysis rather than faithful modes of analysis. In the social sciences, they seek explanations in materialistic terms of aggrandizement, whether economic or political or psychological. In philosophy and literature, they increasingly emphasize the arbitrariness and subjectivity of standards of goodness, truth, and beauty. Underlying these modes of analysis is the tendency of the analyst—the social scientist in particular—to arrogate to himself a power to treat humans as objects, a tendency to "play God" with his intellectual systems. He stresses causation instead of creation, facts instead of acts. He looks only at the temporal things which are seen and not at the eternal things which are unseen. He denies the reality of God's self-revelation in the intellectual process itself. Pride of intellect is the besetting sin of the modern university, whether it takes the form of the professor's skepticism or the student's idle curiosity.

There is a need for Jews and Christians to cultivate Judaic and Christian methods of thinking about life—Christian modes of analysis of society, of history, of economic life, of the human psyche. This means, at the very least, bringing back into the classroom the simple truth that our entire cultural and intellectual heritage derives historically from our religious tradition.

From a Judaic or Christian standpoint, intellectual understanding is intimately connected with faith, with hope, and with love. There is a faithful, a hopeful, and a loving mode of scholarship which it is the task of the scholar to cultivate. Though the unbeliever will classify such a mode of scholarship as "unscientific," it will come much nearer than dispassionate objectivity to the truth about human nature and social life. For the truth is that God does not call us to be merely observers of life; rather he calls all of us—even the scholars—in all that we do, to participate with him in the process of spiritual death and resurrection which is the fundamental religious experience.

The non-Jewish or non-Christian reader may be puzzled by this conclusion and may wonder whether it does not exclude him from the intellectual community of his Jewish and Christian fellow-scholars—or, more precisely, whether it does not excuse those relatively few persons who seek to practice a Jewish or Christian mode of scholarship from the intellectual community of the great majority who prefer to dwell in the academic grove where facts are simply facts. Fortunately, however, the modern university, despite its more dogmatic beginnings, is (at least when it is at its best) hospitable to fundamentally diverse concepts of the nature of truth. Indeed, it thrives on such diversity, leaving it to each scholar to relate his intellectual convictions to his personal convictions in his or her own way.

Yet this very pluralism makes it appropriate, and even necessary, for participants in the scholarly community to share with one another, from time to time, their personal experiences. This is a difficult and humbling thing to do, especially in a university where people hardly ever discuss truth and first principles which ought to be fundamental to our dialogue. Yet to be a scholar is to search for truth. And to search for truth is to be open to the possibility that some discovered truth will lay claim to one's allegiance.

In my own case, the truth that "set me free" first appeared to me at the outbreak of World War II, when I was twenty-one years old. I was in Europe, where I had been studying European history for a year. While I visited Germany, Hitler announced on the radio that Germany had invaded Poland. It was literally the outbreak of the world war, and many of us fled for France. The stations were crowded with peasants carrying potatoes and animals and personal effects. The earliest train I could catch left at midnight.

I thought that Hitler's invasion of Poland would lead to the total destruction of human civilization. I felt as one would feel today if all the major powers were to become involved in a full-scale nuclear war. I was shattered—in total despair. There, alone on that train, Jesus Christ appeared to me in a vision. His face reminded me of one of the Russian icons that I would later see—heavily scarred and tragic—not suffering but bearing the marks of having suffered. I suddenly realized that I was not entitled to such despair, that it was not I but another, God himself, who bore the burden of human destiny, and that it was rather for me to believe in him even though human history was at an end.

When the train arrived in Paris early that morning, I walked straight to the Notre Dame cathedral, and I prayed a personal prayer to God for the first time in my life. My wife, who is Protestant, asks me how I could become a believer in Christ without having read the Gospels. My answer is that that is how the first disciples became believers.

And so this experience of "amazing grace" not only made me a Christian believer—against my will and against my heritage—but also freed me from that pride and illusion of intellect which is the besetting sin of academic scholarship.

Feasting at the Table of the Lord

৯৫

— PETER FEAVER —

Ralph cut me off with a bored wave of his plastic cup, "How many books does Lehigh's library have? Harvard has well over ten million." I would like to think it was superior spiritual maturity that kept me from popping him one in the face.

Peter Feaver, Ph.D. in government, class of 1990, is an assistant professor of political science at Duke University. In 1993–94 Feaver held a Counsel on Foreign Relations fellowship to serve as director for defense policy and arms control on the National Security Counsel staff at the White House. He writes widely on national security issues, and his most recent book is *Guarding the Guardians: Civilian Control of Nuclear Weapons in the United States* (Cornell Univ. Press, 1992).

After graduate school and against all odds, he says, he succeeded in marrying above his station. His wife Karen (nee Geers), a "beautiful, intelligent, sensitive, and strong-willed woman," has a passion for human rights and political activism.

Dr. Feaver also boasts of his parents. His father, Dr. Douglas Feaver, recently retired from Lehigh University, Peter's alma mater, as professor of classics and now is dean of humanities at Youth With a Mission. There he is ably assisted by his wife, Margaret, an accomplished teacher in her own right. Peter is the youngest of four children and encourages his many gifted nephews and nieces to refer to him as "Favorite Uncle Peter."

Feasting at the Table
of the Lord

— PETER FEAVER —

Start a child in the way he should go,
And when he is old he will not turn from it.
PROVERBS 22:6

❧

Always be prepared to give an answer to everyone
who asks you to give the reason for the hope that you have.
1 PETER 3:15

❧

My Harvard career had what you might call an inauspicious beginning. For starters, I did not really comprehend what I was doing when I applied to the government department in Harvard's Graduate School of Arts and Sciences (GSAS). I knew I had thoroughly enjoyed my life as an undergraduate at Lehigh University in Pennsylvania, and I suspected graduate school would be a good way to prolong the magic a bit. But as for the psychological cost of getting a doctorate, or the pros and cons of a Ph.D. in GSAS versus a masters from Harvard's Kennedy School of Government, such things were a complete mystery to me. In the end I decided against the Kennedy School, because its application form was longer than the one from GSAS. Also, I naïvely thought it would take only four years to get a Ph.D.— a wishful delusion from which a registrar office gnome, rather coldly, delivered me on the very first day of registration.

That was the first day. On the second, one of my colleagues-to-be gave me a most memorable welcome to the ivied towers. The scene was a mixer for new graduate students, second floor, student lounge, Littauer building. Like me, Ralph was a G–1 in the "gov department," and I instinctively felt we could become fast friends and fellow travelers on the road to truth. I approached him with grinning enthusiasm.

Upon hearing I had gone to Lehigh as an undergraduate, he pointedly stated the obvious: "You are in the big leagues now, Peter." Well, he didn't have to rub it in, but I cheerfully agreed and inquired of his undergraduate school. "Harvard College," he replied archly.

Things weren't going too well, so I tried the fawning approach: "That's great. Then you probably know all the professors and the courses, and you can help me find good ones—"

Ralph cut me off with a bored wave of his plastic cup. It was plain I wasn't getting the point. "Look, Peter," he said, looking me straight in the eye. "How many books does Lehigh's library have?" I stared vacantly as he set his beer down and delivered the coup de grâce: "Harvard has well over ten million."

I would like to think it was superior spiritual maturity that kept me from popping him one in the face. Or that great moral courage kept me from running home to Mom and Dad that very evening. But the truth is less noble. Ralph unwittingly had tapped into a feisty strain that runs deep in the Feaver blood—yes, I know, it sounds like an unsavory disease. I may not have been everyone's idea of Harvard material, but his snobbery convinced me to dig in, to stay and fight it out, word for word, *mot a mot*.

Feavers, and especially this particular Feaver, are by nature a disputatious and contentious lot. It is possible that the family gene pool is generally overstocked with this trait, but I trace my cultivation of this endearing quality to our ritual Sunday dinners. Each week, we would pick an unsuspecting church member—usually one of the garrulous young singles—and bring them home for dinner. The aroma from Mom's roast would already have filled our home when we arrived with guest in tow. After the obligatory tour around the house ("bathroom to the left . . . medicine cabinet above the sink"), we would then sing grace—a three-part round composed by Dad. Having herded our guest into the seat of honor, we would settle down to dinner, starting with the roast and, of course, the guest.

Standard operating procedure called for the guest to talk briefly, explaining something about himself, his work, or some other topic he found interesting. Then began the Inquisition. Each of us kids-in-training took turns grilling our guest on the topic *du jour*. We would use the opportunity to show what we knew about the subject the guest had picked and to challenge the visitor on untested assumptions, unnoticed parallels, and uncertain ramifications. Usually the hapless individual would wilt in the heat of this combined onslaught and yield the field to us and our own considerable egos. Two hours later, after sopping up the last bit of Norwegian apple pie à la mode, Dad would close the dinner-debate with a Bible reading carefully selected to comment on the recent proceedings.

This weekly ritual was an integral (and much anticipated) part of my primary education. It taught me that everyone is interesting and that

everyone, if sufficiently pressed, teased, or cajoled, could make a contribution to knowledge—or at least make dinner worthwhile. It also taught
me the finer points of rhetoric and, later in life, the importance of standing up for what you believe in, even when the apparent evidence of your
own personal life seems to be going against it. Above all, it taught me
that scriptural principles lay at the foundation of any serious quest for
knowledge.

So when Ralph, the fellow G–1, mentioned the bit about Harvard's ten
million books, I cleared my throat and slowly refilled my cup. It may not
have been Sunday dinner, indeed it wasn't even Sunday, and Ralph and I
later did become friends, but right then and there I could smell Mom's roast
bubbling fiercely in the oven.

Debate around the family dining table, if not my undergraduate college's modest collection of library books, had prepared me for the hurly
burly of graduate school at Harvard, a special community of emphatically
fragile egos and testily untested credos. The next seven years was an extraordinary time. I hit some great highs and sank to some new lows and along
the way learned a lot about God, myself, and, as time permitted, the arcane
trivia that eventually became my doctoral dissertation.

I went through what I now euphemistically call my early-Augustinian
phase, a prodigal path that disturbed the alignment between my *doxis* and
my *praxis*. But through it all I remained pugnacious about my Christian
faith—even when the discrepancy between my walk and my talk was pal-
pable. I don't excuse myself, but I am grateful that, at least confessionally,
I clung to what I knew to be true, Feaver-style, even when I was doing
whatever I damn well pleased.

Naturally, I was combative about a lot of other things too. As a raging
moderate on the political spectrum, I often found myself at odds with the
liberal orthodoxy embraced by a majority of my peers. It is a curious Harvard veritas that one can be squarely to the left of middle America and yet
be branded a right-wing reactionary by one's colleagues in Cambridge. And
yet it was a comfortable place for me to be. Given my early childhood training, I was ever poised to defend—and sometimes be impaled on—a
provocative policy position or to chip away at some sacred shibboleth.

But what I also remember, and what I hope those with whom I inter-
acted will remember, is that I made a point of defending the faith. Whether
it was with Abhijit, the brilliant Marxist from India, or John, the debater
from Scotland who boasted of a world championship title, I tried to explain
what I believed and why it was worthy of their consideration. I made a
point of bringing up the subject with my mentors. I challenged my dissertation advisor on his Unitarian omnidoxy. I exhorted my (Dudley House)

housemaster, who happened to be that rarest of Harvard eccentrics—a Divinity School professor *and* a believer in Jesus Christ. And when the opportunity presented itself, I encouraged my Dudley House tutees to confront the unique claims that Jesus had made.

Sometimes my actions took on quixotic proportions, such as the time I went to President Derek Bok to protest Harvard's structural discrimination against evangelical Christians. He listened to me graciously. I doubt that he changed his mind after hearing my indictment of the restrictions enacted by a particular potpourri of Harvard chaplains. But who knows if, somewhere down the line, that small act of chutzpah did not inspire others who heard about it to express their faith, maybe by sharing the gospel or by applying biblical principles to modern social problems.

My prayer is that as much as friends and colleagues and indeed the very university system influenced me, I too had a similar impact on them. The claims I made on Christ's behalf were undoubtedly stronger than those I could have made for my own spiritual life. Yet there I was, an educated person willing to "give a reasoned defense for the hope that is in [me]" (1 Peter 3:15)—surely a novel experience for many I met at Harvard. By directing attention heavenward, I at least rattled some old cages and perhaps even moved a few complacent friends to consider the message of the gospel.

I sometimes think about it myself. Why would a red-blooded young American boy, trained at school and at home in the rigors of debate, in the methodologies of postgraduate political science, in techniques of exposing assumptions and laying bare the skeleton of an opponent's arguments, embrace a set of extravagant allegations made by someone who lived two thousand years ago? The fact is that in professing Christ, I have *not* abandoned intellectual rigor. Those who embrace Christ do not do so because they have abandoned rigor, any more than those who reject him do so because rigorous thinking requires it. There is no necessary connection between modern scholarship and atheism, any more than there is a necessary opposition between love for Jesus and the life of the intellect. If Christ's sacrifice never occurred, or if I could be persuaded that it didn't, then I would join other agnostic Harvard alumni in adopting my own subjective, cynical (and, if I may add, often solipsistic) theology. But it did happen, as surely as I scraped through graduate school. And the whole world is the better for it.

For Christ's atoning sacrifice, that is. The jury is still out on the ultimate worth of my own modest miracle.

Called to Teach

৯৫

— BOBBY FONG —

Teachers bore witness to the truth, not only by their words but also by their lives.

Truth is not only that which awaits discovery but also that which was once known but is now threatened by forgetfulness.

Bobby Fong is the dean of faculty at Hamilton College in Clinton, New York. He has served as a national fellow with the American Association of Colleges in Washington, D.C., and as dean of arts and humanities, and professor of English, at Hope College. A son of Cantonese immigrants, he was born and raised in Oakland, California's Chinatown, where at age six he first heard the gospel of Jesus Christ in a basement used by a Chinese missionary for conducting worship services. Dr. Fong attended Harvard in 1969 and concentrated in English. He participated in antiwar activities and was active in the Harvard-Radcliffe Christian Fellowship, where he met his wife, Suzanne, a Wellesley student. Graduate work followed at UCLA, and after receiving his Ph.D. in English, he spent eleven years on the faculty of Berea College in Kentucky.

Professor Fong reflects that his life has been filled by three abiding passions: God, family, and the educational enterprise. "The presence of God is the constant that gives direction and meaning to these endeavors," he says. "The Lord is the point of unity in my own shifting world."

Called to Teach

— ROBERT FONG —

For I delivered unto you first of all that which I also received.
1 CORINTHIANS 15:3 KJV

ᚦᚴ

I teach. As a professor of English, I also research and write and serve on committees and speak at conferences, but the heart of my work is that I am a teacher. I make this affirmation deliberately, for as a witty colleague of mine has noted, "In the American university system, one begins by teaching undergraduates; after the first successful books, one need only teach graduate students; after one becomes a name, why, one may choose not to teach at all!"

Professors too often find themselves with divided loyalties: on the one hand, there is the lure of the subject, the boundaries of which they want to extend by new insights; on the other hand, there are the students, who wait to be initiated into knowledge that seems at times so rudimentary. The common ideal is that of the scholar-teacher as one who successfully serves both masters. But the reality is that in modern higher education the scholars are the more honored. The consequence is that teaching seems a distraction from the "real" work of academia—research. So teaching gets short shrift.

As a Christian, I find two continuities between my faith and my work that impel me to affirm the primacy of teaching. The first has to do with a particular esteem for knowledge of the past. The emphasis on research rests on a regard for the "new"—new paradigms yielding new insights and new discoveries about the world and ourselves. By no means do I want to disparage this enterprise, for the record of its achievements is indubitable. At the same time, there is a custodial aspect to knowledge that is too often taken for granted. This custodianship is best exemplified for me by the rabbis of the Diaspora who compiled, preserved, and passed on, from generation to generation, the Scriptures and commentaries that form the heart of Jewish faith and culture. The basic impulse underlying this transmission of knowledge was the belief that the revelation of God is immutable, never outmoded, never to be left behind, at least in this world, for more complex sophistications. God's truth is truth for all time, to be spoken from age to age. The rabbinical commentaries were not in themselves "new learning" but ways of adapting eternal truths to new times.

Christians are inheritors of this custodial attitude, the belief that what was revealed to Moses, proclaimed by the prophets, and finally embodied in Jesus Christ is still sufficient for today. Christians too recur to the past to find accommodation with the present and hope for the future. Christianity, like Judaism, has been Janus-like: speaking to the present with the wisdom of the past. As the prophets of old sought to call Israel and Judah back to renewed faithfulness to the Lord, so did Luther and Calvin, who fractured Catholic hegemony in Europe, do so in the name of returning to the beliefs and practices of the first-century church. In this understanding, truth is not only that which awaits discovery but also that which was once known but is now threatened by forgetfulness.

In turn, the humanistic knowledge of history, philosophy, and the arts and letters has traditionally been bathed in a similar light. The learning of the European Renaissance was sparked in part by the rediscovery of Greek and Roman authors, and renewed interest in their ideas.

For the Christian and the humanist, the past is not a mausoleum of dead knowledge best left behind. Neither is it a treasure-house full of baubles to be hoarded but never spent. I am not interested in passing on to my students dead canons. On the contrary, I believe with Sidney that true poetry teaches while delighting, that it vividly addresses the needs, questions, aspirations, and pleasures of my students. The great classics, sacred and secular, have the common quality of transcending time, space, and culture to convey visions of human life and possibilities that still move us, aesthetically and morally, today. And beyond the well-known, we should be open to hitherto neglected works that have this same quality of moral immediacy, works neglected because they were written by women, by minorities, by the oppressed, by all who ran against the grain of the dominant culture in which they composed (in the Old Testament they were sometimes called prophets). Donne, Melville, and Edward Taylor were recovered from obscurity. A similar process of recovery goes on today for Kate Chopin and Zora Neale Hurston. Matthew Arnold could speak of the "best that was known and thought in the world," of texts ancient and recent that spoke so truly to human experience that their visions remain undimmed. As a Christian and as a teacher, I believe in the mimetic and moral worth of texts that allow my students to rehearse their lives in their imaginations, to know themselves in versions of what they might have been in different times and circumstances and what they desire to be. My work as a teacher is to open these texts, and to make them meaningful and useful to the students who trust themselves to me.

This trust represents the second continuity between my faith and my work. In the medieval university, the "professor" was exactly that—a monk who professed, made public declaration of both knowledge and the Creator of knowledge. To teach was a spiritual "vocation" to which one was set apart. These words, "professor" and "vocation," have all but lost their spiritual resonance in the modern world, but originally they were descriptive not simply of a job but of a divine commission. Teachers bore witness to the truth, not only by their words but also by their lives. Pupils were charges from God, to be nurtured in faith and knowledge. A professor was concerned not only with communicating the facts of the subject but also with the edification—the building up—of the student for service. Teachers were "entrusted" with students.

American education in general needs to regain a sense of teaching as "vocation," of teaching as a calling. By transmitting the knowledge of the past, and the culture of the present, to our students, we enable and equip them to continue the world and perhaps even to change it—for the better, we hope. Beyond the low pay, the long hours, the infrequent recognition, teachers need to affirm a devotion to values, intellectual and moral, inherent in the profession.

In this regard, it was no small point with me that at my ten-year Harvard reunion in 1983, I renewed acquaintance with many doctors, lawyers, and businesspeople. The teachers and professors, however, were few and far between. Perhaps some were too busy or too poor to come. More ominously, I suspect that many of my peers did not seriously consider teaching as a life's work, because it did not seem to pay, either in money or in fame. And yet for this very reason, "the harvest is plentiful, but the laborers are few, pray therefore the Lord of the harvest to send out laborers into the harvest."

One does not have to be a Christian to share my regard for the knowledge of the past, and my notion of teaching as a calling. Christians, however, are especially behooved and particularly privileged to claim these continuities as their own. In any event, we who are called to teach do so out of conviction that what we teach is important, those whom we teach are precious, and that the reason why we teach reaches to the very core of our place and mission in the world. In Robert Bolt's *A Man for All Seasons,* a young Cambridge scholar named Richard Rich approaches Sir Thomas More for some vocational advice. Rich is ambitious, anxious to rise in the world. He is nonplussed when More suggests, "Why not be a teacher? You'd be a fine teacher. Perhaps even a great one." Rich contemptuously retorts, "And if I was, who would know it?" More replies, "You, your pupils, your friends, God. Not a bad public, that. . . . " Not bad at all.

A Sense of Mystery:
Reflections of a Monk

— BROTHER JOHN —

The true scientist or scholar cannot work without a sense of mystery or intellectual humility.

Born in Philadelphia in 1950, **Brother John** graduated from Harvard College in 1972, having concentrated in social relations. While traveling in Europe as a Sheldon Fellow (1972–73), he visited Taizé, an ecumenical Christian monastic community based in France that attracts tens of thousands of visitors each year for periods of spiritual renewal. When he returned to Taizé, it "suddenly became clear that in the U.S. I had been trying to run away from my own deepest self."

Having entered the Taizé community in 1974, Brother John welcomes young pilgrims and facilitates Bible studies in five languages, often to hundreds of people at a time. This has led to the publication of three books: *The Pilgrim God: A Biblical Journey*, *The Way of the Lord: A New Testament Pilgrimage*, and *Praying the Our Father Today*, all published in the U.S. by the Pastoral Press, Washington, D.C. Taizé's "ministry of listening," helps people "discover what lies hidden in their heart of hearts and clarifies their priorities."

Brother John has traveled to Africa, Latin America, and Eastern and Western Europe to visit Christians and lead retreats and other gatherings. Since 1983 he has served along with a small group of brothers living in New York City. "The past nineteen years have gone by in a flash," he says, "which is probably a sign that I'm in the right place."

A Sense of Mystery:
Reflections of a Monk

— B R O T H E R J O H N —

Why did I "become a monk"? A difficult question, certainly not one to be answered exhaustively in the confines of a short essay. But to set one popular cliché to rest at once, let me say right out—and I think I can speak for a legion of other monks as well—that I never had any sense at all that I was "running away from the world."

So why did I leave William James Hall for the hills of Burgundy? As far as I can see, my ultimate life-choice had something to do with a search for existential consistency, with the feeling that the life one leads should be as congruent as possible with the beliefs one professes. I profess the gospel of Jesus Christ. Therefore life in community—a community centered on prayer and service—still seems to me the best living translation possible of that gospel. I think I was horrified by the thought of a split existence, of having my faith confined to the "private" realm while being forced to subscribe—or at least make accommodations—to a whole series of antagonistic values in the rest of my "public" life.

Of course, given the realities of a broken world, no one, whether in a monastic community or elsewhere, can live a perfectly unified life. And thus I have the utmost admiration and respect for many I know who attempt to live out the demands of their faith in an uncomprehending, indifferent, and even hostile environment. Suffice it to say that my own "still, small voice" within slowly convinced me that in order to live and not merely to subsist, I needed to focus on the essential, and at that moment of my pilgrimage the Taizé community appeared and made manifest a concrete alternative.

At the same time, I was attracted by the "sign value" of an intentionally religious community. Far from turning one's back on society, such a community seeks to be a living sign, a kind of parable of an alternative way of living. It "says" that a life centered on God and founded upon such values as simplicity rather than consumption, sharing rather than accumulation, and solidarity rather than "success" does not have to remain an abstract possibility. It can be a lived-out reality rather than a wished-for idea, one empowered and sustained by the wholeness that the resurrection of Jesus Christ makes possible for the inner self. Here, and perhaps elsewhere also, utopia enters into history. Belief is clothed in concrete lifestyle. An "intentional" community such as Taizé speaks to tens of thousands of people each year, mostly young, Western and non-Western, who come to visit us from across the world and who discover Christianity not just as an idea, an ideal, a theory, but as an actual experience in time and space. If I had indeed come to Taizé with the idea of "running away," I would have been deeply disappointed: very few other vocational choices could have provided so many intensive contacts with people from Chile to China, from Norway to South Africa.

Had other circumstances supervened, my life might have taken a very different path. In any case, since I have no regrets after nineteen years of communal life, my purpose here is not to criticize Harvard College, American higher education, or the social sciences (although in passing I will do a bit of all three). It is simply to reflect on a peculiar notion of knowledge and learning I encountered in late adolescence, a notion that to my mind cannot fail to lead in the long run to unfortunate results.

As far as I can remember, what disappointed me during my first year at Harvard was not the absence of a specifically Christian worldview. Such disappointment would have been signally perverse on my part, to say the least: one of the reasons I had chosen Harvard was to broaden my outlook. Nor was it the failings of any particular professor, most of whom were capable and congenial enough. It was rather a certain intellectual climate that I can now best characterize as the absence of a sense of mystery.

What do I mean by that? Every intellectual discipline offers its own way of viewing the world, which one may benefit from without necessarily having to agree with all of its claims or assumptions. The physicist may learn from religion something about the nature of ultimate knowledge and the limits of the scientific enterprise. The psychologist may learn from literature something of the layered subtlety of human expression. Knowledge can be viewed as more unified than specialized, more complementary than antagonistic. No single field is complete—or completely neutral—in its perspective. What reclaims this sense of reverence for the integrity and diversity of human thought is what I would like to call a sense of mystery.

Sociology attracted me because of its claim to understand the human enterprise—especially the concept of knowledge—from a particular approach, that of placing it in the context of group behavior. By using particular methods, sociologists could make unexpected parallels and hidden patterns of human dynamics emerge. But that approach was, or should have been seen as, merely one out of several.

Had sociology justified itself as one among many possible viewpoints, with its own advantages and weaknesses, its own assumptions and blind spots, my life might have turned out differently. Yet no one I encountered at Harvard ever made an attempt to relate the sociological endeavor to the rest of human knowledge—to literature, history, economics, and all the varied ways by which we make sense of the world. The fact that no one ever did so, I suggest, was not just an inevitable outgrowth of academic specialization. It testifies to an existential vacuum at the heart of the modern secular university. We turn out scholars and scientists, each busily working to amass a small but concentrated lode of knowledge in his or her own field yet scarcely able to place that work in any larger meaningful context. As a result, there is no common vision of the status of that knowledge, or its relation to the whole enterprise of the university. No one *really* knows what on earth anyone else is doing. Or why it is important that he or she is doing it.

If a sense of mystery is predicated on finding some common ground, one might ask, what hope is there to achieve it, when there is essentially no practical common thread between Derrida, marginal cost analysis, and the molecular biology of gene replication? What chance is there that business school lecturers and professors of feminist literature will sit at the same table and respectfully exchange ideas—or even just sit at the same table?

The answer lies in distinguishing substantive common ground and attitudinal common ground. A sense of mystery begins with a disposition of mind, not with specific unifying themes. It is based on the idea that reality is an inexhaustible source of meaning, that it is accessible to the present tools and methods of scholars and scientists but most certainly not limited to these, and that it is capable of being approached from a multitude of complementary directions. A sense of mystery does not imply a denigration of any particular intellectual pursuit but rather the recognition that there is more to the universe, to paraphrase Hamlet, than is dreamt of in one philosophy. It means that the world is not rational or irrational but rather superrational, that it always holds in reserve a surplus of meaning.

Some professors at Harvard did operate, consciously or unconsciously, with such an understanding. The true scientist or scholar, in fact, cannot work without a sense of mystery or a certain intellectual humility, because in order to unlock reality's secrets, he or she must be open to the world as it is and not impose his or her own meanings on it or claim to have understood everything in advance.

But the general trend I encountered seemed to run against this view of things. Humility was, sadly, a disappearing trait. With each scholar locked into his or her own area of expertise (and competing for what was strongly perceived to be a limited and nonexpandable pool of funding), there was little cross-fertilization of ideas, little of a shared sense of mystery, and often little respect for other scholars who might approach knowledge in a radically different way. In place of a sense of mystery was a sense of self-justification and a grasping after self-acknowledgment. It was far easier to run into scholars who saw meaning not as something we discover and submit to but as something that is wrenched from general chaos by the superior power of the mind and placed under human control, at our beck and call. Our time is particularly susceptible to the destructive fiction that reality is what we choose it to be. And yet what ravages has this "myth of control" not caused in the century that is currently approaching its end! How ironic, and tragic, that a civilization that prides itself on its rationality and on "being in control" has unleashed some of the most dangerous irrationalities the world has ever known, a veritable Pandora's box of perils to the planet and its inhabitants.

In the social relations department, what I found hard to explain was that no one seemed to imagine—or if they did, they kept it to themselves—that the same methods used by social scientists to analyze and relativize other belief systems could be applied to the social sciences themselves!

The secular institution of higher learning has seemed to disintegrate into isolated islands of knowledge, each reinventing the wheel, each justifying its own small patch of turf as the new center of all there is.

The nurturing of a sense of mystery will go some way to bring a pluralistic university together and ground it in a common enterprise, without forcing partisan choices that would alienate portions of its clientele. Cultivating such a sense—the idea that reality is neither so small a domain that it cannot accommodate us all, nor such an unrelated collection of personal spaces that we can only tolerate, not share deeply in, each other's differentness—would not be easy. But we must at least start with its possibility. What is needed is not a set of formulated truths and values to which all must subscribe but an active sharing of visions of reality underlying different disciplines, a mutually interpretive collaboration. What is needed is a meaningful exchange among scholars and scientists about what it is they are really doing and what implicit understandings of our world emerge from their work or make their work possible.

A sense of mystery such as I am suggesting is therefore in no way exclusively Judeo-Christian. Any true seeker will be able to grasp it. It requires only the openness to question and be questioned and the humility to tolerate one's own ignorance, temporary or long-term. Indeed, a certain type of agnostic might very well find it more congenial than would some theistic believers. And yet I believe that those who have cultivated a deep religious sensibility in their lives will do especially well in the task of fostering such a sense of mystery. I would venture to suggest that if they are true to their roots, Christians and Jews, because of their belief in a creator God distinct from and yet intimately concerned with the world, already possess a philosophical framework for a universe understood as a repository of inexhaustible meaning.

In fact, one of the sources of the very notion of mystery is the Wisdom tradition of the Hebrew Bible and of Judaism, where it refers to the gradual revelation of God's compassionate designs in the course of human history. Thus, the scriptural notion of mystery actually refers not to something eternally *inaccessible* or perplexing but to the progressive movement of increasing *revelation*. It is ironic that in the highly secularized and in some ways post-Judeo-Christian academic world of today, the word mystery has come to stand for superstition, anti-intellectualism, and obscurantism. Yet correctly understood and sought, a sense of mystery—by linking head and heart—is, in the long run, the only effective safeguard of rationality itself.

The seventeenth-century founders of Harvard College understood something about mystery: they understood the interdependency between wisdom and knowledge, between part and whole, between revelation and discovery. They understood the collaborative nature of private worship and public scholarship, and the attitude of humility necessary for striking accurate proportions in one's analyses and avoiding "knowledge" that is simply bloated opinion. The reasons why this perspective has fallen by the wayside are complex. But Flannery O'Connor stated it most succinctly when she said, "Mystery is a great embarrassment to the modern mind."

Here in Taizé a vast process of osmosis takes place through innumerable discussions, formal and informal, within and across cultures, and simply by living and working together. Thousands of people, mainly young adults, arrive each week with their tents and sleeping bags to spend a week joining in the worship of the brothers, washing dishes, listening to introductions on the sources of the Christian faith, and sitting on the grass in small groups to share their searching with people their own age from around the world. Taizé has likewise organized gatherings in the capitals of Europe and other continents, bringing together up to one hundred thousand young adults for five days of prayer and sharing. Such meetings are, in their own small way, preparing the world of tomorrow, that planetary village where we will have to learn to live together in order to survive. Should this not be one of the vocations of the modern university as well? But more than goodwill is needed to achieve authentic modes of discussion: the practitioners of intellectual disciplines must look beyond their partial truths, beyond their self-justifying pockets of thought, to some kind of vision of the whole.

CHAPTER 10

CONCLUSION: VERITAS, HOPE FOR THE TWENTY-FIRST CENTURY

A Hunger For God   *Mother Teresa*

On Abundant Life   *Phillips Brooks*

Alternative to Futility   *Elton Trueblood*

The Wonder of Being   *Charles Habib Malik*

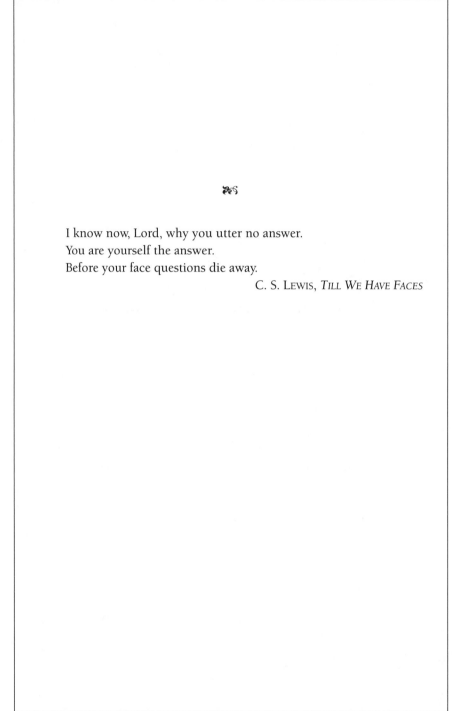

I know now, Lord, why you utter no answer.
You are yourself the answer.
Before your face questions die away.

C. S. LEWIS, *TILL WE HAVE FACES*

A Hunger for God

— MOTHER TERESA —

For God, it is not how much we give but how much love we put in the giving. That love begins at home, right here. Holiness is not the luxury of the few; it is a simple duty for you and me.

The following talk is adapted from the address of **Mother Teresa** at the 1982 Class Day exercises at Harvard College. A founder of the Missionaries of Charity in Calcutta, India, she received the Nobel Peace Prize in 1979 for her service to the poorest of the poor. The sisters work in dozens of cities throughout the world.

An Albanian nun, she became a citizen of India. "How can I know what God is calling me to do and to be?" she asked in the biography *Mother Teresa of Calcutta.*[1] "Profound joy of the heart is like a magnet that indicates the path of life. One has to follow it, even though one enters into a way full of difficulties," she answered.

Some time ago Mother Teresa was visited by a group of American professors. "They said to me, 'Tell us something that will help us to become holy.' And I said to them, "Smile at each other—because we have no time even to look at each other.'"

She recalled that in 1948, twenty years after she came to India, "God wanted me to be poor with the poor. They are our very lovable people who help us to learn love. I try to give to the poor people for love what the rich could get for money." She continued, "When I see how the poor remain neglected and unrecognized all around us, I understand the sadness of Christ at not being accepted by his own."

---

[1]Ed. Gonzalez-Balado and Playfoot (New York: Ballantine, 1985).

A Hunger for God

— MOTHER TERESA —

How wonderful it is! We all long, we all want, even the unbeliever, to love God in some way or another. But where is God? How do we love God, whom we have not seen? To make it easy for us, to help us to love, he makes himself the hungry one, the naked one, the homeless one. You will, I'm sure, ask me: "Where is the hunger in our country?" Yes, there is hunger. Maybe not the hunger for a piece of bread, but there is a terrible hunger for love. There is a terrible hunger for the Word of God.

I will never forget when we went to Mexico and visited very poor families. They had scarcely anything in their homes, and yet nobody asked for anything. They only asked us: "Teach us the Word of God? Give us the Word of God." Here too, in the whole world, there is a terrible hunger for God, especially among the young. We must find Jesus and satisfy that hunger. Nakedness is not only for a piece of cloth. Nakedness is the loss of human dignity, the loss of respect, the loss of that purity which was so beautiful, the loss of that virginity which is the most beautiful thing that a young man and young woman can give each other because of their love. The loss of that presence, of what is beautiful, of what is great—that is nakedness. And homelessness is not only the lack of a home made of bricks but the feeling of being rejected, being unwanted, having no one to call your own. I will never forget one day I was walking the streets of London and I saw a man sitting there looking so sad, so lonely. So I went right up to him. I took his hand and I shook it. He looked up at me and said, "Oooh, after such a long time I feel the warmth of a human hand." That little action was so small, and yet it brought a radiating smile on a face which had forgotten to smile, a man who had forgotten the warmth of a human hand. This is what we have to find in this country and in all other countries around the world.

And where do we begin? At home. And how do we begin to love? By prayer. Prayer always gives us a clean heart, and a clean heart can see God. And if we see God in each other, we will naturally love one another. We must help each other to pray.

And where do our sisters get the strength to take care of lepers and the people dying in the streets of Calcutta, New York, London, and around the world? From their union with Christ, the Bread of Life, who feeds us and gives us life. Make time to be alone with Jesus, and you will find the strength, joy, and love that your heart hungers for.

Love, to be true, must hurt. Some time back in Calcutta, we had difficulty getting sugar, and a little four-year-old boy heard, "Mother Teresa has
no sugar." He went home and told his parents, "I will not eat sugar for three
days. I will give my sugar to Mother Teresa." After three days the parents
brought this little one to our house. They had never been to see me before,
and they had never given anything. But this little one, with a little bottle of
sugar in his hand, brought his family to our house. That little one loved
with great love. Not because he gave so much. For God, it is not how much
we give but how much love we put in the giving. That love begins at home,
right here.

Just a few days before I left Calcutta, a young man and a young woman
came to our house with a big amount of money. I asked them, "Where did
you get this money?" because I knew that they gave their money to feed
the poor. (In Calcutta we feed about seven thousand people each day.) They
gave me the most strange answer: "Before our wedding we decided not to
buy wedding clothes, not to have a wedding feast, but to give you the
money to feed the poor." Then I asked them one more question: "But why,
why did you do that?" That is a scandal in India, not to have a wedding
feast and special clothes. And they gave me this most beautiful answer:
"Out of love for each other, we wanted to give each other something special,
and that special something was that big sacrifice, the wonderful something."
How beautiful to love each other with a pure heart. On your wedding day,
resolve to give each other something beautiful. The most beautiful thing is
to give a virgin heart, a virgin body, a virgin soul. That's the greatest gift
that the young man can give the young woman, and the young woman can
give the young man. The joy of loving gives us joy in sacrifice. And if a
mistake has been made, it has been made. There is healing in God's love
which renews us. One must have the courage to accept and love one's child
and not to destroy the most beautiful creation of God that is life. Let us
pray for each other that we may love God as he loves us. It is our turn to
give that lifelong, faithful tenderness and personal friendship to him in
each other.

So let us thank God. I have no gold and silver to give to the American
people, but I give my sisters. I hope that together with them, you will go in
haste, like Mary, to find the poor. And if you find them, if you come to
know them, you will love them; and if you love them, you will do something for them. You may have the poor right in your own family. We get
many young people who come to our place in Calcutta to share the joy of
loving, and it's beautiful to see how devotedly they serve the poorest of the
poor, with so much love, with so much care. But many families need to see
in their own family the suffering, the pain, and the loneliness. I will never

forget when I went to thank a family in Venezuela for a plot of land they had given us to build a children's home. When I went to see the family, I saw one of their children—I've never seen anyone so disabled, so completely handicapped—and he had the most beautiful, black, shining eyes, radiating full of joy. I asked the mother: "What is the name of your child?" And the mother answered: "We call him Professor of Love, because he keeps teaching us how to love." Such a wonderful spirit of joy in that family, because they had someone who taught them how to love.

So let us thank God for the beautiful things God has given to your children, and with your help, with your prayers, they have been able to stand on their feet, and you are sending them, like Jesus sent his apostles: "Go and preach the good news." Today let us pray that they will go out and preach the good news, not just by words but by their example, by the love they give to each other, especially to the unwanted, the unloved, the uncared for. You have many poor people here. Find them, love them, put your love for them in living action; for in loving them, you are loving God himself.

As the new graduates go out, I thought that the prayer of Cardinal Newman is most fitting for them, so that in going into the world, they go with Jesus, they work for Jesus, and they serve him in the distressing guise of the poor:

> Dear Jesus, help us to spread your fragrance everywhere we go. Flood our souls with your spirit and life. Penetrate and possess our whole being so utterly that all our lives may only be a radiance of yours. Shine through us and be so in us that every soul we meet may feel your presence in us. Let them look up and see no longer us, but only Jesus. Stay with us and then we shall begin to shine as you shine. To shine so as to be a light to others. The light will be all from you, dear Jesus. None of it will be ours; it will be you shining on others. Let us thus praise you in the way you love best, by shining on those around us. Let us preach you without preaching; not by words, but by our example. By the catching force, the sympathetic influence of what we do, the evident fullness of the love our hearts bear for you.

This is exactly what the parents have worked for, that their sons and daughters will become the carriers of God's love. Today God loves the world through each of us, for we know in the Scripture it is written that God loved the world so much that he gave his Son, Jesus (John 3:16), who became like us in all things except sin. And he came to give us good news. He came to the poor, you and me, the poor, to give that good news that God loves us, that we are somebody special to him, that he has created us for greater things: to love and be loved. And we read in Isaiah where God speaks: "I have called you by your name. You are mine. You are precious in my sight. You are honored and I love you." And to prove that, he says: "Even, even if a mother could forget her child, I will not forget you. I have curled you in the palm of my hand."

It is good to remember this, especially in these days when there is so much fear, so much pain, so much suffering, so much distress. It is good to remember that he will not forget you, that he loves you, loves me, and that Jesus has come to give us that good news. When we look at the cross, we will understand how he loved us by his actions. And he wants us to love one another as he has loved each one of us. And when he came into the light of Mary, she accepted him as the handmaid of the Lord, and she did not speak, but what did she do? Immediately in haste, she went to her cousin's home, to do what? Just to serve. To do the small works of a handmaid. And something very strange happened: the unborn child in the womb of Elizabeth, six months old, leaped with joy. That child recognized the presence of Christ. He was the first human being to welcome Jesus, to rejoice that God's son has come.

And today it is unbelievable that we are afraid of having to feed one more child, afraid to educate one more child. A nation, people, or family that allows the death of a child, they are the poorest of the poor, because they are afraid—even of their own child.

You and I have been taught to love, to love one another, to be kind to each other, not with words but in real life. To prove that love in action as Christ has proved it. That's why we read in the gospel that Jesus made himself the Bread of Life, to satisfy our hunger for love. For he says, "whatever you do to the least of my brethren, you do to me."

My prayer for you is that you may grow in love for each other. That you grow in the likeness of Christ, in the holiness of Christ. Holiness is not the luxury of the few; it is a simple duty for you and me. And where does it begin? Right at home. God bless you.

On Abundant Life

᛭

— PHILLIPS BROOKS —

There are the men who cry, "Do not think, for it is dangerous."
Against them Christ is always crying, "No, live your fullest."

Phillips Brooks graduated from Harvard College in 1855. In 1869 he came to Trinity Episcopal Church in Copley Square, Boston, and began receiving invitations to teach and preach at Harvard. Though he declined permanent positions, he did preach and was twice a Harvard Overseer, and ministered to students including Helen Keller when she was at Radcliffe. He published hundreds of sermons, including a collection called *The Influence of Jesus*.

At Brooks' suggestion, chapel became voluntary in 1886. As he had hoped, spiritual life began to thrive under this freedom. In the same year, the largest and in many ways most effective organization in the college's history was founded: the Harvard Young Men's Christian Association. The Harvard YMCA's need for its own building led to the formation of Phillips Brooks House (PBH). Five-hundred-fifty-nine donors in twenty-nine countries made PBH a reality by 1901.

After Brooks' death and memorial in 1893, hundreds of students helped to carry his casket three miles between Harvard Yard and Trinity Church. Phillips Brooks was one of the most vital and beloved figures in the history of Harvard College. He embodied his own knowledge that "the great hunger everywhere is for life." Thus, he pointed people to Jesus Christ. It was said that Brooks' face showed the kindness of Christ, and students felt that his life was his clearest sermon. This talk, given to the freshman class of 1883, encapsulates Brooks' vision for the gospel in, and far beyond, Harvard College.

On Abundant Life

— PHILLIPS BROOKS —

"I am come that they might have life,
and that they might have it more abundantly."
JOHN 10:10 KJV

☙

A new term, a new year, has begun in the old place. Once more the gates which have opened and closed themselves upon so many coming and going companies of students have unfolded their welcome to this new assemblage, to some of whom everything is familiar and already dear, to others of whom all is as yet very strange, but who together are to make the college world of this new year.

It is right that this chapel, which we hold to be in some true sense the spiritual center and soul of the university and to express the deepest motives of her life, should have its welcome too, should open its doors anew on this Sunday evening of the term and try to echo some great word of our Master, which should declare his presence in the very midst of our life and let us know, in the largest way, what it is that he desires to do for his Father's children.

What art thou here for, O wonderful, mysterious, bewildering Christ? "I am here that men may have life, and have it more abundantly." Among all the words of Jesus I do not know where we shall find larger words than these. They are very primitive and fundamental. They go back to the very beginning and purpose of his presence on the earth. Could words go further back than that? Behind all special things which he wanted men to learn, he wanted men, first of all, to live; they are the words of a Creator. It is that craving of life to utter itself in life which makes the beauty and glory of the universe. He who speaks these words is very brave. He recognizes that the danger of men is not in too much life but in too little. It is deficient vitality, not excessive vitality, which makes the mischief and trouble of the world. Below the question whether a being is living well or living ill, there is the deeper question whether he is living at all. The great hunger everywhere is for life. All things are reaching up towards it. All living things are craving an increase of it.

Into this world comes Christ and announces himself as that world's Savior and satisfier, in virtue first of his bestowal of vitality. "I am come that they might have life, and have it more abundantly."

As we begin to think about these words of Jesus, we need not trouble ourselves too much about definitions. Of course we know that life is undefinable. No power of language has ever yet gathered up its vastness and its mystery into a compact and portable phrase. Of course we know that life is undiscoverable. No surgeon's knife has yet pursued life to its secret chamber and dragged it forth and said, "Lo! Here it is."

But nonetheless, we know what we mean when we say that behind all the activities of living there lies life, and that beside and beyond the benefactor who teaches men a certain lesson, or who fits men for a certain task, there is the Life-Giver, the Inspirer of the vitality of men, who makes the amount of life greater in the world and so makes all special achievements of life more possible. Life is effectiveness. The live tree is the tree that bears the apples. The live brain is the brain that thinks. The live truth is the truth that makes character and action. All dead things are fruitless. Dead men tell no lies, but neither do they tell truths. The entrance of life is the beginning of effectiveness. Life enters into a factory, and its wheels move, and it sends forth its product of cloth or iron. Life enters into an institution, and it becomes productive of the fortunes, the happiness of mankind. Life enters into a man, and that man's effectiveness, his power of doing something which no other man that ever lived could, becomes a reality in the world. Behind all the infinitely various results and forms and activities of living lies this one great same thing which we call Life, in which the possibility of all those results abides, as the ocean lies behind the countless waves which it sends up against a thousand shores.

And now do we not know that there are certain persons in the world whose recognizable purpose and office it is to increase the amount of this vitality or life in the regions where they have been set? In every circle or community where you have ever lived, has there not been some man whom you knew as the life-giver? He was not, perhaps, the wisest man, so that he specifically directed action. He may or may not have been a learned man who gave varied and definite instructions, but he increased vitality. He caused men to be their best. He quickened languid natures. He made the streams run full. He called the dead to life. Such men are everywhere. There is no place where their presence is more notable than here in college. By them the thinker thinks, the student studies, the artist paints, the athlete runs. They create condition in other men. They inspire the great primary emotions—hope, shame, desire—in the class, the college, the world wherein they move. All other men do their best because of these. You can say nothing more of such a man than this: he is the life-giver. He comes, and things have life. Such men there are in history. Such a man, I doubt not, there is in the little group which makes your world. "The desert and the solitary place are glad of him, and the wilderness rejoices and blossoms as the rose."

When we have realized such a man as that, and seen just what he is in the great world, then we have come where we can understand Christ and see just what was the meaning of his self-description. Sometimes people count up Christ's acts and stand with the little group of jewels in their open hands, looking at them with something like puzzled wonder and saying, "Is this, then, all that he did?" Other people gather Christ's *words* together and feel, through all their beauty, a bewildering sense that they do not account for the marvelous power of his life. But sometimes there comes a truer apprehension. The things he did, the things he said, were only signs and indications of what he was. He was not primarily the Deed-Doer or the Word-Sayer. He was the Life-Giver. He made men live. Wherever he went, he brought vitality. Both in the days of his incarnation and in the long years of his power which have followed since he vanished from men's sight, his work has been to create the conditions in which all sorts of men should live. He hates death. He hates death everywhere. He took men in Jerusalem and poured in behind their torpid faculties the fiery vitality which stung them all to life. This was his redemption of mankind. Whatever else came from his words and actions, everywhere this was true—men lived by him. "Ye will not come unto me that ye might have life," was his cry of keen momentary disappointment. "He that eateth me, the same shall live by me," was his consummate definition of his power. At the head of all life-givers stands the life-giving Son of Man.

Fill yourself with this conception of the work of Christ, and then go on and see how perfectly clear is his conception of the way *in which* he is to give life to men, to complete the vitality of the world. It is not by stirring up the powers of each individual, as if each carried his vitality lodged within himself and could live as an independent unit of life. Not that but something different. He is always religious, always the preacher of a great religion. There is a great reservoir and source of life with which each being is to be brought into contact, into which each being is to be bound, so that *its* vitality can be poured through the channels of the bound, the related, the consecrated, the religious being. All life is God's life. This is Christ's splendid doctrine of the fatherhood of God. He realized it first in himself. *He* was the Son of God. His life was God's life. What, then, he would do for every man was to set that man's nature into the divine nature so that the divine life could live in it. He would put the tree into the soil. He would put the star into the system.

This setting of the finite into the complete infinite nature Christ calls by various names. Sometimes it is faith. You must believe in God. Sometimes it is affection. You must love God. Always what it means is the same thing. You must belong to God. Then his life shall be your life. I am come to bring you to him so that you may have life, and have it more abundantly.

Sometimes he seems to gather up his fullest declaration of this vital connection of man with God and call it in one mighty word, "obedience." You must obey God and so live by him. How words degrade themselves. This great word "obedience" has grown base and hard and servile. Men hate the sound of it. Men dread the thought of it as a disgrace. "I never will obey," men say, as if so they asserted the greatness of their souls. Is it not true that what they really assert is the meagerness of their lives? He who obeys nothing receives nothing. Obedience, in the purity of its idea, is the setting of life into life, as the tree is set into the living ground. You set your life into a dead thing, and it pours into you its death. You obey a living thing (and to such only have you a right to give yourself in obedience), and at once you are a sharer in its life.

This is the principle under which the strength of the strongest becomes the possession of the weak, and the whole universe throbs with the mutual ministries of all its parts. The man who comes here without the spirit of obedience comes with his eyes shut and goes away after four fruitless years with his heart empty.

When God says to his people, "Do this and live," he is not making a bargain. He is declaring a necessary truth. He is pronouncing a necessity. "He who does my will, possesses me." For my will is the broad avenue to the deepest chambers of my life. "Son, thou art ever with me, and all that I have is thine." So speaks the infinite God to the obedient child. But to the disobedient, the door is closed. Whatever wealth there may be is none of his. Therefore let us glorify obedience, which is light and life, and dread disobedience, which is darkness and death.

We have reached then, I think, the two principles of Jesus which are included in his great announcement of himself—that he came in order that men might have life. These two principles are: first, the necessity of life; and second, the glory of obedience.

These are the key principles of all success and effectiveness. In the day when their power shall be complete, the world shall really at last unfold its strength. Surely they are the principles which it is good for us to insist upon here and now as we hail the beginning of a new period of life in this venerable place.

Let us think how those principles, together, assert their power alike in the thought and in the action of mankind. Consider man's thought. There are the men who cry, "Do not think, for it is dangerous." Against them Christ is always crying, "No, live your fullest. The only safe thing to do with the mind is to use it. My spirit shall lead you into all truth. Thou shalt love the Lord thy God with all thy mind." And when men, other men, say, "Yes, think for yourself, be original, be solitary, be defiant, think in denials, find all men wrong and say, 'I, I alone, am right,'" once more Christ might speak to us and say, "Obey, believe, find all the truth that is in everything. Set your mind close to the eternal unity of truth and hold it there till the two grow together and the truth that is universal and eternal, the truth that is God, flows into you, and you live by it." That is Christ's urgency of faith which is also hope and love. That is Christ's urgency of faith which is the mind's obedience and so the mind's life.

If Christ is right, if that is true, then how much strange and foolish talk there is which praises unbelief as if it were the true life of the human soul. To believe is to live. Skepticism as a habit, as a condition, is a sign of deficient vitality. It is a vastly nobler fear which dreads lest it should lose some truth than that which trembles lest it should believe something which is not wholly true. "Seek truth and pursue it."

Then think about *action*. Christ crowded it all into his parable of the talents. Action shunned because action is dangerous—that is not life but death. "Act, act, turn power into deeds," is the perpetual exhortation of the Lord of life. There should be no stingy caution which will do nothing for fear of doing wrong and so does wrong all the time. For all the time the talent still is the Lord's talent, to be used in obedience to him. "Thou oughtest to have put *my* money to the exchanges and then at my coming I should have received *mine own*." Every deed is part of one great drama through which flows one vast purpose, by union with which purpose alone does any deed be strong. What folly it is to be selfish! It is one wheel out of the vast engine unbelting itself from the great shaft, untoothing itself from all its brother wheels, saying, "I will spin my own music; I will not be obedient." And lo! It whirls wildly into space a minute and then drops into the sand and dies. That is dissipation. That is what men sometimes call life. Blessed is it if the poor, wrecked, wasted, dissipated wheel is taken up again by and by, by the kind Master of the engine, and reforged in any hot furnace of pain and set once more in its true place from which it flew. That is blessed; but a thousand-fold more blessed is it for the wheel which catches from the first the glory of service, makes every revolution delight in responding to the throb and beat of central power, finds every deed dignified by all worth of the entire motion of the whole, loses itself and so finds itself, and lives by obedience—and lives ever more and more abundantly.

Our Christian faith, in its high optimism, holds that whatever ought to be, some day will be. If we are truly Christians, we believe that the great truths which Christ made known are legitimately masters of the earth and are steadily taking possession of the life of man. Before us, then, there shines the vision of a perfect world, where these two principles on which we have dwelt tonight shall be the unquestioned elements in which all thought, all action, all progress, shall go on. In that world no man shall ever dream that peace or safety or goodness or happiness is to be secured by stifling life, by forbidding free activity to any of the physical or social or spiritual or intellectual powers of mankind. Only by freedom, only by vitality given its liberty and encouraged to its fullest energy, only so in that perfect world shall the great hope and attainment of mankind be expected and secured.

But with this first principle, the second also shall be ever present as its friend and complement, the glory of obedience. Along with the insistence upon life shall run the deep conviction that life is not life, that freedom is not freedom, unless the free thing is set in the ground of its true nourishment and keeps ever open connection with the eternal sources of its strength. The body does not live save in obedience to the soul. The real lives only in obedience to the ideal. Man is not living except he lives in God. Through all the system in that perfect world of which we dream spreads *obedience,* as a subtle ether uniting each to each in vital union and making the life of all.

Everything best which comes into the world as it is now opens some glimpse and vision of that complete world which shall be someday. Every outburst of freedom, every triumph of faith over superstition, every new glorification of self-sacrifice, every disappointment of the senses in the self-indulgence, every misery which makes man at once ashamed of what he is and conscious of what he was made to be—they all open glimpses of the new heaven and the new earth which are to be radiant and strong with the vitality which is by obedience.

Friends, if there is any place in the world where that vision of the abundant life of man ought to be most real and vivid, it seems to me that it is *here.* I say it in all soberness.

My friends, let us think clearly; let us speak plainly. The world has no use for this place unless here all that I have been trying to say to you tonight finds its perpetual illustration and enforcement. The world thinks that it has a use for this place. Therefore it has provided and sustained it. Therefore it has lavished on it the richness of its endowments. Therefore it throws open the doors of it more widely every year.

For what purpose has the world built and sustained Harvard College? It is all nonsense to say or think that it is in order that a few privileged young men may be prepared to earn an easy living and grow rich someday above their fellow men. Of course, it is not that those same young men may first spend here four years of idle luxury or wanton dissipation. It is—it must be—that first here and then wherever they who have been educated here may go, there may be seen a pattern and picture of the highest life of man.

And if the highest life of man consists in the predominance of these two principles, the necessity of vitality and the glory of obedience, then what the world expects, what the world has a right to expect, as she looks into the new gates of the old yard, is to see here students, above all other students, abounding in life and glorying in the task of finding and obeying the true mastery of their souls.

We rejoice to believe that this sight may increasingly be seen in the university. Freedom has come where compulsion once ruled. Not the denial of the evil but the assertion of the good in man, and release from petty regulations, that men might be free to find the great Lord whom they ought to serve. These have been the directions in which the ideas of the policies of the college have for many years been moving.

He who comes here in sympathy with what he finds, catching the spirit of the place he comes to, must feel himself drawn up and on to live his fullest and to give himself to obedience to truth and fellowman and to God.

If any do not so, if there is any man so false to the spirit of this place that he grows timid or grows reckless here, that he seeks freedom in sluggishness, or thinks that freedom means self-will instead of loyalty to the Eternal Master, if there is any man of whom this place makes a skeptic or a profligate, what can we sadly say but this: that he was not worthy of the place to which he came. He was not up to Harvard College. The man whom the college ruins is not fit for the college. He should have gone elsewhere.

"I have come to you here where men have dreaded and said that I could not come. I come to you here that you may live, that you may have life, and that you may have it more abundantly." So speaks the Christ to the student. And with great trust and great hope and happy soberness, giving himself into the power of whatever is diviner than himself, believing truth, rejoicing in duty, the student goes forward into ever-deepening life. Of such life, and of brave, earnest students entering into its fullness, may this new year of the old college life be full.

Alternative to Futility

৯৵

— ELTON TRUEBLOOD —

How is civilization changed? By the creation of fellowships which eventually become infectious in the entire cultural order. These ancient believers were accused of turning the world upside down.

In 1900 **Elton Trueblood** was born in Iowa, an eighth-generation Quaker. He studied at William Penn College before earning his S.T.B. at Harvard in 1926, after which he earned a Ph.D. from Johns Hopkins. Throughout his lifetime he received fourteen honorary doctorates and authored thirty-six books, including *The Philosophy of Religion, A Place to Stand, Abraham Lincoln: Theologian of American Anguish,* and *Essays in Gratitude.*

Trueblood has been a professor of philosophy and religion at Haverford, Harvard, Stanford, Mt. Holyoke, and Earlham. He is the founder and former president of Yokefellows International. First published in the book *Alternative to Futility* (Harper & Row, 1948), this essay is here adapted and included that the reader might consider the persistent nature of evil, the consistent freshness of the gospel, and the radical possibility of the church in culture.

Alternative to Futility

— ELTON TRUEBLOOD —

Concerning the sickness of Western man, the doctors agree. Most who think seriously about the matter are agreed even on the reasons for this decay. There is marked similarity even in the titles of books.[1] But there must be some path of recovery and renewal. I am now convinced of the truth of the first axiom of the philosophy of civilization, the axiom that no matter how powerful a civilization may be in military strength and no matter how rich it may be in physical resources, it *can* go down if other conditions of survival are lacking.

It is now time to pay equal attention to the second axiom of the philosophy of civilization, the axiom that nations and peoples, even after long decay and corruption, can be revived and redirected into productive lines of human advance. The most needful thing at this hour is the concentration of the best thought of our time on the demonstration of this second axiom. Now that we have lost the delusion of health, we may be in a position to accept a cure, providing there is any wisdom pointing in this direction.

As we seek a cure, it is perfectly clear that what is needed lies in the realm of the intangibles. We need many *things,* but we need a new spirit far more, because without such a spirit the *things* we already have often become a curse rather than a blessing. Actually we are well supplied with material resources. Our failure in housing comes not from any lack of clay to make the bricks; there is plenty of clay, but the will is lacking. With our present resources we could have a magnificent standard of living in a short time if only men and women would put their backs into the undertaking with enthusiasm, vision, and unstinted loyalty; but this is what we will not do. Our incentive is not equal to our skill.

We realize more fully the direction from which a cure must come when we note that what we have is fundamentally a loss of nerve. Today's men and women are often bewildered and confused. Joy has gone out of much of our lives. Millions go through the motions as though they were waiting for a catastrophe. We cannot live well either in poverty or in abundance unless we see some meaning and purpose in life, which alone can be thrilling. Lacking the joy which comes from meaning and purpose, we turn to all kinds of wretched substitutes.

---

[1]Two popular titles of that period were *The Annihilation of Man* and *The Abolition of Man.*

The growth of the sensual arts, including the marked increase in the consumption of alcohol, helps us to see what it is that modern man needs. Scientific studies of the use of alcohol, notably those carried on at Yale University, show conclusively that alcoholism is the result of spiritual lack or emptiness. Men drink to excess not because they love the drug but because of failures of personality. A man for whom life has lost its meaning turns to alcohol as a substitute and as a temporary escape from an intolerable sense of futility.

Bad as alcoholism may be, it is not the worst that can occur in a society suffering from a sense of futility. The deepest danger in this connection is war. In our efforts to build enduring peace, people of goodwill often go on the gratuitous assumption that most people hate war and wish to remove it from the world. But many like war, because it saves us from boredom, from mediocrity, from dullness. It is instructive to note that great numbers of people in Britain say openly that they look back to 1940–41 with nostalgia. There was the constant danger of invasion and bombing; but there was more. People stood shoulder to shoulder, united by a common pride. They were sustained by great rhetoric and by great deeds. Life had significance. Now all is different. Now there is no danger but only a constant round of petty restrictions. Another war would be a glorious escape for a little while. There would again be the thrill of a crusade; again the common man would wear a uniform and be a temporary hero; again, no matter how fantastic the national debt, money would flow freely.

If the insight based on studies in alcoholism is a valid one—and there is much to support it—our industrial trouble may also be spiritual. Our economic problems are worsening, but we can be utterly sure that it will never be solved on the basis of economics alone. The Achilles' heel of our economic system is the question of incentive, and this is not primarily an economic question. And we have lost incentive because, in our entire manner of living, our psychological and spiritual needs are not fulfilled. We go back and forth to our places of employment, beget children, and try to pay our bills, but we do not feel that all these details are steps toward some great and dignifying end. Even work, whether manual or clerical, that is intrinsically repetitive could be ennobling if it were seen as part of something larger, but this is precisely what we have lost.

We may have not yet turned to another war as an escape from ourselves, but we are finding other lesser ways of escape.

All of this suggests that our central problem is moral and spiritual. The central problem is not political, for it is clear that any political system will be destroyed if the life of the citizens has lost its meaning. The problems of world government, on which so many thoughtful people pin their ultimate hope, are really spiritual problems, since it is clear that there cannot be world government without world community. Moreover, the central problem is not the problem of science. Science can do wonders, but it cannot do what is required now. It is not by reference to science that we decide *whether* we are to feed our former enemies or millions of needy children. That is a question of quite another kind. It is a question which concerns both mercy and justice, which constitute no part of the scientific vocabulary.

It has been popular, in some intellectual quarters, to refer to the present situation as a cultural lag in which social science and moral philosophy have not been able to keep up with natural science and, accordingly, to blame the moralists for the existence of the lag. The moralists, we are told, must be stupid and slow. Why don't they match the physicists in brilliance?

This conception of the relative situation as between science and ethics has a certain superficial plausibility but turns out to be almost meaningless on careful analysis. For one thing, the materials which the ordinary scientist handles are not free to act on the basis of choice, whereas in the reconstruction of the moral life, we are always dealing with freedom in this important sense. For another, no matter how perplexing problems in physics, chemistry, or even biology may be, they are all elementary when compared with those dealing with the human heart and its amazing capacity for self-deception. We are more successful in building bridges than in building a good society because bridges are easier to build.

When we realize that we are faced with something far more profound than a "cultural lag," we will be better prepared for the future. No amount of intelligence will give us the certainty of a good world, even though a modest amount of intelligence *will* give us excellent science. There will be self-centered men in any society. But knowing this, we are not thereby stopped in our efforts to discover and effect a cure. Every great renewal of life is God's doing, and there are some lines along which divine renewal is more likely to come than others.

What we seek is a situation in which we are filled with a vibrant truth. If we could believe greatly in truth, life would become more radiant than we can now imagine. Then, working to redeem the rubble and lack of housing, we could live joyously and victoriously. There are two chief ways in which spiritual solidarity comes, one temporary and the other enduring. The temporary way is by response to a common danger. We see this vividly in time of flood or fire. An entire community, when seriously threatened, will work together, temporarily neglecting all divisions of party or ancestry. Later we usually look back on such times as high moments, but the tragedy lies in the fact that the experience is so truly momentary. After the source of danger is removed, the old life returns with its divisions and its animosities. This is therefore no enduring way.

The other way in which there can be spiritual solidarity is by common devotion to a great cause. This is frequently not so exciting in the beginning, but it involves remarkable endurance and releases deep springs of power. It is ultimately the only true way in which men can be united and inspired. If we can find a truth to inspire our loyalty and if we can learn and offer it in such a way that millions are committed to it, we shall be on our way toward a cure for the sickness of the human family. What I believe we need more than anything else is a restoration of faith in that which dignifies our lives. This is the way of salvation. But how is this to be found, and to what or whom shall we be committed?

There have been, within some of our lifetimes, two remarkable attempts to *create* for people a sense of meaning in life, and if we are wise, we shall observe these most carefully. These are, as everyone knows, nazism and communism. We may have heard much about these two systems in the spirit of denunciation, but we have not heard enough about them in an attempt to understand the mysteries of the human spirit. Both are remarkably revealing about humans—and revealing in a similar way. The nazi system is revealing in that it shows what "achievements" can be wrought by a people possessed of a burning faith, even when it is a fantastically evil and monstrous faith.

We, however, seek a faith which can dignify each life by grounding it in essential bigness, in love, without divisiveness of class, race, or nation. There have been periods when a vigorous faith has swept like a prairie fire. It is this, and no less than this, which our sagging age requires. But the burning faith might do more harm than good if it were not a faith which involved "liberty and justice for all."

Once, long ago, there was such a faith, and it swept the ancient world with remarkable speed. It began in such a modest manner, in such an out-of-the-way place, that the unbiased observer, at the beginning, would have considered any suggestion of its success a fantastic proposition. Once there were a few unlettered men and women in an obscure province, and their movement was obviously a failure, for their leader had been executed! Yet something so remarkable happened that, within a generation, these men and others like them were beginning to make a difference in the entire Hellenic-Roman world. They brought to a civilization suffering from a sense of futility a genuine lift, and finally, when the Roman power fell into decay, they provided the main structure of faith upon which civilization could be rebuilt.

If we ask how this most remarkable of the miracles of history was performed, we are amazed at the simplicity of God's method. The world needed a saving faith, and the formula was that such a faith comes by a particular kind of fellowship. Jesus was deeply concerned for the continuation of his redemptive work after the close of his earthly existence, and his chosen method was the formation of a redemptive society. He did not form an army, establish a headquarters, or even write a book. All he did was to collect a few unpromising men and women, inspire them with the sense of his vocation and theirs, and build their lives into an intensive fellowship of affection, worship, and work.

One of the truly shocking passages of the gospel is that in which Jesus indicates that there is absolutely no substitute for the tiny redemptive society. If this fails, he suggests, all is failure; there is no other way. The Sermon on the Mount is largely directed to making the little band understand this momentous fact. Here the key passage is the metaphor of salt. He told the little bedraggled fellowship that they were actually the salt of the earth and that if this salt should fail, there would be no adequate preservative at all. He was staking all on one throw.

That these unqualified words were addressed to a small group is part of our amazement, especially when we know how weak and fallible its members were. The group at that time included Judas, who turned out to be a traitor, Peter, who showed himself a coward, and the sons of Zebedee, who were crudely ambitious of personal advancement. Sometimes we picture the Sermon on the Mount, which is the charter of the redemptive society, as being given to a great crowd, but the New Testament distinctly says otherwise. "And seeing the multitudes, he went up into a mountain: and when he was set, his disciples came unto him: And he opened his mouth, and taught them, saying, ' . . . You are the salt of the earth.'"

The entire burst of new life was undoubtedly the work of God, a gift of divine grace, but in partnership with his dedicated children. Not only are portions of the Gospels devoted to the careful elaboration of this intensive fellowship but, likewise, the epistles of Saint Paul are given over, in considerable measure, to creative thought about what the nature of a redeeming fellowship might be. The fellowship was marked by mutual affection of the members, by a sense of real equality in spite of difference of function, by inner peace in the face of the world's turmoil, and by an almost boisterous joy. The members were filled, not with the intoxication of wine but with that of the Spirit. Such people could hardly avoid, as the sequence in the fifth chapter of Ephesians suggests, breaking out in psalms and hymns. In the early Christian community the people sang, not from convention but from a joy which overflowed. Life for these people was no longer a problem to solve but a glory to discern.

We are so hardened to the story that it is easy for us to forget how explosive and truly revolutionary the Christian faith was in the ancient Mediterranean world. The church at first had no buildings, no separated clergy, no set ritual, no bishops, no pope, yet it succeeded in turning life upside down for millions of unknown men and women, giving them a new sense of life's meaning and superb courage in the face of persecution or sorrow. It is our tragedy that we are living in a day when much of this primal force is spent. Our temper is so different that we hardly understand what the New Testament writers are saying. Once a church was a brave and revolutionary fellowship, led by the Holy Spirit, changing the course of history. Today it is a place where many go and sit on comfortable benches, waiting patiently until time to go home to their Sunday dinners.

But a cardinal point in the redemptive fellowships was that all human barriers must be transcended. There is no longer Jew nor Gentile, no longer bond nor free. The work is grounded in history, but it involves no struggle against other races or other classes. It takes a human being as a human being, wherever the person may be, and welcomes that person into a loving fellowship which acknowledges Jesus Christ as the Lord of life. This faith is accepted intellectually and formally by millions in the modern world, but it has not caught the imagination of more than a very few. Much of the salt has lost its savor.

What we need is not intellectual theorizing or even preaching but a demonstration. There is only one way of turning loyally to Christ, and that is by loving others with the great love of God. Abstract and unembodied Christianity is a fiction. We cannot revive the faith by argument, but we might catch the imagination of puzzled men and women by an exhibition of a Christian fellowship so intensely alive that every thoughtful person would be forced to respect it. If again there appears a fellowship of men and women who show, by their vitality and moral sensitivity and overwhelming joy, that they have found something so real that they no longer seek a means of escape, the seekers will have something to join without disappointment and without embarrassment. If there should emerge in our day such a fellowship, wholly without artificiality and free from the dead hand of the past, it would be an exciting event of momentous importance. A society of loving souls, set free from the self-seeking struggle for personal prestige and from all unreality, would be something unutterably precious. A wise person would travel any distance to join it. This, and this alone, will take us beyond diagnosis to cure.

The Wonder of Being

— CHARLES MALIK —

There goes on in the soul of each of us a most fateful struggle between the person of being and the person of not being.

After earning his Ph.D. in philosophy from Harvard in 1937, **Charles Malik** was awarded more than fifty honorary doctorates. He served as president of the General Assembly of the United Nations, as president of the Security Council of the United Nations, as chairman of the Human Rights Commission of the United Nations, and as the Lebanese ambassador to the United States. He taught at the American University in Beirut and in Washington, Dartmouth College, Harvard University, and the Catholic University of America. His many books include *A Christian Critique of the University* and *The Wonder of Being,* from which this essay is adapted.

Describing his conversion, he said, "I came to know Christ directly in my life, forgiving my sins, strengthening me in trials when everything was dark and repulsive and when terrible loneliness and deep darkness were all around."[1]

Trained in an Orthodox-Byzantine tradition, Dr. Malik said, not long before his death, "I really do not know what will remain of civilization and history if the accumulated influence of Christ is eradicated from literature, art, practical dealings, moral standards, and creativeness in the different activities of mind and spirit."

---

[1]Dr. Malik's testimony first appeared in "One Man's Debt to the Bible," U.S. Bible Society's *Bulletin* and the American Bible Society's *Record*.

The Wonder of Being

— CHARLES MALIK —

There goes on in the soul of each of us a most fateful struggle between two persons—the person of being and the person of not being. Which has the upper hand is the deepest question that can be asked about us at any given moment.

The person of being stands in awe before the wonderful plenitude of being, with its variety and wealth and content, its diversity of levels and orders. The person of not being dissolves this plenitude into smaller and smaller parts until they finally merge indistinguishably into one another and vanish in not being.

The person of being affirms—and rejoices—in every positive being. The person of not being is afraid to affirm, or only affirms in order to contradict—that is, to destroy some positive being.

The person of being sometimes stops talking altogether, because he is lost in contemplation and wonder. The person of not being never stops talking, because that is his way of destroying or suspending or covering up or drowning his sense of amazement at being.

The person of being rejects magic and chance and random happenings and sees everything ultimately grounded in some meaning, some essence, some agency, some objectively existing independent being. The person of not being is easily discomfited—if he ever gets discomfited—when shown that at every turn he is espousing magic and chance as his ultimate principle of explanation, and that this is simply a device, perhaps even a disease, by which his fundamental sense of wonder is set aside or even abrogated.

The person of being is always taken by the norm, the rule, that which for the most part is the case; he never averts his gaze from it to the abnormal and exceptional. On the contrary, he understands these only in terms of it. The person of not being appears not to be interested in what is true as a rule, but always hunts the abnormal, the aberrant, the exotic, and in terms of these he feigns to understand the rule and the norm. He does not see the wonder of being true as a norm to be aspired to or as a rule to be upheld. His behavior seems to indicate that he hates the sight of being, that he does not want to see being at all, especially being as a rule of existence. And since there is no rule to the abnormal, he is always essentially without a rule himself.

The person of being moves about in the world freely and joyously, wholly unentangled in himself, sometimes even wholly oblivious of his own existence—he is all the time out there, living and loving and laughing. The person of not being cannot take a single step without tripping and stumbling upon himself—he simply cannot let go; he simply cannot be out there, living and loving and laughing.

The person of being is free and lighthearted, because things carry on quite apart from him, because he is not weighed down by the burden of having to sustain being, because being carries its own burden, or has someone else to carry that burden for it. The person of not being breathes a pathetic air of heaviness and unfreedom, as though the whole world rested on his shoulders, as though the whole of being depended on him.

The person of being trusts, because there is essential integrity at the heart of existence to free him from worry and give him peace of mind. The person of not being cannot trust, because he is at all times suspecting and sniffing danger and disintegration and disaster, and therefore you never find him enjoying rest and peace.

The person of being is not afraid because he rests his gaze on the wonderful sight of being, because at all times and everywhere he is supported and sustained by the ecstasy of some independent existence. The person of not being is full of dark fears, scenting ghosts at every turn, perpetually expecting someone or something to jump out and annihilate him any day.

The person of being rejoices in every achievement, in every truth, in every positive existence, wherever and however it turns up and regardless of the amount of falsehood and not being with which it may be mixed, wishing it from the bottom of his heart stability and continuance, and himself aiding it where necessary towards that end. Therefore he never envies, his eye is not evil because somebody else is good, and he recognizes no enemy whatever except darkness and not being. The person of not being cannot stand the sight of being. Let any being turn up before him, and he is goaded toward pulling it down and reducing it to nothing. He has declared war on all being.

Put a being before a person of being: the first thing he sees is what that being is, and he rejoices in it. Put a being before a person of not being: the first thing he sees is what that being is not, and in a perverse way he rejoices in that. Put a being before a person of being, and he would not even touch it lest he desecrate it; he submits to its being in adoration and love. Put a being before a person of not being, and his first impulse is to manipulate it, to use it, to bring it under his control; he wants *it* to submit to him.

To the person of being there are holy things which should not even be touched. To the person of not being there is nothing holy—the world is one drab continuum, every part of which may be trodden under foot, touched, mangled.

The person of being knows perfectly the absolute insufficiency and precariousness of his being and of every being—he needs nobody to point that out to him. He therefore seeks, expects, pants for, thirsts after, and demands some secure independently existing good to sustain and guarantee his being and all being. The person of not being appears quite self-sufficient and secure in himself, and when you point out to him his essential insecurity, he will take no notice of that, and therefore you will never find him panting or longing for anything "above himself."

Because he is turned, in his inmost heart, toward the fullness of being, the person of being is full of hope. Because he is turned, in his inmost heart, toward the darkness of not being, the person of not being is fundamentally hopeless. The person of being believes so deeply in being that he cannot believe that his being ends with this earthly life. What a meaningless waste of being that would be, what a cosmic joke. The person of not being ultimately believes so deeply in not being that he is incapable of looking forward in hope to anything beyond this life. Thus, the person of being takes the notion of his death in stride, because he lives in hope, if not for himself, at least for others who will carry on beyond him; whereas the person of not being feels and thinks and acts as though his death will signal the end of the world, as though his death were the end of being. So he lives in quiet terror of the very thought of his death.

The person of being rejoices in the least bit of being and is deeply thankful for it. The person of not being is almost incapable of thanking anybody or being thankful for anything. The typical act of a person of being is stillness and adoration, as with Jesus' friend Mary. The typical act of a person of not being is business and activity and analytical obfuscation, as with her sister Martha.

When you show a person of being Florence or Rome or the great cathedrals, when you take him to El Prado or the British Museum or to the Metropolitan Museum of Art, when you place in his hands Plato or Shakespeare or Tolstoy or the Psalms or the Gospels, he is profoundly grateful. When you put before him the great manifestations of culture and art, life and civilization, in ancient China, and Athens before Christ, in Rome in the first century, in Europe in the thirteenth century, in England in the Elizabethan period, in Paris in the seventeenth century, in North America in the nineteenth and twentieth centuries, he is filled with awe. When the person of being stands face-to-face before these wonders and really and concretely takes them in, he finds himself filled with ecstatic amazement, transported into another world full of stillness and meaning—a world of peace and creativity and life, a world of being, of God—a world of which these marvels, wonderful as they are, are nevertheless mere shadows and reflections and merest fragments, and he is profoundly grateful. But put these same things before the person of not being, and in little time he dissolves them into socioeconomic "conditions," and you will look in vain for wonderment on his face or for gratitude in his heart.

The greatest being is a total person, a whole person. And that is why politics is such a real business; at its best it deals not with ideas and objects and things but with real persons. Put a human person before a person of being, and the person of being comprehends him as a whole, absolutely amazed at his being. Put this same human person before a person of not being, and the latter at once breaks him up into his elements, into his different aspects, into the influences that shaped him, into his net worth, into the functionings of body and mind and background and society. He deconstructs and decomposes him in this way until nothing of his being is left before him. That is why the person of not being can never wonder and love, because one can only love and wonder at being.

What is it that calls forth the person of not being in us, and what is it that calls forth the person of being? This too is a tremendous question which, if it were given the attention it deserved, would occupy more than half of theological anthropology. I mean the attempt to understand the history of human existential choice in the light of the living God. My answer is that only Jesus Christ of Nazareth calls forth the person of being in us, whether or not we know it. I know why he does it—he does it because he loves us—but I do not know how.

No person of being will fail to be arrested by the phenomenon of Jesus Christ; no person of being can have enough knowledge and experience of Jesus Christ. He will therefore seek everything he can possibly find on him and about him—in the Bible, in the church, and in every historical-cultural manifestation. Here you have personal existence in history and time, confident, sure, unhesitating, full of matter and content, without the slightest attempt at coercion. Here you find yourself engaged personally-existentially at your deepest.

The person of being has no desire to explain Jesus Christ away. He is attracted by him as by nothing else. Jesus Christ powerfully convicts us of our sin and rebellion, yet no matter how much the person of being is thus convicted and shattered in the presence of Christ, he is never tempted to replace him with someone or something "safer"; he is never frightened or driven away by him. There is a strange bifurcation among people: there are those who are not frightened by him, in fact love him, even though they be the worst sinners; and there are those who are somehow frightened at the least trace of him and hate the very sight of him, even though they may seem to be the most perfect human beings.

Blessed are those who see him simply in faith behind the workings of the universe. Twice blessed are those who, having suffered in "the depths of Satan," return to God "while it is still called today." When both kinds of pilgrim meet Jesus Christ in person—whether in the Bible, in the living church, or in the faces and lives of those who love him—the first will at least begin to wonder whether it was not he who was lurking behind the universe when they felt its insufficiency. The second will wonder whether it was not they who brought on their own sufferings because they alienated themselves from him whom they now meet for the first time or from whom they fell away. Each will recognize him as the "Yes!" of God, behind either their sense of insufficiency or their sufferings.

This we can never understand in abstraction; this we can only understand when we really meet him. He is the ultimate affirmation in history that "all the promises of God in him are yes"—promises of relief from suffering and estrangement, promises of freedom and salvation, promises about the absolute conquest of fear and death.

This is a very strange situation—that one brought up in Galilee some two thousand years ago should be the clue to the being and order of the universe, the way out of every self-entanglement. Let us not be poetic or sentimental, or fall into all sorts of idealistic-metaphysical interpretations. Above all, let us not demythologize. What is here affirmed, what the church affirms—not I, or this or that recondite theologian—is that a man born near Jerusalem and crucified just outside the city wall is literally, truly, himself, and none other, the answer not only to the question of the origin and order of the universe but for all those who are lost in the wilderness of existence, those who worship wealth or acclaim or power or country or culture, who worship mind or art or spouse or children or scientific theory or political cause or anything you can name, and who thereby proceed unwittingly on the path of corruption.

But such is the inscrutable way of God. He takes the initiative from the other side without consulting us. This is how he graciously surprises us, keeps us off balance from our perch of self-assurance. This is how our sense of wonder is kept freshly on the alert, in order that we may give thanks, ascribing nothing to ourselves.

Certainly I cannot "prove" these things—but I believe them more surely than what my senses present me with, more than any mathematical or scientific proposition. How insipid and trivial all such propositions are by comparison. I am not here "proving" my faith. I am only bearing witness to what I know and believe. For the grounds of my faith are of a different order than any scientific, philosophical, or theological proof.

In his tremendous speculations about the teleology of the universe, Aristotle was really seeking Jesus of Nazareth, and if only he had met him, he would have understood why that is so. In his insistence on a supreme and beneficent "good" behind all phenomena, full of solicitude for humankind, Plato was really seeking Jesus of Nazareth, and if only he had met him, he would have understood why that is so. In his wonder about the *nous* behind the order of the universe, Anaxagoras was really seeking Jesus of Nazareth, and if only he had met him, he would have understood why. All people of ambition—the conquerors and scientists and philosophers, the industrialists and statesmen, the celebrities and media moguls—are really seeking Jesus of Nazareth, and if only they would meet him, they would understand why. Every alienated person who is profoundly unhappy with himself and with the world, every drug addict trying to escape the burden of existence, every prostitute who does not realize what is happening to her, every victim of a terminal illness facing the grave in terror of the unknown, is really seeking Jesus Christ of Nazareth, and if he or she would only meet him, he or she would understand why.

These are bold statements, some might say absolutely mad. Yet nothing less than this—and much more—is asserted by Christian doctrine, whether or not the world believes it, whether or not "the theologian" these days believes it. But the mania here is that of love and gratitude; it is inspired by the radical mystery and sense of paradox that surround the man from Nazareth, about whom Saint Augustine writes:

> The Maker of man was made man, that the Ruler of the stars might suck at the breast; that the Bread might be hungered; the Fountain, thirst; the Light, sleep; the Way, be wearied by the journey; the Truth, be accused by false witnesses; the Judge of the living and the dead, be judged by a mortal judge; the Chastener, be chastised with whips; the Vine, be crowned with thorns; the Foundation, be hung upon the tree; Strength, be made weak; Health, be wounded; Life, die. To suffer these and suchlike things, undeserved things, that He might free the undeserving, for neither did He deserve any evil, who for our sakes endured so many evils, nor were we deserving of anything good, we who through Him received such good.[2]

There is nothing in this whole life that compares in mystery and seriousness with the things Jesus Christ of Nazareth says of himself. Yet the mystery that confronts us has a sweetness about it, for we feel we had been

---

[2]"Sermones CXCI," i, 1 in *An Augustine Synthesis*, pp. 180–181.

expecting it all our life, from the womb. Secretly we have always wanted someone to say these things to us, and now comes this person who says them exactly as we have wanted to hear it. Our heart's deepest desire has now been fulfilled but the question becomes, can we now believe what we have always wanted to hear?

There is this strange thing about humankind, that although deep down we crave the fulfillment, in practice we love the longing more than the fulfillment, so that when the fulfillment comes along, we cannot believe our eyes and ears, and we nostalgically recreate the longing and fall back upon it. This is the secret of all unbelief—a mysterious force holds us back from believing, and we long again to return to the state of longing. We seem unable to bear the truth for long, even truth that brings joy.

How well Jesus knew this. Time and again those talking with him would wander off into some anxiety, some fear, some cosmology, some distant hope, some doubt and uncertainty, some darkness—all perfectly human, perfectly natural. And time and again he would bring them back to face the truth—namely, to face him himself. He told the world, in effect: "The truth is I myself—not philosophy, not the law, not some vague theory, not human reason, not some human technique, not even so-called life and activity, not even my teachings and acts." But this was so astounding and unbelievable that people always "changed the subject," always wandered off into something else.

But he would not let people change the subject. For anyone to get stuck in anything short of him was to him the gravest tragedy and the most egregious sin. In fact, to him sin was not at all what we usually call sin—he forgave all that—but simply and only being away from him. And so, in effect, he would tell his listeners, "Here I am, right here—and you are still seeking something else?" This is the most striking thing in the whole New Testament, which no higher criticism or search for "the historical Jesus" and no demythologizing can possibly explain away.

What is really new, what is radically new, is the embodiment of the living truth in Jesus Christ, not ideas or systems or theories or even theologies. There is no end to these things, and they all more or less regurgitate the same thing. (They all see through a glass, darkly, for all thinking is a form of mediation or indirect reflection and not *the thing itself* that is thought or mediated.) Do you think that it is only in these latter days that people are demythologizing the data of our faith or romanticizing or humanizing or secularizing them or denying or explaining them away? There is nothing new in these attempts. The church faced similar movements in its first seven centuries and dealt decisively with them; we need to restore in our thinking the historical dimension of our heritage. People today are worried or impressed, as though something awful has happened, because throughout the world there is so much rebellion by "the new theology" against orthodox Christianity. But throughout history all such rebellion has been very well known, and in fact it was precisely on the basis of facing and refuting and declaring it as nonsense that councils and doctors and saints built up the church's solid and enduring orthodox heritage.

What is really new, radically new, is the new creature in Jesus Christ—the outcome of the great encounter. How you and I confront and react to Jesus Christ—that is the only really new thing that occurs in history; that is the only really important thing that happens to us in our life. In this there is no "eternal recurrence" whatever—that horror of horrors of which Nietzsche speaks. There are no generalities and no universals here. There are no wishy-washy "ideas." For as Christ is God and therefore absolutely unique, so each one of us, in confronting the otherness of Christ—namely, God himself—becomes absolutely new and unique.

What we desperately need is not *thinking* about God or about Jesus Christ or about the Holy Spirit but these *themselves*. Thinking about them becomes a substitute for living them. Give them to me themselves, and you can have and enjoy all the thinking in the world.

Are we really face-to-face with Jesus of Nazareth? Do we really believe, without any cleverness, without averting our gaze, what he says of himself? Do we absolutely believe, without any "ifs" or "buts," without any rationalistic or metaphorical interpretations, in his resurrection? These are the real questions.

In our heart of hearts we crave nothing more than to become authentic persons, to become intimately relational, to be repentant, to be forgiven, to enter life eternal. And yet modern existence diminishes and dissolves the person into his components, has no room whatever for repentance, never seeks forgiveness, and as for life eternal, this existence "lives" only for the moment or, at most, for the near future. This measures the magnitude of the anti-Christian revolution amidst which we are living and have been living for two thousand years. For Jesus Christ evokes in us nothing other than personal being, repentant being, forgiven being, and eternal being.

The greatest event in history is not the birth of Jesus of Nazareth, celebrated on Christmas Day, but his resurrection on the first Easter morning. This event utterly debunks the world and everything in it, proves its absolute lack of self-sufficiency, and provides the greatest real hope there is.

Do we find Jesus Christ everywhere—in nature, in history, in art, in our personal trials and sufferings, in our miseries and in our triumphs, in every human law and culture? Only the new creature, born from above, "born of the Spirit," can see everything in Jesus Christ and Jesus Christ in everything. And only this new birth and this mode of seeing in and through Jesus Christ is new in history. If you take him at his word, then nothing can be the same again for you in the world and in your life.

The Maker of heaven and earth is before you; the Creator of everything in the universe, visible and invisible, is before you; the Fullness of Being is before you. God himself, who took on human form to free us from not being, adopts us and grants us, through his resurrection, life everlasting with him, and victory over the Devil and his works. He is before you. What can the thankful believer then do but fall on his knees and repeat from the Divine Liturgy:

> For unto thee are due all glory, honor and worship,
> to the Father, and to the Son, and to the Holy Spirit,
> now, and ever, and unto ages of ages.

Epilogue:
A Taste of New Wine

Kelly Monroe

AUTHOR'S NOTE:

This book is an exploration of the possibility, unity, and beauty of truth, as gracefully revealed in these lives. In 1992, three years into the writing process, we tried a kind of live version of the book called "The Harvard Veritas Forum." Both the book and the Forum have been uphill climbs with beautiful views, bouts with fog, and even a few rests. We now rejoice to see the Veritas Forum emerging in universities around the world, arising out of grassroots curiosity and community.

Todd Lake and I first wrote an Epilogue as a sketch of the tenacity of those who sought to live out the gospel at Harvard within the course of four centuries—from *In Christi Gloriam* through spiritual "declension," the Great Awakening, independence, Unitarianism, Emerson's transcendentalism, naturalism, modernism, the world wars, Marxism, secularism, to signs of grassroots revival as we enter the new millennium.

Instead of history, I have been asked to introduce you to our present story, including something of my own journey here. As my editor knows, it was easier for me to write a history than a documentary including stories that are personal and subjective, with little critical distance and few neat categorical "isms." Though so many wonderful people are not mentioned, I hope that this will at least give you a feel for the courage and vitality of students and friends who share this time together. My love for them is deepened by time and respect. I begin by describing the context and community out of which the book and the Veritas Forum have grown. In this place new wine is fermenting.

DIVERSITY AND IRONY

In 1987 I left home and came to Harvard Divinity School (HDS) to research and write a thesis entitled "The Gospel in the Information Age." I had hoped to be challenged by one or two Christian professors, students, and a broad curriculum, but at an orientation lunch, I gathered that one was not to speak of Jesus or the Bible without a tone of erudite, even if irrational, cynicism.

I am a lot like my mother—I like people and hate conflict. Though people were often pleasant, HDS seemed, to this hayseed from Ohio, an eclectic and somewhat confusing mix. Professor Henri Nouwen had just left to work with mentally retarded adults, calling HDS a spiritual desert. Liberal Christianity was fractured into denominational cul-de-sacs, while the "full moon circle" (self-defined as neo-pagan, pre-Christian, eco-feminist, and Wiccan) filled the chapel. Da Vinci's *Last Supper* promoted HDS' weekly pub, with Jesus and his disciples drinking Budweisers. "Dames Divinitas" posted invitations to evenings of "dancing, drinking, and debauchery, for women only." Diversity. (Though the Div School prided itself on its diversity, we had to wonder how sincere that was when someone mysteriously cleared all bulletin boards just before a tour for potential donors.)

I was glad for new friends and the chance to see through their eyes, but there was a joyless caution about the place. What could have been a rich and respectful exchange of ideas felt more like walking on eggshells—or minefields.

The buzzwords masked weak realities. "Pluralism" usually meant mere cohabitation. Emphasis on "diversity" heightened our differences rather than common ground. A passive "tolerance" usually ignored the ideas and beliefs of isolated others. Ironically, all seemed tolerated except that for which Harvard College was founded—Truth for Christ and the Church.

One bold student, Steven Craft, an African American who ministers in the inner city, said in 1995:

> Everything is taught at HDS except for the gospel of Jesus Christ. Why? Because the gospel would transform their behavior and other mockeries of God and his Word. HDS tries to shipwreck Christians, but I am not ashamed of the gospel.

Steve suggests that Harvard's founders were prophetic when they wrote in the 1642 "Rules and Precepts to be Observed in the College":

> ... [students] study with good conscience, carefully to retain God and the love of His truth in their minds, else let them know that (notwithstanding their learning) God may give them up to strong delusions, and in the end to a reprobate mind, 2 Thes 2:11; Romans 1:28.

I later met Muslim and Jewish students who also felt that they did not belong. Any earnest believer seemed like a real threat to prevailing relativism, deconstruction, and mysticism.

Perhaps HDS merely reflects the world as it is becoming, but I had hoped to find, or help contribute to, a culture dynamic enough to explore many ideas about reality and hope, and liberal enough to consider classical Christian faith. Like many within the "Div School," I was first timid and a little lonely. When I gave up the effort to fit in, life became richer and more adventurous.

THE FERMENTING OF NEW WINE—
A COMMUNITY OF SCHOLARS AND FRIENDS

Later that year, a persuasive friend dropped me at a Cape Cod weekend gathering of something called the Harvard Graduate School Christian Fellowship (GSCF). There the gospel was passionately discussed by students in the Schools of Law, Business, Medicine, Government, Design, Arts and Sciences. For the first time since coming to Harvard, I saw joy.

The reach of this gospel amazed me. Here were musicians, physicists, historians, architects, and athletes sharing the goodness of God in friendship, the life of the mind, life. We discussed our research. We considered our vocation, *vocare*, as our calling from God—the place, as Frederick Buechner said, where our deep joy and the world's deep hunger meet.

Like many retreats to come, this was a time for hours of beach soccer and ultimate Frisbee, Bible study, laughter, prayer, and the confluence of old and, for me, new friends. We sang,

All good gifts around us are sent from heaven above.
So thank the Lord, yes, thank the Lord for all his love.

The retreat marked a turn of seasons. Wood smoke scented cool air. Autumn leaves changed the season of their observers, though we sensed a promise of spring—just as ours was a time out of time to prepare for a world which, we believed, would soon become alive to us.

This was my introduction to an iconoclastic subset of graduate students—out of Harvard's ten thousand—who seem more interested in making a life than in making a living. They are attracted to Jesus because Jesus knows that our danger is not in too much life but in too little. They come from many countries to integrate great ideas with lives of service—truth for the art of life. They are people, as Charles Malik says, "of being."

Over the next two years, I met Graduate School of Education (HGSE) students whose love excites classrooms and children about life. Kindred spirits at the Kennedy School see how humility, creativity, and forgiveness can resolve international conflicts as justice is sought—and conversely, how fundamentalism, apart from love, produces tyrants and delusions.

I met business students like Andy Webb, who quit a lucrative job to begin a Third World reforestation project and then a bungee jumping business in Dallas, where he lives and ministers in the inner city.

When I asked a law student named Kurt Alme to write for this book during spring break, I learned that he would instead be wandering around

Boston, without money or possessions, sleeping in shelters—trying to understand how his "Little Brother" grew up.

I remember the sheer enthusiasm of friends like Katie Smith Milway, a journalist who came to the Kennedy School. With writers Bob Massie and Becky Baer, Katie began the Harvard Coalition Against Apartheid and later became the Africa liaison for Food for the Hungry. There are no dull moments with Katie, who might burst into a nearly endless repertoire of songs in almost any language or location—sea kayaking with whales off Vancouver or in a San Salvador barrio.

Many have come to a faith through the physical and natural sciences. With their sense of wonder intact, the universe fascinates them. They explore chaos, energy, and order. They see design that suggests a Designer. They advance ethics and epistemology in their fields. They too are learning to see.

Behind a telescope, Jennifer Wiseman prays with her eyes and mind open. When peers attribute the discovery of the "Wiseman-Skiff comet" to her, she credits God and colleagues.

Eager to see the invisible, students image the interior of the human body in nuclear engineering at M.I.T. They map the subsurface of the earth with radar, looking for an ancient Chinese city with Harvard archaeologists.

Students like Elisabeth Overmann, Debbie Edgar, and Trish Lyons in the social sciences and humanities begin to discover the gospel's inspiration in civil rights, jazz, women's suffrage, international schools and hospitals, scientific inquiry, literature, and intellectual history.

Another such student is our first writer, Rebecca Baer. With shining eyes, she is the first to skinny-dip in Walden Pond (at night), the first to dive into Harvard dumpsters to rescue and recycle goods lazily abandoned by graduates (and give them to homeless), the first white woman to join a Soweto church and gospel choir. Once I found her sound asleep beside her bed, on her knees, "just praying."

The GSCF coordinator, Jeff Barneson, studied at the Kennedy School of Government (KSG), races on the cycling team, and dominates the doubles volleyball court. As you might have suspected from his essay, Jeff habitually calculates in favor of others. A student once wrote about Harvard's beloved preacher and overseer, Phillips Brooks, "We saw in his face the most uncommon kindness." This also brings to mind the face of Jeff Barneson.

As I packed to return to Ohio after finishing my thesis, Jeff asked me to stay and work with him as a chaplain to grad students. After nine years in Cambridge, I still felt like a cyclist on his rear wheel, drafting off his work and energy (with a few diversions). Then again, we all hoped that we were drafting off the work of God's Spirit, who brings us along for the ride.

AT PLAY IN THE LIGHT OF THE LORD

In much of our life together as students, we felt the joy of the Lord with Saint Paul, who said in the book of Acts, "In him we live and move and have our being."

Heather Tallman, a Kennedy School student from Whitefish, Montana, glorifies God as an elite athlete in skiing, cycling, and tae kwon do. She taught us, more by her manner of quiet beauty than by her words, to be at peace with life and to welcome discipline. We lived together and often headed north or west with friends, depending on the price of gas, or student discounts on airline tickets. On a father-daughter fly-fishing trip in Glacier National Park (with GSCF friends), we sang to keep the grizzlies away (on a seventeen-mile hike), and we sang for joy:

Sing ho for the life of a bear . . .
For the beauty of the earth . . .

Likewise, on a hike up Mt. Lafayette in New Hampshire, Brian Ruhm, a relentlessly energetic air force and Kennedy School student, now married to Heather, made footholds to the snowy summit for me to follow in. I was reminded of the One who goes before us—"Fix [your] eyes on Jesus . . . who for the joy set before him endured the cross, scorning its shame," according to the writer of Hebrews.

New England barn dances, sleigh rides, ski and rock climbing trips get students out of the ivory tower.

Winter 1995 journal entry:

> We skied Whiteface before the snow entirely melted and rushed down the mountain faster than we could race it. Alex, Robin, David, and I sang Scottish ballads on the chairlift as we rose up through the fog and the verdant crags. That night our sing-along drew in other lodge guests. We sang David Wilcox, James Taylor, Joni Mitchell, hymns, and "Young Life" songs. A guest asked, "Why do you sing like this? I haven't heard such singing since I was a boy." Late-night readings of Pooh, all six of us piled on my bed.
>
> The next day we hiked Mt. Joe. Between ambushes we discussed bioethics, luge, just war theory, geophysics, landscape painting, and the beauty of the earth. I ran my hands and face down a sunlit and melting ice sculpture against a cliff in a white birch forest. Winter. A strange time to celebrate the birth of Christ in the world, but such may be God's nature—life and birth in what seems to be the dead cold of winter.
>
> I was thinking of Wendell Berry's "Standing Sabbath of the Woods" and the complete reordering of life that can freely flow from the love of God. Any seed knows that obedience to the earth and sky is life and fruit—for it is rooted in the source of life, just as branches draw from

the vine, just as a child nurses from her mother. Rebellion and autonomy are death. And so T. S. Eliot said that "man without God is like a
seed upon the wind."

All of our ventures were knit together into the larger adventure of holiness—being restored to the image of God in which we were created, loving
and creative caretakers of the earth and of each other. Were it not for the
coming of Christ, we couldn't know the Creator's image and intent, and
wouldn't know what it is to be human. But the Word has become flesh, and
God's nature and glory is now clearly seen in the eyes and heart and mind
of Christ. Were it not for his cross, we would remain lifeless in our guilt
and distance from God. Were it not for the resurrection, we would remain
powerless to become like Christ, fully human once again. But since life is
the final word, we are learning the freedom to live without fear of all that
death can touch, though not also without sorrow.

TO SEE THROUGH THE EYES OF STRANGERS

God's love leads us to try to see through the eyes of strangers, and so we
travel and attempt to learn from and to be of some use to people whose
wisdom has come at a high price. Though first more motivated by curiosity and a kind of self-important altruism, God lets us travel to have our
hearts broken in the right ways, to know his power to give life, and to see
our own spiritual poverty.

Knowledge of truth is painful for me, because it reminds me of my natural preferences. Someone once said that Jesus came to comfort the afflicted
and to afflict the comfortable. As an extreme but not sole example, the night
before a mission trip, my friend John Sage and I went with friends to the
Newport Ball held at Rosecliff, where *The Great Gatsby* was filmed. Hosted
by the HBS European Club, we were greeted in many languages. We found
in each room a new musical ensemble, international cuisine, and the beautiful people of Harvard Business School.

The next morning, we traveled with GSCF friends to build a medical
clinic and church for Haitians, including little children, who were forced to
cut sugarcane each day. In six months they might earn three hundred dollars—the amount we had just spent on a party—yet they shared with us all
that they had. Later that week, in a burned-out cane field, we were invited
to sing a song with them, written by a slave trader who was changed by
Jesus Christ:

Amazing grace, how sweet the sound that saved a wretch like me ...

Afterward, during a Bible study inclusive of uninvited tarantulas, our
bunkhouse door was smashed in by drunk men with a rifle. They did no

harm but further inspired us to consider the value of life, and the tragedy of decadence, addiction, violence, and fear—forms of poverty by which the rich and the poor suffer. Whether in Newport or in Haiti, it is level ground at the foot of the cross. In seeing my own poverty apart from Christ, I need to know how God gives a special grace—and song—to the poor.

The following year, our team of fourteen was invited to build houses with Guatemalan women and children whose husbands and fathers were killed, and houses destroyed, in the war against them. There is no greater gift to folks stuck in the ivory tower than new friends, a hammer and some nails, the earth, and a chance to get dirty.

May 26, 1990, The Ixil Triangle, Guatemala, journal entry:

Our day begins at 5:30 a.m. Jeff, Cecely, Will, Jutta, Nick, and Heather sink posts in solid rock. Eric and John work while sick from bad mangos and heat. The Guatemalan women, rarely five feet tall, haul boards up the mountains, passing us in mud slides. Parades of children bring flowers, carry tools, and sing to us in Ixil. Their laughs suggest that we are the largest and silliest people in Central America.

Nathan Estruth and I took on four boys, two horses, and a pig of unusual size, in soccer during the afternoon rain. Girls appeared in the mountains above the field and became cheerleaders for the female gender, screaming whenever there was a remote possibility of me coming in contact with the ball.

Around the fire, with Bibles open, we considered one of Harvard's favorite concepts—development. "Development of what?" we discussed. People? Land? Faith? Economics? We sang and we prayed. Heads bowed, we held the hand of the One who holds the widow and the orphan. Firelight warmed our dirty hands and faces, tan and tranquil from a day worth living.

We climbed you, hill of Sisyphus, in the heat of day with wood for houses; higher, alongside aged and smaller women, yet stronger, alongside children, somehow older.

We beat you, Tower of Babel. We understood the words beneath the words that we do not share with the Ixil. The eyes of Mayan women and their children, breathing time, the eyes of our judges, saw us white as friendly ghosts begin to grow weathered and real.

The following year, we worked with World Relief in El Salvador, helping to redeem the condition of eight thousand people living in the city dump. Writer Peter Clark introduced us to a man who forgave his torturers and visited them in prison. As I relayed this story to Becky Baer, she told me about her South African friend who threw himself around a boy who was about to be burned, "necklaced," for being an informer. He knew it was a gamble, because they might have killed them both. "As Christians, we have many freedoms," said Becky, "one of which is the freedom to die because of the hope we have in the resurrection from the dead." This life has no hold on us, so we are beginning to live it with courage.

NEW WINE, THE COLOR OF CRIMSON

In this book, in the Veritas Forum, and in campus fellowhips, those who share a belief in the gospel as the hope of the world, despite reductionism and the politics of competition to say something "new," are beginning to meet each other and to engage the deep questions of students and the university. They are "at risk," and they are emerging.

Though many Christians do not find a physical center at Harvard, they have learned to stand alone, and now they are coming together as coals for a fire providing light and warmth.

This book was begun in 1989 as a collection for fellow graduate students. Around the margins of my thesis, the GSCF, and service projects, there were many revisions, roadblocks, and hundreds of letters and conversations with patient writers.

For example, I met Brent Foster in the John Harvard Brew House meeting of the C. S. Lewis Society. We later spoke together at the Freshman Union on the subject "Christmas and Suffering." Before he left for home, I asked if he would write his story as a sophomore with bone cancer. Brent is one of the clearest thinkers I've ever met. He says that facing your own death tends to have that effect.

Writers in this book have become catalysts for renewal at Harvard. Students invite, for example, Owen Gingerich, Bill Edgar, and Poh Lian Lim to speak at their gatherings. A series entitled "A Mind Awake" was led by writer Todd Lake with fellow writers Dick Keyes, Lamin Sanneh, and Krister Sairsingh.

Students wait several years to take a course by Professors Armand Nicholi and Rodney Petersen on the conflicting ideas of Sigmund Freud and C. S. Lewis. Leading Catholic intellectuals, like Professor Robert Coles, explore with students the literature of social reflection, and the spiritual wisdom of children. Father Brian Hehir teaches international peacekeeping and public policy.

In October 1991 a new Catholic Center was dedicated. The keynote speaker, the Honorable John Noonan, a Harvard overseer, recognized that Christian churches are on the road to ecumenical unity.[2] He went on to say

---

[2]John T. Noonan, "The Catholic Community at Harvard," *New Oxford Review* (March, 1992).

that the Catholic community at Harvard believes, with Saint Augustine and Saint Paul, in "a real, not metaphorical, Christ and church. The faith of this community is thus at odds with that of the university." To explain the tension, he pointed to Harvard's spiritual indifference, its heritage from the Enlightenment, and its sense of itself as its own church celebrating its own rituals and festival rites; as the song has it, "the herald of Light" and "the bearer of Love."

A growing community of students join local churches and help lead thriving Christian fellowships. In 1990 these fellowships hosted a conference at the Kennedy school called "Revolution in Eastern Europe: The Role of the Church." Those involved in five liberation movements testified to the prayer and catalytic work of indigenous churches. Panelists spoke of the courage of perhaps millions killed as they stood for human dignity against a totalitarian and atheistic regime.

In December 1991 two hundred and fifty students gathered to explore the subject "Jesus and the Dynamics of Diversity: Ethnic Strife in America." Students and speakers spoke of the need for confession, forgiveness, and sacrificial love wherein lies hope for unity in the context of increasing ethnic diversity.

Fellowships joined for a spring "Jubilee" uniting hundreds of students in worship, prayer, and friendship for things to come. Filing into the Yard, InterVarsity's Andy Crouch led the singing:

I will build my church, and the gates of hell shall not prevail against it.

In March 1993 the "Gospel Jam" drew over three hundred New England students in three feet of snow.

Even the *Harvard Crimson* ran a story called "Christian Groups Blossom."[3] A senior biochemistry concentrator explained that the growth of fellowships is because students are attracted to "the joy of Christian students, and the way they live. . . . It's not just about eternity, it's about today." The reporter found that "many point to the growing attendance at the annual Veritas Forum" as an indicator of spiritual intellect and interest.

THE VERITAS FORUM

We were starting to learn about the founders' concept of veritas as the truth of Jesus Christ in vast relation to all of life.[4] At the same time, to use the metaphor of a symphony, it seemed as if the latest findings in many

---

[3]Victor Chen, "Christian Groups Blossom," *Harvard Crimson* (December 1, 1994).

[4]The Hollis Professor of Divinity, Emeritus, George Hunston Williams, had asked me to research Harvard's evangelical heritage for his final book on Harvard history.

fields harmonized with a biblical view of reality. We believed that if the gospel is true, then it would be revealed by exploration. Likewise, if the gospel is false to the nature of reality, we also wanted to know and to live our lives accordingly.

God brought us together with a kindred spirit and supporter named Jerry Mercer. After three visits to the Licensing Office, I was granted permission to use the nineteenth-century shield—*Veritas, Christo et Ecclesiae*—to propose a "Harvard Veritas Forum" as a grassroots effort to explore the truth and relevance of Jesus Christ by "raising the hardest questions of the university, society, and the human heart." Like a live version of this book, the Veritas Forum is a gathering of people from many cultures and disciplines. The greatest challenge was to find willing partners. Law students offered to host the first forum in the historic Ames courtroom in Austin Hall.

For the next three autumns, nearly a thousand students, faculty, alumni, and friends met to discuss *Veritas, Christo et Ecclesiae* and the possibility of comprehensive and personal truth in our postmodern world. Though most seminars and events are led by students and alumni, excellent keynote addresses have been given by apologist Ravi Zacharias (1992), philosopher Peter Kreeft (1993), journalist David Aikman (1994), professor Ron Sider (1994), and the Reverend John Stott (1995).

At the organizational meeting hours before this year's forum, several hundred of us met to pray and to sing, "O God, our help in ages past, our hope for years to come. . . ." When a thousand people filled Sanders Theater, we began with the words of historian Samuel Eliot Morison:

> *In Christi Gloriam* declared the unity of purpose with the Middle Ages. *Veritas* proclaimed the principle that the founders held greater than knowledge. . . . Her presidents and tutors insisted that there could be no true knowledge or wisdom without Christ.

Highlighted on the front wall were three identical shields bearing the Harvard motto—*Veritas, Christo et Ecclesiae*. After journalist David Aikman spoke on the topic "Truth, Consequences, and History," a panel of fourteen scholars, artists, and scientists engaged student questions about gender, race, suffering, evolution, chaos, deconstruction, pluralism, and the reliability of the Bible.

Students on a "Treasure Hunt for Veritas" discovered early Christian symbols in Harvard Yard (most tours perpetuate revisionist history with thousands of visitors each year). Kay Hall and Todd Lake described the meaning of the shield, the gates, inscriptions on buildings. "What Is Man That Thou Art Mindful of Him?" from Psalm 8, is inscribed over the front door of Emerson Hall, the philosophy building. (The faculty had apparently requested Protagoras' famous "Man Is the Measure of All Things.") Students asked, "What does the shield symbolize?" "Is that a Bible on John Harvard's knee?" (referring to the landmark in the center of the Yard).

A hunt for veritas in the Fogg Art Museum was given by Mrs. Annalise Harding, a lovely German docent. The week before she told me, "No one has ever asked for a tour like this. Even if only one person comes, I will do this for God." During the tour, she paused in front of an Italian Madonna and child. "You want to find veritas? This is veritas," she said, pointing to the child, asleep to foreshadow his sacrificial death.

We viewed and discussed films including *Babette's Feast*, *Shadowlands*, *Crimes and Misdemeanors*, and *Chariots of Fire*. Words of encouragement were given by China Inland missionary David Adeney, fifty years after he helped begin Harvard-Radcliffe Christian Fellowship (advised by InterVarsity) in 1942.

Pierce Pettis performed in concert during a lightning storm heard and seen through Paine Hall's arching windows. Alluding to 1 Corinthians 13, he sang,

> *Knowledge and prophecy will fade and tongues will all fall silent.*
> *Love that lives is here to stay solid and defiant.*
> *I know it's hard to see these things like through a dark glass straining,*
> *but when we're standing face-to-face the truth won't need explaining.*

THE CROSS IN THE IVY

Many of us were cared for by Harvard-Radcliffe Christian Fellowship (HRCF) faculty advisors of five decades, Mrs. Vera Shaw and Professor Jim Shaw, who are legends in every mind but their own. Like resident grandparents, their quiet influence is incalculable. Students, alumni, and friends are beginning to join the Shaw's legacy of prayer and love for Harvard.

We are beginning to understand Bobby Fong's words in his essay: "Truth is not only that which awaits discovery but also that which was once known and is now threatened by forgetfulness." We are beginning to see that the history of Christian students at Harvard, as in colleges throughout the world, is about those who sought by the grace of God to follow Christ with all their heart, mind, soul, and strength and to love their neighbor as themselves.

In learning about the past, we are sad to find that some who gave their lives and estates for the gospel here are now forgotten or actively dishonored. After three years of quiet requests of the university, we are still asking for an account of substantial gifts that the Divinity School appears to have misplaced. One such gift was given to the college for lectures on the inspiring meaning of *Christo et Ecclesiae*. Meanwhile students and alumni involved in the Veritas Forum and weekly fellowship activities contribute personally or find funding outside of the university. At the same time, we are grateful, because we see how the church can suffer more from comfort than from need.

After five years of near silence on the subject, I raise this point because I believe that the process of thinking about such problems is more important than the funds themselves. With students around the world beginning to discover similar challenges, I commend the Shaws' example—their first impulse is always to pray. They do not protest in anger and demand "rights." Though some believe that we have erred on the side of complicity, we are trying to find a Christlike balance of justice and mercy. We want to temper knowledge with humility and grace, knowing our own imperfections and oversights.

We ask to meet with administrators in order to consider the right path together with them, as friends. When ignored, we don't give up, because we think that the principles involved are worth the long wait. We pray that God would teach us in the university about our responsibilities to the past as he speaks to our consciences. We pray that alumni would be honored, that students would be nourished, and that justice and mercy would be seen in this place and time.

It is beautiful to see that nothing can stop the love of God among students. Without proportional faculty representation, a physical center, or the use of endowments to support teaching and programs, the faith and joy of many Harvard students now shoots up like flowers between sidewalk cracks. Their joy is not dependent upon externalities such as money, for in Christ they are free from the love of it. As one student said: with or without gifts, it is Christmas morning, and the Whos down in Whoville are joyfully still singing.

With the Veritas Forum developing in other universities, I meet students who are beginning to explore the place where they study and live. Yale seminarian Donald Dacey leads a group of students who are developing a *Lux et Veritas* Forum to discuss the light and truth of the gospel. Princeton alumnus Bill Grady gathers alumni who pray for their university. Though tiger alumni like to translate the current motto *Dei Sub Numine Viget* as "God Went to Princeton," it actually means "Under God's Power She Flourishes." For the first 150 years, while the College of New Jersey (founded in 1747), the motto on the seal was *Vitam Mortuis Reddo*, "I Restore Life to the Dead."

Dartmouth was founded in 1769 as "A Voice Crying in the Wilderness," *Vox Clamantis In Deserto*. After learning of the Veritas Forum, graduate student John Murray began his thesis as a documentary script on the

Christian origins of the early colleges (the term "Ivy League" is of more use for football than for history). When I visited John and Navigator fellowship leader Craig Parker, we wondered why the stained-glass windows that include Jesus are completely boarded over in Dartmouth's Rollins Chapel. Other students are beginning a *Voces Clamantium* Forum to raise dialogue on truth at Dartmouth.

By God's grace and the hard work of planners, Veritas Fora have emerged in major universities, including Ohio State, Virginia, Florida, Indiana, Texas, Yale, Colorado, Michigan, Wisconsin, Oregon State, and Stanford. In each case, hundreds and often thousands participate.

The Harvard Fellowships' newsletter, written for years by students with the Halls and the Shaws, encourages alumni and friends to pray for each other and for universities in Korea, Sri Lanka, Nigeria, Japan, and Moscow, many of which were founded for the free pursuit of truth and for the gospel.

In my search for God at Harvard, I expected to find something new, something *beyond* Jesus, but instead I have found *more* of him. I have begun to see how the pure light of God's truth refracts and falls in every direction with color and grace. I found the memory of this truth in the color of crimson, in the iron Yard gates, and in the symbols on the college seal. I began to see him in the work and eyes of fellow students, in rare books, in a friend's chemistry lab, in recent astrophysical abstracts, and in the lives and legacies of founders and alumni who, whether living or beyond this life, would befriend and teach us.

The fact of pluralism is wonderful because it takes the whole family of God—every set of eyes, every color and culture and discipline—to see and to reflect the mind and heart of God. I am learning to see, and I can tell you that all is not lost for those who like treasure hunts.

AND SO WE SING

There is a lot of sound at Harvard, and some students make a noise that is, well, full of hope and even joy. It is a strange sound in this place, always beautiful, sometimes haunting, and I have heard it many times.

I hear it at the Dunster House *Messiah*-sing, where diverse students are thawed by hot cider, the fire in the hearth, and the presence of each other as they pack in and sing,

> *All we like sheep have gone astray . . . and the iniquity of us all is on*
> *him.*

I hear it in the snowy Yard, in the Square, and in Widener Library after hours, with voices wafting up through the stacks that hold its millions of volumes:

O Come O Come Emmanuel and ransom captive Israel....
Mild he lays his glories by, born that man no more may die ...

I hear it on Good Friday:

O Sacred head now wounded, with grief and shame weighed down

And in the Yard on Easter:

Jesus Christ is risen today, alleluia.

I have only about three notes to contribute, but I join in. We sing while hanging drywall with Habitat for Humanity in Boston and while ski-hiking Tuckerman Ravine. We sing while quilting in Cambridge and while building a school for kids with polio in the rain forest of Peru. We sing while riding low in the back of a dusty pickup across war-torn El Salvador. We sing at the weddings and funerals of friends. The Lord is our song, and so we sing.

I have found here a beginning of what writer, Elton Trueblood, knew would heal the world: "A society of loving souls, set free from the self-seeking struggle for personal prestige and from all unreality." It is indeed something unutterably precious. Wise persons do "travel any distance to join it." Wiser persons become this where they are.

With the eyes to see, we find a great cloud of witnesses to which we all belong. We sing with them, warmed by the knowing that all manner of thing shall be well, One Day. We remember the prophet Jeremiah, to whom the Lord said, "Do not say 'I am only a youth'. . . Be not afraid . . . for I am with you to deliver you." And so we find courage in ages past, the age to come, and this age which, by grace alone, is ours.

ॐ

With the drawing of this Love and the voice of this Calling
we shall not cease from exploration
And the end of all our exploring will be to arrive where we started
and know the place for the first time.
Through the unknown, remembered gate
when the last of earth left to discover
is that which was the beginning. . . .[5]

T. S. ELIOT, CLASS OF 1909

---

[5]T.S. Eliot, *The Complete Poems and Plays*, "The Four Quartets" (San Diego: Harcourt Brace Jovanovich, 1980), 117–45.

POSTSCRIPT

Finding God at Harvard, in its original form, became a *Boston Globe* bestseller and was in print for ten years. It helped to catalyze Veritas Forums at more than seventy research universities. The book was also given to hundreds of diplomats within the United Nations, and translated into Chinese and Korean.

Thanks to a friend's network of zippy cargo jets, a wonderful staff of helpers, and thousands of volunteers and participants, Kelly led the Veritas Forum beyond Harvard, advising planners throughout the United States, Canada and the United Kingdom. In her memoir and Veritas story, *Finding God Beyond Harvard: The Quest for Veritas* (IVP, 2006), Kelly shares adventures of the Veritas movement from Harvard to Berkeley and many schools in between. We find students in the prisons of Bolivia and the jungles of Brazil, serving the poor. Readers discover them on mountain bikes and skis throughout New England and the Rockies. She weaves into the story a deep thread of her own life, heartache, and struggles beneath the surface of the Veritas story, and how "having disappeared into a lonely cabin in the woods north of Boston, the questions of Veritas became my own questions, from the inside out." We then see how God revived Kelly's story and grew the Veritas movement. After many years in Boston, Kelly returned to her hometown of Columbus, Ohio, and married David Kullberg, a businessman, novelist, and widower raising five children. Along with the joys of family life, Kelly remains the Director of Project Development for the Veritas Forum, and she teaches high school English literature in a private/public "hybrid" school alternative she helped to found.

An update on the writers of *Finding God at Harvard: Spiritual Journeys of Thinking Christians:*

Going on three decades at Harvard, Jeff Barneson continues to lead the Graduate School Christian Fellowship, now with the help and added gifts of wife, Tara, and sons Zach and Ezra. Jeff continues to introduce Harvard grad students to opportunities to serve the poorest of the poor in Central and Latin America and India.

In approximate order of essays and chapters as they appear in the book (some are in the conclusion):

Becky (Baer) Porteous finished her doctorate at Duke in theological ethics. She and her husband, David, moved for a decade to South Africa and then back to Boston where they are raising two sons, Jonathan and Benjamin. Robert Coles, child psychiatrist, Pulitzer Prize-winning author, and former Agee Professor of Social Ethics, recently edited the anthology *A Life in Medicine: A Literary Anthology.* Todd Lake was a dean at Baylor University, and is now vice president for spiritual development at Belmont University in Nashville where the Lakes are raising three children. Todd has authored many articles on faith and social change. Eve Perera retired after teaching Christianity and literature for fifteen years at the Berkshire Institute for Christian Studies. Bill Edgar is professor of cultural apologetics at Westminster Seminary near Philadelphia, a jazz pianist, Veritas speaker, and advisor. His recent books are *Reasons of the Heart* and *Truth in All Its Glory.*

Glenn Loury is professor of economics, and director of the Institute on Race and Social Division at Boston University. Dick Keyes published *Seeing Through Cynicism* and *Beyond Identity: Finding Yourself in the Image and Character of God.* Dick and Mardi Keyes direct the Southborough L'Abri study center near Boston, where Dick is a cultural apologist, author and musician. Aleksandr Solzhenitsyn, Nobel laureate in literature, left America for his Russian homeland where he now writes history and short stories in Moscow.

Olympic medalist Paul Wylie is a husband and father in New England, and is still gracefully skating.

Armand Nicholi, Harvard Medical School professor, authored *The Question of God,* which explores the conflicting worldviews and life consequences of Sigmund Freud and C. S. Lewis and was the topic of a recent PBS special. Michael Yang is a pediatric ophthalmologist in Cincinnati. Led toward atheism by the novels of Ayn Rand, Michael came to faith as a student at Harvard Medical School. He recently published the book *Reconsidering Ayn Rand.* Brent Foster appears in the conclusion. Poh Lian Lim Yap, an infectious disease specialist in Singapore, was named the 2005 Malaysian Woman of the Year for her pioneering work on SARS. Her husband, Vong, was in small part inspired to meet Poh Lian after reading her God at Harvard story on sexuality and intimacy. They are raising three children.

Kathryn Wiegand's tribe is mostly out of the home, and she still finds parenthood a great intellectual and spiritual challenge. Nicholas Wolterstorff was the Noah Porter Professor of Philosophical Theology at Yale from 1989-2001, and has recently joined the philosophy department of the University of Virginia as a scholar-in-residence. His interests include metaphysics, aesthetics, and epistemology. Rodney Petersen has led the Boston Theological Institute as executive director for more than a decade. Betsy Dawn Inskeep Smylie is mentioned in the conclusion.

Habib Malik divides his time teaching at the Lebanese American University and, with the Library of Congress, researching his late father's archives. He is a leading voice in many conferences on the Middle East, Lebanon, Christianity in the Arab world, human rights and democracy. He recently married and is raising children. Krister Sairsingh is a professor in Moscow at the State University Higher School of Economics, and at the Russian-American Christian University. Lamin Sanneh's story of conversion from Islam to Jesus, "Jesus More Than a Prophet," has been used to introduce Jesus to Muslims and to begin explaining Islamic faith and culture to Christians. Lamin remains at Yale University as the D. Willis James Professor of Missions and World Christianity, with a concurrent courtesy appointment as professor of history at Yale College. John Rankin continues to engage America's leading secularists in public dialogue. He teaches the Love of Hard Questions seminar, the Only Genesis seminar, and has developed an eight-course curriculum called Theological Education Institute.

Robert Massie Jr. went on to become a founding fellow and executive director of Ceres, the Coalition for Environmentally Responsible Economies. Ruth Goodwin-Groen works as an independent consultant specializing in microfinance on behalf of women in poverty. Ruth and Paul are raising two sons. Jeff Barneson is mentioned previously.

Elizabeth Dole has served five United States presidents and now the people of North Carolina in the United States Senate. Senator Dole has been named numerous times by the Gallup Poll as one of the world's top ten most admired women.

Peter Clark leads ARCA Associates International, aiding community development and helping to rebuild lives and communities in regions including Central America, Afghanistan, Iraq, and Rwanda (sometimes riding his bicycle across entire countries). Robert Beschel Jr. consults in international governance with the World Bank.

Charles Thaxton is a physical chemist, a Fellow of the Discovery Institute, and teaches at Konos Academy. Owen Gingerich, author of the recent book *God's Universe,* is Research Professor of Astronomy and of the History of Science at Harvard University and a senior astronomer emeritus at the Smithsonian Astrophysical Observatory. Greg Hammett is a professor and researcher in plasma physics at Princeton. Vera Shaw is discussed at the conclusion.

Harold Berman remains at Emory University and The Carter Center. Peter Feaver is professor of political science and public policy at Duke University and director of the Triangle Institute for Security Studies. Peter is on leave from Duke and is working as the Special Advisor for Strategic Planning and Institutional Reform on the National Security Council staff at the White

House. Bobby Fong is the president of Butler University. Brother John is a member of the Taizé Community in the small village of Taizé in the Burgundy region of France. Founded by Brother Roger as a "parable of community" in the darkest days of the World Wars of the last century, today the Taizé Community is made up of over a hundred brothers, Catholics and Protestants, from more than twenty-five nations.

All writers in chapter ten are mentioned in the conclusion.

A few of the many friends in the epilogue were also instrumental in the growth of Veritas. Jennifer Wiseman, a speaker at the first Veritas Forum, married and went on to become the lead scientist for the Hubble Space Telescope Program. Glenn Lucke is completing his Ph.D. in sociology at the University of Virginia. Elisabeth (Overmann) Baumann is a mother and a doctoral student in English literature at the University of Virginia. Debbie Edgar attended the Fuller School of Psychology and is a counselor near Pasadena. Katie (Smith) Milway earned her M.B.A at INCEAD in France, authored several books and is the Global Editorial Director for Bain & Company. She and Mike are raising three children. Heather (Tallman) Ruhm is a mother practicing medicine and is back in New England where Brian serves in the Air Force. John Sage began Pura Vida, a gourmet coffee company that gives 100 percent of its profits to coffee growers and to the poor.

Lastly, several in our community of coauthors have already moved on to see Veritas face to face. To be with him. Whole books could be (or have been) written on each of their lives. D. Elton Trueblood. Mother Teresa. Betsy Inskeep Smylie. Sophomore Brent Foster. Phillips Brooks. Charles Malik. Vera Shaw, who with her husband, Jim, were faculty advisors to the Harvard-Radcliffe Christian Fellowship for fifty-five years.

When Kay Hall and I visited Vera in hospice, Vera let go of the morphine pump in order to hold our hands. Jim looked adoringly at Vera, as he had for sixty-five years. The nurses had fallen in love with her, quite naturally. Vera's eyes were never brighter, though her body was failing, and though she was deeply pained that Harvard's administration had still not honored its mission and endowments given for Christ's glory. She asked us to pray with her, but during that time she only prayed *for us,* for our circle of friends now in many countries, and for Veritas and the gospel in universities (as she'd been praying each day for years). After her "Amen," I asked through tears, "But Vera, how might *we* best pray for *you?*" She looked at me with knowing, shining eyes. She smiled and said, "Honey, the future is as bright as the promises of God. Just give thanks, dear. Just give thanks."

INDEX
───── ॐ ─────

 *The* · VERITAS · FORUM

Mission Statement

We create forums for the exploration of true life.
We seek to inspire the shapers of tomorrow's culture
to connect their hardest questions
with the person and story of Jesus Christ.

About The Veritas Forum

The Veritas Forum helps create university events that engage students and faculty in discussions about life's hardest questions and the relevance of Jesus Christ to all of life. We seek to restore an understanding of the Gospel to promote intellectual, spiritual and communal vitality for tomorrow's leaders. The forums are created by local university students, professors and ministers while guided by the national Veritas Forum team.

The Veritas Forum believes that the search for truth, which is the search for reality, is our human responsibility and privilege and the principle endeavor of the university. Each Veritas Forum is an opportunity for the entire university community to explore the possibility of truth, beauty and goodness in every aspect of our academic and personal lives. By asking the pressing questions on campus and seeking answers with respected university voices, we hope to engage the entire university in fruitful discussion and restore to culture a sense of wonder, meaning and true life.

Our story began at Harvard University in 1992 when a group of students and ministers, challenged by the emptiness around them, decided to face their hardest questions about life and truth. At the first Veritas Forum writers of the book *Finding God at Harvard* gathered to share of their own sufferings, journeys and discoveries with the Harvard community. Students, faculty and friends came together to discuss how the pursuit of knowledge in the university related to the truth claims of Jesus Christ.

Veritas Forums have now emerged on more than seventy campuses across the country, involving almost a quarter-million student and faculty participants and hundreds of speakers. Veritas Forums have been featured on ABC's *World News Tonight,* C-SPAN Book TV and National Public Radio, and in books and many campus newspapers. *Finding God at Harvard: Spiritual Journeys of Thinking Christians* won a Christian Booksellers Association Book of the Year award and appeared on the bestseller list of the *Boston Globe.*

You are invited to join the Veritas journey in three ways: in person at campus forums, on the web with recordings of hundreds of Veritas talks, and in this book and others that are forthcoming from InterVarsity Press. To find out more about The Veritas Forum, visit our website at www.veritas.org.

VERITAS FORUM BOOKS
FROM INTERVARSITY PRESS

As a partnership between The Veritas Forum and InterVarsity Press, Veritas Forum Books connect the pursuit of knowledge with the deepest questions of life and truth. Established and emerging Christian thinkers grapple with challenging issues, offering academically rigorous and responsible scholarship that contributes to current and ongoing discussions in the university world. Veritas Forum Books are written in the spirit of genuine dialogue, addressing particular academic disciplines as well as topics of broad interest for the intellectually curious and inquiring. In embodying the values, purposes and mission of The Veritas Forum, Veritas Forum Books provide thoughtful, confessional Christian engagement with world-shaping ideas, making the case for an integrated Christian worldview and moving readers toward a clearer understanding of ultimate truth.